D0872305

The Mad Among Us

A History of the Care of America's Mentally Ill

Gerald N. Grob

THE FREE PRESS
A Division of Macmillan, Inc.
NEW YORK

Maxwell Macmillan Canada
TORONTO

Maxwell Macmillan International
NEW YORK   OXFORD   SINGAPORE   SYDNEY

The Free Press
A Division of Macmillan, Inc.
866 Third Avenue, New York, N.Y. 10022

Maxwell Macmillan Canada, Inc.
1200 Eglinton Avenue East
Suite 200
Don Mills, Ontario M3C 3N1

Macmillan, Inc. is part of the Maxwell Communication Group of Companies.

Printed in the United States of America

printing number

1 2 3 4 5 6 7 8 9 10

Library of Congress Cataloging-in-Publication Data

Grob, Gerald N.
  The mad among us: a history of the care of America's mentally ill/Gerald N. Grob.
    p.   cm.
  Includes bibliographical references and index.
  ISBN 0–02–912695–9
  1. Mentally ill—Care—United States—History. 2. Psychiatry—United States—History. 3. Mentally ill—United States—Public opinion. I. Title.
RC443.G747   1994   93–40806
362.2'0973—dc20   CIP

To Lila

with love and gratitude

Contents

List of Illustrations

McLean Asylum for the Insane (Massachusetts General Hospital, *Annual Report*, 1844).

Bloomingdale Asylum (New York Hospital and Bloomingdale Asylum, *Annual Report*, 25 [1845]).

Worcester State Lunatic Hospital. (*Reports and Other Documents Relating to the State Lunatic Hospital at Worcester, Mass.* [1837]).

Dorothea Lynde Dix (1802–1887). (Houghton Library, Harvard University, Cambridge, Mass.)

Utica State Lunatic Asylum (Utica State Lunatic Asylum, *Annual Report*, 14 [1856]).

Isaac M. Hunt, *Three Years in a Mad-House* (1852).

Elizabeth W. Packard, *Modern Persecution, or Insane Asylums Unveiled* (1873).

New York City Lunatic Asylum, Blackwell's Island ("Blackwell's Island Lunatic Asylum," *Harper's*, 33 [February 1866]).

Danvers State Lunatic Hospital, Massachusetts (Danvers State Lunatic Hospital, *Annual Report*, 1 [1878]).

Willard Asylum for the Insane, New York (Willard Asylum for the Insane, *Annual Report*, 10 [1878]).

Eastern Hospital for the Insane, Kankakee, Illinois (Illinois Eastern Hospital for the Insane at Kankakee, *Biennial Report*, 5 [1885–1886]).

Buffalo State Hospital, New York (Buffalo Psychiatric Center collection of photographs).

Philadelphia State Hospital (Philadelphia *Bulletin* photos in Temple University Urban Archives, Philadelphia, Penn).

St. Elizabeth's Hospital, East Campus, 1941 (National Archives, Washington, D.C.).

The Snake Pit (Twentieth Century-Fox motion picture [1948]. Film Stills Archive, Museum of Modern Art, New York, N.Y.).

The Three Faces of Eve (Twentieth Century-Fox motion picture [1957]. Film Stills Archive, Museum of Modern Art, New York, N.Y.).

William C. Menninger meeting with John F. Kennedy in the White House on February 9, 1962 (John F. Kennedy Library, Boston, Mass.).

John F. Kennedy signing into law the Mental Retardation Facilities and Community Mental Health Centers Construction Act, October 31, 1963 (John F. Kennedy Library, Boston, Mass.).

One Flew Over the Cuckoo's Nest (United Artists motion picture [1975]. Film Stills Archive, Museum of Modern Art, New York, N.Y.).

Joyce Brown (Billy Boggs) and Norman Siegel (Associated Press Wide World Photos, Inc., New York, N.Y.).

Homeless men in Los Angeles (Associated Press Wide World Photos, Inc., New York, N.Y.).

Preface

Serious and chronic mental illnesses are among the most pressing health problems in America. Statistics on the prevalence of such disorders are striking. Recent estimates indicate that the total number of seriously mentally ill persons may run as high as three million; the direct and indirect costs of their care and treatment run into the tens of billions of dollars. The human dimensions of the problem are even more stunning. The mentally ill include individuals suffering from a variety of disorders that erode or prevent their ability to cope with daily life and preclude economic self-sufficiency. Their inescapable presence poses tragic choices for their families as well as for American society generally.

More than thirty years ago a chance question by a colleague led me to undertake a scholarly odyssey to study the ways in which Americans responded to the presence of the mentally ill. The journey proved exciting and extraordinarily lengthy. I found that the history of the care and treatment of the mentally ill was both complex and shifting, and rarely supported many of the assertions of those involved in shaping policy, providing services, or using the subject to illuminate broader social trends. My findings were presented in a series of articles and books addressed largely to a scholarly and professional audience.

In this work I have attempted to summarize for a more general public my thinking about the subject. In so doing I have drawn materials from four previous books: *The State and the Mentally Ill: A History of Worcester State Hospital in Massachusetts, 1830–1920* (University of North Carolina Press, 1966), *Mental Institutions in America: Social Policy to 1875* (Free Press, 1973), *Mental Illness and American Society, 1875–1940* (Princeton University Press, 1983), and *From Asylum to Community: Mental Health Policy in Modern America* (Princeton Uni-

ix

versity Press, 1991). This volume, however, is written as an independent work and incorporates both my most recent thoughts about the problems posed by mental illnesses and the contributions of other scholars. The focus is less on the mentally disordered themselves (although they are not ignored) and more on the ways in which Americans have responded to the presence of such individuals in their midst.

No historian writes in a social and intellectual vacuum, and I am surely no exception. I should therefore like to call the reader's attention to some personal assumptions that undoubtedly influence the ways in which I interpret the past. I have never held to the modern belief that human beings can mold and control their world in predetermined and predictable ways. This is not to suggest that we are totally powerless to control our destiny. It is only to insist upon both our fallibility and our inability to predict all of the consequences of our actions. Nor do I believe that human history can be explained in deterministic or quasi-deterministic ways, or that solutions are readily available for all problems. Tragedy is a recurring theme in human history and defines the very parameters of our existence. I have tried, therefore, to deal sympathetically with our predecessors who grappled—so often in partial and unsuccessful ways, as we still do ourselves—with the distinct problems relating to the mentally ill and mental health policy.

Over the years I have incurred many debts to friends who have given me the benefits of their knowledge. Roger Bibace introduced me to the subject of mental illnesses, and Jacques Quen offered the perspective of a clinician. David Mechanic provided me with an entry into the sociology of health, and sensitized me to the many currents that shape the development of the mental health system. George Billias for more than three decades helped me to sharpen my thinking about historical problems. Lawrence Friedman shared with me his knowledge of American history and twentieth-century psychiatry. Allan Horwitz contributed to my work in many informal conversations, and Alexander Brooks exposed me to the complexities of mental health law. I should like to acknowledge as well the indispensable assistance of Joyce Seltzer, whose editorial and substantive comments have made this into a much better book than it might have otherwise been.

My research on the history of mental health policy spanning more than three decades has made me indebted to so many archivists and librarians that I cannot possibly acknowledge them individually. No scholar, however, can be unaware of their contributions in ensuring that records are kept, preserved, and organized. Finally, I owe a debt to several organizations that have supported my research and writing. The National Institute of Mental Health has been extraordinarily generous in providing a succession of grants, and fellowships from the National Endowment for the Humanities, the American Council of Learned Societies, and the Guggenheim Foundation gave me free time to think and to write. Without such generous assistance, scholarly work of this kind would be far more difficult, if not impossible.

Gerald N. Grob
Rutgers University

Abbreviations Used in Text

AMSAII   Association of Medical Superintendents of American Institutions for the Insane

AMA   American Medical Association

APA   American Psychiatric Association

CMHC   Community Mental Health Center

CPZ   Chlorpromazine

ECT   Electroconvulsive therapy

GAP   Group for the Advancement of Psychiatry

JCMIH   Joint Commission of Mental Illness and Health

NIMH   National Institute of Mental Health

SSDI   Social Security Disability Insurance

SSI   Supplemental Security Income for the Aged, the Disabled, and the Blind

VA   Veterans Administration

Prologue

At present most severely and chronically mentally ill persons are no longer confined in mental hospitals. Some are housed with parents and relatives; some find shelter in residential facilities supported by a combination of private and public funds; and some are confined in penal and correctional institutions. Others have joined a large mass of homeless persons who live on the streets amidst tragic circumstances. The latter, noted one critic in 1987,

> are an inescapable presence in urban America. In New York City they live in subway tunnels and on steam grates, and die in cardboard boxes on windswept street corners. The Los Angeles City Council has opened its chambers to them, allowing them to seek refuge from the Southern California winter on its hard marble floors. Pioneer Square in Seattle, Lafayette Park in Washington, the old downtown in Atlanta have all become places of refuge for these pitiable figures, so hard to tell apart: clothes tattered, skins stained by the streets, backs bent in a perpetual search for something edible, smokable, or tradable that may have found its way to the pavement below.[1]

Such observations echo the words of Dorothea L. Dix one hundred and fifty years ago. "I come to present the strong claims of suffering humanity," she informed members of the Massachusetts legislature in 1843. "I come as the advocate of helpless, forgotten, insane and idiotic men and women; of beings, sunk to a condition from which the most unconcerned would start with real horror." Everywhere she looked she found large numbers of insane persons "in jails and poor-houses, and wandering at will over the country." Such a state of affairs was inexcusable, since the remedy was available in the form of *"rightly organized*

1

Hospitals, adapted to the special care of the peculiar malady of the Insane."[2] In her eyes public mental hospitals, which represented enlightenment and social progress, would provide a judicious combination of humane care and medical/psychiatric treatment for all mentally ill persons. Those who recovered would return to their homes; chronic cases would remain in hospitals dedicated to supplying all of their basic human needs.

The dreams and aspirations of those who were staunch advocates of treating insane persons in mental hospitals were quickly realized. By 1875 there were sixty public (state and county) institutions in thirty-two states. Eighty years later there were 265 public institutions with an average daily resident population of more than half a million. The average annual per capita expenditure per patient in 1955 was $1,017, and total state expenditures exceeded $1 billion. The commitment to institutional care and treatment was also reflected in the fact that on the eve of World War II more than two-thirds of the members of the American Psychiatric Association (APA) were employed in mental hospitals.[3]

A century after Dix's death in 1887, however, it was clear that the mental health system was in disarray. State mental hospitals—institutions that had occupied center stage in public policy for more than a century and a half—had lost much of their legitimacy. Once perceived as harbingers of progress, mental hospitals in our own time have been identified as the "problem" rather than the "solution." Correspondingly, community mental health policies are heralded as a means of avoiding the negative consequences of protracted institutionalization. Since the early 1970s Americans have seemingly committed themselves to a policy of deinstitutionalization.

Recent policy shifts, however, have given rise to ambiguous consequences. Many mentally ill persons, to be sure, found that the quality of their daily existence was enhanced when they lived in the community. Others, especially young adults who were mobile and had a dual diagnosis of mental illness and substance abuse, became part of a large homeless population that was especially visible on the streets of the nation's largest cities.

From the seventeenth century to the present American society has had to face the dilemmas posed by the presence of severely and chronically mentally ill persons. This group included individuals who suffered from schizophrenia, recurrent depressive and manic-depressive disorders, organic brain syndrome, paranoid disorders, and other chronic conditions. These conditions often eroded their ability to deal with "personal hygiene and self-care, self-direction, interpersonal relationships, social transactions, learning, and recreation," which in turn hindered or prevented them from becoming economically self-sufficient.[4] In some cases the illness was episodic, in other cases persistent and long-term. Many severely disordered persons were unable to function with any degree of independence, and their bizarre behavior frequently stimulated public fear and apprehension.

The inescapable presence of the mentally ill has always raised important issues. What is society's obligation toward them? What is the most effective way of meeting their varied needs? Should the protection of the public take precedence over the human needs of the mentally ill? The responses to these and other questions have varied sharply over time. Public policies have often blended such contradictory elements as compassion, sympathy, rejection, and stigmatization. In like vein, psychiatrists have vacillated between emphasizing curability and chronicity, between extreme optimism and a more fatalistic pessimism, and between a commitment to deal with the severely mentally ill and a search to find other kinds of patients. Families of mentally ill persons also have been affected in profound ways; their desire to care for members has been tempered by a recognition that their presence threatens the very integrity of the household.

The history of the care and treatment of the mentally ill resembles a seemingly endless journey between two extremes—confinement in a mental hospital versus living in the community. The chapters that follow are designed to describe, analyze, and evaluate the American experience in dealing with the often intractable problems posed by severe and chronic mental disorders. If a knowledge of the past does not offer a precise prescription for the future, it can nevertheless yield insights and knowledge that provide a context against which to measure and to evaluate contemporary policies and issues.

1

Caring for the Insane in Colonial America

I n modern America the mentally ill are highly visible and therefore of public concern. In the seventeenth and eighteenth centuries, by contrast, mentally ill—or, to use the terminology of that age, "distracted" or "lunatick"—persons aroused far less interest. Society was predominantly rural and agricultural, and communities were small and scattered. Mental illnesses were perceived to be an individual rather than a social problem, to be handled by the family of the disordered person and not by the state. The very concept of social policy—the conscious creation of public policies and institutions to deal with dependency and distress—was virtually unknown.

The absence of systematic policies did not imply that insanity* was of no significance. On the contrary, the presence of mentally ill persons was of serious concern to both families and neighbors. The behavior of "distracted" persons might prove a threat to their own safety or that of others, and the inability to work meant that others would have to assume

---

*No doubt some readers will be offended by the use of the terms *insane* and *mad*. Although they have acquired an odious connotation, they were perfectly good terms in the past. My use of them and other similar language is historical and is not intended to suggest any hidden meanings. After all, it is likely that *mental illness* is becoming a pejorative designation; witness the current effort to substitute *brain disease* in its place.

responsibility for their survival. Nevertheless, the proportionately small number of "distracted" persons did not warrant the creation of special facilities. Nor had insanity come under medical jurisdiction; concepts of insanity in that period were fluid and largely arose from cultural, popular, and intellectual sources. Mentally disordered persons, therefore, were cared for on an ad hoc and informal basis either by the family or community. Insanity was an intensely human problem, and families and neighbors made whatever adjustments they deemed logical and necessary to mitigate its consequences to themselves and the community.

––––––––––

Before the American Revolution mental illnesses posed social and economic rather than medical problems. The care of the insane remained a family responsibility; so long as its members could provide the basic necessities of life for afflicted relatives, no other arrangements were required. Yet in many instances the effects of the illness spilled outside the family and into the community. Sometimes the behavior of "lunatics" or "distracted persons" threatened the safety and security of others. James Otis, Jr., an important eighteenth-century Massachusetts politician, went berserk and began "madly firing the guns outside of his window." For the remainder of his life he alternated between lucidity and bizarre behavior. Sometimes afflicted individuals were unable to work and earn enough for sustenance. In other cases the absence of a family required the community to make some provision for care or for guardianship. When one "distracted" person wandered into a Massachusetts town "in most distressed circumstances in most severe weather," local officials insisted that "humanity required [that] care should be taken to prevent her from perishing." She was placed with a local family and provided with the basic necessities of life at public expense while an effort was begun to discover her original place of residence.[1]

Throughout the seventeenth and eighteenth centuries most cases involving the insane arose out of this inability to support themselves. Illnesses, particularly those that were protracted, created unemployment, which in turn had a disastrous impact upon the individual as well as the immediate family. If either the husband or wife was affected, the remainder of the family, including dependent children, faced dire economic consequences. Under such circumstances the community was required to assist the insane person and his or her family.

Early colonial laws were based on the English principle that society had a corporate responsibility for the poor and dependent. As in England, most colonies required local communities to make provision for various classes of dependent persons. Since illness and dependency were intimately related, the care of the mentally ill fell under the jurisdiction of the local community. Various codes and laws enacted in Massachusetts, for example, touched upon the care of the insane in one form or another. The first legal code, adopted in 1641, contained several references to "distracted" persons and idiots. One section authorized a "generall Court" to validate the transfer of property made by such persons. Another provision stipulated that "Children, Idiots, Distracted persons, and all that are strangers, or new commers to our plantation, shall have such allowances and dispensations in any Cause whether Criminall or other as religion and reason require." By 1676 the legislature, noting the rise in the number of "distracted persons" and the resulting behavioral problems, ordered town selectmen to care for such persons in order that "they doe not Damnify others." Another statute in 1694 made all insane persons without families the legal responsibility of the community. Its officials were enjoined "to take effectual care and make necessary provision for the relief, support and safety of such impotent or distracted person." If the individual was destitute, the town was required to assume financial responsibility.[2] Other colonies, including Connecticut, New York, Rhode Island, and Vermont followed suit and often copied Bay Colony statutes outright. Even Virginia, which had laws dealing only with the property and status of the insane, cared for them under a poor law system modeled after that of England.[3]

Virtually none of this legislation referred to the medical treatment of the insane; the emphasis was strictly upon the social and economic consequences of mental disorders. This omission was not an oversight. To the limited extent that contemporary medical literature even discussed insanity, the concern was focused largely on the nature rather than treatment of mental disorders. Indeed, specific therapies were rarely mentioned before 1800. The frequent use of bleeding and purging reflected the influence of the Galenic humoral tradition. Disease, according to this tradition, was general rather than specific; it followed an excess in the production of any one of the four humors (blood, yellow bile, black bile, and phlegm). The physiological imbalances that resulted were treated by general nonspecific therapies, of which bleeding and purging were the most common. The distinction between mental and physical diseases, therefore, was tenuous at best. The relatively small numbers of trained physicians militated against medicalization as well. Sick individuals were often treated by ministers and women rather than doctors.

Although insanity was not yet defined exclusively in secular and medical terms, explanations about its origins or manifestations abounded. Most individuals who migrated to the New World brought with them the beliefs, traditions, and practices common in England as well as on the continent. Madness in early modern England was a term that conjured up supernatural, religious, astrological, scientific, and medical elements. The boundaries between magic, religion, medicine, and science were virtually nonexistent, and those who wrote about madness could integrate themes and explanations from all to explain mysterious phenomena.

The life of Richard Napier, an early seventeenth-century astrological physician, is illustrative. Napier treated five to fifteen patients per day between 1597 and 1634. During his career thousands of patients consulted him, of whom more than two thousand were either mad or deeply troubled. Like others of his generation, Napier believed that mental disorders could flow from both natural and supernatural sources. Stress, for example, could lead to either physical or mental disturbances. But mental disorders could also follow from the intervention of God as well as the Devil. Napier employed medicaments, psychology, environmental manipulation, and astrology in his armamentarium. He also exorcised those patients he believed to be possessed. When Edmund Francklin was brought before him, Napier ended with the following incantation:

> Behold, I God's most unworthy minister and servant, I do charge and command thee, thou cruel beast, with all thy associates and all other malignant spirits in case that any of you have your being in the body of this creature, Mr. E. Fr[ancklin], and have distempered his brain with melancholy and have also deprived his body and limbs of their natural use, I charge and command you speedily to depart from this creature and servant of God, Mr. E. F[rancklin], regenerated by the laver of the holy baptism and redeemed by the precious blood of our Lord Jesus Christ, I charge you to depart from him and every part of his body, really, personally.[4]

Napier's therapeutic and theoretical eclecticism was by no means unique. Robert Burton's famous *Anatomy of Melancholy*, published in 1621, was a compendium that incorporated beliefs and concepts drawn from a millennium of experience. The category of melancholia dated from antiquity, and its symptoms included depression, suspiciousness, weeping, muteness, and death wishes. Burton's interest in melancholy grew out of his own sufferings, and he wrote his classic text both to assist others and to rid himself of its debilitating symptoms. Melancholy could arise from a wide range of causes, including (but not limited to) faulty education, stress, childhood experiences, and heredity. Secular explanations, however, did not imply the absence of supernatural elements. To Burton and many of his contemporaries the Devil was a reality. Religious melancholy, therefore, symbolized ensnarement by Satan and was but a measure of human mortality. Indeed, the line between sanity and insanity was at best murky; the presence of melancholy was but a reaffirmation of human fallibility. Similarly, therapy for ordinary melancholy could include music ("a tonick to the saddened soul"), avoidance of solitude and idleness, and pharmaceuticals. One treatment consisted of a decapitated head of a ram ("that never meddled with an Ewe") boiled with cinnamon, ginger, nutmeg, mace, and cloves. For three days the concoction was to be given to "the patient fasting, so that he fast two hours after it. . . . For fourteen days let him use this diet, drink no wine, &c." Religious melancholy, on the other hand, could not be expelled by "physick," but required instead faith and a willingness to seek divine forgiveness.[5]

Those who settled in America were the heirs of Elizabethan thought, and brought with them the intellectual and cultural perceptions of the homeland. The rigors of creating a society in a radically different environment left little time to produce elaborate and original treatises on madness comparable to those published in England. Yet colonial perceptions of madness did not differ in fundamental ways from those of the mother country. Like their English brethren, colonial Americans integrated religious and secular themes in an effort to render insanity intelligible.

Few individuals devoted as much time and thought to the problems posed by madness as Cotton Mather. An eminent Puritan minister who played an important role in late seventeenth- and early eighteenth-century Massachusetts, he straddled the two worlds of the natural and supernatural. As a minister, Mather emphasized that Satan could tempt individuals into madness by exploiting their moral weaknesses. Sin, after all, was at the heart of the human condition, and one of its more obvious consequences was madness. But even saints could be smitten by divine intervention, for the will of the Almighty was beyond human comprehension. In *Magnalia Christi Americana*, published in 1702, he recounted the travail of John Warham, a pious man whom Satan "threw into the deadly pangs of melancholy" and whose "terrible temptations and buffetings" were relieved only by death.[6]

Nevertheless, by the 1720s Mather's religious explanations of insanity had begun to be modified to include naturalistic and biological elements. His treatise, *The Angel of Bethesda* (written in 1724 but not published until the twentieth century), was indicative of this shift. In it, he supported inoculation, a technique whereby a healthy person was exposed to the smallpox virus. This controversial intervention followed the observation that naturally occurring cases of smallpox had far higher mortality rates than induced cases. When strong opposition to inoculation threatened to divide the Boston community, Mather denounced speculative thinking and argued in favor of experience. "A few *Empirics* here," he added, "are worth all our Dogmatists."[7]

The Angel of Bethesda included as well a discussion of insanity even though the bulk of the text was devoted to other physical illnesses. Mather continued to affirm that madness was of divine origin, and therefore required repentance and the confession of guilt and unworthiness. But he linked mania (a category that included disturbed reasoning, excited and agitated behavior, and general irritability) to "*Animal Spirits* inflamed" and melancholia to "*Flatulencies* in the Region of the *Hypochondria*." He also accepted naturalistic therapies derived from traditional folk medicine, including "Living Swallows, cut in two, and laid reeking hott unto the shaved Head" as well as the "Blood of an *Ass* drawn from behind his Ear." Mather was also aware of the burdens caused by such illnesses. "These *Melancholicks*," he observed,

> do sufficiently *Afflict themselves*, and are Enough their *own Tormentors*. As if this *present Evil World*, would not *Really* afford Sad Things Enough, they create a World of *Imaginary Ones*, and by *Mediating Terror*, they make themselves as Miserable, as they could be from the most *Real Miseries*.
>
> But this is not all; They *Afflict others* as well as *Themselves*, and often make themselves Insupportable *Burdens* to all about them.
>
> In this Case, we must *Bear one anothers Burdens*, or, the *Burdens* which we make for One another.[8]

Like other Puritan divines, Mather was both articulate and prolific. Whether or not his views were representative is problematic. The similarities between his ideas and those of his ministerial brethren as well as his English contemporaries, however, suggest that his were by no means idiosyncratic. The shift in the nature of Mather's thinking was reflective of a more general decline in supernatural explanations of most phenomena during the eighteenth century. Enlightenment thought had led to more naturalistic ways of explaining human behavior. God and Satan, hitherto central elements in popular perceptions of madness, were now relegated to a more remote position. A naturalistic interpretation of insanity merged with a moral component. Insanity no longer followed divine intervention, but rather was a penalty for the willful violation of natural law. Admittedly, natural law was of divine origin, but not beyond human comprehension. All individuals, precisely because they were endowed with rational minds and free will, could understand the moral imperative that constituted its central core.

Slowly but surely the traditional distinction between supernatural and secular interpretations of madness began to disappear. If moral irregularities and excessive passions hastened the onset of insanity, then at the very least the illness was amenable to human intervention. Human beings were no longer passive pawns in the hands of an inscrutable and mysterious Deity whose actions defied human comprehension. Eighteenth-century explanations of insanity, therefore, were less likely to employ the language of faith and theology. Even in Massachusetts—a colony in which religion continued to play a vital role—the clergy stressed not the inscrutable will of God, but rather the personal responsibility of the individual. In a sermon delivered at the burial of an individual who had committed suicide in 1740, Solomon Williams emphasized how "the ignorance and perverse desires of the Mind" ultimately gave rise to bodily illness, which in turn reacted back upon the mind to weaken the power of reason. Madness thus involved an interaction of moral excesses and physical illnesses.[9]

As supernatural explanations receded, popular perceptions of insanity and a long-standing medical tradition dating from Hippocrates that emphasized biological and psychological elements began to converge. Lay and medical explanations of madness as well as somatic illnesses, to be sure, tended to be eclectic. Yet they all shared a holistic pathology that eschewed any effort to define the precise relationship between body and mind. The focus was rather on the interaction between body and mind, between the body and external environment, and between emotions and physiological processes. The body and the mind were seen as mutually interdependent; both played a vital role in maintaining the balance that was so necessary for good health. A disturbance in the digestive tract or other organs could affect the brain and cause mental disturbance, just as morbid or perverse thoughts could lead to adverse physiological consequences. Insanity could either follow misfortune beyond the control of individuals or result from the willful and purposeful violation of moral norms.[10]

Indicative of the growing significance of naturalistic interpretations of insanity was William Buchan's famous *Domestic Medicine*. From its initial publication in Edinburgh in 1769, Buchan's manual enjoyed phenomenal popularity in America. An American edition appeared in 1772, and the book remained in print for nearly a century. Like most of his contemporaries, Buchan believed that the human body functioned as an equilibrium system. Diet and climate shaped intake; behavior and clothing affected process; and urine and feces represented an effort to rid the body of potentially harmful wastes. Any imbalance would lead to illness; health was synonymous with balance. The role of the physician was to assist in restoring an equilibrium. In a like vein morbid thought patterns or excessive passions could weaken the body and thus lead to insanity. "Violent anger," he wrote, "will change melancholy into madness; and excessive cold, especially in the lower extremities, will force the blood into the brain, and produce symptoms of madness." Regimen—a balanced diet, exercise, and an avoidance of such substances as hard liquors, tea, and coffee—played an important role in both prevention and treatment. Buchan emphasized psychological factors; equally notable was the absence of any hint that insanity had supernatural origins. He also described Bedlam—the famous English asylum—in harsh terms. These institutions, he insisted, "are far more likely to make a wise man mad than to restore a madman to his senses."[11]

Explanations and perceptions about the nature and etiology of insanity, however important, did not by themselves shape the ways in which society dealt with disturbed individuals. Indeed, there was often a disjuncture between theoretical pronouncements and the reality of everyday life. Insanity, whether caused by an inscrutable Deity, immoral behavior, physiological factors, or even chance, nevertheless had a profound impact upon the immediate family as well as the neighboring community. The presence of distracted persons rarely remained a purely private matter and often required some kind of public intervention. Yet the unique circumstances of a newly-settled society meant that colonial Americans would have to develop novel ways of dealing with the problems associated with insanity. The decentralized nature of colonial society and government, as well as its rural character, mandated informal solutions to the intensely human problems that involved the immediate community and—if the afflicted person had one—the family.

In early 1651 Roger Williams addressed his fellow citizens of Providence regarding one Mrs. Weston, whom he described as "a distracted person." He appealed to the town to assume guardianship of her property and to make arrangements for her support. His reasons proved revealing. Such an act of mercy would in part reciprocate for the "many mercies from Heaven," he declared. Williams also enjoined his fellow citizens to remember "that we know not how soone our wives may be widowes and our children Orphans, yea and our selves be deprived of all or most of our Reason, before we goe from hence, except mercy from the God of Mercies prevent it." All individuals were at risk, and the presence of misfortune would hopefully arouse a charitable response. The citizens of Providence were receptive to his appeal and voted to take custody of Weston's property and to provide for her maintenance. Weston died shortly thereafter. The coroner's jury report offered further evidence that she was not in possession of her faculties, since they found "so neare as we can judge, that either the terriblness of the crack of thunder . . . or the coldness of the night, being she was naked, did kill her." Williams's sentiments and the town's favorable action suggested an awareness of human frailties and a recognition that society had a moral obligation toward all individuals in distress.[12]

The colonists who settled America brought with them English traditions and practices, including a poor law system that mandated local responsibility for distressed persons. Yet local responsibility had a quite different meaning in America, which lacked large urban areas and complex institutional arrangements characteristic of the mother country. Even outside London—by far the largest metropolitan area in England—population was sufficiently dense as to permit the creation of workhouses and poorhouses (which often held mad persons). London had an elaborate institutional network to care for the mentally ill, including the famous Bethlehem Hospital (often referred to as Bedlam), which held large numbers of dependent insane persons. In America, by contrast, population was widely dispersed. As late as 1790 there were only six areas with more than 8,000 residents; these held only 3.35 percent of the total population. Only two (New York and Philadelphia) had more than 25,000 residents, and none had more than 50,000. Such diffuse populations could not support large institutions to care for the insane. Confinement was the exception rather than the rule.

Unless they threatened public safety, people who were mad resided in the community. Those able to work were often afforded the opportunity to do so. Joseph Moody, a Harvard graduate and minister to a Maine church, wore a handkerchief over his face because of his feelings of unworthiness. During the services he turned his back on the audience for the same reason. His congregation accepted his bizarre ministry for three years, and even after he was removed from his pulpit and preached occasionally, his behavior was unchanged. Similarly, James Otis, Jr., occupied a series of public offices and maintained a law practice even though his obviously irrational behavior placed him beyond the bounds of sanity. Indeed, individuals who could manage their jobs or who recovered from episodes of madness were quickly absorbed into the community even though insanity was by no means free of stigma. Daniel Kirtland, a Yale graduate, lost his ministerial position after becoming insane. Upon his subsequent recovery, he received a comparable appointment from another Connecticut church.[13]

Ministers and political leaders, of course, represented high status occupations, and their behavior was perhaps more likely to be tolerated by a respectful community. Nevertheless, even ordinary individuals who had become insane were rarely incarcerated. In rural areas or small villages the number of disordered persons was far too small to permit institutional care. Charles Leonard, a resident of Taunton, Massachusetts, wandered about the town in "filthy clothes, deranged," and on occasion "frightened people." After cutting a Bible in half, he burned it. His conversation was garbled and he laughed in a "wild, insane manner." Yet local residents never confined him and even provided support at public expense.[14] In the colonial period, insanity was above all a problem involving the victim's dependency on those around him. A family might be devastated if an insane member was unable to work or else disrupted the household. On the other hand, if an individual had no family, the issue of support became paramount. In a society that lacked a central government or an elaborate bureaucracy, it was understandable that responsibility for dealing with distressed and dependent persons fell to local overseers of the poor or other town officials. Virtually all who served in these positions held other jobs; public service was an honor that carried few pecuniary rewards. Local officials usually dealt with insane and other dependent persons on an ad hoc basis.

The presence of "distracted" persons or "lunatics" in colonial America—perhaps due to their small numbers—aroused few expressions of public concern or fear. Insanity was not perceived as a *social* problem requiring formal public policies. Expediency more than anything else shaped the ways in which individuals and communities responded to perceived problems. In 1676 Jan Vorelissen, a resident of Amesland, Pennsylvania, complained that his son Erik was "bereft of his naturall Senses and is turned quyt madd." Given the father's admission that he lacked the resources to support his son, the community levied a tax to build "a little block-house at Amesland for to put in the said madman" and to provide support. Twelve years later the residents of Braintree, Massachusetts, voted to provide funds to Samuel Speere to "build a little house 7 foote long & 5 foote wide" adjacent to his own home for his distracted sister. The town also obligated itself to pay for her maintenance. By modern standards such accommodations would be regarded as evidence of brutality. In the seventeenth century, however, it was quite common for entire families to be housed in single rooms. Confining the insane in close quarters was only a reflection of the prevailing standard of living rather than an expression of callousness.[15]

Insanity placed many families under extreme emotional and economic duress. If it was not always possible to alleviate psychological tensions, it was certainly feasible for the locality to provide funds to permit a family to maintain itself. Many communities offered subsidies to families in order to enable them to care for insane members, particularly those whose behavior was perceived as benign. A town meeting in Providence in 1655 presided over by Roger Williams received an application from "our neighbor Pike", whose wife was "distracted." She had fallen "downe into a former distempure of Weakness & distractjon of mind," and the entire town had "to take our Turns & to watch with her, day & night least by her Distemp & Bitterness of ye Season she should p[e]rish amongst us." Those present voted to give Pike fifty shillings and promised "upon his further want & Complaint, he shall be supplied though to ye value of 10£ or more." Such actions were by no means uncommon, if only because there were few other alternatives. In particular, the absence of threatening behavior was generally accompanied by tolerant attitudes, particularly if the afflicted individual was a long standing resident. It was not uncommon for the community to provide such necessities as food and clothing to insane persons living in the community.[16]

But these tolerant attitudes had limits. When the behavior of insane persons appeared to threaten public safety, more stringent actions followed. Seventeenth- and eighteenth-century legislation often contained clauses empowering local officials to limit the freedom of "distracted persons" who menaced other residents. A Virginia court in 1689 took notice of John Stock, an individual "whoe keepes running about the neighborhood day and night in a sad Distracted Condition to the great Disturbance of the people." To prevent "his doeing any further Mischiefe," the court ordered the sheriff to place Stock "in some close Roome, where hee shall not bee suffered to go abroad untill hee bee in a better condition to Governe himselfe." Fear and benevolence were inextricably intertwined. When a colonial soldier who killed his mother was acquitted by reason of insanity, the court ordered him confined for life to a "small place" erected by his father in his home, but at public expense.[17]

Other communities reacted in a negative manner when confronted with the responsibility of providing for nonresident dependent persons. Such concerns gave rise to the legally sanctioned practice of "warning out"—a practice based on the proposition that towns had the right to exclude strangers. Legal residency during the colonial period was not an inherent right, but rather a privilege granted by existing residents. The distrust of strangers reflected both the relative absence of formal mechanisms of control to deal with behavior that might menace public order and a desire to absolve towns of any financial liability for the support of ill or unemployed strangers. Hence it was not uncommon for local officials to force the return of insane persons to the community in which they were legal residents. As residents of the largest town in New England, Bostonians sometimes found nonresident insane persons in their community. Officials frequently attempted to return such individuals to the town from which they originally came. When sending Edward Eveleth to Ipswich, the Boston selectmen noted that he was "disposed to wander" and requested Ipswich officials to "take care to prevent his returning to us, which if he should will occasion a charge to your Town." The overwhelming majority of individuals "warned out," however, were not insane, suggesting that fiscal concerns rather than fear of insanity shaped this practice. Efforts to avoid or to shift welfare costs became a tradition that was to play a major role in shaping public policy toward mental illnesses during the nineteenth and twentieth centuries.[18]

To most colonial Americans insanity was of concern because of its economic ramifications and potential threat to public safety. Medical considerations played virtually no role in shaping practices and customs. Given prevailing standards of living, available resources, and the absence of institutions, there is every reason to believe that the fate of the insane was not appreciably different from that of other dependent groups. Like widows, orphans, handicapped, aged, and sick persons, insane individuals required public assistance. Although always present, fiscal concerns were softened by long-standing ethical and moral values that assigned an unyielding obligation to assist those unable to survive independently.

By the early eighteenth century institutionalization of the insane in the colonies first appeared. Demographic factors had begun to hasten changes in the pattern of welfare in larger towns. The growth of population in several colonial towns led to a proportionate increase in the number of sick and dependent persons. The informal manner in which communities had cared for such persons no longer seemed adequate. To assist a variety of dependent groups, a few of the larger towns began to create undifferentiated welfare institutions such as almshouses. These institutions were intended to fulfill humanitarian and moral obligations while simultaneously effecting economies by virtue of their size and efficiency. Eclectic in nature, they accepted the very young, the aged, the infirm, and the mentally ill, among others.

In Boston the first almshouse was built with private bequests in 1662, even though the first inmates were not accepted until several years later. As early as 1729 Boston officials sought authorization for a separate facility in order to keep "Distracted Persons Separate from the Poor," perhaps because the indiscriminate confinement of inmates proved disruptive. In 1764 Thomas Hancock, a wealthy and prominent Boston merchant and uncle of John Hancock, left a bequest of £600 for the establishment of an institution for insane persons alone. The bequest, which had a three-year limitation, was never used for the purpose; the town failed to raise the necessary supplementary funds. The developing crisis between the colonies and Britain had shifted attention to more pressing problems, and a separate institution for insane persons did not become reality for more than half a century. The increase in illness and dependency ultimately moved community leaders in the major colonial cities to support the creation of institutions for dependent persons. But the undifferentiated nature of these facilities generated novel problems of their own. The subsequent efforts to create specialized facilities for the insane proved temporarily unsuccessful.[19]

As in England, many areas in this period developed a mixed system in which public welfare and private benevolence mutually reinforced and complemented one another. Out of this system emerged the first urban hospitals in mid-eighteenth century America. The eighteenth (and nineteenth) century hospitals, however, differed in fundamental respects from their twentieth century counterparts. The hospital in its origins was more akin to the almshouse than the modern medical center. Before 1880 it provided care for socially marginal groups of sick and aged individuals, and, to a lesser degree, served as a training facility for aspiring physicians. "The hospital," Charles E. Rosenberg has noted, "was something Americans of the better sort did for their less fortunate countrymen; it was hardly a refuge they contemplated entering them-selves." As late as 1873, there were only 178 hospitals in the United States (of which one-third were mental hospitals) containing fewer than fifty thousand beds. Nonpaying patients constituted the majority of admissions, and control resided not with physicians, but with affluent trustees who supported the institution. The functional line between the hospital and almshouse was vague at best and often nonexistent; the lat-ter was supported by public funds from the local community, the former by private philanthropy.[20]

It was in Philadelphia, the largest city in mid-eighteenth-century America, that the first hospital was founded. The presence of affluent people, urbanization, immigration, and the resulting social problems provided the breeding ground for institutional growth. Quakers no longer dominated the political life of the colony, although they were seeking to influence society by creating a network of private, voluntary, and nonsectarian organizations that met perceived social needs. They were instrumental in founding a new hospital.[21]

The idea originated with Dr. Thomas Bond, a man who, in fact, had been disowned by the Friends in 1742 for taking an oath. (Quakers rejected oaths on the ground that they were committed to a unitary stan-dard of truth which did not allow them to be less honest in everyday life than in a court.) Having visited London, Bond was impressed with the care provided the mentally ill at Bethlehem Hospital. He secured the aid of Benjamin Franklin, who launched a colony-wide fund raising effort and applied to the provincial Assembly for assistance at the same time. The petition to the Assembly opened with the following declaration:

> THAT with the Numbers of People the Number of Lunaticks, or Persons distemper'd in Mind, and deprived of their rational Faculties, hath greatly increased in this Province.
>
> THAT some of them going at large, are a Terror to their Neighbours, who are daily apprehensive of the Violences they may commit; and others are continually wasting their Substance, to the great injury of themselves and Families, ill disposed Persons wickedly taking Advantage of their unhappy Condition, and drawing them into unreasonable Bargains, &c.

Proper treatment, Franklin added, could restore many of the insane to health. Although the province had made provision for the relief of the poor, it still required facilities to care for needy persons whose plight had been worsened by illness.[22]

In spite of opposition, the legislation passed. Under its provisions the hospital was granted a charter as well as a subsidy of £2,000 when matching private funds had been secured. The hospital, according to the act, would save and restore "useful and laborious Members," provide "Relief for the Sick Poor," and care for the insane. Quaker control notwithstanding, the institution quickly outgrew its sectarian character and became a benevolent and philanthropic institution that served the whole community.[23]

Throughout the eighteenth century the hospital cared for insane patients, but the number was never large. Between 1752 and 1754, 18 out of 117 persons admitted were classified as insane, and during the same period fifteen were discharged. By 1787 the number of such persons had grown to 34. In general, the patient population was not unrepresentative of the community. Some were admitted by the overseers of the poor and supported by public funds; others were private patients who in some instances had private attendants. Although the latter received special care, the hospital never formally adopted a differential policy. Unequal care developed as a result of the class and social relationships that existed between staff and patients.[24]

Within two decades New York City followed Philadelphia's lead. The first suggestion for the creation of a hospital came from Dr. Samuel Bard, whose physician-father was intimately acquainted with Franklin and the Pennsylvania Hospital. Bard had already persuaded the governors of King's College (later Columbia University) to establish a medical school. Mindful of the need for a hospital that could provide teaching facilities as well as serve the community, he secured the support of the royal governor. In 1771 a charter was granted to the "Society of the Hospital in the city of New-York in America." Shortly thereafter construction of a physical plant began which included provision for "wards or cells for the reception of Lunatics." The project came to an abrupt halt in 1775, however, after a fire destroyed the structure. The Revolutionary War halted any further action, and the New York Hospital did not open until 1791. In the ensuing decade fewer than one hundred insane persons were admitted, and some were housed in basement cells. The care and treatment of the insane remained distinctly secondary to the hospital's central mission.[25]

The first public hospital devoted exclusively to the care and treatment of the insane, ironically enough, was established in Virginia—a colony that had no urban center. British tradition in this most English of the colonies probably provided the impulse. Having adopted the English poor law system, the colony cared for its insane within the framework of the poor laws. The initial call for a hospital came from the Royal Governor in 1766, but the project languished for several years when the legislature failed to act. With the support of the colony's governing elite, a bill authorizing a new public hospital located in Williamsburg passed in late 1769. The wording of the act was revealing—"to make provision for the support and maintenance of ideots, lunatics, and other persons of unsound minds." The opening clause provided a justification for the creation of a public hospital by observing that "several persons of insane and disordered minds have been frequently found wandering in different parts of this colony," and that "no certain provision" had "yet [been] made either towards effecting a cure of those whose cases are not become quite desperate, nor for restraining others who may be dangerous to society."[26]

Four years later the hospital received its first patient. That the institution served a caring rather than a medical function was evident by the choice of a layperson—not a physician—as its principal officer. This "keeper" generally deferred to the visiting physician insofar as any medical treatment was concerned. Before 1800 the hospital remained small and was rarely filled to capacity. Between late 1786 and 1790 only thirty-six patients were admitted. A French traveler was impressed with the hospital building during a visit in 1796, but added that

> the unfortunate maniacs are rather abandoned to their wretched state than subjected to any treatment which might tend to their recovery. From the observations made in Virginia on maniacal complaints, the principal causes assigned for them are enthusiastic devotion [to religion] and spirituous liquors; and it appears that such as arise from the latter of these causes are less difficult of cure than those which owe their origin to the former. There are only fifteen lunatics of both sexes in this hospital, which is capable of containing thirty.

Novel in character, the Virginia Eastern Asylum (to use its later name) had relatively little influence. Its isolated location, small size, and local character ensured that it would not become a model for other states to follow.[27]

The absence of hospitals and other formal institutions in colonial America was a product neither of callousness nor ignorance. Indeed, Americans were acutely aware of the threats that epidemic infectious diseases—smallpox, yellow fever, diphtheria, malaria, measles, dysentery—posed to health and life. But with the exception of a few urban areas, population density was so low that the need for formal mechanisms of care was minimal. Under these circumstances responsibility for providing care for the insane remained in the hands of families or local communities. There was widespread recognition that madness was an inescapable if undesirable part of the human condition, and that insanity did not strip individuals of their status as members of a community. Colonial Americans also believed that they had a collective moral obligation toward individuals whose illness made them dependent upon others for the very means of survival. In future decades and centuries Americans would continue to debate how best to meet such responsibilities.

2

Inventing the Asylum

In the half century following 1800 demographic and economic changes forced Americans to reappraise many of their traditional arrangements and practices of caring for mentally ill people. In 1790 there were only six cities with 8,000 or more residents, amounting to only 3.35 percent of the total population. By 1850 there were eighty-five such urban areas containing 12.5 percent of the population. In 1790 no city had more than 50,000 residents; sixty years later New York had more than half a million persons; four others held between 100,000 and 250,000; and twenty more ranged in size from 25,000 to 100,000. The process of urbanization was even more complex than these figures suggest. Because of high rates of geographical mobility, perhaps two to six times as many individuals and families passed into and out of cities as lived in them at the beginning of each decade.[1]

Urbanization was only one aspect of the changes that altered individual and class relationships and reshaped family structure in America, thus necessitating new means of caring for the insane. The artisan system of labor was being undermined by the rise of merchant capitalism and the emergence of a national and international market, and a system of wage labor was taking its place. At the same time the nature and responsibilities of the family were being redefined. In preindustrial society the family provided not only the basic necessities of life, but assumed responsibility as well for educating children, caring for the aged and infirm, and for supporting dependent members. The separation of home from the workplace—a characteristic of nineteenth-century industrial society where labor was often centralized in factories and other industrial or commercial workplaces—led to the privatization of family life. This change in turn led to a diminution of the educational and welfare functions of the family, both of which were transferred to public or quasi-public institutions. The weakening of traditional means of socialization within the family and control by the family ultimately fostered the creation of public structures to take its place.[2]

In the emerging urban-industrial society the care of the insane proved far more complex than it had been in the rural areas and villages of seventeenth- and eighteenth-century America. The dramatic growth in population was accompanied by a proportionate increase in the number of insane persons. In densely populated areas insane people were more visible, and public concern about security increased. The spontaneous and informal manner in which most rural communities dealt with sickness and dependency did not operate as well in urban areas. High rates of geographical mobility tended to weaken social cohesion as neighbors became more anonymous, and the efficacy of informal and traditional means of alleviating distress diminished. These considerations militated against reliance on informal responses by families and community, and favored more systematic policies to deal with mental illnesses. In its origins, the mental hospital—irrespective of its specific medical role—was primarily an institution designed to serve more densely populated areas and to assume functions that previously had been the responsibility of families.[3]

In experiencing rapid social change, the United States was by no means unique. But the migration to America of large numbers of lower-class persons from minority ethnic backgrounds exacerbated problems arising out of disease and dependency. Between 1830 and 1850 population increased from nearly thirteen to twenty-three million. During these same years more than two and a third million immigrants landed in the United States, of whom about 44 percent were from Ireland. Often lacking skills, the Irish worked in low-paid, dangerous, and unhealthful occupations, and lived in crowded urban slums; high morbidity and mortality rates were common. When a cholera epidemic struck Boston in 1849, it had a devastating impact in Irish districts, which were the "least perfect in drainage, the worst ventilated and the most crowded." Of seven hundred fatalities, no less than five hundred occurred among the Irish and their children. Mortality rates during epidemics, however, paled into insignificance when compared with high infant mortality rates from common intestinal disorders, which one physician attributed to "overcrowding and imperfect drainage." Many Irish came to America without spouses, and therefore lacked any supporting family network. Consequently, they were generally dependent on public assistance when unemployed or ill.[4]

––––––––

Changes in the economy and social structure, however important, could not by themselves have created the mental hospital. What was required was the idea of such an institution, an awareness of an alternative to the informal modes of care that had resulted from the colonial poor law system. As Enlightenment values permeated Europe and America, a peculiar blend of intellectual and scientific currents gave rise to a secular faith that long-standing problems could be solved by conscious and purposeful human intervention. Preindustrial people tended to accept their fate; the ways of an omnipotent God were beyond human understanding. The Enlightenment outlook, by contrast, stressed the desirability of innovation, condemned stagnation, and sought to apply intelligence and rationality to social problems. The belief that the conquest of disease was only a matter of time, that perennial dilemmas of humanity—poverty, vice, and ignorance—could be minimized if not abolished, became popular. Faith in reason and science and in the ability of humanity to alleviate problems and change its environment slowly began to influence theories of insanity and prevailing practices.

By the mid-eighteenth century changes in explanations of and attitudes toward insanity were already evident. Madness, wrote Dr. William Battie in 1758, was "as manageable as many other distempers, which are equally dreadful and obstinate, and yet are not looked upon as incurable . . . and such unhappy objects ought by no means to be abandoned, much less shut in loathsome prisons as criminals or nuisances to the society." As one of the founders and first physician at St. Luke's Hospital for Lunaticks in London, he noted the existence of spontaneous recoveries. Insisting upon the importance of "regimen," Battle stimulated the founding of lunatic hospitals in other English cities.[5]

In France Philippe Pinel, born in 1745, moved to Paris in 1778, where he set out to rethink medical and psychiatric assumptions and goals. In 1798 he insisted that medicine should employ the same methods and criteria used in natural history. Rejecting speculations about the ultimate nature of disease, Pinel confined himself to the accumulation and analysis of data. "The time, perhaps, is at length arrived," he proclaimed,

> when medicine in France, now liberated from the fetters imposed upon it, by the prejudices of custom, by interested ambition, by its association with religious institutions, and by the discredit in which it has been held in the public estimation, will be able to assume its proper dignity, to establish its theories on facts alone, to generalize these facts, and to maintain its level with other departments of natural history.[6]

Loathing speculation, Pinel avoided abstract questions, including the nature of mental disease or the relationship between mind and body. Concentrating upon the behavioral aspects of insanity, he observed and analyzed patients and kept extensive case histories. He recognized that madness could either be "continuous or chronic" or "show long remissions" and be "interremittent" in character. His own classification of mental disease was not particularly original; his four major categories (melancholia, mania, dementia, and idiotism) had been used before. Similarly, his etiological explanations were hardly novel. He identified a variety of situations that could lead to insanity, including "ungovernable or disappointed ambition, religious fanaticism, profound chagrin, and unfortunate love." Certain professions "in which the imagination is unceasingly or ardently engaged, and not moderated in its excitement by the exercise of those functions of the understanding" placed its members at high risk to become insane.

> Here is the father of a family whom unexpected losses have thrown into despair; here a son exhausted by work and vigils to provide for his parents' subsistence; elsewhere a passionate and sensitive young man, victim of unrequited love; there a tender husband, distracted by suspicions and the justified or false umbrage of jealousy; a young warrior thirsting for glory whose vast and ambitious projects failed, his spirit crushed by the harsh experience. Religious zeal claims its victims, as does ardent military fervor, which often expresses all the reveries and excesses of manic fanaticism.[7]

If Pinel's contributions to theory were modest, his therapeutic innovations played a major role in the development of institutions. As an empiricist, he tended to judge therapies in terms of their outcome. Thus he found bleeding, corporal punishment, and other traditional practices used to treat the insane ineffective. He was equally opposed to prevailing modes of confinement. "To detain maniacs in constant seclusion," he observed, "and to load them with chains; to leave them defenceless, to the brutality of underlings . . . in a word, to rule them with a rod of iron . . . is a system of superintendence, more distinguished for its convenience than for its humanity or its success." Because he rejected the idea that insanity was solely the result of physical lesions, he made room for a psychologically-oriented therapy. Seeking to gain the patient's confidence and instill hope, he developed what he called *traitement moral*, which in England and America became known as "moral treatment" or "moral management." It must be understood, however, that the French word *moral* had no moralistic content; within Pinel's analytic framework it meant a psychologically oriented therapy. *Traitement moral* reflected his innovative assumption that environmental changes could affect individual psychology and thus alter behavior. "Moral treatment," one of Pinel's most famous students wrote, "is the application of the faculty of intelligence and of emotions in the treatment of mental alienation."[8]

Moral therapy assumed that confinement in a well-ordered asylum was indispensable. In such an institution the regimen could be employed in ways that would persuade patients to internalize the behavior and values of normal society and thus promote recovery. Pinel rejected the prevailing belief that madness was incurable. To insist upon incurability, he observed, "is to assert a vague proposition that is constantly refuted by the most authentic facts." Pinel's *traitement moral* held out the possibility and probability of recovery. Since madness did not "imply a total abolition of the mental faculties," it became theoretically possible to appeal to the patient's reasoning abilities. Pinel's approach, however, was by no means libertarian or democratic. The physician occupied a demanding and dominant position; patients were expected to comply with all medical directives. "One of the major principles of the psychologic management of the insane," he wrote, "is to break their will in a skillfully timed manner without causing wounds or imposing hard labor. Rather, a formidable show of terror should convince them that they are not free to pursue their impetuous willfulness and that their only choice is to submit." The hospital, retreat, asylum—whatever its designation—which focused on the insane alone was at the heart of his therapeutic system. The institution, he concluded in his seminal essay in 1794, "should reflect a well-ordered wisdom corresponding to the varied needs of the insane and proclaim from afar the respect due to distress and misfortune."[9]

Although Pinel played a vital role in the medicalization of insanity and conferring legitimacy on the asylum, he was by no means alone. The general humanitarian currents that had grown out of the Enlightenment produced other figures who helped transform the ways in which society dealt with the problems of mental illnesses. In Italy Vincenzio Chiarugi and in the United States Benjamin Rush played roles in modifying theory and practice. More important than either of these individuals was William Tuke, an English Quaker and merchant, whose efforts led to the founding of the York Retreat in 1792. That Quakers would be involved with the insane was understandable; the Society of Friends was already dedicated to moral reform and was seeking to abolish slavery, assist the poor, and promote prison reform. The establishment of the York Retreat, however, was not solely a humanitarian and philanthropic act. The Society was concerned because insane Friends

> are often from the peculiar treatment which they require, necessarily committed, wholly, to the government of people of other societies: by which means the state of their own minds, and the feelings of their near connexions are rendered more dissatisfied and uncomfortable. . . . It appears therefore very desirable that an Institution should be formed, wholly under the government of Friends. . . . This would . . . alleviate the anxiety of the relatives, render the minds of the patients more easy in their lucid intervals and consequently tend to facilitate and promote their recovery.[10]

The therapeutic system developed at the Retreat was similar in some respects to the one advocated by Pinel. Like Pinel, the leaders of the Retreat were distrustful of indiscriminate use of drugs, bleeding, emetics, and cathartics, and thus tended to minimize their use. The basic objective of the Retreat's regimen was to assist patients in developing internal means of self-restraint and self-control. The religious foundations of the York Retreat nurtured the belief that those who worked there were instruments of God's will; the moral character of its managers and staff was indissolubly linked with therapeutic efficacy. Religion promoted self-restraint as well as social harmony and stability. The Retreat's regimen—presided over by a layperson—was designed to create an environment in which internal self-restraint and discipline replaced external fetters. While expressing religious and benevolent ideals, the managers of the Retreat also employed more authoritarian means. "There is much analogy," Tuke observed, "between the judicious treatment of children, and that of insane persons." Hence "the principal of fear . . . when moderately and judiciously excited . . . has a salutary effect." Since the founding of the Retreat reflected Quaker beliefs, abstract speculations were largely absent; Tuke and his associates were not particularly concerned with theoretical explanations about the nature of insanity.[11]

Pinel and Tuke provided an alternative to local means of care or to confinement in undifferentiated welfare institutions such as poorhouses and prisons. Thomas S. Kirkbride, a Quaker and a very important nineteenth-century American psychiatrist, understood their contributions when he wrote that both figures, "by a singular coincidence, without any knowledge of each others movement, were at the same time, in different kingdoms, engaged in the same noble work of discarding time honoured prejudices and abuses, and from actual practice, giving to the world a code of principles for the moral treatment of Insanity, which even now can hardly be improved."[12] The work of Pinel, Tuke, and others led inescapably to a radical conclusion; insanity was not necessarily a chronic illness, that with appropriate treatment recovery was probable, and that investment in mental hospitals would yield a high proportion of cures.

Within a few decades educated and upper-class laypersons, physicians, intellectuals, and others had become aware of the newer views associated with the advocates of a hospital-based system of care. The existence of a translantic intellectual and scientific community facilitated the rapid dissemination of such views. Some Americans were educated abroad and brought back with them first-hand knowledge of European and English practices. Others were influenced by the printed word. Language proved no barrier, for Pinel's classic work appeared in an English edition in 1806, and the York Retreat was memorialized in Samuel Tuke's influential *Description of the Retreat* in 1813. Not only did American Quakers establish the Friends' Asylum in Pennsylvania in 1813, but they played important roles at other nonsectarian institutions. Thomas Eddy, a well-known New York Quaker, played a key part in reorganizing the care of the insane at the New York Hospital, and acknowledged his debt to Tuke. Indeed, half of the hospitals in the United States founded before 1824 borrowed heavily from the Quaker example.[13]

Alternatives to community or almshouse care, however, were but one element in the emerging transformation of public policy toward the insane. Another was the Second Great Awakening—a religious revival movement that in its efforts to revitalize American Christianity and enhance its relevancy created a climate conducive to institutional change. Beginning about 1800, the Awakening further weakened the Puritan and Calvinistic emphasis on the depravity of human nature and the futility of human intervention which had long held sway over American religion. In place of such pessimistic tenets, some Protestant leaders substituted the ideal of a loving and beneficent God. The central theme of their liberalized theology was the belief in a moral universe and the doctrine of free will. When the concept of the free individual was fused with the millennial vision of a perfected society, evangelical Protestantism was transformed into an active social force seeking the abolition of the restraints that bound individuals. Ministers and laypersons alike began to work actively to rid society of restraints that shackled individuals, of which slavery was an outstanding example. The result was a generalized faith that institutions could be improved and that individuals could be perfected. Within this context madness lost its aura of permanence; appropriate therapy within a well-ordered asylum could in many cases lead to the restoration of sanity. In his first inaugural speech in 1829, Andrew Jackson gave eloquent expression to many of the ideas of the Second Great Awakening.

> I believe that man can be elevated; man can become more and more endowed with divinity; and as he does he becomes more God-like in his character and capable of governing himself. Let us go on elevating our people, perfecting our institutions, until democracy shall reach such a point of perfection that we can acclaim with truth that the voice of the people is the voice of God.[14]

The cause of reform was also aided by the growing financial support of wealthy elites in urban communities. Philadelphia and New York had already benefited from the moral and financial support given to their new hospitals by wealthy individuals in the latter part of the eighteenth century. Even Virginia's hospital had been created by an indigenous elite. By the early nineteenth century these older elites found that their hegemony was being challenged by affluent newcomers whose rise reflected economic change. This rivalry, stimulated by sectarian differences, fostered philanthropic giving. Revering virtues like ambition, thrift, hard work, personal responsibility, and honesty, these new elites believed that they had a responsibility to use their wealth and power in socially beneficent ways. The concept of stewardship was central, and its members played important parts in the founding and support of such institutions as hospitals, colleges, museums, and other enterprises.

Alongside new ideas, new methodologies, and new elites, there was a growing consensus that government—particularly at the state level—had an obligation to foster the welfare of its citizens. There was broad agreement in the United States that government was, in the words of Orestes S. Brownson, "a positive good . . . never" to "be dispensed with." Most state governments retained many reform and police functions. Under such circumstances it was not surprising that states would emphasize important social policy functions and play a critical part in the creation of asylums, prisons, schools, and almshouses. In so doing they would broaden their regulatory and welfare functions and responsibilities as well. If individuals were free to pursue their private interests, then the state would have to exercise police and regulatory authority in order to ensure that some sort of cohesion prevailed.[15]

The first suggestion that traditional and informal modes of care for the insane were weakening came with a short-lived but significant spurt in the founding of private asylums in the Northeast. Created largely by contributions from affluent elites—which were often supplemented by public subsidies—these new institutions were for the most part intended, at least in theory, to serve the entire community. Those who could afford to pay for their upkeep were required to do so. All others, whether from middle- or lower-class backgrounds, were to be subsidized by a combination of private and public funds as well as by higher charges paid by well-to-do patients. Between 1811 and 1822 three new institutions—the McLean Asylum, Friends' Asylum, and the Hartford Retreat—were founded, and the Bloomingdale Asylum was given an autonomous identity at the New York Hospital.

Although indigenous circumstances shaped each of these hospitals, there were some threads common to all. In one form or another religion was an operative element. In Boston religious rivalries stimulated Congregationalist support for an asylum. Both the Friends' and Bloomingdale Asylums owed much to prominent Quakers. In Connecticut the Second Great Awakening shaped the background of those involved in the founding and subsequent history of the Hartford Retreat. Similarly, the involvement of prominent physicians aware of newer concepts of care and treatment of the insane was evident in Massachusetts, New York, and Connecticut. Finally, affluent elites not only contributed funds, but mobilized political support that resulted in state subsidies.

The first of these new asylums was established in Boston. By 1800 the city's population had reached 25,000, complicating informal means of caring for insane persons. As early as 1801 Jedidiah Morse, an eminent conservative Congregationalist minister, called for the creation of a "hospital for Lunatics." Some insane persons, he emphasized, "are committed to close confinement, under circumstances of great wretchedness. Others are left, forlorn and friendless, to roam through the country, exposed to the insults of the thoughtless and wicked; to hunger, cold, and various calamitous and fatal accidents, a terror to female delicacy, and a grief and a continual cause of anxiety to their relations." Nine years later Reverend John Bartlett, chaplain of the city almshouse, and two prominent physicians, John Collins Warren and James Jackson, called for the founding of a general hospital. Warren and Jackson were concerned with the devastating nature of protracted illnesses such as insanity; the inability of family to pay for long-term care often led to neglect, which in turn transformed an acute into a chronic illness. The ideal solution was a hospital that would accept insane patients, and derive its support from private donors and public funds.

The following year the General Court passed an act of incorporation and contributed a private estate valued at $20,000 as an endowment if the corporation raised $100,000 from private sources. Fund raising was delayed by the War of 1812, but by 1817 the trustees had raised the requisite funds. The bulk came from affluent citizens associated with the Congregational Church; the thirteen largest gifts amounted to $56,000. Denominational rivalries were evident in the appeal of the clergy. "Shall the Congregational scion alone be barren of the sweetest fruits which the tree of Christianity had produced?" they noted when calling attention to the charitable activities of other Christian denominations.

Even before the Massachusetts General Hospital had opened, the trustees had already decided to separate insane from other patients. The hospital was placed in Boston; the asylum for the insane in nearby Charlestown. After receiving its first patients in 1818, the facility was officially renamed McLean Asylum for the Insane in 1826 after John McLean, who had donated $25,000 and made the hospital his residual legatee. Eventually the corporation received nearly $120,000 from his estate—a huge bequest by prevailing standards.[16]

While the Boston elite was founding the Massachusetts General Hospital and McLean Asylum, Philadelphia Quakers were in the process of creating an institution modeled along the lines of the York Retreat. Concerned with members of their own denomination, the Society of Friends began to discuss the issue in 1811, and by 1813 had adopted a constitution and launched a fund-raising drive. Although admission would be limited to members of the Society, ability to pay was excluded as an element. Located in Frankford, a suburb of Philadelphia, the new facility opened in 1817. It was administered by a lay superintendent, and the responsibilities of a resident physician were limited to strictly medical problems. Small in size and sectarian in character, the Asylum did little to shape public attitudes even though its existence stimulated interest in institutional care.[17]

The third corporate hospital to appear was the Hartford Retreat in Connecticut. Unlike the founders of the Boston and Philadelphia institutions, those who promoted asylum care in Connecticut tended to come from the ranks of physicians. Between 1812 and 1816 the members of the Connecticut Medical Society had discussed the possibility of establishing an asylum and even had appointed a committee to take a census of the insane. The concept was resurrected in 1821 when the Society authorized another investigation of the number of insane persons in the state. Composed of five physicians, including Eli Todd and Samuel B. Woodward, the committee found nearly 1,000 insane persons. "Their situation," they wrote,

> is wretched in the extreme. . . . Sometimes he [the poor maniac] wanders from place to place without food and without decent apparel; sometimes he occupies an apartment in the family mansion, at once the monument and the source of wretchedness, the victim, and in many cases the cause of insanity. . . .
>
> The wretchedness of those families upon whom devolve the care and maintenance of the insane can be estimated only by those who, from personal observation, have become acquainted with its extent. Their peace is interrupted, their cares are multiplied, their time is engrossed, and their fortunes reduced or entirely dissipated in attempting to restore to reason one unfortunate member. . . . The misery which they suffer is communicated to a large circle of friends and the whole neighborhood is indirectly disturbed by the malady of one.

Insisting that a hospital could prevent the advent of chronicity, the committee urged the creation of a "Society for the Relief of the Insane." Its draft of a constitution was quickly accepted by the assembled colleagues.[18]

By 1822 the legislature had approved of the act of incorporation. Although the superintendent had to be nominated by a committee of the State Medical Society, a complex system of governance was adopted that weakened his authority and resulted in protracted internal conflict for more than five decades. Within months a fund-raising drive was launched. The lead was taken by the original five physicians who were assisted by eminent members of the clergy. The support of the latter was understandable, since the Second Great Awakening had a profound impact within Connecticut. Indeed, many of the physicians active in the efforts to establish the Retreat had been influenced by their religious background and upbringing. Less affluent than their Massachusetts counterparts, Connecticut citizens had only contributed $12,000 by the spring of 1822. That same year the legislature provided a subsidy of $5,000, and gave the Society for the Relief of the Insane the authority to operate a lottery. Fund raising proved more successful than the lottery, and the Retreat finally opened in 1824. Financial problems, however, continued to plague the Retreat throughout its early years.[19]

At the same time that institutions were established in Boston, Frankford, and Hartford, the insane department of the New York Hospital was undergoing a series of reorganizations that by 1821 had given it a somewhat autonomous character. Opened in 1791, the hospital did not segregate the insane. By 1808, however, a separate facility, built for about $50,000, was opened. Although an administrative reorganization provided for a physician to visit patients, a lay caretaker exercised the powers of a superintendent, suggesting that the reorganization was hardly informed by the newer views about the care and treatment of the mentally ill associated with Pinel and Tuke.

Thomas Eddy, influenced by his Quaker brethren, presented the governors of the New York Hospital in 1815 with a series of far-reaching recommendations that reflected the influence of Samuel Tuke and the York Retreat. His views prevailed, and the governors purchased a thirty-eight acre tract on Manhattan's upper west side, then known as Bloomingdale (and now the site of Columbia University). They also sent a petition to the state legislature, citing the large numbers of applications for admission, the lack of facilities, and the "indiscriminate mixture . . .

of persons of different character, of various and opposite religious sentiments, the serious and profane, the profligate and virtuous." Prodded by
Eddy's skillful lobbying, the legislature granted the hospital an annual
subsidy of $10,000 until 1857, giving the institution a quasi-public char-
acter. In July of 1821 patients were moved into the newly named Bloomingdale Asylum. A division of authority between a lay superintendent
and a resident physician would create internal strife for nearly three
decades.[20]

These early hospitals generally cared for a severely incapacitated
population. William Handy, who served as the visiting physician at the
asylum of the New York Hospital in 1817 and 1818, kept records on
about seventy-five patients. Two-thirds were male, and half were no
more than thirty years of age. Handy was obviously little interested in
nosological categories; most of the inmates were described as maniacs.
Many were violent, and were perceived to represent a danger to themselves or their families; others were clearly depressed. One twenty-two
year old male admitted in 1817 had received a good education, but
declined to join his father's tannery business. Unable to hold a job, he
became "gloomy, sullen, discontented, and hypochondriacal," and his
mind "appeared to be left a prey to the gloom of solitude." During a trip
to the South he became "mentally deranged," and he was confined in a
straight jacket. Upon his return "his maniacal symptoms returned and
overwhelmed him, [and] he became frantic and has ever since been subject to paroxysms of madness" so severe as to require the use of
restraints. A forty-five year-old female who had been ill for three years
came to the conclusion that she "must kill one of her family and must
be imprisoned and executed, that the devil reigned and they must pray
to him." Most of the patients were institutionalized by their families,
who found themselves unable to deal with behavior that was often disruptive in the extreme.[21]

Treatment in hospitals tended to be empirical and eclectic. Handy, for
example, preferred mild cathartics and warm baths, and expressed hostility to "drastic purges." Hyoscyamus, camphor, and opium were used
to sedate violent patients. Patients who refused to eat were fed by a fun-
nel. The time-honored practice of bloodletting was occasionally used,
although Handy expressed doubt about its efficacy. Recreation and
employment were highly valued for their therapeutic effects. In extreme
cases solitary confinement and restraining devices were employed,
although they were discontinued as soon as was feasible. The means of

restraint were easily available, Handy conceded, "but it should be the supreme object of those who have assumed the supreme responsibility of governing the insane, to restore to their reason and to society the greatest possible number of these afflicted beings . . . [which] will be most certainly accomplished by strict attention to a moral regimen."[22]

Popular in their respective communities, these early hospitals did not become models that were widely emulated, but they did influence subsequent developments. They were instrumental in spreading and popularizing some of the newer concepts of mental disorders, including the belief that early treatment implied a hopeful prognosis. Moreover, some of the physicians associated with them helped to create a medical specialty concerned with mental illnesses that subsequently shaped policy. Yet the structure, limited financial base, and affluent clientele precluded these institutions from becoming the foundation of a comprehensive system of hospitals serving the entire community.

Although in the mainstream of early nineteenth-century psychiatric thought and practice, these private or quasi-private asylums accepted relatively few patients. McLean, for example, admitted about sixty-one patients annually in the first twelve years of its existence. Discharging about fifty-five cases yearly, the average number of resident patients was usually under fifty. Bloomingdale treated twice as many as McLean, but the Hartford Retreat in the 1820s admitted only forty-one patients yearly and the Friends' Asylum somewhat over twenty. Their small size notwithstanding, these hospitals claimed striking successes. Of the 666 patients discharged between 1818 and 1830, McLean listed 247 as recovered, 96 much improved, and 91 improved; the figures for Bloomingdale between 1821 and 1844 were comparable. Though seemingly exaggerated, there is good reason to take these claims seriously. The criteria for recovery, after all, were by no means vague or unrealistic. When discharging a patient as recovered, early nineteenth-century alienists (to use the terminology of that era) were simply stating that the individual could function at a minimally acceptable level in a family and community setting. To be sure, some individuals discharged as recovered were subsequently rehospitalized, but many never reentered a mental hospital.[23]

The seeming success of early hospitals had some unforseen consequences. In their early years they attempted to make provision for patients who could not afford the costs of protracted hospitalization, a reflection of the belief that such institutions should serve the whole community. Once opened, however, they faced serious financial problems. What would be the source of operating funds, as compared with capital expenditures? Should those unable to pay be denied admission? Should the state or local community subsidize such cases? Or should trustees seek private funds?

At the outset these hospitals (excepting the Friends' Asylum) sought to admit a heterogeneous patient population. Yet economic realities ensured that ability to pay would become an important element. By the time McLean opened, for example, the earlier stipulation in its charter that public subsidies would support poor patients had been repealed, and only more affluent patients were admitted. As early as 1822 the trustees expressed regret at their inability to accept free patients and the need to discharge others who could pay their bills. Although superintendents had leeway to use private donations to subsidize patients, they did not necessarily do so on the basis of need. Such funds were sometimes used to support private patients when relatives who could afford to pay refused to honor their responsibilities. Luther V. Bell, McLean's eminent superintendent, found that he could retain partially recovered patients when relatives were assured that "*there will be no more bills.*" "Even the question of ability," Bell added, "does not necessarily enter into [the issue of a subsidy] . . . as it unfortunately is true, that selfishness of responsible relatives might sacrifice a most valuable and interesting patient." By the middle of the nineteenth century McLean was the most exclusive hospital in the nation; average annual expenditure per patient was double that of its public counterparts.[24]

Similar situations prevailed at Bloomingdale and the Retreat, although exclusiveness evolved more slowly than at McLean. At Bloomingdale an annual state subsidy ensured the admission of nonpaying patients. In 1828 17 percent of patients were supported by public and charitable grants; by 1838 the figure had risen to 40 percent. But when the city and state opened their own institutions in 1839 and 1843, respectively, Bloomingdale—in the words of its superintendent—sought to serve "the wealthy" and "indigent persons of superior respectability and personal refinement." The latter included "families of clergymen, and other professional persons . . . teachers and business men who have experienced reverses . . . [and] dependent unmarried females." With the aid of a public subsidy, the Retreat also accepted poor insane patients. Following the opening of a state institution in 1868, however, admissions were limited to an affluent clientele.[25] Despite an initial commitment to serve a heterogeneous population, trustees of these institutions were confronted with the relatively high costs that accompanied protracted confinement. For this and other reasons, therefore, they preferred to admit patients whose families were willing and able to pay for the costs of care and treatment.

The growing exclusiveness of private hospitals became a widespread phenomenon and included institutions founded later in the century, such as the Pennsylvania Hospital for the Insane (reorganized and given autonomy within the structure of the Pennsylvania Hospital in 1841) and Butler Hospital in Providence, Rhode Island. The latter, opened in 1847 with a large bequest from Cyrus Butler, accepted poor patients with the assistance of a substantial state subsidy. When chronic pauper patients were removed following the opening of the "State Farm" in 1870, Butler adopted a more selective admission policy that emphasized ability to pay. Dr. John W. Sawyer, its superintendent, approved of the new policy. "I think," he wrote to Dorothea L. Dix, "it will result in increased usefulness and a firmer hold upon the interest and good will of the people."[26]

That these hospitals catered to affluent patients is not difficult to understand, given their narrow base of support. Private philanthropy during the first half of the nineteenth century was limited in scope. Moreover, a variety of projects competed for available funds, including general hospitals as well as welfare, educational, and religious institutions. Private mental institutions could not secure sufficiently large operating funds to enable them to accept a heterogeneous rather than a homogeneous patient population. Few local communities were willing to pay the costs of treating their residents. Indeed, even families with means often found it difficult to keep paying for protracted confinement.

The shift to a homogeneous and affluent patient body, however, was not merely a function of economics. Americans, like most peoples, tended to live within the relatively narrow parameters of a cohesive and clearly defined ethnic or economic group. The arrival in the United States of minority ethnic groups in the early nineteenth century only accentuated the process of group identification and solidarity. Affluent families sent their members to private hospitals with the expectation that they would not mix with ethnic or racial minorities. In this respect mental hospitals were no different than other institutions that differentiated between individuals on the basis of class, race, status, and educational level.

As a group, few medical superintendents expressed opposition to a class-based system of private institutions. Samuel B. Woodward, superintendent of the most important public hospital in the 1830s and 1840s and first president of the Association of Medical Superintendents of American Institutions for the Insane (AMSAII, which ultimately became the American Psychiatric Association), was aware of the social distance that separated private and public hospitals. Patients at the Hartford Retreat, he noted, "are of a higher order, and would afford, I should think, a larger sphere of operation for the exercise of skill and ingenuity, and for the accumulation of results which would benefit mankind." In a similar vein Bell defended McLean. "It is not unreasonable," he wrote in 1839, "that one Institution in New England should be designed for the reception of those whose pecuniary ability justifies their enjoying not only the necessaries and comforts, but the luxuries and superfluities of life to which they may have been accustomed. . . . To the polished and cultivated it is due as much to separate them from the course and degraded, as to administer to them in other respects." John Butler at the Hartford Retreat echoed these opinions in 1867. "It is evident," he wrote,

> that different classes will require different styles of accommodation. The State should provide for its indigent insane, liberally and abundantly, all the needful means of treatment, but in a plain and rigidly economical way. Other classes of more abundant means will require, with an increased expenditure, a corresponding increase of conveniences and comforts, it may be of luxuries, that use has made essential. This common sense rule is adopted in other arrangements of our social life—our hotels, watering places, private dwellings and various personal expenditures.[27]

With the opening of the Hartford Retreat in 1824 the initial phase of the movement to create asylums ended. To be sure, similar institutions were founded in the 1840s (notably the Pennsylvania Hospital for the Insane and the Butler Hospital), and other private and religious asylums came into existence during and after midcentury. Yet the limited resources of private philanthropy, the high costs of protracted confinement, and the growing exclusivity of admission policies all but destroyed the hope that such asylums could serve the entire community rather than the affluent. When it became clear by the 1820s that such institutions, no matter how striking their successes, would be unable to meet perceived social needs, the stage was set for the emergence of the public mental hospital.

During the second quarter of the nineteenth century responsibility for the care and treatment of the insane slowly fell under the jurisdiction of asylums established and administered by the states. The process of asylum building was rapid in some areas and slow in others; indigenous circumstances often shaped the responses of individual states. Yet within several decades a broad consensus had taken shape around the concept that the insane should receive care and treatment in public mental hospitals, and that ability to pay should not be a criterion for admission.

The belief that mental health policy was the responsibility of the state was not solely a product of benevolent and humanitarian concerns or a recognition that private hospitals could not meet existing needs. On the contrary, the founding of public institutions was an expression of the growing conviction that population growth, depression and unemployment, widening class distinctions, and immigration of minority ethnic groups—all of which were accompanied by a seeming increase in poverty, indigency, disease, and crime—required the creation of formal institutions to replace older ad hoc mechanisms that were ill-suited in a rapidly changing society. Fear and optimism combined to shape the ways in which Americans responded to social problems.

The preoccupation with the need to rationalize public policy was evident in several early nineteenth-century public investigations into the nature, causes, and extent of pauperism and its ramifications. In Massachusetts the influential Josiah Quincy chaired a legislative investigation in 1820; three years later New York Secretary of State John Yates conducted another inquiry. Local officials shared similar concerns; the Philadelphia Guardians of the Poor appointed a committee in 1827 to review welfare practices in other urban areas. Virtually all of these investigations began with two assumptions. First, that there was a fundamental distinction between the "impotent poor," a group that included those "wholly incapable of work, through old age, infancy, sickness or corporeal debility," and the "able poor . . . capable of work . . . but differing in the degree of capacity." Secondly, that pauperism was increasing, and, unless checked, would weaken if not destroy the fabric of American society. "It is well known to the General Court [i.e., Massachusetts legislature]," Quincy observed, "that the evils of pauperism, in Great Britain, have of late years, become so desperate and malignant in their nature, as to have been a subject of parliamentary investigation, and that the causes of those evils and their remedies, have been the source of more controversy . . . in that nation, as perhaps any other subject whatsoever." His committee urged that towns no longer subsidize paupers in their homes, for this was "the most wasteful, the most expensive, and most injurious to their morals and destructive of their industrious habits." Its members recommended instead that the state authorize the creation of a poor relief system that rested on public almshouses and workhouses. Yates went beyond the Quincy Committee; he urged that each "house of employment be connected with a work house or penitentiary, for the reception and discipline of sturdy beggars and vagrants." Discipline, he added, should consist of either "confinement on a rigid diet, hard labor, employment at the stepping mill, or some treatment equally efficacious in restraining their vicious appetites and pursuits." At the same time Yates held out the hope that the"growing evils of pauperism" could, "with proper care and attention, be almost wholly eradicated from our soil." The existing system, he added, penalized idiots and lunatics, who did not receive sufficient care and attention in towns that lacked suitable asylums for their custody. Virtually all of these investigations were based on the belief that new problems required innovative and formal institutional solutions. The activities of figures like Quincy, Yates, and other like-minded individuals, led to a dramatic increase in the number of almshouses and workhouses.[28]

The effort to rationalize public welfare by creating formal institutions was by no means an isolated phenomenon. In the early nineteenth century Americans were preoccupied with creating new organizational structures—including schools, prisons, juvenile homes—designed to assume functions previously assigned to families and neighbors. The creation of a system of public asylums reflected the same concerns that underlay the growth of institutions; fears that traditional informal mechanisms no longer sufficed, and a faith that new institutions would resolve long-standing problems.

Ironically, the first public hospitals appeared not in the populous Northeast, but in the more rural South where the absence of an affluent elite committed to a stewardship ideal of wealth promoted receptivity toward public action. Yet these institutions were somewhat removed from the optimism associated with Pinel, Tuke, and others who emphasized the possibility of cure in a well-ordered asylum. Consequently, they tended to assume a custodial character; their primary function was to protect both the individual and community from behavior that was either obstructive or dangerous. In Virginia, for example, the high costs and difficulty of transporting patients from the more remote western section to the Williamsburg institution led the legislature to establish the Western Lunatic Asylum in Staunton, which opened in 1828. During the first eight years of its existence, Staunton lacked the resources to implement many of the newer therapeutic ideologies, and therefore developed a custodial character. "Every thing has been provided, which humanity could prompt, for the protection and support of the insane," noted Francis T. Stribling (a physician who subsequently became superintendent and presided over its transformation), "but nothing has been done for the purpose of removing their affliction and enabling them to resume the care of themselves." The institution, he added, "deserves no higher appellation, than *a well-kept prison*."[29]

Much the same was true of the Kentucky institution, which opened in 1824. By dividing authority between a lay keeper and an attending or resident physician, the institution made it clear that custodial functions took precedence over therapeutic requirements. As late as 1844 nearly 80 percent of its 236 patients represented chronic cases with histories of insanity ranging from five to forty years. The patients, observed the first medical superintendent appointed in 1844, "were generally from the lower classes of society" and had "no desire for mental or moral enjoyment." Rational classification was all but absent. "Appalling indeed was the spectacle, to the rational mind, upon entering the halls of our Asylum," he added, "to behold the promiscuous and heterogeneous assembly of associates. . . . The same gallery resounded with the discordant sounds of maddened ravings, giddy laughs, senseless chatter, sepulchral moanings, earnest prayers, fiendish oaths and pious songs."[30]

The South Carolina Lunatic Asylum, on the other hand, was founded in 1828 by individuals familiar with private hospitals in the Northeast and hence aware of the newer therapeutic concepts associated with Pinel and Tuke. Designed to care for both the affluent and impoverished, the asylum attracted patients from neighboring southern states lacking comparable institutional facilities. Its officers sought to maintain an equilibrium between paying and pauper patients; to shift the balance toward the latter, they believed, would eventually discourage admission of the former. They also sought to implement the principles of moral treatment while simultaneously employing such traditional medical interventions as sedative and purgative drugs, hydrotherapy, and special diets. If structural and financial barriers inhibited striking therapeutic successes, the South Carolina Lunatic Asylum was nevertheless a har-binger of things to come.[31]

Although the first public institutions appeared in the South, the foun-dations of an institutionally oriented mental health policy were laid in the Northeast. Cultural, intellectual, scientific and medical leadership was for the most part concentrated in its more populous metropolitan areas. In the century following the American Revolution a few states—notably Massachusetts and New York—inaugurated a series of innova-tive social, economic, and educational policies and practices; other states, with but few exceptions, tended to follow their example. The founding of a state asylum in Massachusetts in 1830, therefore, acted as a catalyst that set in motion a movement designed to make state hospi-tals the focal point of mental health policy.

In the seventeenth and eighteenth centuries the citizens of Massa-chusetts had manifested more concern with insanity than residents of other colonies, and this interest persisted. In 1797 and 1816 the Massa-chusetts legislature enacted statutes mandating that welfare and penal institutions accept "lunatics, and persons furiously mad" whose behav-ior threatened the welfare of others or who were so impoverished as to require public assistance. The confinement of the insane in welfare and penal institutions, however, raised troubling problems, which were ulti-mately brought to public attention by the Reverend Louis Dwight.

An agent for the American Bible Society, Dwight had visited prisons while dispensing Bibles to inmates. He was appalled by the conditions he observed in most local jails, and came to the conclusion that they served no useful purpose as then structured. "You will probably know, at some future day, if my health is spared, what I this day witnessed," he wrote in impassioned words after visiting a Baltimore jail in 1825. "There is but one sufficient excuse for Christians, in suffering such evils to exist in prisons, in this country, as do exist; and that is, that they are not acquainted with the real state of things." As a vehicle for change he founded the Boston Prison Discipline Society in 1825, an organization dedicated to the redemption of criminals. During his travels Dwight also found lunatics housed in local prisons where they lived under shocking conditions. In a jail with ten insane residents, one was con-fined in a room that he had left but twice in eight years. Food was fur-nished through a small hole in the door, and there was no heat. "As he was seen through the orifice in the door," Dwight reported, "the first question was, is that a human being? The hair was gone from one side of his head, and his eyes were like balls of fire." In another jail a lunatic had been in the same room for nine years.

> He had a wreath of rags around his body, and another round his neck. This was all his clothing. He had no bed, chair, or bench. Two or three rough planks were strowed around the room: a heap of filthy straw, like the nest of swine, was in the corner. He had built a bird's nest of mud in the iron grate of his den. Connected with his wretched apartment was a dark dungeon, having no orifice for the admission of light, heat, or air, except the iron door, about 2 ½ feet square, opening into it from his Prison. The wretched lunatic was indulging [in] some delusive expectations of being soon released from this wretched abode.[32]

Since the Society was composed of prominent citizens, Dwight was able to call upon a member who was also a prominent legislator. He was instrumental in convincing the legislature to appoint an investigating committee. Within a year its members had recommended either that the Massachusetts General Hospital accept lunatics or that McLean construct a separate building with appropriate public support. Nothing occurred until young Horace Mann, then on the threshold of an eminent career as an educational reformer, proposed that the state establish an asylum for the insane. Like others of his generation, Mann believed that to be a social activist was to fulfil a religious mission. He persuaded his legislative colleagues to appoint him to chair a committee charged with enumerating the insane and developing a recommendation. At the same time he familiarized himself with European and English theories and practices relating to the care and treatment of the insane. In urging the state to establish a hospital, Mann delivered an impassioned peroration.

> While *we* delay, they *suffer*.—Another year not only gives an accession to their numbers, but removes, perhaps to a returnless distance, the chance of their recovery. Whatever they endure, which we can prevent, is virtually inflicted by our own hands. . . . It is now . . . in the power of the members of this House to exercise their highest privileges as men; their most enviable functions as legislators, to become protectors to the wretched, and benefactors to the miserable.[33]

As a result of his efforts, the legislature in 1830 overwhelmingly approved a bill providing for the erection of a state lunatic hospital for 120 patients and appropriated $30,000 for the project.

Located in Worcester, the new hospital opened in 1833. Under the leadership of Samuel B. Woodward, its first superintendent, the hospital quickly acquired a national reputation. Unlike existing asylums, it admitted relatively large numbers of patients; between 1833 and 1846 its average daily census rose from 107 to 359. More important, the hospital was structured in such a way as to maximize moral and medical treatment, for Woodward was intimately acquainted with contemporary psychiatric and medical theory. Above all, the hospital seemed to prove that insanity—with prompt medical and moral treatment—was as curable, if not more curable, than "any other disease of equal severity."* Between 1833 and 1845 Woodward reported that the number of recoveries of recent cases (insane for a year or less) averaged between 82 and 91 percent (based on the number discharged). His affirmations about the curability of insanity received national attention and played an important role in hastening the founding of hospitals in other states. His claims, noted Pliny Earle, "were widely circulated, and he soon became known, not only throughout the States, but likewise in Europe, and was generally regarded as the highest living American authority in the treatment of mental disorders." His prominent role was recognized by his colleagues, who elected him to the presidency when the AMSAII was founded in 1844.[34]

The example set by Massachusetts was quickly emulated by other states experiencing comparable problems. The significance of the Bay State experiment was that it offered an alternative model, namely, publicly supported institutions dedicated to providing restorative and effective therapy. Only in a few states did the drive to establish public asylums succeed immediately. Characteristically, two to five years (and sometimes more) were required before legislatures passed an enabling act and appropriated funds. Usually an additional three years was required for planning and then constructing physical facilities. Consequently, only Ohio and Vermont had functioning hospitals before 1840. Between 1840 and 1849, however, Maine, New Hampshire, New York, New Jersey, Indiana, Tennessee, Georgia, and Louisiana all opened public hospitals. In the next decade sixteen new state, one federal, and four municipal institutions were opened. Even in states like Connecticut and Rhode Island—neither of which had public hospitals before the Civil War—alternative arrangements were made to have the Hartford

---

*A detailed description of the internal regimen of mental hospitals can be found in chapter 3.

Retreat and Butler Hospital accept indigent patients in return for public subsidies.[35]

Between the 1840s and 1860s leadership in the movement to make public asylums the foundation of public policy was assumed by Dorothea L. Dix, an individual whose name became indissolubly linked with institutional care and treatment. A woman whose most striking characteristic was her determination, she devoted her career to the cause of the mentally ill and other distressed groups. In mid-nineteenth century America females had few career choices available to them. They lacked political power, did not have the right to vote, and were legally subordinate to their male counterparts. The belief that women were shaped by biology and fulfilled their destiny by becoming wives and mothers was pervasive. Social activism—precisely because it fulfilled expectations that females were the repository of morality and virtue—was the one public role that was acceptable. Women like Dix, therefore, could forge careers as activists without seeming to defy convention.

Like others of her generation, Dix's life was molded by her religious commitment to a liberal Unitarian theology. Following a protracted illness in 1836, she traveled to England where, through mutual friends, she may have met Dr. Samuel Tuke and learned firsthand about the York Retreat. Returning to America, she agreed to teach a religious class in the East Cambridge jail. Finding insane persons confined with hardened criminals, she decided to become an advocate for the insane. For more than a year she traveled throughout the Bay State inspecting the places where the insane were housed. In 1843 she sent her first petition to the legislature to support Samuel Gridley Howe's efforts to expand the Worcester hospital. "I come to present the strong claims of suffering humanity," she wrote in a moving plea.

> I come to place before the Legislature of Massachusetts the condition of the miserable, the desolate, the outcast. I come as the advocate of helpless, forgotten, insane, idiotic men and women; of beings sunk to condition from which the most unconcerned would start with real horror; of beings wretched in our prisons, and more wretched in our almshouses. And I cannot suppose it needful to employ earnest persuasion, or stubborn argument, in order to arrest and fix attention upon a subject only the more strongly pressing in its claims because it is revolting and disgusting in its details.

Combining passion, knowledge, and sheer determination, she insisted that the state had a moral, humanitarian, medical, and legal obligation toward the mentally ill to provide the benefits of asylum care.[36]

Successful in her first venture, Dix pursued the same strategy elsewhere. After arriving in a state, she would gather data and then present her findings to the legislature, generally in the form of a lengthy petition or memorial. Unconcerned with developing a mass following or arousing public opinion, she turned with unerring political instinct to persuade elite leaders both within and without the legislature. Like others who committed themselves to moral causes, she was not above employing exaggerated rhetoric or embellishing facts. Amariah Brigham, a prominent alienist and hospital superintendent, felt that during Dix's visit to New York State she "did hurt by *coloring & by* not accurately observing. She was often mistaken & this has thrown a doubt over all her statements with many." Time and age did not change Dix. Isaac Ray, one of the two most important psychiatrists of these decades and a close friend, observed in 1873 that she often censured "without good judgment, but has generally a basis for her censures."[37]

Dix's devotion to the cause of asylum building gave her a key position in shaping public policy. Indeed, her influence extended to the emerging specialty of institutional psychiatry. When superintendencies became vacant, she played an important role in deciding upon replacements. Younger physicians seeking a career in asylums often consulted with her about their aspirations and plans. Nor was her position as a powerful figure honorific; she was often called upon to adjudicate or to pass judgment on internal institutional conflicts. Her personality and persistence made it difficult for legislators to ignore her efforts. Pursuing a strategy of deliberately ignoring such issues as the abolition of slavery, she was able to exert influence in all regions of the nation. By the close of her career she had been responsible for founding or enlarging over thirty mental hospitals in the United States and abroad.

To be sure, Dix's achievements reflected the society in which she lived. In early and mid-nineteenth century America government activity, particularly at the state level, was expanding. There was broad agreement that the creation of public institutions to deal with poverty, crime, and insanity represented a valid and desirable policy choice. In committing themselves to schools, colleges, asylums, houses of refuge, and almshouses, Americans demonstrated their belief that the customs and practices associated with smaller, more rural societies were no longer appropriate. Dix's insistence upon the need for large-scale institutions for the insane, therefore, struck a responsive chord among a generation persuaded that public and quasi-public institutions had to assume functions once contained within the jurisdiction of the family.

The adoption of institutionally oriented policies was national rather than sectional in scope. The pattern of hospital founding in the newer states of the West, for example, differed but little from the East. Even in the South a commitment to institutions was characteristic, although hospitals in this region had lower levels of funding and were plagued by more severe internal problems. In Georgia, for example, the Milledgeville asylum cared for idiotic and epileptic patients as well as the insane. Dr. David Cooper, its first superintendent, was highly eccentric, and, indeed, perhaps insane. Upon reading Cooper's bizarre and barely comprehensible first *Annual Report*, the editor of the new *American Journal of Insanity* questioned its very authenticity. Dix wrote to one correspondent that she had been informed that Cooper "is really insane, but being harmless, the Trustees consent to his remaining in charge of the Institution." The appointment of a new superintendent in 1847 did not improve conditions at the asylum; as late as 1872 two physicians who conducted a study for the legislature remarked that they "commended nothing, for the very simple reason, *that we saw nothing to commend. . . .* We can say nothing about the Asylum but that in the past it has been a failure, and now needs a thorough reorganization."[38] The experiences of Georgia provided dramatic evidence that the mere founding of a hospital did not necessarily resolve existing problems; the internal administration and levels of financing played equally vital roles.

The opening of a new asylum in virtually every state was generally followed by a steady rise in admissions and resident populations. The presence of a mental institution had the inadvertent effect of altering both the expectations and behavior of the surrounding population. When offered an alternative to home or community care, many families and local officials opted to use institutional facilities with far greater frequency than was originally anticipated. New asylums, therefore, found that admissions tended to exceed capacity. When the Worcester hospital opened in 1833, for example, it had 120 beds. Within thirteen years it tripled in size as a result of two major additions to its physical plant. In 1840 eight asylums admitted an average of 180 patients; a decade later twenty-two institutions admitted nearly 329 persons. That there were limits to the size of individual asylums was obvious. Over time, there-fore, most states established additional facilities. By 1875, for example, California, Illinois, Iowa, Kentucky, Missouri, New York, Ohio, Pennsylvania, Virginia, and Wisconsin, had two or more institutions. This process of expansion would continue for more than a century; not until 1955 did the total inpatient population peak at nearly 559,000.[39]

The creation of a system with the asylum at its center, however, was not the result of systematic planning, at least in the modern sense of the term. Mental health policies throughout the nineteenth century were the result of an incremental but haphazard process. In most state legislatures there was little continuity in either personnel or deliberations from session to session; a high proportion of members served only a single term. Between 1830 and 1858 about three-quarters of the membership of the New York State Assembly were in their first term, and even the Speakers of the Assembly averaged only about two and a half years of prior legislative experience.[40] Bills were often introduced by petitions or memorials from private individuals or organizations and the enactment of specific laws rarely reflected broad public demands. Investigating committees were sometimes composed of the very individuals who petitioned the legislature on behalf of a particular cause, or else made up of individuals who did not even serve in the legislature. Standing committees were generally ineffective, and the inexperience of their membership and lack of permanent staff inhibited their autonomy and significance. Consequently, the legislative process weakened rather than promoted long-range policy-making. The laws that were enacted thus reflected individual and immediate concerns.

Nor did the legislative process draw upon permanent staff charged with gathering and analyzing data. Although individual legislators were aware of the need for information that would inform their deliberations, a professional staff and procedures to meet this need were not available. More importantly, there was little awareness that insanity, dependency, legal and financial systems, and social and class relationships interacted in complex and profoundly difficult ways. Consequently, the focus was on short-term and immediate issues. Legislative actions were often shaped by external factors or unexamined presumptions. Moreover, there was little or no disposition to scrutinize the arguments and claims of those who insisted upon the superiority of asylum care. Nineteenth-century legislators were neither incompetent nor malevolent, but the prevailing structure of deliberative bodies and the absence of broad theoretical models often led to policies that in the long run had unintended consequences. There was no way of predicting that the founding of a hospital, for example, would change public attitudes and dramatically increase admissions.

Nineteenth-century state legislatures were generally responsive to constituent demands for land grants, charters, and other benefits. These demands usually came from individuals or small and transient interest groups. Although specific groups benefited from government action, the costs were widely distributed. An expanding economy also created a context in which a large number of groups could receive public subsidies, thus minimizing group conflict. Hence there was little or no incentive to oppose public expenditures. Under such circumstances a Dorothea Dix encountered little opposition in persuading state legislatures to appropriate funds for mental hospitals. The outcome of such an incremental process was the passage of individual legislative acts, each having little or no connection with what preceded or followed. The broad framework of public policy could only be derived from the sum total of a series of unrelated decisions. Policy, to put the matter somewhat differently, did not necessarily rest on the analysis of a body of empirical data.

In 1850 Edward Jarvis, a prominent alienist and statistician, pointed out that the assumption that state institutions would serve all citizens equally was an erroneous one. In a careful study that took into account nearly every mental hospital in the United States, the place of residence of all patients, and the total population by county and state, he demonstrated conclusively that areas adjacent to hospitals used their facilities at a far higher rate than more distant places. This finding called into question the assumption that placing hospitals in the geographical center of a state would ensure equal access. In another study he also noted that the mere existence of a mental hospital tended to sensitize the local population to the very concept of mental disease and thereby promoted greater use. "Consequently," he observed, "more and more persons and families, who . . . formerly kept their insane friends and relations at home, or allowed them to stroll abroad about the streets or country, now believe, that they can be restored, or improved, or, at least made comfortable in these public institutions, and, therefore, they send their patients to these asylums, and thus swell the lists of their inmates."[41]

Such findings contradicted the widely held view that one or two state hospitals, centrally located so as to ensure equal access, represented an appropriate and adequate policy. In fact, large urban areas were often located far from the geographical center of a state where asylums were placed. Since access was largely determined by proximity, urban areas were unable to use state facilities to any significant extent, and were forced to rely on their own meager resources. The consequences were often devastating, since urban areas created institutions that did not differentiate between the insane, the unemployed, and other dependent groups, and even individuals who were incarcerated because of criminal activities.

New York City is a case in point. Before 1825 its insane poor were housed either at the almshouse or at Bloomingdale. In 1825 they were brought together on Blackwell's Island (later Welfare Island), where the city had begun to centralize its welfare and penal institutions. For the next decade and a half the city maintained what was designated as a "Lunatic Asylum" as part of its almshouse and prison complex. Its officials conceded in 1837 that the asylum

> yet remains, a witness of the blind infatuation of prejudice and miscalculation; affording to a class more deserving commiseration than any other among the afflicted catalogue of humanity, a miserable refuge in their trials, undeserving the *name* of an "Asylum," in these enlightened days. These apartments, under the best superintendence, cannot be made to afford proper accommodations for the inmates . . . and a portion of the rooms seemed more like those receptacles of *crime*, "to whose foul mouth no healthsome air breathes in," than tenements prepared for the recipients of an awful visitation of Divine Providence, justly considered the worst "of all the ills that flesh is heir to."

In 1839 the asylum was moved to a separate building, but there was little improvement. Overcrowding was characteristic; convicts were employed as attendants; patient abuse was not uncommon; substandard diets were characteristic; and epidemics were frequent. Charles Dickens and Kirkbride, both of whom visited the hospital in the 1840s, were extremely critical in their comments. "As evidence of the kind of attendants employed," observed Kirkbride in his notes, "it may be stated, that a large red-faced masculine woman, was pointed out, as an 'admirable hand'—her only fault being that she was a drunkard!"[42]

Yet when New York State embarked upon a policy of constructing public hospitals, it placed them at a considerable distance from the city.

The first state asylum was built in Utica and opened in 1843; the second institution a quarter of a century later (Willard Asylum) was placed hundreds of miles to the north of New York City. The location of state asylums thus ensured that the city would continue to be left on its own, since relatively few of its residents were sent to far away state facilities. By 1870 the city's asylum housed no less than thirteen hundred patients. A second asylum on Ward's Island opened in 1871, but it differed but little from its counterpart on Blackwell's Island. Indeed, the opening of the former did little to improve conditions at the latter. The medical staff often consisted of only two or three physicians; attendants—many of whom were convicted criminals—were inadequately supervised; abuse of patients remained a recurring problem; the institutional diet was inadequate; crowding was endemic; and the lack of occupational and recreational facilities gave the asylum a depressing character. Much the same state of affairs existed in Kings County (Brooklyn), which was not a part of the city until the turn of the century. In a report issued some twenty-five years after its own asylum opened in 1852, an investigating committee concluded that the superintendent, his assistants, and the nursing staff were incompetent, and the institution was "a reproach and disgrace to Kings County."[43]

Conditions in other urban areas were similar. Like New York State's, Pennsylvania's first state hospital, opened in 1851, was located at a distance from its major cities, in Harrisburg. Left on its own, Philadelphia kept its poor insane in the municipal almshouse before 1859. In that year an organizational change gave the insane department a measure of autonomy, but did little to alter its character. By 1875 it had more than a thousand inmates. John C. Bucknill, the eminent English psychiatrist, concluded during a visit to the United States in 1875, that the Philadelphia and New York asylums were among the poorest in the country. Isaac Ray, who settled in Philadelphia after retiring from the superintendency of the Butler Hospital, expressed a similar sentiment. Philadelphia, he insisted, needed a "strictly State Institution," for the "insane poor are the wards, not of the city, but of the Commonwealth." So long as the city maintained its own institution "just as long will it be a field for jobbery [corruption in public office] and meanest parsimony."[44]

Unlike Brooklyn, New York, and Philadelphia, Boston created a separate municipal asylum in 1839. The opening of the Worcester hospital some forty miles away had done little to alleviate the problems posed by the presence of insane persons. The history of the Boston institution was similar to those in other urban areas; crowding and other difficulties precluded any efforts to provide a more humane and therapeutic environment. Nor were the experiences of northeastern urban areas unique. In Ohio the first state asylum was located in Columbus, and the city of Cincinnati had to fall back upon its own resources. In 1857 the state legislature passed a somewhat novel statute that made Hamilton County (in which Cincinnati was located) a separate district; all taxes paid by the county for the support of the insane due the state were returned for the support of the county asylum.[45]

Virtually every urban area in the nineteenth century faced similar dilemmas. Some recognized their problems but—as in the case of Baltimore—took no action. Others established "temporary" asylums that remained in operation for many years. A New Orleans facility, for example, functioned for three decades despite the fact that it resembled, in the words of one observer, a "lock-up, calaboose or man-kennel."[46] Still others—St. Louis, Newark, Chicago—founded municipal institutions in the face of a state policy that promised equal access but in practice worked to the disadvantage of cities.[47]

By the second half of the nineteenth century the mental hospital had become the foundation on which mental health policy rested. With few exceptions, most states had at least one (and most more than one) public institution. More populous urban areas were impelled by circumstances to establish their own asylums. In addition, corporate and proprietary hospitals served affluent groups disinclined to use public institutions. The piecemeal manner in which these asylums had been founded, however, would have a profound impact in future decades when a series of unanticipated consequences would give rise to a mental health system that had but faint resemblance to the goals of its founders.

3

The Emergence of
American Psychiatry

The founding of asylums was accompanied by the emergence of psychiatry, arguably the first medical specialty (excluding surgery). The creation of a new medical specialty—a development that placed madness within medical jurisdiction—was not a function of new discoveries or changes in the ways in which the nature of insanity was understood. Nor was psychiatry responsible for the establishment of asylums, which preceded rather than followed. The outlook and functions of asylum physicians were shaped by the setting in which their specialty was conceived and grew to maturity. Psychiatrists—unlike the rest of their medical colleagues—were for the most part employed in public institutions and not in private practice at this time. The ensuing identification of the specialty of psychiatry with asylums and state medicine would have a lasting effect. It not only helped shape professional and popular perceptions about insanity, but it contributed also to the prevailing consensus that institutional care and treatment for mental disorders represented the appropriate and professional policy choice. Psychiatry and asylums, therefore, enjoyed a symbiotic relationship for more than a century; each reinforced and conferred legitimacy upon the other. Had both not been so closely related, it is conceivable that subsequent developments might have followed a quite different path.

As public sentiment for institutional care was gathering momentum in the 1830s, there were not yet physicians who specialized in diseases of the mind to lead and direct asylums for the insane. In some instances laypersons directed asylums. In others, physicians were selected as superintendents for qualities not directly related to the care and treatment of mental disorders. Within two decades, however, a medical specialty had emerged to treat the new asylum populations. By mid-century it was taken for granted that asylum superintendents would be physicians with prior experience in dealing with insanity. These same individuals generated a systematic body of concepts dealing with insanity and asylums as part of their rationale for autonomy. They forged as well a sense of professional unity that defined the boundaries of their specialty. Despite internal differences on specific issues, they successfully established a general consensus on fundamental principles dealing with the nature and treatment of insanity.[1]

The eighty-three individuals who served as asylum superintendents before 1860 came from middle-class backgrounds and were by the standards of their day well-educated. More than half had attended leading colleges and medical schools. Most had been reared in devout households where they absorbed the tenets of Protestant Christianity and the belief that they had a mission to assist less fortunate individuals and groups. Their introduction into the world of medicine, however, was often troubled. In the early nineteenth century medicine was a divided profession. Internal conflicts were bitter and acrimonious; proprietary medical schools competed for students; and standards for degrees and practice were virtually nonexistent. Nor were the boundaries of medicine clearly defined. Regular or allopathic physicians faced challenges from a variety of "unorthodox" groups that included homeopathic and botanical practitioners as well as popular health reformers who emphasized the critical importance of lifestyle. Indeed, regular physicians came under sharp criticism because they were committed to dogmatic principles and employed such "heroic" therapies as bleeding even in the absence of evidence that demonstrated their efficacy. From a strictly economic point of view, medicine was an insecure occupation. Under such circumstances a career in asylum medicine seemed attractive, for compensation and benefits were both secure and above average. The economic opportunity as well as the chance to explore novel ways of healing in new public institutions which provided a clean slate helped to make the specialty of asylum medicine attractive to a new generation.

The careers of Samuel B. Woodward and Thomas S. Kirkbride

embodied many of the characteristics of antebellum asylum superintendents. Born in 1787, Woodward studied medicine under the tutelage of
his physician father, and by the 1820s was one of the leading medical figures in Connecticut. Influenced by a liberalized Congregationalism
stripped of its Calvinistic pessimism, he accepted a religious obligation
to help less fortunate persons. He rejected the mere pursuit of worldly
goods and insisted that human beings had a duty "to contribute to the
happiness and welfare of all the creation of God . . . and to exhibit in our
lives and conversation the influence of the principles of christianity, and
the love of God in our hearts as the governing motive of our conduct."
"Natural and moral evil will cease together," he wrote in a peroration to
medical science, "when man shall have learned the laws of his constitution, the nature, extent and proper use of his intellectual and moral powers, and shall have acquired a knowledge of the means which Infinite
Wisdom has provided for his happiness." His close ties with Eli Todd
and the Hartford Retreat made him an obvious candidate to head the
new state asylum in Worcester when it opened in 1833. Although his
salary was a modest $1,200, all living expenses for himself and his large
family were provided gratis. The prospect of not having to compete with
other physicians, to say nothing about difficulties of collecting patient
fees, no doubt proved an added attraction.[2]

Kirkbride, who did more to shape the asylum than perhaps any other
figure, was raised in a devout Quaker family. When the Society of
Friends split into two groups in the late 1820s, Kirkbride joined the
more orthodox wing, which rejected radical separatist tendencies and
perceived no incompatibility between adherence to religion and pursuit
of a secular career. After serving an apprenticeship with a local physician, he studied at the University of Pennsylvania Medical School. He
was subsequently introduced to insanity while serving as resident physician at the Friend's Asylum. When offered the superintendency of the
soon-to-be opened Pennsylvania Hospital for the Insane in Philadelphia
in 1840 at a "rather liberal" salary of $3,000, he accepted and quickly
became one of the leaders of the emerging specialty of psychiatry. A
patron's description of him as a "Christian and Physician" was revealing.[3]

The creation of the specialty of psychiatry was accompanied by an
extensive literature designed to illuminate the etiology and nature of
insanity, and to provide a rationalization for institutionalization as well as

a model of the ideal asylum. In articulating their views, psychiatrists employed language derived from science and medicine as well as religion. The absence of persuasive empirical data was largely overlooked; the psychiatric claim to legitimacy and authority derived from the character of practitioners and their institutional position as superintendents. In spelling out their views, members offered both a critique of society and a program for the future.

Most psychiatrists, like physicians generally, conceived of disease in individual rather than general terms. Health was a consequence of a symbiotic relationship or balance among nature, society, and the individual. Disease represented an imbalance that followed the violation of certain divine natural laws that governed human behavior.[4] Insanity occurred when false impressions were conveyed to the mind because the brain or other sensory organs had been impaired. Mental illnesses were perceived to be somatic and to involve lesions of the brain, the organ of the mind. To have argued otherwise would have broached blasphemy. If the mind itself (often equated with the soul) could become diseased, it might conceivably perish. The immortality of the soul, upon which Christian faith depended, would thereby be denied or negated. Reared in a Protestant culture, most psychiatrists instinctively rejected a model of disease that threatened traditional moral and religious values.

Such reasoning provided asylum physicians with a model of mental illnesses that was especially compatible with a belief that they were precipitated by psychological and environmental factors interacting with the constitution or predisposition of the individual. Insanity thus was provoked by willful violation of certain natural laws that governed human behavior. Immorality, improper living conditions, or unnatural stresses that upset the natural balance of the individual could also precipitate mental disorders. Mid-nineteenth-century psychiatrists managed to infuse moral values and science into their model of insanity.

The holistic concept of mental illnesses which saw physical disorder of the brain as the cause of the insanity required of most American psychiatrists an act of faith. Except for a few cases in which autopsies revealed the presence of a brain tumor or other gross abnormality, the link between the brain and madness remained a mystery. Given their inability to demonstrate a relationship between anatomical changes and behavior, psychiatrists identified mental disorders by observing external signs and symptoms. In this respect they were no different from other physicians who defined pathological states in terms of visible and external signs (such as fever). Although disagreeing on the diagnosis of diverse signs and symptoms, few physicians questioned this approach, if only because they could conceive of no alternative. Psychiatrists accepted disease as a given; the inability of patients to function, combined with severe behavioral symptoms, was sufficient evidence of the presence of pathology.

Most asylum doctors were vaguely aware of the intellectual and logical difficulties that followed from their somatic view of insanity. Their references to lesions generally lacked empirical support, and acceptance of their presence rested on faith rather than observation. Classification of mental disorders (nosology) was equally problematic, for there was no way to relate brain physiology to specific behavioral patterns. Indeed, nomenclature and classification aroused little enthusiasm among mid-nineteenth-century American psychiatrists, if only because diagnosis was not related to specific therapies. No system of classification, conceded Amariah Brigham in 1843, appeared to be of "much practical utility." All categories based on symptoms "must be defective, and perhaps none can be devised in which all cases are arranged." Nor were Brigham's views unique. Woodward had observed earlier that insanity was a "unit, indefinable . . . easily recognized . . . [but] not always easily classified." He believed that therapy was independent of any nosological system and had to reflect the unique circumstances presented by each individual case. And when Pliny Earle, one of the most important American psychiatrists, was approached toward the end of his long career on the possibility of developing a universally accepted classification of mental disorders, he took issue with the idea. "In the present state of our knowledge," he observed,

> no classification of insanity can be erected upon a pathological basis, for the simple reason that, with but slight exceptions, the pathology of the disease is unknown. . . . Hence, for the most apparent, the most clearly defined, and the best understood foundation for a nosological scheme for insanity, we are forced to fall back upon the symptomatology of the disease—*the apparent mental condition*, as judged from the outward manifestations.

Nineteenth-century psychiatric nosologies—unlike their twentieth-century counterparts—were simple, and employed such categories as mania, monomania, melancholia, dementia, and idiocy.[5]

Recognition of the difficulties that blocked the formulation of a comprehensive system of classifying mental disorders did not in any way impede discussions of the origins and causes of disease. Despite an inability to demonstrate meaningful relationships between physiology and the presence of particular behavior signs or symptoms, the social and cultural role of medicine required that physicians—psychiatrists and others—provide some explanation of disease processes.

The causes of insanity, most psychiatrists agreed, could be subsumed under two general headings—physical and "moral." The physical causes, noted Edward Jarvis, produced "their primary effect on the physical structure of the brain or some other organs, and disturbing the cerebral actions, produce their secondary effect on the mental operations; as a blow on the head, or epilepsy, or a disordered stomach." The moral causes, by way of contrast, acted "directly on the mind itself; as excessive study, disappointment, grief, trouble, &c."[6]

Etiological speculation tended to emphasize the moral more than the physical causes of insanity, if only because the latter were not only obscure but generally not preventable. A blow to the head or an illness, for example, had little to do with individual choice. The "moral" causes of insanity (which seemed to account for the majority of cases), on the other hand, appeared to be amenable to human interventions and hence preventable. Lifestyle thus became a key analytic category in causal explanations. Psychiatrists tended to interpret insanity as an inevitable consequence of behavioral patterns that departed from their own normative model of behavior, a model derived from Protestant Christianity and prevailing bourgeois standards. Disease—irrespective of its particular manifestations—was perceived to follow violation of natural, that is conventional, behavior, and was therefore seen to be related in part to immorality, vice, and filth.

The major causal factors in mid-nineteenth-century psychiatric thought included intemperance, masturbation, overwork, domestic difficulties, excessive ambitions, faulty education, personal disappointments, marital problems, excessive religious enthusiasm, jealousy, and pride. Woodward's case records at the Worcester hospital offer dramatic evidence of the belief that deviations from acceptable lifestyles could lead to insanity. Thus Woodward willingly accepted family explanations of the cause of insanity. A woman with a history of mental disorder had been experiencing domestic strife, which in turn was listed as the cause of the illness. The first patient entering the institution in 1833 also had a history of insanity. He claimed "to be a sacred ambassador from Heaven" and to have direct communications with Christ and God. From time to time he exhibited violent behavior even though rational on subjects other than religion. The cause of the disease was listed as religious fanaticism. The records also indicate that recidivism could involve different causes. A male admitted in 1833 because "pecuniary embarrassment" had precipitated the disease was subsequently hospitalized because of "hard labor" (i.e., overwork). In the latter confinement the record noted that he had inherited the disease, since his mother had been insane on at least three occasions. In analyzing more than 2,300 cases admitted to the Worcester hospital between 1833 and 1845, Woodward identified seven causes that accounted for 60 percent of the total: intemperance (278), ill health (318), religious excitement (191), masturbation (145), domestic affliction (219), loss of property and fear of poverty (131), and some form of personal disappointment (101).[7]

Individual lifestyle, however, was not the only determinant of illness and health. Social relationships and institutions also played a role. The argument that there was a link between insanity and civilization was not original; many early nineteenth-century romantic writers believed in the existence of an uncorrupted golden age in a remote past. Most founders of American psychiatry shared this illusion. "Insanity is rare in a savage state of society," wrote the trustees of the Worcester hospital in 1845, echoing their superintendent. "One reason for this disparity undoubtedly, is, the substitution of the luxurious and artificial, for the more simple and natural modes of life. Another and more important one is, that among the ignorant and uncultivated, the mental faculties lie dormant, and hence are less liable to derangement."[8]

Edward Jarvis, a psychiatrist who pioneered in using statistical analyses to understand social reality, could not verify the claim that there was an increase in the incidence of insanity. The question, he insisted, had to be restated in a more qualified form. Those causes related to the "malignant and evil passions, anger, hatred, jealousy, pride and violent temper" remained the same, affecting savage and modern society alike. The increase in mental labor as well as social and economic mobility, on the other hand, heightened chances of becoming insane. Insanity, therefore,

> is then a part of the price which we pay for civilization. The causes of the one increase with the developments and results of the other. This is not necessarily the case, but it is so now. The increase of knowledge, the improvements in the arts, the multiplication of comforts, the amelioration of manners, the growth of refinement, and the elevation of morals, do not

of themselves disturb men's cerebral organs and create mental disorder. But with them some more opportunities and rewards for great and excessive mental action, more uncertain and hazardous employments, and consequently more disappointments, more means and provocations for sensual indulgence, more dangers of accidents and injuries, more groundless hopes, and more painful struggle to obtain that which is beyond reach, or to effect that which is impossible.[9]

Etiological explanations ranged far and wide. Some psychiatrists pointed to defects in the American educational system: rigidity in some instances; permissiveness in others; or else the tendency of schools to raise expectations to unreasonable levels, thereby diminishing a child's capacity to deal with reality. William M. Awl believed that the Anglo-Saxon race was especially vulnerable to insanity because of high intellectual achievements. Jarvis, on the other hand, believed that lower-class Irish immigrants were more susceptible. "There is good ground for supposing," he wrote,

> that the habits and condition and character of the Irish poor in this country operate more unfavorably upon their mental health, and hence produce a larger number of the insane in ratio of their numbers than is found among the native poor. Being in a strange land and among strange men and things, meeting with customs and surrounded by circumstances widely different from all their previous experience, ignorant of the precise state of affairs here, and wanting education and flexibility by which they could adapt themselves to their new and unwonted position, they necessarily form many impracticable purposes, and endeavor to accomplish them by unfitting means. Of course disappointment frequently follows their plans. Their lives are filled with doubt, and harrowing anxiety troubles them, and they are involved in frequent mental, and probably physical, suffering.
>
> The Irish laborers have less sensibility and fewer wants to be gratified than the Americans, and yet they more commonly fail to supply them. They have also a greater irritability; they are more readily disturbed when they find themselves at variance with the circumstances about them, and less easily reconciled to difficulties they cannot overcome.
>
> Unquestionably much of their insanity is due to their intemperance, to which the Irish seem to be peculiarly prone, and much to that exaltation which comes from increased prosperity.[10]

Even war could be absorbed into the psychiatric critique of American life and institutions. Before the Civil War, the superintendent of the

Connecticut Retreat for the Insane observed, "we were as a people sinking into a selfish materialism . . . [with] the consequent rapid increase of insanity. . . . Now in this new and higher life upon which we have entered, wealth seems as if deemed but the handmaid of a charity that never faileth. . . . A war, wisely conducted to a successful issue and in defense of the right, tends directly to the elevation and development of the nation conducting it."[11]

Having interpreted insanity as a consequence of lifestyle, environment, and chance, psychiatrists understandably defined a prophylactic and educational role for themselves. Their concept of prevention involved a synthesis of medicine, religion, morality, and social activism. Medicine, observed Jarvis in revealing terms, was too preoccupied with the cure of disease rather than the preservation of health. Indeed, physicians had neglected to identify the attributes of health, an understanding of which was indispensable if the body was to be returned from its "wanderings in the devious path of disease." Persuaded that disease was generally the consequence of ignorance and sin, he devoted much of his time to enlightening the public about appropriate modes of behavior. The harmonious processes of the human body would function efficiently if people followed proper diets, breathed pure air, exercised properly, and maintained a clean environment. Too many people, by contrast, lived amidst filth and pollution; they breathed air fouled by industrial fumes and tobacco; they substituted stimulants and narcotic beverages for water; they ate improper foods and indulged themselves; and they refused to bathe regularly and carried instead a "corrupting waste." "There is a general ignorance of the laws of vitality," he informed the members of the Massachusetts Medical Society in 1848. Whether human beings lived a full life or died prematurely was dependent "upon our obedience to those laws which God has stamped upon our frames." Health was dependent upon personal behavior; the laws of health were self-evident to all rational persons. Few of Jarvis's psychiatric brethren would have dissented from these opinions. Indeed, the psychiatric commitment to statistical analysis reflected a commitment to an orderly and objective external order, which was consistent with a teleological interpretation of the universe.[12]

———

To define the nature and causes of insanity was only a beginning, not an end. The goal of psychiatry, like that of medicine generally, was the alleviation and cure of disease. Despite their recognition that disease processes remained shrouded in mystery, most asylum physicians believed that insanity was curable. "No disease, of equal severity," wrote Woodward in words that were echoed by other physicians, "can be treated with greater success than insanity, if the remedies are applied sufficiently early."[13] Since the disorder was in large part precipitated by improper behavioral patterns or a deficient social environment, it followed that treatment had to begin with the creation of a new and presumably appropriate environment. Home treatment was ineffective, for the physician had no means of controlling or eliminating the causal elements that produced the disorder. Institutionalization, therefore, was a sine qua non. Once in a hospital, the patient could be exposed to a judicious mix of medical and moral treatment.

The complex therapeutic systems employed by asylum physicians were derived in part from their social background, institutional experiences, and concepts derived from French and English sources. Yet psychiatry did not develop independently of medicine, and those who made careers for themselves in treating the insane were also heirs to a rich medical tradition dating back to antiquity. Although committed to institutionalization and environmental therapies, they never rejected the medical understanding of how the human body functioned or therapies commonly employed by their brethren in private practice. Disease in the early nineteenth century was perceived by physicians and laypersons alike as a holistic entity that could not be disaggregated into specific categories. Health represented a physiological equilibrium; disease occurred because of imbalance. The goal of treatment was the restoration of balance. Within this framework drugs played an indispensable role in regulating the digestive and intestinal tracts and tonics played an equally compelling part in rebuilding a weakened body.

The therapies employed by Woodward at the Worcester hospital typified the eclectic nature of early and mid-nineteenth-century asylum practice. Expressing confidence in the "utility and importance of moral management," he nevertheless affirmed the undisputed utility of "medical treatment." Insanity, as he often wrote, arose "from disease of the brain, disturbing the healthy performance of its functions, and is exhibited in illusions, hallucinations, undue or morbid excitement of the feelings and propensities, perversion of the senses, or estrangement of the moral feelings." His therapeutics included medications designed to counter specific symptoms and conditions associated with insanity. Active and violent patients received narcotics such as opium or its alkaloid derivative, morphine, although a variety of other substances were also widely used. Melancholic (i.e., depressed) patients received laxatives, baths, and counterirritatives such as digitalis. He also prescribed a variety of tonics and laxatives designed to rebuild and strengthen the patient's general health. Since mind and body were inseparable, it was obvious that ill physical health could precipitate mental symptoms.[14]

Woodward may have emphasized somatic therapies more than other superintendents, but he was not idiosyncratic. The prevailing emphasis on the significance of inflammation as a sign of disease, for example, led to the widespread use of depletive or antiphlogistic (i.e., antiinflammatory) measures such as general bloodletting. By the 1830s most alienists believed that heroic* depletive measures were harmful, but they continued to employ local bleeding. "The greatest error I have seen committed in the medical treatment of the insane," Amariah Brigham observed in 1840, "is the neglect of depletion in the early stage, and of narcotics and tonics in the subsequent." Brigham believed that madness involved an inflammation of the brain, and that bloodletting would "arrest the disease." The subsequent use of narcotics and tonics would both calm the patient and rebuild bodily strength. Most asylum physicians were enthusiastic about drugs, including such narcotics as opium and morphine (especially for cases of mania), tonics, and cathartics.[15]

Although moral treatment was seen as conceptually distinct, mid-nineteenth-century psychiatrists did not in practice distinguish between it and medical therapy. The indissoluble linkage of mind and body required that careful attention be paid to both; to neglect one for the other would only perpetuate the continued presence of the disease process. In effect, they were reiterating the ancient faith that health involved both mind and body. Woodward tended to emphasize the autonomy of medical treatment, whereas Kirkbride believed that drugs were preliminary interventions that prepared the foundation for moral treatment. Nevertheless, there were virtually no institutional psychiatrists who rejected the importance of either therapy.

While susceptible to many interpretations, moral treatment meant kind, individualized care in small institutions. Such care consisted of occupational therapy, religious exercises, recreation, and the employment of mechanical restraint infrequently and only when absolutely

---

*Heroic medicine involved the deployment of active and drastic interventions designed to alter the course of an illness as quickly and dramatically as possible.

necessary. Since insanity was precipitated by both prior behavior and environment, the goal was to reeducate the patient by inculcating those internal controls and external activities that enabled individuals to live in normal society. Hence the daily institutional regimen became the key to recovery; for it created a framework which enabled patients to begin to transform themselves into normal people.

Luther V. Bell of the McLean Asylum offered a definition of moral treatment that few of his colleagues would have rejected. In his view, its major elements were separation, direction, classification, and occupation. Separation from home and friends was essential; Bell even felt that letters and visits had to be interdicted. Direction included "the application of such measures as . . . are calculated to save from noxious influences upon mind and body, to change and divert diseased action, to secure as much personal comfort as practicable, to retain as long as, and no longer than the real interests of the sufferer require." Classification was also of vital importance. Patients had to be placed in situations where their interpersonal relationships with other patients and staff would have beneficial effects. The contacts of insane persons, he insisted, had to be limited "to such persons, patients and assistants as are most likely to exert a favorable, or save from a noxious influence during the period of mental disorder; the principles of self esteem and emulation and forbearance, being also brought into action upon the character of the insane individual, by means of such classification." Finally, occupation—including work as well as play—was an indispensable component. These measures, judiciously and appropriately applied, led inevitably toward improvement and ultimate recovery.[16]

Within virtually every institution the superintendent played a key role in establishing the daily routine of each patient and overseeing the staff. Indeed, his role was widely perceived to be that of a stern, authoritarian, yet loving and concerned father. Like a good father, he was expected to reason with a patient in order to persuade, and even punishment, while necessary on occasion, was never to be arbitrary, cruel, capricious, or unjust. Ideally, the goal was to appeal to an individual's rational sense. The ideal hospital itself was seen as a cohesive and closely knit family, within whose confines the superintendent would treat patients with consideration and respect in the hope of eliciting a response in kind. "If there is any secret in the management of the insane," Woodward wrote in 1839, "it is this: respect them and they will respect themselves; treat them as reasonable beings, and they will take every possible pains to show you that they are such; give them your confidence, and they will rightly appreciate it, and rarely abuse it." After more than a decade at Worcester, he added that "the 1800 patients that have been and are now under my care, *seem like children and kindred.*"[17]

In many early nineteenth-century hospitals the day commenced at about six in the morning. Patients initially attended first to their personal needs, and then were required to put their beds and possessions in the ward in neat order; breakfast was served shortly thereafter. Medical visitation then commenced. The superintendent and assistant physicians checked on the mental and physical condition of each patient, prescribed whatever medication was deemed appropriate, and suggested a variety of activities. All patients were encouraged to find meaningful jobs within the institution, which generally were organized along gender lines. Males worked on the hospital farm and grounds or did general maintenance labor; women were likely to be assigned to housekeeping duties or engage in sewing. Exercise, amusements, games, and religious observances were also part of the regimen. The evening meal was often followed by organized programs. At the Pennsylvania Hospital, for example, Kirkbride introduced an imaginative program of magic lantern slides that used a large and varied collection of glass stereopticon slides. The shows often included visiting speakers on a variety of topics designed to appeal to a broad audience. The goal was to create a comfortable way of life that made patients accept prolonged confinement. Although violent behavior sometimes disrupted the daily routine, the majority of patients were able to adjust to their surroundings and create an environment that was at the very least tolerable.[18]

Some superintendents encouraged patients to issue their own newspapers and journals. The *Retreat Gazette* was published at Hartford; the *Asylum Journal* at Vermont; and *The Opal* at Utica. In these publications patients often revealed their own inner feelings. One individual used the pages of *The Opal* to express resentment at visitors who derived "a morbid satisfaction upon looking on scenes of human misery." Another regretted the fact that institutionalization sometimes involved abandonment by family and friends alike.

A year is gone, and five months more,

My parent, since thy face I saw,

And full twelve months have past me o'er,

Since news from thee I heard or saw.

If you had loved me as you ought

A being you had given life,

Some note or message would you not

Have sent to cheer my prison life?[19]

Superintendents were sensitive to the importance and need for incentives and rewards. Wards were generally organized along graduated lines. The lower and more restrictive wards were for violent and destructive patients as well as those whose habits—including masturbation and incontinence—went beyond conventional boundaries. As behavior improved, patients were moved to higher wards, which were less restrictive and provided greater amenities. Since the rules governing behavior were generally spelled out in detail, patients who willfully violated them had to accept the consequences that followed. "In spite of repeated warnings, given in the kindest spirit and in the most respectful manner," Kirkbride reported to one family, the patient had been removed to a lower ward "to show to others as well as to convince him that some order and discipline were to be observed in this institution, and that conduct of the most unbecoming kind could not be passed over, from week to week, without some notice." Those who manifested responsible conduct, on the other hand, received a series of privileges. In 1839, for example, 93 out of a total of slightly under 400 patients at Worcester were granted freedom to walk anywhere on the grounds without supervision; some, upon a promise to return, were able to walk in town. Such trust was usually justified; only one individual given this freedom broke his word and escaped.[20]

Institutional privileges, however, were not merely a function of behavior. Social status and class also shaped the institutional lives of patients. To be sure, the greatest differential was between corporate and public institutions. Nevertheless, the presence of private patients as well as individuals from quite different walks of life within public hospitals led to subtle differences in care. At Worcester middle-class patients and those with higher educational levels were permitted to keep their trunks in their own rooms, to have greater independence over their possessions, and given better choices of work. Superintendents were especially concerned, as Woodward noted, "that no one shall associate with those particularly obnoxious to him." Ethnicity and class, in other words, often shaped the ways in which patients were treated and the ways that they interacted. Denying that he drew invidious distinctions, the head of the Kentucky Eastern Lunatic Asylum noted that it was "exceedingly unpleasant to be almost compelled to associate with those whose education, conduct and moral habits, are unlike and repugnant to us. Because persons are insane, we must not conclude that they always lose the power of appreciating suitable associates, or are insensible to the influence of improper communications." Isaac Ray, one of the most influential figures in nineteenth-century American psychiatry and author of a classic work on the jurisprudence of insanity, believed that poor and working-class patients required less attention than those from "educated and affluent" backgrounds. With some isolated exceptions, inequality within hospitals was the norm rather than the exception, although differentials were always confined within relatively narrow parameters.[21]

That institutional regimen was crucial to the success of moral treatment was self-evident. Yet moral treatment was equally dependent upon effective physician-patient communication. The groundwork began with a dialogue with family members. If hospitals were to retain their social legitimacy, families had to be persuaded that commitment was a sine qua non for recovery, and that the superintendent's choice of treatment modalities was appropriate. Equally important, the patient had to acknowledge that the family's decision to institutionalize was proper. At that point the superintendent could focus on the thinking and emotional state of patients, and to help them to recognize the irrational nature of their delusions. "I have stated to him," Kirkbride wrote to a family, "that they were delusions and that no one could consider him well while he entertained them." Nor was it improper to repress or escape from troubled familial relationships. When dealing with a son's "unnatural feelings" toward his father, Kirkbride suggested that the youth "say little about them . . . [and] introduce the subject rarely if ever." Such hostile expressions, he concluded, "can do good to no one and may do you much harm." The influence of the superintendent upon the patient—reinforced and mediated by the medical and lay staff—represented a crucial part of moral treatment.[22]

The emphasis on moral treatment gave mid-nineteenth-century psychiatry a distinctive character. It implied the legitimacy of custodial as well as therapeutic functions. Moral treatment was based on the presumption that under certain conditions care—including counseling and regimen—was a form of treatment, while in other respects care (i.e., food, clothing, and shelter) was distinctly custodial. As a matter of fact,

mid-nineteenth century psychiatrists generally opposed the establishment of separate institutions for chronic or incurable cases. They were
not persuaded of their ability to distinguish between curable and incurable persons, and feared that the prevention of abuses in strictly custodial asylums would be too difficult. The only advantage was the relative
cheapness of custodial institutions as they would not require therapeutic interventions, and this presumed advantage had validity only if moral
and humanitarian obligations were ignored. In his classic and influential
book on hospital organization and architecture in 1854, Kirkbride
summed up the case against separate asylums for chronic patients. "The
first grand objection to such a separation is," he wrote,

> that no one can say with entire certainty who is incurable; and to con-
> demn any one to an institution for this particular class is like dooming
> him to utter hopelessness. . . . When patients cannot be cured, they
> should still be considered under treatment, as long as life lasts; if not with
> the hope of restoring them to health, to do what is next in importance, to
> promote their comfort and happiness, and to keep them from sinking still
> lower in the scale of humanity. Fortunately, almost precisely the same
> class of means are generally required for the best management and treat-
> ment of the curable and incurable, and almost as much skill may be
> shown in caring judiciously for the latter as for the former. When the
> incurable are in the same institution as the curable, there is little danger
> of their being neglected; but when once confined to receptacles especial-
> ly provided for them, all experience leads us to believe that but little time
> will elapse before they will be found gradually sinking, mentally and
> physically, their care entrusted to persons actuated only by selfish
> motives—the grand object being to ascertain at how little cost per week
> soul and body can be kept together—and, sooner or later, cruelty, neglect
> and suffering are pretty sure to be the results of every such experiment.

When Kirkbride published a second edition of his book a quarter century later, his views remained unchanged. "What is best for the recent,"
he insisted, "is best for the chronic."[23]

Moral treatment imparted to psychiatry an administrative and managerial character. The very concept of moral treatment was synonymous
with the creation of a specific environment that would facilitate recovery. The vagueness of etiology and the inability to locate presumed
somatic changes that accompanied disease meant that psychiatric theory often had little direct (or even indirect) relationship to practice. Consequently, the imperatives of the hospital as a social system—its size and

structure, physical plant, patterns of authority, and relationships between physician and attendant as well as between staff and patients—became dominating factors.

If any single symbol represented mid-nineteenth century psychiatry, it was the architecture and organization of the asylum. The physical plant was not merely the place where the mentally disordered were confined and treated; it was the embodiment of a moral ideal of a caring profession. The asylum was designed in such a way as to facilitate moral and medical treatment. Its very existence was intended to inspire public faith in the state and to reinforce the institutional and professional legitimacy of psychiatry. American psychiatrists developed a very specific form of asylum architecture and a clear set of guidelines to govern its administration. Indeed, an early twentieth-century psychiatrist was not far off the mark when he used the term "domiciliary psychiatry" to refer to his predecessors.[24]

The attributes of the ideal asylum were spelled out in a series of propositions adopted at the meetings of the AMSAII in 1851 and 1853 and amplified and elaborated by Thomas S. Kirkbride in the first edition of his famous and influential book. For more than three decades most public and private hospitals were modeled along the lines of the "Kirkbride" (or congregate) plan, which unified the theory and practice of asylum medicine by integrating it with a specific physical and organizational form. To be sure, Kirkbride did not create the hospital structure that bore his name, but he surely rationalized prevailing psychiatric beliefs into a coherent, consistent, and unified body of thought.[25]

Physical structures and administrative rationality were central to the care and treatment of the mentally ill. Mid-nineteenth century Americans believed in the redemptive ability of institutions to alter and shape human behavior in socially and ethically desirable ways. Institutions such as schools, hospitals, prisons, and asylums were intended to serve as patent-office models of the good society; all required appropriate physical structures and rules of governance if they were to serve their proper function.[26] Form, in other words, had to follow function. An asylum could not be the random design of an idiosyncratic architect, but rather had to embody psychiatric concepts that gave the physical and moral environment a central position.

The ideal hospital had to begin with the selection of an appropriate site located outside a populated urban area, but accessible by trains and roads. Such features as good drainage, an abundant water supply, and fertile land were important, for they promoted healthful living and provided opportunities to engage in meaningful agricultural and outdoor labor. The aesthetic quality of the landscape was important, for it exercised a beneficial influence on patients. Equally significant, a pleasing site and physical plant fostered a sense of confidence among the families of patients, and thus strengthened their belief in the legitimacy of the institution.

A good site was a necessary prerequisite but an aesthetically pleasing set of buildings designed for specific functions had to complement the landscape. Physical structures were not solely intended as places to provide shelter and other basic necessities; rather they assisted in the creation of a therapeutic environment and enhanced appropriate classification of patients. The linear plan, formalized by Kirkbride, spelled out in minute detail the design of the hospital. The center building housed the superintendent, his family, and the administrative offices and quarters. Extending laterally on both sides for about 150 feet were the patient wings, each segregated by sex. Each wing contained wards subdivided from lower to higher. As patients improved, they moved closer to the center building where personal liberties were correspondingly greater. If additional accommodations were required, a similar structure could be repeated, either joining existing wings at right angles or else lapping on at the end and extending in a parallel line. The interiors had to be attractive and yet provide for the safety and security of patients whose sometimes bizarre behavior threatened personal and collective security. Finally, the separation between hospital and society—aside from geographical location—was achieved by a high but attractive wall that surrounded the entire site. The separation between institution and society was, at least in theory, never absolute; once cured, patients would return to the communities from whence they came.[27]

Physical structures embodied a set of assumptions which were evident in the rules and procedures governing mental hospitals defined by the AMSAII and elaborated by Kirkbride. There was a general consensus that hospitals should never contain more than 250 patients; that superintendents should have complete control of the medical and moral regimen; and that all staff, professional and supporting, should remain under the unfettered control of the superintendent. Although a public hospital had to have a legally sanctioned governing board, its role ideal-

ly was to select the superintendent and oversee its finances and operations in order to give "to the community a proper degree of confidence
in the correctness of its management." The superintendent was clearly
the dominant figure; his authority grew out of his position and his expertise in and knowledge about insanity. Indeed, the placement of his physical quarters at the very center of the institution symbolized and
confirmed his crucial role. In its famous Propositions, the AMSAII put
the matter in simple and succinct form.

> The Physician should be the Superintendent and chief executive officer
> of the establishment. Besides being a well educated physician, he should
> possess the mental, physical, and social qualities to fit him for the post.
> He should serve during good behavior. . . . He should nominate to the
> board suitable persons to act as Assistant Physician, Steward, and
> Matron. He should have entire control of the medical, moral, and dietet-
> ic treatment of the patients, the unrestricted power of appointment and
> discharge of all persons engaged in their care, and should exercise a gen-
> eral supervision and direction of every department of the institution.[28]

In their annual reports, private correspondence, articles, books, and
professional discussions, these superintendents spent an extraordinary
amount of time elaborating the principles that governed their institutions. No details were too minute; they analyzed sites, water supplies,
sewerage, drainage, size of buildings, materials, heating and ventilating
systems, lighting, and occupational facilities. Their involvement in such
matters reflected a deeply rooted faith that asylums, appropriately constructed and administered, could facilitate beneficent outcomes. "The
location of a hospital for the insane," wrote Kirkbride, "its general
arrangements and official organization, must ever exert so important an
influence on the comfort and happiness of all its patients, on the
prospects for a recovery in those that are curable, and on the mental and
physical well-being of those that are incurable, that no apology is
required for any one, who having some practical knowledge of the subject, desires a general dissemination of the views and conclusions which
have resulted from actual experience among those for whom these institutions are specially intended."[29] During the third quarter of the nineteenth century virtually every public hospital conformed in large
measure to the Kirkbride plan. Since each new plant was built only after
committee visits to existing institutions and consultations with members
of the AMSAII, it was understandable that hospital architecture was

uniform and homogeneous and reflected a shared consensus among members of the specialty as well as the larger society that sanctioned and financed these institutions.

———————

As superintendents developed a sense of common identity and purpose, they moved to create an organization that would facilitate regular contacts among them, permit the sharing of experiences and discussions of common problems, and formalize and legitimate the principles that were the foundation of the specialty. In October, 1844, thirteen superintendents met in Philadelphia and organized the AMSAII, the first medical specialty organization in the nation. The meeting was convened by Woodward (who also was elected the first president), and included such figures as Bell, Brigham, Earle, and Ray, all of whom played key roles in shaping the character of early American psychiatry. Meeting annually thereafter, the association developed guidelines and standards relating to the care and treatment of the mentally ill that confirmed and strengthened an institutionally based policy.

Prior to 1860 eighty-three men served as asylum superintendents, and thus were eligible for membership in the AMSAII. Most had been born between 1775 and 1815 when the rise of a market economy had begun to transform family and community and to foster geographical and occupational mobility. They had come from families that were neither rich nor poor. They were all influenced by a pietistic Protestantism, and often expressed concern about the decline in traditional moral values. The asylum thus represented both a vehicle for personal advancement and a means of elevating society. The organization that they created in 1844 offered them an opportunity to reach out to and educate a larger public and simultaneously create a positive image of their specialty and the institutions which they led.[30]

For more than a quarter of a century the AMSAII followed in the traditions laid down by the founding fathers. Its members adopted rules governing the size of institutions, architectural standards, modes of governance, and the personal and professional qualifications of practitioners. They also helped to develop a set of uniform statistical reporting procedures in order to create a body of quantitative data that would assist in uncovering the etiology and nature of mental disorders as well as formulating more effective public policies. Membership was limited only to those occupying the office of superintendent; others with reputations as alienists or who were employed as assistant physicians in mental hospitals were excluded. Above all, the new organization promoted close personal relationships, and enabled its members to speak with a united voice to the larger society.[31]

From the very beginning the AMSAII had a vehicle to disseminate its opinions and thus strengthen its social and medical legitimacy. Even before its first meeting, Amariah Brigham had founded the *American Journal of Insanity*. Although owned and published by the Utica State Lunatic Asylum in New York State, the new journal immediately became the representative of the Association. It printed the proceedings of the annual meetings, and most of its articles were written by members. The journal quickly acquired a reputation as the most authoritative American periodical dealing with insanity, and it had a broad audience both in the United States and Britain.

The growth of the organization strengthened the belief that the problems associated with insanity could only be resolved by individuals possessing character, knowledge, and expertise. Mental disorders, averred its members, were no different from physical diseases and required ever more training and experience, a point of view that was conducive to an emerging professionalism. Many of the difficulties pertaining to commitment procedures and asylum management, they insisted, were related to the fact that policies were often shaped by those lacking the requisite knowledge and competency. Although the imposition of licensing and educational requirements would have to await the rise of a new bureaucratic society toward the close of the nineteenth century, asylum physicians had already achieved these goals through informal means.

An early indication that psychiatry was developing a distinct professional identity was the rupture between prison reformers and hospital superintendents following the creation of the AMSAII in 1844. Since the 1820s individuals and organizations concerned with prison reform had also provided support for the creation of asylums. Two decades later superintendents were expressing reservations about the conflation of prison and insane asylum reform. Woodward, for example, was critical of the Boston Prison Discipline Society's reports for providing "an account of the Insane Hospitals, associating crime with misfortune." When a new Pennsylvania prison reform journal published an article on public mental institutions, Brigham was furious. "I cannot say," he wrote to Earle, that "I like the *comingling* of the *insane* and the *criminal* and to be *catalogued* with Sing Sing and Auburn. . . . It tends to keep up a notion we strive to do away with—that Asylums and Prisons are alike." Nor were Brigham's feelings restricted to his private correspondence; the feud was carried on in print. Indeed, by mid-century such figures as Kirkbride and Earle sought to have the term "asylum" replaced by "hospital."[32]

The success of asylum physicians in creating an influential (and well paying) specialty was reflected in their status within the medical profession generally. In the mid-nineteenth century the practice of medicine had become increasingly problematic. The supply of orthodox physicians far exceeded demand, and the presence of hundreds of proprietary medical schools with few entrance or graduation requirements diminished the ability to create minimum professional standards. The equal rights and democratic ideology of the Jacksonian era, moreover, led to a sustained and successful attack on licensing and legal monopolies, and seemed to confirm the prevailing belief that learned and exclusive professions were more of a danger than an asset. Mid-nineteenth-century orthodox physicians, therefore, were constantly beset by challenges from within and without, and often had precarious careers that offered little in the way of material reward or personal satisfaction.

Asylum medicine, by contrast, was secure, well-paying, and provided status and prestige. Superintendents—unlike their brethren in general practice—had far greater authority and control over their patients and institutions. Under such circumstances asylum physicians were prone to distance themselves from their colleagues in private practice. The AMSAII, for example, had little interest in associating with the American Medical Association (AMA), which had been founded in 1847. In 1853 a motion to affiliate with the AMA was defeated. Subsequent efforts to persuade asylum physicians to merge their organization with the AMA also failed. An unwillingness to lose their favored position and a belief that their interests would be subordinated to broader concerns undoubtedly reinforced the desire to maintain a distinct identity.[33]

By mid-century the physicians who presided over a growing public asylum system had laid the foundation for a professional identity that provided them with status and a secure economic position. They created a coherent literature concerned with the nature, causes, and treatment of mental disorders; staked out a claim for authority in dealing with this dreaded malady; provided the American public and their governmental representatives with information and policy recommendations; spelled out the principles that shaped their specialty and even delineated the qualities that members ideally possessed; and created an organization to further their goals. Above all, they contributed to the legitimization of the emerging commitment to an institutionally based policy for the insane that would remain in place for the succeeding century.

4

Realities of Asylum Life

The early claims and achievements of asylum enthusiasts and supporters exerted a powerful influence. By the second half of the nineteenth century a broad consensus had taken shape that the care and treatment of the seriously and chronically mentally ill ought to take place in public asylums rather than in community settings. These institutions, which accepted all insane persons irrespective of their financial status and were under medical jurisdiction, had a dual responsibility: to cure if possible and to provide humane custodial care for those who failed to respond to therapy. By meeting these obligations, hospitals were seen to serve both the interests of society and those of the individual patient.

Intended as small curative institutions that fostered close relationships between the medical and lay staffs and patients, hospitals grew in size and complexity, and considerations of order and efficiency began to conflict with therapeutic imperatives. The vision of a harmonious institution proved difficult to implement. The realities presented by an increasingly diverse patient population that included individuals who sometimes behaved in bizarre and disruptive ways led to friction with the medical and lay staff. In theory all patients were to receive the same quality of care. In practice the variables of class, race, ethnicity, and gender resulted in internal distinctions. Conceived as self-contained and independent institutions, asylums in fact were shaped by legal, administrative, political, and fiscal environments in which they existed, and consequently faced problems similar to those at other public and social institutions. In short, major differences developed between the ideology of asylum care and the realities of institutional life.

Nowhere were the complexities of an asylum-based policy better illustrated than in the process of committing an individual to an asylum. In theory commitment was a complex legal process designed to safeguard against wrongful confinement and at the same time to ensure that insane persons threatened neither the safety of themselves nor others. In practice commitment was an informal process that involved human decisions rather than strictly legal ones. The decision to commit was largely made by the family of the mentally ill person. Public officials responsible for caring for dependent persons without relatives had a distinctly secondary role. Those involved with the criminal justice system also played a peripheral if not an inconsequential role. During the nineteenth century, commitment in New York State (which had the largest mental hospital system in the nation) was overwhelmingly a family responsibility. In 1846 and 1847, for example, three-quarters of all commitments to the Utica Asylum were begun by the family. This figure changed but little over time. An analysis of commitment proceedings in San Francisco at the turn of the century revealed that 57 percent were begun by relatives, 21 percent by physicians, and only 8 percent by the police. Books and articles written by former patients—many of which were extremely critical of their institutional experiences—also revealed that families were deeply involved with commitment.[1]

The decision to commit was normally undertaken with a great deal of reluctance. Indeed, most families did everything within their power to find alternative means of dealing with mentally disordered members. The final decision generally came after prolonged tensions had created a crisis, and forced a choice between institutionalization and the very destruction of the family unit. A variety of behavioral patterns often precipitated family action, especially the threat or actual use of violence and possible suicidal behavior. A wife admitted to Utica in 1848 initially had ceased to perform household tasks. Shortly thereafter she expressed a desire to give away her four children in the belief that they would come to a bad end. Tragedy then followed when she drowned two of them and attempted suicide. In another case a blacksmith devoted to his work and family became melancholic (i.e., depressed) and threatened his family with an axe. One family was forced to keep a deranged member "under our observation continually by day and night" to prevent violence or suicide, but eventually committed her to Thomas Kirkbride's care. Sexual abuse was not uncommon. A husband with seemingly insatiable "sexual desires" masturbated frequently and manifested a tendency to call upon his wife "at all hours and in any presence to gratify his inclinations." After threatening his spouse with violence, he was committed.[2]

The pleas of family members to asylum superintendents suggest the tragic dimensions in which decisions to hospitalize occurred. A husband whose wife refused to eat brought her to Kirkbride in the hope that "some means may be found to force her to take nourishment immediately." "I reluctantly enclose application filled out for admission of my mother," wrote a bank employee to the superintendent of the Wisconsin Hospital for the Insane in 1875, using very typical language.

> Of late she has grown materially worse, so that we deem it unsafe for the female portion of the family to be left alone with her during the day and especially unsafe for the little 2 year old that is obliged to remain continually there, as she has stated several times of late that she or the children must be sacrificed. Should she destroy another us [sic] could never forgive ourselves if the state has a place provided for their comfort and possible need.[3]

The death of primary caretakers, especially parents, also led to institutionalization, since siblings and more distant relatives were either unable or reluctant to assume responsibility. The first national data in 1880 revealed that 54 percent of patients in hospitals were unmarried and an additional 9 per cent were widowed.[4] To be sure, there were allegations that sane persons were confined in hospitals because of the desire of families to control their estates or husbands to control overly independent wives. While wrongful commitment was by no means unknown, it was relatively rare. In the nineteenth century, confinement followed some form of extreme behavior, including violent, suicidal, and occasionally homicidal acts, hallucinations, excitement, agitation, delusions, and deep depression.[5]

Admission to a mental hospital was often a frightening experience. Cut off from familiar circumstances, patients were thrust into a radically new environment. However intended and designed, asylums did embody a form of coercion in that confinement diminished individual autonomy and freedom. Authority over the daily regimen began with the superintendent, whose directions were transmitted vertically downward to assistant physicians and staff. The goal was clear; to serve patients and thus to facilitate their recovery.

Practice, however, deviated sharply from the ideal. The ability to direct and control the environment was severely restricted by both internal and external constraints. The directives of superintendents often met with the determined resistance of patients. Attendants who were on the wards for hours on end had to deal with noncompliant patients, and the interaction between the two groups created tensions that were hardly conducive to a therapeutic environment. Inadequate levels of funding, deteriorated physical plants, and overcrowding also diminished the ability of managers to shape the institution in desirable ways. Institutional autonomy was also circumscribed by state governments, which exercised authority by virtue of their control over legislation and policy.

Without doubt the most important element in shaping the character of the asylum was the patients themselves. However lofty the intent of organizational rules and regulations, patients' behavior and their relationships with the medical and lay staff more than anything else shaped the internal environment. Patients lived in an atmosphere in which personal liberty was constrained and behavior regulated. As a group, inmates were by no means quiescent or accommodating; their actions often reflected a refusal to conform to defined behavioral norms. Consequently, the character of the asylum was shaped by the uneasy and turbulent relationships of the patients among themselves and with the staff.

The outstanding feature of asylums was the diverse population of inmates. Institutional populations were divided about equally between male and female. In terms of age, the overwhelming majority of patients were in their twenties, thirties, and forties. A substantial proportion were immigrants, and so social and class backgrounds varied in the extreme. And, being committed for different disorders, they exhibited divergent behaviors. Admissions fell into one of four categories; mania, melancholia, monomania, and dementia (which correspond to such contemporary diagnoses as schizophrenia and mood disorders). The heterogeneous nature of the patient population, therefore, presented a formidable challenge to the goal of maintaining institutional order and fostering a therapeutic environment.

Many patients responded favorably to their hospital experiences. Their prior existence had been turbulent and marked by conflict with family and friends. At the asylum they often found physicians and staff who rekindled a sense of hope for the future. The authoritative demeanor of the superintendent-physician generally fostered warm and trusting relationships and led patients to accept medical interpretations of their condition. That patients responded in positive ways was evident in their correspondence after they left the asylum. "*I see now clearly that it was disease* which led me to pursue the course of conduct I did," wrote one woman to Kirkbride, expressing wonderment at her ability to accept delusions as reality. "How in the wide world I ever believed in them so firmly as I did I cannot now imagine . . . owing to your constant and unvarying kindness . . . I was first led seriously to reflect, to reason with myself about it." "I have made every exertion to keep up my spirits," wrote another, as "well as to do many other things for the improvement of my health." Even recalling Kirkbride's demeanor often helped former patients. "When I sometimes tremble for the *future* there arises a strong feeling of confidence in looking towards you." The warm feelings manifested by patients toward Kirkbride were not at all idiosyncratic; Woodward and other superintendents received equally laudatory letters.[6]

Undoubtedly the towering figures of the first generation of superintendents, when combined with the novel character and relatively small size of asylums, created close interpersonal relationships and resulted in positive experiences for many patients. Superintendents were quite conscious about the significance of such personal relationships, and hence tended to fight against institutional growth. Well before the AMSAII adopted its propositions dealing with hospital size and organization, Luther V. Bell insisted that no asylum have more than two hundred patients. "I believe," he wrote to Dorothea L. Dix, "that if there is any circumstance which has elevated our American institutions to the present position of confidence before the community it is their moderate extent and having the head of the establishment domiciliated with his family in the midst of his charge, where he can have a certain paternal relation to them, and can know their characters, feelings, connections and interests with a good degree of intimacy."[7]

For other patients, however, confinement was a traumatic experience. Removed from a familiar environment, deprived of personal liberty, and forced to associate with persons from different backgrounds who often behaved in bizarre ways, some developed profoundly negative attitudes toward the hospital. In extreme cases they published exposés of their experiences. In 1833 Robert Fuller, a former patient at McLean, charged that there were no barriers to commitment and that institutional abuse and maltreatment were common. In his eyes there was but little difference between McLean and the Spanish Inquisition; both suppressed liberty and freedom. At the asylum patients were isolated and the staff practiced "constant deception." Confinement, he charged, was generally injurious and "a vast majority [of patients] would obtain relief in half the time, if permitted to stay with their friends."[8]

The most spectacular attack on legal incarceration came from Elizabeth W. Packard, who challenged both the subordination of women to their husbands and a male political and psychiatric establishment. Packard had been stricken at the age of nineteen with "brain fever," and spent six weeks under the care of Woodward at the Worcester hospital in 1835. Four years later she married Theophilus Packard, a Protestant minister who was nineteen years her senior. An unhappy marriage was exacerbated by sharp religious differences. Elizabeth Packard adhered to a liberal theology, while her husband was a devout Calvinistic who accepted the total depravity of humanity. When Packard refused to play the role of an obedient wife and expressed religious ideas bordering on mysticism, her husband had her committed in 1860 to the Illinois State Hospital for the Insane at Jacksonville, where she remained for three years. After being released, she was confined by her husband in a locked room. To preclude further commitment proceedings, a friend secured a writ of habeus corpus. In a trial that received national publicity, Packard was declared sane. She then spent nearly two decades campaigning for the passage of personal liberty laws that would protect individuals and particularly married women from wrongful commitment to and retention in asylums.[9]

Whatever their reactions, most patients found the asylum environment to be difficult and ambiguous. The idiosyncratic behavior of patients tended toward social disorganization, if not anarchy. Although the ward system was structured to correspond to behavioral patterns that varied from total withdrawal and bizarre and violent behavior on the one hand to quiet cooperation on the other, immediate problems often disrupted this arrangement. Under such circumstances, much of staff time and energy was devoted to dealing with outbreaks of behavioral problems and the maintenance of a minimum degree of order.

Therapeutic considerations by necessity receded into the background. Indeed, staff—whether medical or lay—tended to react to inmate initiative rather than the other way around.

Consider, for example, the problems posed by patients often described as the "filthy insane." Virtually all hospitals had their share of such persons. Upon entering their wards in the early morning, reported one New York State official, "the sight was most repulsive, and the odors intolerably sickening. . . . Some of the patients were literally wallowing in their own excrements. They had besmeared their beds, their heads and faces, and even the floors and walls of their rooms." In some instances three or four attendants were required to overcome the resistance of such patients and to wash and dress them. The result was "unfavorable in every respect." Indeed, the need to maintain institutional routine and order often contradicted the imperatives of moral treatment, thus creating perpetual and seemingly unresolvable tensions.[10]

Complicating the therapeutic regimen still further were problems relating to deficient physical plants. The codification of the principles governing the construction of asylums was based on an ideal type. The actual implementation of these principles, however, often left much to be desired. "The tendency now is," Isaac Ray complained to Dix in 1851, "not to make hospitals as good as possible, but as cheap as possible." Three years later he used the pages of the *North American Review*—one of the nation's most respected and influential periodicals—to express his dismay. Hospital building, he complained, was "too much controlled by economical considerations, and . . . too often the question has been, not how well, but how cheaply, the thing can be done." Economy often led to the elimination of day rooms; bathing facilities and water closets were forced into obscure corners; furnishings were sparse; ventilation and heating were inadequate; and the "whole scene was cheerless, dismal, and forbidding." Even exteriors were "unsightly" and "monotonous," a result perhaps of "an uncultivated taste" rather than strictly economic considerations. Ray urged that building committees advertise for plans, which would then be submitted "to the examination of men practically conversant with these institutions." Only then would asylums "have the merit of being intelligent and well matured."[11] Ray's critique was echoed by many of his colleagues, who agreed that their therapeutic goals were being undermined by dysfunctional physical plants.

The problems of administering a complex institution were further exacerbated by the presence of a heterogeneous population that included individuals separated by social class, ethnicity, race, and sex. To be sure, asylums—precisely because they were supported by public funds—did not engage in overt discrimination. The absence of blatantly unequal practices, however, concealed distinctions that mirrored larger social tensions and that played a role in shaping the lives and experiences of their inmates.

In many public hospitals native-born poor and indigent patients did not receive the same care as private patients whose families paid for their support. Though differences in care were subtle, they reflected the widespread belief that patients should not be forced to associate with those who made them uncomfortable. Consequently, the assignment to wards reflected both behavioral as well as socioeconomic considerations. Middle-class and private patients sometimes were given more luxurious accommodations and received special privileges. At Worcester such patients were permitted to accept responsibility for their own clothing, books, and work.[12] With only a few exceptions, asylum physicians saw no reason why hospitals should not provide certain amenities for private patients even though they were cognizant that differential treatment might arouse a negative response among those from less affluent backgrounds.

The psychiatric rationalization for distinguishing between individuals on the basis of social class reflected a concern with the need to maintain public support. Cognizant that purely welfare institutions sometimes aroused antipathy, they were mindful of the need to avoid being stigmatized. They were especially fearful that their institutions might become glorified poor houses. Such a development would serve neither the interests of their patients nor of the institutions. Justice and wisdom, therefore, required that hospitals serve a representative cross-section of the community. In an admittedly extreme action, the directors of the Ohio Lunatic Asylum abolished all charges for private patients in 1851. "The distinction was invidious; its bad consequences were manifold, and far outweighed all pecuniary advantages," observed the superintendent, "Often did our halls resound with the exclamation, 'You are only a pauper, I pay for my board.'"[13] Although asylums distinguished between native-born indigent and private patients, a common religious and cultural background kept differences within a relatively narrow range.

At precisely the same time that states were founding public asylums, the pace of immigration quickened. The movement of peoples included large numbers of Catholics, particularly from Ireland, a development that stimulated a powerful nativist movement and reawakened long-standing Protestant suspicions of the Papacy. To many native Americans, Irish Catholics followed clerical teachings that were hostile to republican ideals; their very presence seemed to menace social harmony. That asylums, prisons, and welfare institutions held large numbers of foreign-born persons (especially Irish) reinforced existing stereotypes. Although the foreign-born constituted less than half of its population, for example, the New York City Lunatic Asylum on Blackwell's Island in 1850 held 534 foreign-born patients as compared with only 121 native Americans.[14] Such data fueled fears that the United States was being threatened by hordes of persons incapable of being assimilated.

The growing number of immigrants in public asylums exacerbated internal problems of management and administration. The reaction of asylum physicians tended to be mixed. Some explained high rates of insanity as a consequence of circumstances, including dislocation from familiar surroundings, poverty, and absence of supporting family networks. Others, however, were more ambivalent and came to different conclusions. Ralph L. Parsons, superintendent at Blackwell's Island, described the Irish as "persons of exceptionably bad habits." Separated from family and friends, they had suffered from indigent circumstances, an inadequate diet, substandard living conditions, and intemperance. "The majority of such patients," he concluded, "are of a low order of intelligence, and very many of them have imperfectly developed brains." At the annual meetings of the AMSAII in 1857, one superintendent described foreigners as "more noisy, destructive, and troublesome," while another commented on the low curability rates of the Irish in particular. A few years later Ray noted that "very ignorant, uncultivated people" often lacked insight into their delusions, a trait particularly prevalent "among the lower class of the Irish."[15]

Nowhere did the combined influence of class and ethnicity have as great an impact upon asylums than in Massachusetts, a state that received large numbers of Irish immigrants. By 1854 the trustees reported that the Worcester institution "is fast becoming a Hospital for foreigners." Insanity, they insisted, did not change the sensibilities of men and women.

Among the insane of this State are wives and daughters, widows and orphans, of farmers, mechanics, ministers, schoolmasters and the like. . . . [H]owever ready and willing they might have been, when sane, to help the poor, and elevate the humble, of whatever race or color, they would have shrunk most sensitively from living next door even to a wretched hovel, and from intimate association with those who are accustomed to, and satisfied with filthy habitations and filthier habits. Now, they do not lose their sensibilities by becoming insane, and they ought not to have them wounded by being herded together in the same apartment with persons whose language, whose habits, and whose manners, offend and shock them.[16]

Such attitudes undoubtedly had an impact upon care and treatment. The superintendent of the Worcester hospital, for example, conceded in 1847 that he was more successful in treating native than Irish patients. A decade later his successor had reorganized the wards in order to maintain "a complete separation" of foreigners and natives, although he insisted that this action did not reflect a discriminatory intent. Opposite in "religion and all the notions of social life, it would not be well to class the two races in the same wards," he explained. This extreme action was criticized by the *American Journal of Insanity*, which maintained that no compelling justification for such a practice existed. Though nativist sentiment had its greatest impact upon the treatment of foreign-born patients in Massachusetts, the impact of ethnicity was not absent elsewhere. Urban asylums—which had large numbers of foreign-born—tended to be among the worst in the nation. Underfinanced and understaffed, they were generally shunned by native middle-class Americans.[17]

The most significant differentials in care and treatment were clearly a function of race. African-American insane persons were either denied admission to asylums or else were confined in rigidly segregated quarters. Such practices, however, were rarely justified by theories that purported to relate race and insanity. Concerned with maintaining the legitimacy of their institutions, superintendents followed prevailing mores and community practices. Charles H. Nichols, a prominent asylum superintendent, wrote that there was general agreement "that it *is the duty* of the State, County, & City Hospitals for Insane . . . to receive col'd patients"; that separate quarters be provided in order to effect "all desirable separation of the races; . . . [and] that such an arrangement may be carried into effect without prejudice to either party."[18]

Outside of the South, African-American insanity aroused but little interest because the black community was so small. The general practice in most areas was either exclusion or segregation. Shortly after opening in 1833, the Worcester hospital admitted several African-American patients and constructed quarters for them in the brick shop. Some states—Indiana and Ohio—excluded them entirely. Urban areas such as New York and Cincinnati created segregated public facilities—including jails and almshouses—that accepted all dependent black persons. Separate facilities, however, were rarely equal. At the New York City Almshouse, for example, a segregated building was described by officials as "an exhibition of squalid misery and its concomitants. . . . Here, where the healing art had objects for its highest commiseration, was a scene of neglect, and filth, and putrefaction, and vermin. . . . It was a scene, the recollections of which are too sickening to describe."[19]

In the South, on the other hand, a quite different situation prevailed. On the eve of the Civil War about four million out of a total population of eleven million were African-Americans. Under such circumstances asylums were unable to ignore the problems posed by insanity among blacks. The paternalism that was characteristic of antebellum slave society led to somewhat different policies. Indeed, the pattern of institutional care of insane blacks—slave or free—was somewhat more variegated in the South than other regions. Some states did not segregate patients; others provided separate quarters; and some simply followed an exclusionist policy.

Under the leadership of John M. Galt, for example, the Williamsburg hospital after 1841 placed African-American females in separate quarters while black males were housed with their white counterparts. Since all of the institution's servants were slaves, white patients, according to Galt, regarded black residents "pretty much in the same light as they do the servants." A decade and a half later, however, Galt had to abolish the practice of integrated wards. At the Virginia Western Lunatic Asylum, by way of contrast, African-Americans were denied admission; its superintendent favored separate institutions. Similar inconsistencies prevailed throughout the entire region. Following the end of slavery after the war, most southern states created entirely segregated institutions or else constructed separate, but generally unequal, quarters for black patients within the same institution.[20]

Irrespective of their policies, many asylums found that internal racial conflict was often unavoidable. Even strict racial segregation did not guarantee harmony. One former patient recalled an instance in which a white patient wandered into a black area and began to abuse its residents. He was struck by a black inmate, who began to pursue him. Other white patients, having witnessed misbehavior of their colleague, originally manifested no disposition to interfere. "But to see a white man fleeing before a negro foe, and the latter audaciously pursuing him in the midst of his friends, was too much for their self-control"; the result was a violent fight. The asylum environment thus replicated the racial tensions found in the larger society.[21]

Gender also shaped the character of asylums, albeit in more subtle ways. Commitment rates did not vary by sex; there is little or no evidence to suggest that women were more likely to be committed than males. At the Utica hospital, for example, the sex ratios for most of the nineteenth century were virtually even. At the Willard Asylum—an institution devoted to the care of the chronic insane in New York State—the population was 56.3 percent female. The slight differences in the sex ratio did not reflect any particular concern with female madness. Chronically mentally ill females were more likely to be sent to a state hospital, while males who fell into the same category were more likely to be confined in penal or welfare institutions. Early twentieth-century national data indicated that males had higher first admissions rates than females. Within asylums, however, the organization, structure, and daily regimen reflected gender roles typical of the larger society. Until the late nineteenth century, asylum medicine was exclusively male; even when female physicians broke the gender barrier they could never rise to a hospital superintendency. Wards were segregated along gender lines. More importantly, occupational therapy and recreation were molded along gender and class lines. Working-class women worked in the kitchen, laundry, and did general housework; more affluent females spent their time in recreational activities, reading, and sewing. Men tended to labor outdoors, and hence had somewhat shorter work days. The regulations to limit sexual relationships were rarely successful; fragmentary evidence suggests that illegitimacy remained a perennial problem in hospitals with a young patient population.[22]

The character of asylums, however, was molded not only by the nature of and interaction among patients, but by other elements beyond the control of its administrators. Institutional growth in particular led to the

construction of larger and larger physical plants, which inevitably affected the very quality of asylum life. Hospitals limited to about two hundred patients could more likely impose a regimen than those twice or
triple in size. Staff quickly found that they were forced to compromise
with and adjust to new realities.

From their very inauguration asylums were faced with unremitting
pressure to expand beyond their physical capabilities. In many states
institutions had little discretionary authority to limit admissions, and
were generally reluctant to discharge patients prematurely. Even
though surveys to determine the need for institutions were common,
most underestimated the demand. The very founding of a hospital in an
area often transformed community attitudes and made families more
receptive to institutionalizing troubled relatives. Within a half century
following the founding of the influential Worcester institution, the
majority of state and urban institutions exceeded the upper limit of
200–250 recommended by the AMSAII in its famous mid-century
propositions. By 1875 state and urban asylums founded before 1870 had
an average resident population of 432; about a third had between 500
and 1300 residents.[23]

Steadily and seemingly inexorable growth had dramatic consequences for institutional structure and functions. The theory of moral
treatment assumed that hospitals—like families—would remain small,
and that superintendents—like firm but loving fathers—would have the
ability and flexibility to shape the environment in order to arrest and
then reverse the course of mental disorders. Therapeutic objectives
mandated the creation and maintenance of close and intimate interpersonal relationships without the interposition of mediating influences
that might vitiate patient-physician interaction.

As long as asylums remained small, superintendents were able to
supervise the care and treatment of patients and meet their administrative responsibilities; there was no inherent conflict between the two.
But as institutions grew in size and the patient population became more
heterogeneous, states found themselves in an increasingly difficult situation. The informality that existed at the outset could no longer be maintained. With four and five hundred or more patients, the social
organization had to be more rigid and coercive. The theory of moral
treatment offered few guidelines in these new circumstances, for it rested on largely individualistic premises. Since asylum physicians were
unable to reconcile an individualistically oriented therapy with a com-

plex social system, the demands of the latter began to take precedence over the requirements of the former. They were thus faced with a cruel dilemma; their concern for the welfare of their patients collided with the larger goal of maintaining order and administrative rationality in the asylum. "I confess my inability," George Chandler, successor to Woodward, told a legislative committee about 1848,

> to do justice to my feeling in its management. I cannot sufficiently keep myself acquainted with the various departments to act understandingly. I cannot know the daily changes in the symptoms of 450 patients—the operations on the farms and in the workshops—the domestic operations—direct the moral treatment—conduct the correspondence with friends—wait upon such visitors as demand my personal attention and various other things. . . . The patients expect and desire frequent intercourse with the Superintendent. . . . He, if any one, has their confidence and he can usually control them better than any one else. If he has under his charge more than one hundred he finds it difficult to know their personal history and the daily changes of their condition.[24]

As institutions grew in size and complexity, psychiatry was transformed increasingly into an administrative and managerial specialty. An intricate social institution like an asylum required formal regulations and procedures to ensure order and efficiency; formal mechanisms, in turn, often militated against the aims of moral treatment, which was based on the ability of the physician to manipulate the environment of both the individual and the group. As might be expected, the transformation of asylums engendered a parallel change in the character of their superintendents. Whereas the first generation of asylum physicians tended to be charismatic and creative leaders, their successors were often selected for their managerial and administrative abilities.

Nowhere was the ambiguity of institutional life better illustrated than in the debate over the wisdom and desirability of restraint. In theory the goal of institutionalization was the inculcation of means of self-control. In reality disruptive behavior was omnipresent and was exacerbated by the steady growth in the number of resident patients. The so-called nonrestraint system, popularized by Robert Gardiner Hill and John Conolly in England, aroused considerable interest in the United States. Nonrestraint implied that a properly constructed and administered asylum would obviate the need of such mechanical restraints as chains and straightjackets. "*I wish to complete that which Pinel began*," Hill stated in a public lecture in 1838. "I assert then in plain and distinct terms, *that in a properly constructed building, with a sufficient number of suitable attendants, restraint is never necessary, never justifiable, and always injurious, in all cases of Lunacy whatever.* I assert the possibility of the total banishment of instruments of restraint, and all other cruelties whatsoever."[25]

By contrast, American superintendents tended to insist that mechanical restraints, including straightjackets and seclusion in padded rooms, were preferable to arbitrary and often violent action by attendants concerned with maintaining order in their wards. They recognized, of course, that the use of restraints and moral treatment were not always compatible, and that institutional needs might have to take precedence. Most adopted a middle position; they employed restraint only as a last resort while conceding its potential detrimental impact upon individuals. The trustees of the Worcester hospital were acutely aware of the dilemma when they expressed regret that circumstances precluded the adoption of the nonrestraint system.

> There was always a crowd of patients within the Hospital, and more pressing for admission. Those in charge deemed it necessary to use these [strong] rooms. Still, therefore, men and women were thrust into them, and made more furious by the confinement; and still many others were restrained by straps and various mechanical contrivances, who might have had freedom of motion, and the use of their limbs, if sufficient space and sufficient means of medical and moral treatment had been at command, and if there had been fuller faith in the efficacy of milder measures.

The "principal evil" that led to seclusion and restraint, they added, "was the crowd of patients."[26]

Asylum physicians saw restraint as a necessary evil. The only alternative was to rely on attendants to enforce a minimum degree of civility and to protect patients from self-inflicted harm or from violent actions of others. In theory, attendants were invested with formidable responsibilities, for they mediated between the regimen established by medical authority and the patients. In practice, however, their therapeutic responsibilities were supplemented by such mundane tasks as making beds, keeping the wards clean, and bathing dirty and incontinent patients. The work was long and the pay below that of such occupations as shoemakers and woodworkers. Above all, ten or more hours daily work on the wards with the omnipresent threat of violence and social disorganization would have probably tried the patience of anyone. That attendants often responded to disruptive and incontinent patients not as loving parents but as despotic patriarchs was hardly surprising.

Asylum medical staffs were aware of the responsibilities that devolved upon attendants and the difficulties of attracting the right sort of individuals. They were less aware that the assertion of unquestioned medical authority inevitably conflicted with the goal of developing responsible attendants capable of exercising independent and informed judgments in their daily contacts with patients. The result was the creation of competing and perhaps irreconcilable roles. Attendants found themselves at the same time beholden to the medical staff, surrogate parents to patients, and performers of menial household chores. That the ideal of attendant life diverged sharply from reality was perhaps not startling. Extraordinarily high rates of turnover among attendants were characteristic. The most extreme problems were evident at municipal asylums with large patient populations. At the New York City Lunatic Asylum penitentiary inmates served as attendants, thus saving the municipal government substantial sums of money. These individuals, complained the physician in 1843, were

> criminals and vagrants, who have neither character nor discretion to take care of themselves. The bad effects of this system in the introduction of vulgarity and profanity into our halls, is painfully evident. Many of the patients are well aware of their character. Instead of respecting and loving their attendants, they become embittered against them, and consequently irritable and fretful—of course, much to their prejudice. . . .
>
> The impropriety of this arrangement, as well as its sad effect upon these wretched beings, must be apparent to every one.

As late as 1875 only two attendants had served for more than twelve months at the men's asylum on Ward's Island. During that year there were sixty changes, including twenty-two resignations and thirty-eight dismissals (including sixteen for drinking, five for striking patients, and the remainder for other transgressions). To be sure, New York City's asylums were in more desperate shape than other institutions. But even the Worcester hospital—which by the turn of the century had regained some of its national prominence—had to contend with staff instability. In 1912 each female and male position was occupied by 3.2 and 4.4 individuals, respectively.[27]

Asylums were shaped not only by patients and staffs, but by the constitutional, legal, and political environment in which they existed. As public institutions, they could not function as independent and autonomous entities. Their governing structures, admissions policies, and the ways in which they were financed were generally determined by state and local government officials, both elective and appointive. Indeed, the very framework of American government that divided authority between three distinct levels—federal, state, and local—was to have a profound impact not only on asylums, but upon virtually all public institutions and policies dealing with dependency, crime, education, and social welfare generally.

During the 1780s Americans created a unique form of republican government. Two centuries of British imperial rule had created grave mistrust toward centralized authority. The federal Constitution in many respects institutionalized these misgivings by sharply restricting the authority of the federal government and by retaining a large reservoir of power for the states. The Tenth Amendment explicitly stated that the "powers not delegated to the United States by the Constitution" were "reserved to the States respectively, or to the people." However interpreted, the Constitution was based on the premise that responsibility for health and welfare resided with state and local governments and not the national government. Consequently, nineteenth-century social policy involved state and local governments acting in concert with private organizations and individuals. Asylums, although generally established and supported by states, found themselves inextricably enmeshed with local governments as well.

In theory, of course, the powers of local communities derived from and were dependent upon the actions of sovereign state governments. In practice, however, localities had de facto authority to deal with many dependency-related problems. Much of the legislation pertaining to the mentally ill, therefore, was based on the assumption that responsibility would be divided between localities and states. In general, states provided the capital funds necessary for the acquisition of a site and construction of a physical plant for a hospital as well as for subsequent expansion and renovation. Local communities, on the other hand, were required to pay the hospital a sum equal to the actual costs of providing care and treatment. Nor did the system assume that each and every

insane person would be committed to a state institution. Only dangerous mentally ill individuals were required by law to be sent to state hospitals. Others who would presumably benefit from therapeutic
interventions (and thus relieved of the need for public support) could, at
the discretion of local officials, be hospitalized. The system, in short,
involved divided responsibility. For much of the nineteenth century,
therefore, a significant proportion of insane persons continued either to
live in the community or else were confined in municipal almshouses.
Families with sufficient resources could send relatives to state hospitals, provided that they assumed financial liability for their upkeep.
States, moreover, had to reimburse asylums for those patients who had
not established legal residency, such as immigrants. The result was a
variegated pattern. Insane persons were found living with their families,
confined in public asylums, jails, almshouses, and other institutions for
dependent persons. Indeed, the source of funding frequently determined where insane persons resided.[28]

Divided responsibility for the insane had significant repercussions.
The system tended to promote competition and rivalries that were
inherent in overlapping government jurisdictions. In many states the
stipulation that local communities were financially liable for their poor
and indigent insane residents created incentives for local officials to
retain them in almshouses where costs were generally lower. If states
assumed fiscal responsibility for all mentally ill persons, localities were
apt to send individuals to public asylums in order to relieve their con-
stituents of any fiscal responsibility. Many asylums were also adversely
affected by a divided governmental structure. The charge for patient
care and treatment—generally set by the legislature—was often below
actual costs; slow and delinquent payments from local communities for
their residents caused severe cash-flow problems; and inadequate or
tardy state appropriations compounded existing difficulties. Hospital
authorities were sometimes forced to issue scrip (a promise to pay
issued for temporary use in an emergency) or borrow money, and some
states—including Massachusetts and South Carolina—required private
patients to pay above-average charges in order to compensate for below-
average payments for indigent patients. Asylums, moreover, faced
unremitting pressure from communities to discharge patients in order
to save money irrespective of their condition. In extreme instances local
officials sought to force hospital authorities to reimburse them for work
performed by patients even though such labor was generally part of a

therapeutic regimen. The very creation of an institutional-based public policy within a political system that divided authority tended to encourage efforts to shift costs to different levels of government irrespective of the needs of mentally disordered persons.[29]

The only effort to alter the manner in which states financed asylums was launched by Dorothea L. Dix. In 1848 she attempted to persuade Congress to enact legislation that would authorize the distribution of five million acres of federal lands to the states, the proceeds of which would be used to care for the indigent insane. After years of persistent effort, Congress passed a bill in 1854 granting ten million acres. The action was not unprecedented, since the construction of a national railroad system had been subsidized by generous federal land grants. Dix's efforts, however, came to naught after Franklin Pierce vetoed the bill. Should the bill become law, Pierce wrote, "the fountains of charity will be dried up at home, and the several States, instead of bestowing their own means on the social wants of their own people, may themselves, through the strong temptation, which appeals to States as to individuals, become humble supplicants for the bounty of the Federal Government, reversing their true relation to this Union." Pierce's veto, which was upheld by wide margins, ensured that the federal government would have no role in mental health policy for nearly a century.[30]

Public policies were shaped not only by ideology and governmental structure, but by social currents as well. By the mid-nineteenth century there was a growing awareness that the achievements of state institutions had not lived up to the promises and expectations of those responsible for their creation. The distance between the goals of moral treatment and the reality of hospital life, for example, had seemingly widened rather than narrowed; the number of mentally ill persons continued to increase; almshouses and other welfare facilities held even more insane persons than asylums; and the costs of care and treatment inexorably kept rising. Nor had the proliferation of almshouses, penitentiaries, hospitals, schools, and houses of correction stemmed the prevalence of illness, dependency, and crime.

The growing disillusionment of several decades of social and institutional innovation gradually led to a searching examination of the foundations of social policy. A number of states responded by creating new state agencies with investigatory and regulatory authority. Ultimately these agencies became the vehicle by which states imposed a rationalized, centralized, and bureaucratic framework upon their welfare institutions. During the 1850s such influential states as New York and Massachusetts began to experiment with novel regulatory mechanisms in response to the social problems that seemed to accompany the migration of large numbers of impoverished immigrants who came from alien cultural and religious backgrounds. The crucial step in centralizing and rationalizing welfare came in 1863 when Massachusetts created the first Board of State Charities in the nation, the prototype of what eventually evolved into state departments of welfare. Within a decade ten other states had followed the example of Massachusetts. Paradoxically, the goal of these agencies was to rationalize welfare and cut back on the seemingly high expenditures that accompanied institutionally oriented social policies.

Although differing in structure and function, the similarities of state boards of charity were striking. All reflected a pervasive faith in the ability of bureaucratic organizations, when managed by right-minded, intelligent, and educated persons, to deal effectively with social problems and thus to ensure the preservation of a fundamentally moral and healthy society. Possessing investigatory authority, these boards often provided detailed analyses of poverty, indigency, illness, insanity, and crime, all of which they interpreted partly in terms of character deficiencies. That asylums fell under their jurisdiction was significant; to link mental illnesses with welfare led to a subtle form of stigmatization, for it tended to blur distinctions between illness on the one hand and poverty and immorality on the other hand.

On a much more practical level, the creation of state boards inevitably created friction, for public regulation and professional autonomy were not always compatible. Indeed, the formation of the Conference of Charities (later the National Conference on Social Welfare) in 1874—a national organization composed of representatives of state boards of charity—heightened the possibility of conflict. In arguing on behalf of government regulation, its members sometimes came into conflict with the AMSAII. Indeed, in 1864 the latter indicated its opposition to "Lunacy Commissions" or other forms of public supervision. John P. Gray, superintendent at Utica and editor of the *American Journal of Insanity*, echoed his colleagues when he criticized the creation of any agency "having any oversight, charge or control of State or corporate institutions." A decade later Ray persuaded his colleagues to adopt resolutions affirming the necessity for professional autonomy and rejecting the claim that supernumerary officials "with the privilege of scrutinizing the management of the hospital" with either direct or indirect authority could accomplish "an amount of good sufficient to compensate for the harm that is sure to follow." The Illinois Board of Commissioners of Public Charities reacted with equal firmness. "We do not think," its members insisted, that superintendents "should be allowed to dictate legislation, nor do we believe that it is good policy for them to oppose intelligent and honest supervision and inspection by legally constituted authority." Slowly but surely professional autonomy was circumscribed by public regulation. In such bellwether states as Massachusetts and Pennsylvania, friction between central boards and asylum authorities was common. The hope that hospitals would be able to avoid political conflicts and maintain unrestricted autonomy remained an elusive dream.[31]

The founding of asylums had been accompanied by an optimistic rhetoric that emphasized the high probability of recovery among the mentally ill and the eventual conquest of a dreaded malady. Yet within a relatively brief span of time it had become evident that a wide gap existed between the ideals of asylum life and reality. To concede institutional shortcomings, however, is not to imply the absence of any accomplishments. What were the actual outcomes of care and treatment and what role did asylums actually perform, as compared with rhetorical claims? In the early years superintendents claimed striking successes in curing mental illnesses. William M. Awl and Woodward—both of whom played a prominent role in popularizing the concept of curability—claimed a recovery rate in recent cases (defined as ill for less than a year) of 80 percent or higher. Awl, for example, reported that during the first four years of operation at the Ohio Lunatic Asylum 80 percent of recent cases had recovered. Those ill between one and two years and five and ten years had recovery rates of 35 and 9 percent, respectively. The figures at Worcester were not fundamentally different. During its first seven years the proportion of recoveries of recent cases ranged between 82 and 91.5 percent; the comparable figures for older cases were between 15.5 and 22.5 percent.[32]

How valid were such claims? Pliny Earle, one of the founders of asylum medicine, subsequently charged that people like Awl and Woodward employed misleading analyses. The proportion of cures represented the ratio of recoveries to cases discharged rather than to cases admitted. Their claims also did not take into account readmissions; hence the total number of cases was larger than the actual number of patients. Finally, they reported the same individual as recovering on several occasions. Earle suggested that such statistical distortions grew out of a desire to gain support for the creation and expansion of an asylum-based policy.[33]

Woodward and others of his generation undoubtedly were concerned with creating public support for asylums; their data seemed to confirm the claims that cure was a cheaper alternative to confinement of chronic cases in custodial and welfare institutions. "I think the statistics of insanity have done great good," Woodward informed Earle in 1842, "and the extensive and enthusiastic movements in favor of the insane in the United States [*sic*] has been produced by comparing the results of institutions and looking to the success of the best as given in the published statistics." Woodward's insistence that a recurrence of insanity did not represent a relapse also buttressed his data; just as individuals could be ill on many occasions with respiratory diseases, so too could persons have recurring but independent attacks of insanity.[34]

Earle's critical analysis of curability claims was given further legitimacy by mounting complaints after 1850 that asylums were forced to care for large numbers of chronic patients, thus vitiating their therapeutic mission. The chronic population was heterogeneous: some were elderly; some had severe somatic disabilities (e.g., paresis); some appeared to pose threats to themselves or to society; and some were individuals who failed to respond to therapy. For these patients the hospital served as a refuge; many either had no relatives or else their families were unable to cope with their behavior. The presence of chronic patients often had an adverse impact upon asylums. They took up beds that might have been used for several short-term stays, and they tended to create a more pessimistic institutional environment. Nor were asylums able to control admissions, which were largely shaped by legislative and judicial actions.

Yet surviving evidence suggests that the claims of therapeutic successes were not simply imaginary. In the 1880s Dr. John G. Park, then superintendent at Worcester, undertook a longitudinal study of individuals discharged from the hospital on their only or last admission. Influenced by the pessimistic studies of Earle and late nineteenth-century concepts that emphasized the incurability of insanity, Park insisted that "there can be no doubt that the public have been hitherto widely misled as to the meaning of the word 'recovery,' as used in the hospital reports, and as to the permanency of cures from insanity." Yet his own data did not by any means discredit earlier claims about curability. Completed in 1893, Park's study tracked 984 individuals, of whom 317 were alive and well at the time of their reply, while an additional 251 had remained well until their death. Nearly 58 percent of those discharged as recovered never again were institutionalized. Data from other hospitals, including Utica, Williamsburg, and Pennsylvania, suggest much the same state of affairs. Whatever the reasons, a significant number of persons discharged as recovered were able to live in the community.[35]

The claims that large numbers of chronic cases were subverting the therapeutic functions of asylums were also somewhat overstated. Before 1880 hospital populations included large numbers of acute cases whose length-of-stay was less than twelve months. Although national data are lacking, a sample of individual institutions reveals that their custodial functions had not yet become paramount. The experiences of the Worcester hospital are not atypical. In 1842—a decade after it opened—46.4 percent of its patients had been hospitalized for less than a year; only 13.2 percent had a length-of-stay that exceeded five years or more. In 1870 the comparable figures were 49.6 and 13.9 percent. Similarly, in 1850 41.1 percent of patients at the Virginia Western Lunatic Asylum had been hospitalized for less than a year and 29.6 percent for five years or more; the respective statistics for the California Insane Asylum in 1860 were 40.2 and 0.1 percent. For most of the nineteenth century between 35 and 40 percent left the Utica hospital annually. Before the turn of the century, therefore, large numbers of patients who entered hospitals were discharged in less than a year.[36] Such data indicates the half-full or half-empty cup perception; those whose outlooks reflected an underlying pessimism tended to emphasize the problem of chronicity and to ignore substantial discharge rates.

Asylums admittedly failed to live up to the ideals of their supporters. They were shaped in unexpected ways by unpredictable developments: the nature of and interaction among patients, as well as between patients and staffs; the persistence of class, ethnic, racial, and gender differences; the inability of asylum physicians to impose their will; the growth of external public regulation; and policies relating to financing. To acknowledge failures and shortcomings, however, is not to imply the absence of achievements. For many patients hospitalization came at crucial moments in their lives. Substantial numbers were discharged after

5

The Problem of Chronic Mental Illnesses, 1860–1940

The creation of asylums in the early nineteenth century rested on the assumption that mental disorders, if identified early and treated promptly, were curable. This optimistic faith, however, had little basis in fact. Many insane persons—whether treated or ignored—failed to improve or recover, and the duration of their illnesses was often measured in decades rather than weeks or months. An Irish domestic worker, admitted to the Willard Asylum in 1869 with a diagnosis of periodic mania, became so withdrawn that she sat for more than a decade with her head bent and eyes closed. After nearly twenty years of confinement she died of tuberculosis. A reporter who visited the institution in 1886 found the situation "appalling." "It is pitiful," he wrote. "Gray-haired old men playing at innocent games like children of four years. Venerable ladies happy with a piece of string and a bright bit of tin. There is mental ruin everywhere." The inmates sat on the lawn staring at the lake. The most impressive thing was not "the low murmur of the waves," but the omnipresent keeper who stood watch over them. Another reporter described the patients as "happy as any children among the cozy homes of our state."[1]

The growing numbers of severely and chronically mentally ill created

103

formidable problems for both families and the state. Many individuals became mentally disordered in their twenties and thirties. Unable to work, they were entirely dependent upon others for access to such basic necessities as food, clothing, and shelter. Their behavioral problems often magnified the need for supervision. Affluent families might be able to pay for private attendants, but for the overwhelming majority of families this was not a viable option. In many instances mentally ill persons lacked relatives to fall back on for support. Hence the burden of care fell largely on local and state government.

The presence of large numbers of chronically mentally ill persons presented public officials with a profound dilemma. To provide care in mental hospitals required a massive expansion in their number and size. Such a policy contained an element of risk; the character of hospitals might be transformed, perhaps irreversibly, as custodial concerns overwhelmed therapeutic goals. To care for chronic insane persons in the community was also difficult because of the absence of a supportive infrastructure. Chronic mental illnesses, therefore, remained at the center of the debate over the proper shape of mental health policy.

The creation of an asylum-based system failed to resolve all of the problems associated with mental illnesses. From the very advent of mental institutions, the total insane population far exceeded the number of available beds. Even in Massachusetts—the state that had the most extensive system of public hospitals—there was a wide gap between perceived needs and reality. The monumental census of insane persons in Massachusetts in 1854 conducted by Edward Jarvis—a meticulous and compulsive physician and statistician—suggested as much. In agreeing to undertake the census on behalf of the legislature, he attempted to identify every insane person living within the Commonwealth and to gather data on place of birth, sex, race, age, means of support, place of residence or confinement, prior record of hospitalization, and prognosis. He solicited this information by polling every single physician in the state and resident clergymen in localities without a doctor. Included in the survey as well were all the superintendents of public and private hospitals, keepers of jails and houses of correction, as well as hospital officials from other states. The result was the single most revealing census of the insane within a given state. Massachusetts at this time had two state institutions (Worcester and Taunton), one private (McLean) and one municipal hospital (Boston). In 1855 these facilities had an average inpatient population of slightly over one thousand; no other state (taking into account total population) could match the facilities available to Bay State residents.

There were 2,632 insane persons in Massachusetts in the autumn of 1854, according to Jarvis's final tabulations. Of this number, 1,522 were paupers (693 supported by the state and 829 by towns), while 1,110 were supported by their own resources or by friends. Only 625 were foreign-born; 2,007 were natives. No less than 1,284 were either at home or else living in municipal poorhouses; 1,141 were in hospitals; and 207 were in county institutions, houses of correction, jails, or state almshouses. The survey revealed that the overwhelming majority of those polled believed that most insane persons were incurable. Out of the total of 2,632, only 435 were identified as curable; 2,018 were listed as chronic and the prognosis for the recovering 179 was not reported.[2]

The data indicated that the majority of insane persons still remained outside of asylums. The greater part of this group ended up either in other public institutions—notably almshouses—or more commonly in the community from which they originally came. The situation was much the same in New York. In 1854 the County Superintendents of the Poor found that there were 2,419 pauper lunatics at the end of 1854. Only 296 were in the Utica Asylum; the remainder were in county poor houses (1,352) or in the community (771). Of 757 in fifty-one county institutions, 118 were described as "furious and dangerous," 235 as "filthy in their habits," 250 "confined constantly to the house, 180 "confined constantly in strong rooms or cells," and 71 "confined constantly in mechanical restraint."[3]

Most hospitals dealt with their chronic insane by discharging those who failed to improve or recover. Although such practices enabled superintendents to pursue therapeutic goals, it left unresolved how the varied needs of chronically and severely mentally ill persons would be met. "This is not merely a present and temporary evil," Jarvis insisted.

> A large portion of the cases are permanent, because incurable. Others are becoming so, although they may now be restored. Our population is increasing rapidly; and insanity keeps pace with it, and probably runs in the advance. The causes of insanity are still as abundant and as efficient as they have been; and if they are not arrested nor modified, this year and the succeeding years will produce as many lunatics as the last and those that went before it. . . .

It is well, then, to look to the future as well as the present, and lay such a plan for the administration of insanity as will meet all the demands of those who suffer from it, and such as will be the best for the interests of the Commonwealth.[4]

———————

Even though it was evident that there was a very wide gap between the capacity of state hospitals and the total number of chronic insane, there was little disposition to consider alternatives. Indeed, the optimistic rhetoric of asylum physicians tended to minimize the problem, if only because chronic illness seemed to contradict the claims of curability that drove public policy. The ideology of asylum reform was based on the familiar and appealing premise that cure was cheaper than long-term confinement. From time to time there were discussions about the possibility of establishing asylums for incurable patients, but most alienists agreed with Thomas Kirkbride that such institutions were undesirable. Occasionally some states adopted novel policies. Massachusetts, for example, opened a separate department for incurably insane immigrant paupers at one of its state almshouses. This innovation, however, reflected fear of aliens rather than strictly humanitarian concerns; the low level of funding meant that the quality of care was substantially below that provided at state hospitals.[5]

Conditions in the Bay State were by no means idiosyncratic; a comparable state of affairs existed in New York, the nation's largest state. In 1843 it had opened its first asylum in Utica. Failure to create additional hospitals forced such populous urban areas as New York City to develop a parallel municipal system. Nevertheless, the growing numbers of insane persons in local communities and welfare institutions created more pressure for change. By the mid-1850s the county superintendents of the poor had begun to criticize the strategy that consigned the overwhelming majority of chronic dependent insane to the jurisdiction of the welfare system. They urged that additional state facilities be established, including one that would care for chronic patients. But this and other recommendations—all of which were intended to create a system of geographically-dispersed asylums serving all regions—met with resistance from those favoring fiscal restraint.[6]

The increasing number of chronic mentally ill persons outside of asylums slowly but surely led to a modification of the traditional ideology of psychiatric reform. Dr. John B. Chapin, a former assistant physician at

Utica who would play an increasingly prominent policy role, publicly disassociated himself in part from the belief that institutions were only for the curable. Having assisted the New York county superintendents of the poor to draft their petition, he also expressed his dissent with his colleagues in the *American Journal of Insanity*. A supporter of traditional therapeutic asylums, Chapin insisted nevertheless that New York had to make alternative provisions for its nearly two thousand impoverished insane residents, many of whom fell into the chronic category. He called upon the state to create large custodial institutions that would provide humane care for chronic patients and thus avoid incurring the higher costs associated with therapeutic care at Utica. Chapin's proposal indicated that the prior consensus on the need for asylums to accept *both* acute and chronic cases was beginning to weaken.[7]

The economic depression that began with the Panic of 1857 and the Civil War that followed delayed further policy discussions about the care of the insane. In 1864 the New York legislature finally authorized Sylvester D. Willard, secretary of the State Medical Society, to conduct an investigation into conditions among the indigent insane in county poorhouses. Court-appointed physicians gathered data in their localities and forwarded them to Willard. Some of the reports suggested that conditions in county welfare facilities were comparable to those existing in the Utica Asylum. At the Montgomery county poorhouse, ten out of the eighty-three inmates were insane. Each lunatic had a separate cell, and the rooms were "generally clean, and the atmosphere good." The diet, though plain, was substantial. The Jefferson county institution had sixty-one lunatics housed in a relatively new building that was adequate to the task at hand. The report by Dr. L. H. Allen from Tioga county, on the other hand, indicated that the insane were "in a most miserable condition." The washing facilities were inadequate; the insane had little opportunity to leave their cells; the heating was inadequate; the rooms were filthy; and the inmates were rarely visited by a physician. Willard, however, virtually ignored any favorable data and singled out county poorhouses for criticism. There was, he insisted, "gross want of provision for the common necessities of physical health and comfort, in a large majority of the poor houses where pauper lunatics were kept." Willard emphasized that paupers "who in many instances are depraved by vice, cold, sordid, selfish from poverty, utterly incapable of taking care of themselves . . . are employed to oversee and apply moral and physical means of restraint for the insane!" He concluded by recommending the establishment of an institution to care specifically for the incurable insane.[8]

With the support of the governor, the legislature authorized what became the Willard Asylum for the Chronic Insane, which opened in 1869. Located on an isolated site in Ovid on the shores of Seneca Lake, the new asylum represented a sharp departure from the Kirkbride model. A central administrative building included attached wings for the care of the sick and violent. Harmless and quiet patients, on the other hand, lived in smaller detached structures. Within six years after opening Willard held slightly under a thousand chronic patients and functioned as a self-contained, autonomous community. Chapin— Willard's first superintendent—attempted to implement his belief that chronically insane persons could receive decent and humane care in large custodial institutions. He spent less on drugs than his colleagues, and provided work for as many patients as possible. Employment at Willard, however, was not rationalized in therapeutic terms, but rather designed to relieve the monotony of institutional life. Much of the work performed by patients was physically demanding and monotonous but helped to contain costs. Males worked on the farm or helped to construct new buildings; women sewed and washed. Limited resources precluded more variegated work programs. Nevertheless, the quality of care, according to P. M. Wise, who succeeded Chapin in 1884, was superior to that found in county asylums. Willard had a one to ten attendant-patient ratio; county institutions had a one to twenty-five ratio.[9]

The founding of the Willard Asylum immediately precipitated a debate that lasted over a decade and involved asylum physicians, state officials, and critics of an institutional-based policy. John P. Gray, superintendent of the Utica Asylum and authoritarian editor of the *American Journal of Insanity*, published an unsigned article critical of the step taken by the New York legislature. Utica, the article noted, had neither the space nor the resources to carry out the legislative mandate of caring for all recent cases of insanity in the state. Nor did custodial care obviate the need for treatment. Institutions for incurable patients, the article continued, often became unwieldy; the absence of hope created an unhealthy atmosphere; and chronic patients were affixed with the stigma of pauperism even though pauperism was the result rather than the cause of mental disorder. Finally, families would be reluctant to incarcerate members in such a facility. Gray urged instead the creation of additional hospitals for acute and chronic cases that were carefully located so as to serve all geographical areas, and spearheaded a behind-the-scenes effort to persuade the legislature to reverse its action in creating an institution for incurables. Chapin—who was soon to become Willard's first superintendent—responded to critics of the new policy. "Those of us," he wrote, "who have ventured to urge something better than poor houses for . . . [the chronic insane will] persevere. It is idle to suppose all will ever be placed in *hospitals* though the Journal of Insanity proposes to *cure* all. Something must be conceded in style and expense and accommodations to the economic views of our people. In the essentials of care we ask that the standard may be elevated."[10]

The new policy also attracted the attention of the AMSAII. At its annual meeting in 1866 a heated debate ensued. What emerged was a division not so much on the abstract issue of an institution for the incurably insane, but rather on more pragmatic considerations. Even those who had supported the creation of Willard did not think it ideal. One superintendent emphasized that any solution had to take into account both individual needs and community resources. In the end the delegates adopted five resolutions that compromised some of the original principles of the Association, but maintained its opposition to separate institutions for chronic patients. They supported a noncontroversial recommendation that states create geographically dispersed asylums that served all residents, and reaffirmed the propositions adopted in 1851 and 1853 governing the construction, organization, and management of hospitals. The fifth resolution, which passed with a divided vote, modified the association's position by agreeing that the ideal hospital could have as many as 600 residents (as compared with the earlier limitation of 250).[11]

By the 1860s it was becoming apparent that the care of the chronic insane was the single most important issue both within and without the specialty of psychiatry. But the founding patriarchs of the specialty remained adamantly opposed to institutions that limited admission to chronic cases. They never abandoned their faith in the curability of insanity. In their view the size of hospitals and the availability of sufficient resources were the key determinants for an effective policy. Those favoring two kinds of asylums, on the other hand, tended to be younger men who were less committed to the faith in curability. They tended to believe that care in local and county asylums would always be substandard, and hence favored state-imposed and centralized policies that mandated separate asylums for acute and chronic cases. It was possible, they insisted, to provide humane care at a lower cost through efficient administrative and managerial techniques.

These younger physicians found allies among officials responsible for public welfare policy. "It appears to me," observed Frederick H. Wines, the influential secretary of the Illinois Board of State Commissioners of Public Charities, "that the pressing problem with regard to the future of the insane in this country is: how can the chronic insane pauper be most cheaply cared for, consistently with a proper regard to humanity? and must this work be done by the state or by the several counties?" It was obvious to him that state responsibility was preferable to community care. Indeed, Wines emphasized that the policy and principles advocated by the AMSAII were "driving the chronic insane back into county jails and poorhouses, simply because they persist in their adherence to 'propositions,' framed to meet an entirely different condition of public sentiment of affairs."[12]

The older consensus within the AMSAII slowly but surely began to disintegrate. The increasing number of chronic cases led to a growing interest in alternative policies that involved some fundamental changes in the ways in which asylums were structured and administered. As early as the mid-1850s John M. Galt of the Williamsburg asylum called attention to two European models. One was the farm of St. Anne, an experiment conducted at the Bicêtre, the famous French hospital. The other was the colony of the insane in Gheel, Belgium. Concerned with providing an orderly transition from asylum to community as well as providing adequate care for the chronic, Galt proposed several innovations. He favored a parole system that permitted patients to live and work in adjacent communities while remaining under the legal jurisdiction of the hospital; the construction of decentralized facilities for convalescent patients; and the boarding of chronic cases with nearby families. Criticized by his colleagues, Galt's suggestions were all but ignored.[13]

A decade later interest in the colony system in Belgium mounted. More than a thousand years old, the town of Gheel had become famous as a religious shrine where lunatics were sent in the hope that divine intercession might restore their sanity. Its inhabitants became accustomed to their presence and communal responsibility for the welfare of patients became accepted practice. By the mid-nineteenth century Gheel had a formal administrative system that included a medical superintendent who oversaw the welfare of insane persons boarded out in the town. The diet was ample; work was plentiful; and insane persons were granted maximum freedom to move about if their condition so warranted.[14]

Concerned with the problem of chronicity as well as deflecting criticism of their institutions for maximizing confinement and restraint, American superintendents began to seek alternatives to the Kirkbride congregate model. Their search was given urgency by pressure from the new state boards of charity, which disliked a dual system that made localities responsible for chronic patients. The creation of Willard undoubtedly had been influenced by the example of Gheel, and was an indication that the commitment to a traditional model was diminishing. Equally important, Massachusetts and Illinois—states with powerful state boards—began to consider other alternatives to traditional state hospitals.

In the Bay State the initial proposal for a modification of the congregate system came from Dr. Merrick Bemis, superintendent of the Worcester hospital. By the 1860s its physical plant had become obsolete. Both Bemis and Samuel Gridley Howe (chairperson of the Board of State Charities) had visited Europe and were impressed by the Gheel model. In 1869 Bemis persuaded the hospital trustees and state officials to construct a new and decentralized hospital. His plans included a central building that would provide for no more than a third of the patient population. The remainder would be housed in small family-like structures. As patients improved, they would be moved to houses further and further away from the main building, thus gradually facilitating their integration into the community. Bemis called upon the state to assume total responsibility for all insane persons. His plan assumed that the majority of insane persons, especially chronic cases, would reside outside but adjacent to hospitals, thus permitting qualified physicians to exercise supervisory authority. In effect, Bemis proposed a novel plan that incorporated and integrated institutional and community care.[15]

Resistance to Bemis quickly emerged. The Board of State Charities retreated from its initial enthusiasm. But the greatest opposition came from Pliny Earle, superintendent of the Northampton hospital, who received support from Isaac Ray and Kirkbride. In his *Annual Report* Earle condemned all Gheel-like experiments. They transformed superintendents from physicians into "keepers", he wrote, and the self-discipline fostered by moral therapy was undermined by excessive patient liberties. "I read your report with an unusual degree of interest," Ray wrote,

> especially your observations respecting the family and cottage methods of caring for the insane. These projects I regard as the offspring of that class of men (to be found in every community) whose only chance of achieving notoriety is to find fault with everybody else and who suppose they magnify themselves by depreciating others. It is a curious illustration of the prevalent spirit of altruism that while one community, frightened at the cost of furnishing hospital accommodation for all its insane, is disposed to acquiesce willingly in those primitive institutions, the poor house and county jail, another is advocating architectural arrangements far more costly than the old hospital.

By 1872 the trustees of the Worcester hospital had reversed their decision to construct a decentralized hospital. Bemis's resignation followed shortly thereafter, thus ensuring that the new institution would be built along traditional lines. Ray was gratified that "the coup de grace has been delivered at his [Bemis's] preposterous cottage scheme."[16]

The abortive effort to break the sharp distinction between hospital and community care by creating intermediate transitional structures had broad implications. In brief, it suggested that the specialty of psychiatry was unalterably opposed to any plan that might diminish the central role of mental hospitals in providing care and treatment for mentally ill persons. The result was a steady growth in the number and size of public institutions for nearly a century.

Yet the problem of chronic mental illnesses remained as pressing as ever. Although reneging on its initial support of Bemis's plan, the Board of State Charities urged the creation of a dual system based on the Willard model. Failing to gain legislative support, the board won a minor victory in 1877. When the Worcester hospital moved to its new location, the legislature passed a law authorizing the conversion of the old physical plant into what became known as the Temporary Asylum for the Chronic Insane. The institution opened in 1877 with over three hundred patients. Under the jurisdiction of the Worcester trustees, the newly named asylum quickly lost its temporary character. A decade later the legislature, bowing to the inevitable, changed its name to the Worcester Insane Asylum.[17]

The struggle in Massachusetts over the proper shape of public policy was soon repeated in other states. In Illinois Frederick Wines became the catalyst for change. When the legislature authorized the construction of two new hospitals, Wines convened a conference to debate the relative merits of the Kirkbride congregate and family (or segregate) models. Andrew McFarland, superintendent of the sole state hospital, suggested that traditional congregate institutions include as well smaller detached buildings housing forty patients under the supervision of a married couple. To Wines the advantages of such an arrangement was compelling; acute cases could receive intensive therapy, while less costly and more humane facilities would be available for quiet chronic patients. Wines feared that the high costs of small congregate hospitals would only lead to further deterioration in conditions among the chronic insane, and he proposed that the state construct much larger decentralized institutions.[18]

Initially Wines failed to persuade the legislature to mandate changes. In less than a decade, however, his views prevailed. When the legislature authorized a fourth hospital in 1877, it gave him leeway to shape its structure and organization. The new institution, which opened in Kankakee in 1880, marked a sharp break with tradition. The hospital had a conventional central building with the typical wings. But it also had a large number of detached structures housing no more than fifty patients. Under the leadership of Dr. Richard Dewey, Kankakee grew rapidly. By the time of his departure in 1893, the hospital had an average inpatient population of almost 1,900, or twice the total at the other three state hospitals. It was designed to resemble a small village, "highly organized, thoroughly policed, in admirable sanitary condition, and under complete control; but affording to its insane inhabitants a variety, a freedom, and a satisfaction not attainable in any hospital constructed upon the type now prevalent in the United States." Kankakee, observed Dewey, balanced individual needs and institutional and economic efficiency. Its cost—estimated at about a third of that of congregate hospitals—meant that the institution could cater to the needs of the chronic insane, who would no longer be neglected in the community.[19]

In Wisconsin the State Board of Charities and Reform pursued a quite different strategy to deal with the problem of the chronic mentally ill. Initially its members favored the establishment of a Willard-type asylum. But by 1880 they had become critical of institutional psychiatry. If insanity (with some exceptions) was a largely incurable illness—the majority view among asylum physicians—then the psychiatric preoccupation with therapeutic hospitals was unrealistic. A year later the legislature, following the Board's recommendations, enacted a statute that enabled counties—with appropriate state subsidies for maintenance—to create small asylums for chronic patients. Within seven years sixteen such institutions were in existence; their resident population was nearly 1,400. Most were located on small farms ranging from 80 to 350 acres. Inmates had access to both occupational labor and leisure-type activities; there were relatively few limits on personal autonomy; and proximity to families facilitated frequent contacts. The new system had the effect of limiting the size of state hospitals, which discharged patients who failed to improve or recover to the appropriate county asylum.[20]

The Wisconsin system aroused interest despite the hostility and indifference of asylum physicians. But only Pennsylvania emulated its example. During the 1870s and 1880s Pennsylvania had tended to pursue inconsistent policies. The opening of an asylum for chronic cases at the beginning of the 1890s resolved few issues, however, for the burgeoning population of this expanding industrial state meant that institutional capacity remained far below the number of insane persons. Resistance to further expansion finally led the legislature to follow the recommendation of the Committee on Lunacy of the Board of Public Charities to enact a Wisconsin-type statute. Many counties were quick to take advantage of the new law; one year after its passage sixteen counties had either authorized or constructed new buildings or renovated older structures. In both Wisconsin and Pennsylvania the county system persisted for decades, with varying results. As late as 1930 thirty-six Wisconsin county asylums had 7,557 residents, as compared with a hospital population of slightly over 2,000; in Pennsylvania the comparable figures were 12,117 and 12,713, respectively.[21]

The continuing adoption of different policies to deal with the chronic mentally ill indicated the absence of any consensus. Nor was there any unanimity in evaluating the merits and disadvantages of state and county asylum care. If per capita expenditure is a measure of success, there is little doubt that large institutions such as Willard were more cost-effective than traditional hospitals such as Utica. By the 1880s, for example, annual per capita expenditure at the former was 30 to 40 percent below that of the latter. But outcomes also varied. For much of the nineteenth century Utica discharged 35 to 40 percent of its patients annually; at Willard the figure was somewhat under 5 percent. Yet

Mc Lean Asylum for the Insane, Somerville, Mass.

LUNATIC ASYLUM,
Bloomingdale, N.Y.

In the early nineteenth century social and economic changes, as well as new concepts of mental disorders, led to the creation of the asylum—an institution that by removing "lunaticks" from the community could restore them to mental health by creating a therapeutic environment. The McLean Asylum for the Insane, serving the Boston area (above), and the Bloomingdale Asylum in New York City (below) were among the earliest of the private mental hospitals and in general served an affluent clientele.

STATE LUNATIC HOSPITAL, WORCESTER, MASSACHUSETTS.

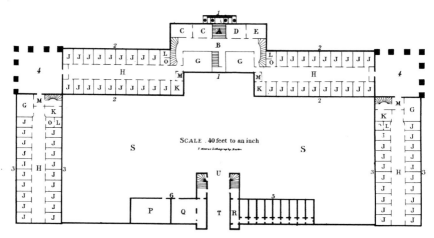

PLAN OF THE PRINCIPAL STORY OF THE STATE LUNATIC HOSPITAL.

The growth in population and inability of private asylums to serve a larger public ultimately led to the emergence of the state mental hospital. The Worcester State Lunatic Hospital, opened in 1833, acted as a catalyst and model for the establishment of comparable hospitals in other states. Its plan symbolized the commitment of the state to provide care and treatment for large numbers of persons irrespective of their financial status. Samuel B. Woodward, its first superintendent, played an important role in disseminating the belief that hospitalization could cure most acute cases of mental disorder.

Finding large numbers of mentally ill persons in jails, almshouses, and wandering about the community in Massachusetts in 1842 and 1843, Dorothea Lynde Dix launched her career by convincing the legislature to expand the Worcester Hospital. For nearly four decades she led a crusade to ensure that all states would create a public mental hospital system, and was personally responsible for founding or enlarging more than thirty public mental hospitals in the United States.

Opened in 1843 to bring the newer concepts of care and treatment to the mentally ill of New York State, the Utica State Lunatic Asylum was located in the center of the state in the belief that it would provide equal access for all its citizens.

Price 25 Cents.

ASTOUNDING DISCLOSURES!

THREE YEARS
IN A MAD-HOUSE!

BY A VICTIM.

WRITTEN BY HIMSELF.

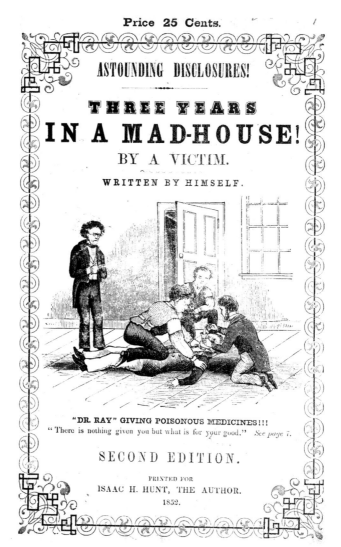

"DR. RAY" GIVING POISONOUS MEDICINES!!!

"There is nothing given you but what is for your good." *See page 7.*

SECOND EDITION.

PRINTED FOR
ISAAC H. HUNT, THE AUTHOR.
1852.

The legal process of involuntary commitment to mental hospitals quickly led to allegations by former patients that they had been unjustly incarcerated even though sane, and that they had been subject to abuse in the asylum by mad doctors. Isaac M. Hunt's pamphlet, *Three Years in a Mad-House!* (1852), was one of the early illustrated publications attacking asylums.

Kidnapping Mrs. Packard.

"Is there no man in this crowd to protect this woman!" See page 59.

No. 1.—"And this is the protection you promised my Mother! What is your gas worth to me!" See page 61.

No. 2.—"I will get my dear Mamma out of prison! My Mamma shan't be locked up in a prison!" See page 62.

Charging that she had been wrongfully committed to the Illinois State Hospital for the Insane by her husband, Elizabeth W. Packard won a court battle, and spent the next two decades crusading for the passage of personal freedom laws to protect individuals against wrongful confinement by their families. In her book *Modern Persecution, or Insane Asylums Unveiled* (1873), she focused on the legal subordination of wives to their husbands, which facilitated wrongful commitment and separation from children.

AT DINNER.

RECEIVING PATIENTS—THE EXAMINATION.

State hospitals were never able to meet the goal of providing care and treatment for all insane persons. Their location at the geographic center of the state often worked to the disadvantage of large urban areas, which were usually located on the coast or navigable waterway and hence were at a distance from state hospitals. A burgeoning urban population of immigrants and working people forced cities to create their own institutions. In New York City, a Lunatic Asylum became part of the almshouse and prison complex on Blackwell's Island. By 1870 the asylum had more than 1,300 patients, and conditions were an open scandal. Convicts from the prison served as attendants; the diet was substandard, epidemics were common; and treatment was nonexistent.

STATE LUNATIC HOSPITAL AT DANVERS.

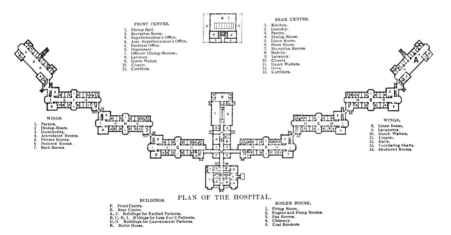

FRONT CENTRE.

1. Dining Hall.
2. Reception Room.
3. Superintendent's Office.
4. Asst. Superintendent's Office.
5. Business Office.
6. Dispensary.
7. Officers' Dining-Rooms..
8. Lavatory.
9. Dumb Walter.
10. Closets.
11. Corridors.

REAR CENTRE.

1. Kitchen.
2. Laundry.
3. Pantry.
4. Dining-Room.
5. Linen Room.
6. Store Room.
7. Reception Rooms.
8. Bakery.
9. Lavatory.
10. Closets.
11. Dumb Walters.
12. Oven.
13. Corridors.

WINGS.

1. Parlors.
2. Dining-Room.
3. Dormitories.
4. Attendants' Rooms.
5. Private Rooms.
6. Patients' Rooms.
7. Bath Rooms.

WINGS.

8. Linen Room.
9. Lavatories.
10. Dumb Walters.
11. Closets.
12. Halls.
13. Ventilating Shafts.
14. Shuttered Rooms.

PLAN OF THE HOSPITAL.

BUILDINGS.

F. Front Centre.
E. Rear Centre.
A, J. Buildings for Excited Patients.
B, C, H, I. B'ldings for Less Exc'd Patients.
D, G. Buildings for Convalescent Patients.
K. Boiler House.

BOILER HOUSE.

1. Firing Room.
2. Engine and Pump Rooms.
3. Fan Rooms.
4. Chimney.
5. Coal Bunkers.

By the second half of the nineteenth century the growth of population had rendered the older ideal of a small and intimate asylum unrealistic. Although following the Kirkbride congregate model, the asylums that came into existence during the second half of the nineteenth century were far larger and in many ways contradicted the therapeutic goals of the early founders of the specialty of psychiatry. Opened in 1878, the Danvers State Lunatic Hospital in Massachusetts was intended to provide relief for the city of Boston and to accommodate a substantial number of insane persons who failed to recover.

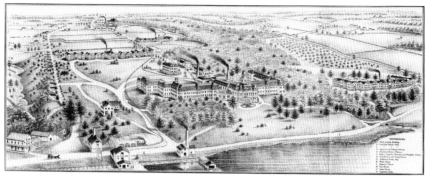

WILLARD ASYLUM FOR THE INSANE.

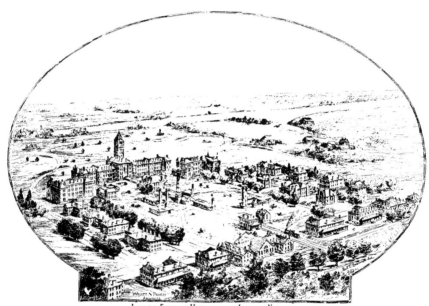

ILLINOIS EASTERN HOSPITAL FOR THE INSANE · KANKAKEE.

The goal of curing all mentally ill persons proved increasingly illusory; a significant proportion of mentally ill persons remained in a chronic stage for decades. Their inability to function in the community and their need for care posed complex problems. Their retention in the asylum threatened to subvert therapeutic goals; their presence in the community posed equally troubling dilemmas. In the latter half of the nineteenth century, New York State and Illinois, among others, moved to create specialized institutions that accepted only the chronic insane. The Willard Asylum for the Insane (above) and Eastern Hospital for the Insane at Kankakee (below) had a thousand or more patients, and functioned as self-contained communities. They were a source of controversy among psychiatrists, since such institutions reflected a growing feeling that insanity was incurable.

Willard had lower mortality rates and provided its residents with more personal freedom.[22]

The experiences of Kankakee were equally problematic. D. H. Tuke, the distinguished British alienist, reacted favorably to the institution during his visit to America in the early 1880s. After working on the farm, patients were able to relax at their cottages. "There was an air of freedom and homeishness," he reported, "which is necessarily more or less lost in an ordinary asylum, especially when of giant proportions." Moreover, a lower-than-average proportion of patients required restraint. Yet Kankakee was by no means free of problems. Overcrowding was characteristic; by 1912 nearly 2,900 patients lived in accommodations designed for 2,200. Even the Board of Public Charities remained ambivalent; it opposed such large institutions, but conceded that the legislature was opposed to a geographically dispersed system of smaller institutions. To psychiatrists institutions that cared for chronic cases represented a scientific and medical backwater. Trained as physicians, they were understandably opposed to an institution dedicated solely to care, as contrasted with therapy. Adolf Meyer, undoubtedly the most influential and important psychiatrist of the early twentieth century, expressed this view in no uncertain terms. He had come to Kankakee shortly after migrating from Switzerland. After eighteen months on the medical staff, he reported in 1894 that

> the atmosphere of the place shows little chance of being improved to such a degree as to make life satisfactory enough to spare energy for the work that I am longing for. Catering towards political effects, towards more show and granting insufficient liberty of action, the administration discourages progress along sound principles. The library facilities are poor and the whole mechanism of medical work little promising although much better than when I came here. My courses on neurology and mental diseases have certainly aroused the interest of the Staff; but the ground does not promise much fruit as long as the simplest means for clinical observation and examination are absent![23]

The county care system, although limiting the growth of state hospitals and ensuring that chronically insane persons would not be confined in jails or almshouses, proved controversial and was not widely emulated. Welfare officials tended to be ambivalent. Franklin B. Sanborn, an influential Bay State figure, was supportive, but Wines preferred a Kankakee-type policy. Similarly, Dr. Charles H. Hoyt—a prominent

New York State official—favored large hospitals, which in his eyes were presumably more economical, maintained higher standards of care and medical treatment, and were more easily supervised. Nor was the AMSAII supportive of a system that left county asylums under the control of laypersons.[24]

Despite its ambivalent reception, the Wisconsin county asylum system persisted even though no state (Pennsylvania excepted) followed its example. Contemporary evaluations of the efficacy of a system that divided responsibility between county chronic care facilities and traditional state hospitals varied widely. Psychiatrists in general were hostile; they were doubtful of their ability to predict patient outcomes with any degree of precision, and also remained committed to therapeutic institutions. State officials in Wisconsin and Pennsylvania, on the other hand, were obviously more favorably inclined. When a Pennsylvania official inspected the Wisconsin system in 1909, he concluded that chronic insane persons were "better fed, better housed, and better cared for" than anywhere else in the United States. Medical care was below that provided at hospitals, but the chronic insane required "very little medical treatment." A similar evaluation of the Pennsylvania system came to similar conclusions. But even the county asylum system was not free of problems. Over time the absence of state supervision led local officials to emphasize economy, sometimes to the detriment of patients. Moreover, some counties refused to accept patients whose behavior posed serious managerial difficulties. Like any system involving human beings, the results of the Wisconsin plan were mixed.[25]

The nineteenth-century debate dealing with the care of the chronic mentally ill proved prophetic. Chronic illness required care and management for periods that could sometimes span decades. But psychiatrists, like their medical brethren, remained preoccupied with acute and episodic rather than persistent and long term disease, and continued to emphasize the paramount importance of restorative therapies. Yet the fact of the matter was that significant numbers of mentally ill persons failed to recover. In one form or another the issue of care for such individuals would continue to dominate all subsequent discussions of mental health policy.

––––––––––

At the same time that the debate over traditional mental hospitals versus special facilities for the chronic insane was taking place, a series of unpredictable developments were rapidly transforming the scene and rendering familiar issues obsolete. Before the turn of the century most chronic severely mentally ill patients—excepting those who posed threats to themselves or others—still remained outside of mental hospitals. Depending on the geographical area, they were dispersed in communities or in welfare (and occasionally penal) institutions. Although hospitals always had chronic cases, the majority of patients fell into the acute category and generally were institutionalized for considerably less than a year. To be sure, institutions such as Willard and Kankakee were custodial in character, but they remained the exception rather than the rule. Despite massive problems related to overcrowding and inadequate funding, state hospital systems in general were committed to a therapeutic ideal even if reality remained quite different.

Beginning in the late nineteenth century, however, mental hospitals were transformed by developments that altered their character in fundamental ways. These changes were neither planned nor anticipated; they were by-products of policies adopted for quite different ends. In brief, inpatient populations began to be made up of chronic rather than acute cases. The consequences were striking, for they set the stage for shattering the century-old and hitherto inseparable links between psychiatry and mental hospitals. At the very same time, these changes ultimately prepared the foundation for a sustained attack on the very legitimacy of an institutional-based policy.

One of the most striking developments involved the rapid growth in both the absolute number and proportion of aged patients in mental hospitals—particularly those sixty years or older. Before 1900 elderly persons, generally speaking, were not committed to asylums. This was true even if their idiosyncratic or bizarre behavior—which at present is subsumed under such categories as Alzheimer's disease, senile dementia, and various depressive disorders—could be identified with a psychiatric diagnosis. In the late nineteenth century physicians distinguished between the psychiatric symptoms of the nonelderly and elderly. Nonelderly persons could become insane for a variety of reasons, few of which were preordained. Aging, by way of contrast, was conceived as a discrete pathological process in its own right, thus suggesting an inevitable loss of mental abilities and functioning. Indeed, few psychiatrists believed that elderly individuals diagnosed as insane belonged in asylums. Insane patients, conceded one physician in 1894, did not belong in almshouses "except in the case of an old person who is pretty senile and can be treated as well at [the] Long Island [Almshouse] as at any other hospital." Three decades earlier the superintendent of the Taunton State Hospital in Massachusetts expressed the belief that the elderly insane should not receive professional attention because "there is no reasonable hope for cure" and advised friends "to retain them at home."[26]

Many elderly persons, however, required care. Indeed, the problem grew increasingly acute throughout the nineteenth century. High rates of individual and family mobility meant that elderly persons had fewer nearby relatives to assist them in times of need. The rise of wage labor and a market economy also altered household structure in profound ways. The separation of home and work tended to create smaller and more specialized families and undermined their capacity to care for needy and especially elderly members. Even if the number of aged in the general population appeared small by contemporary standards, they nevertheless posed serious problems when unable to work because of illness or disability. The very concept of retirement did not exist; individuals were expected to work as long as they lived, and social security systems were lacking. Inability to earn a living—particularly among working-class families where subsistence-level wages precluded savings—represented a major catastrophe.

To permit elderly persons to starve or to die from lack of food or shelter was unthinkable. Few persons advocated a laissez-faire approach to the problem. Religious institutions and private philanthropy often provided assistance, but their resources were limited. The burden of support, therefore, fell on the publicly supported almshouse (or poorhouse), an institution that had become the centerpiece of the nineteenth-century welfare system. Intended to reform and rehabilitate dependent persons, poorhouses by mid-century had acquired an odious reputation. A New York State legislative committee found these institutions to be

> badly constructed, ill-arranged, ill-warmed, and ill-ventilated. The rooms are crowded with inmates; and the air, particularly in the sleeping apartments, is very noxious, and to casual visitors, almost insufferable. In some cases, as many as forty-five inmates occupy a single dormitory, with low ceilings, and sleeping boxes arranged in three tiers one above the other. Good health is incompatible with such arrangements. . . . In one county almshouse, averaging 137 inmates, there were 36 deaths during the past year, and yet none of them from epidemic or contagious disease. Such a proportion of mortality indicates most inexcusable negligence.

The committee noted the difficulty of proper classification. The institution housed children, adults, insane, and aged persons, and the failure to provide separate quarters for men and women led to high rates of illegitimacy. Those who managed these facilities sometimes profited financially by depriving inmates of food, bedding, and fuel; abuse and idleness were characteristic.[27]

Although providing minimum subsistence levels for a variety of dependent persons—widows, children, and the unemployed—these institutions always included large numbers of elderly persons. Younger inmates tended to remain for only short periods of time; for them the almshouse was a temporary refuge in times of crisis or unemployment. But in most areas about a quarter to a third of poorhouse residents were over the age of sixty, a high proportion of them being either single or widowed. In 1880 24.3 percent of the total almshouse population of over 66,000 were reported as insane, and the overwhelming majority were elderly. Many surveys and studies pointed to the growing numbers of dependent elderly persons for whom the almshouse was but a surrogate old age home. In San Francisco, for example, the average age of poorhouse inmates rose sharply from 36 to 59 years between 1870 and 1894. Many aged residents in almshouses suffered from a variety of physical and mental infirmities, and they generally remained in the institution until they died.[28]

By 1900 the problems posed by elderly dependent persons was growing even more acute because of their rising numbers. This development was the result of the decline in mortality among infants and children, which ultimately increased the aged cohort. In 1860 only 4.3 percent of the population was sixty or over; in 1900 and 1940 the comparable figures were 6.4 and 10.4, respectively. In absolute numbers the change was even more striking. On the eve of the Civil War 1.3 million were sixty or over; between 1900 and 1940 the number rose from nearly 4.9 to 13.7 million.

Ironically, the increase in the number of elderly persons occurred at precisely the same time that the almshouse began to decline in significance. By the end of the century there was broad agreement that these institutions had few redeeming features. "Trapped by their contradictory purposes, undercut by poor management and inadequate funds," one historian recently concluded, "poorhouses never could find useful work for their inmates or offer the old, sick, and helpless, not to mention the ablebodied unemployed, much more than a roof and escape from death by starvation. Nor did they reduce pauperism or cut the cost of poor relief." In 1890 73,000 out of a total population of over 62 million were in poorhouses; by 1923 the comparable figures were 78,000 out of 109 million. Even more striking, the proportion of insane persons in almshouses fell precipitously. In 1880 24.3 percent of the almshouse population was insane; in 1923 the proportion had fallen to 5.6 percent.[29]

This seeming change, however, was more apparent than real. What occurred, in reality, was not an effort to deinstitutionalize the aged, but rather a movement to commit them to mental hospitals rather than poorhouses. Indeed, the most striking development during the first half of the twentieth century was the conversion of the mental hospital into a surrogate home for elderly and other kinds of chronic cases. Although national data are lacking, statistics from individual states reveal the magnitude of change. In such diverse states as Alabama, Kansas, Massachusetts, and Washington the percentage of mental hospital patients aged sixty or over rose between 300 and 400 percent. Age-specific first admission rates for the elderly increased far more rapidly than for any other group. In 1885, age-specific first admission rates in Massachusetts for males aged sixty and over was 70.4, and for females 65.5 (per 100,000); by 1941 the corresponding rates were 279.5 and 223.[30]

New York State offers an especially dramatic illustration of the trend toward an aged asylum population. In 1920 18 percent of all first admissions to state hospitals were diagnosed as psychotic either because of senility or arteriosclerosis. By 1940 this group accounted for nearly a third of all first admissions. During these same decades average age of first admissions rose from 42.69 to 48.7 years. The trend toward an older population continued even after World War II, as the experience of the Empire State indicates. Nor was New York unique; data from other states reveal a similar pattern. To be sure, there were exceptions. Because of its county asylum system, Wisconsin state hospitals had a low proportion of elderly inmates. Nationally, however, the trend was clear; as late as 1958 nearly a third of all state mental hospital inmates were sixty-five or older.[31]

Why were elderly persons transferred from almshouses to mental hospitals? Such individuals, after all, generally posed no great threat to the safety of others. Nor could hospitalization alter the underlying somatic elements that shaped their aberrant behavior; restorative therapies for most aged persons were nonexistent. The emergence of the mental hospital as a surrogate old age home, as a matter of fact, was largely unplanned and unanticipated. It grew out of innovative public policies that were adopted for quite different purposes in such states as New York and Massachusetts.

In New York the opening of Willard had resolved few problems. Indeed, the institution grew so rapidly that within two years of its opening the legislature gave the State Board of Charities authority to exempt any county from the requirement that it send chronic cases to Willard if it had the means of providing local care. By 1880 more than 1,200 persons were housed in county facilities. In the ensuing decade a coalition of charity workers and physicians came out in favor of an end to a system that divided responsibility for the insane between localities and the state. Their efforts met with success in 1890 with the passage of the famous State Care Act. The provisions of this piece of legislation were simple. All exemptions granted to counties since 1871 were repealed; county asylums reverted to the status of poorhouses. The distinction between chronic and acute cases was obliterated and all hospitals— including Willard—were placed in an equal footing. Local jurisdictions were required to send insane residents to state hospitals, and a statewide tax to support these institutions was enacted. Those urban areas that maintained their own hospitals (New York, Brooklyn, Rochester) quickly transferred their institutions to the state, thus avoiding double taxation. By 1900 Massachusetts had enacted similar legislation, and other states followed suit. After 1900, therefore, state responsibility for the mentally ill became the general rule even though a few states continued the older system of divided authority. The presumption was that state control would focus responsibility, enhance accountability, and ensure high standards of care.[32]

State care acts, however, had important if unforseen consequences. The most significant result was a change in the behavior of local officials. They quickly recognized the fiscal advantages that flowed from a redefinition of senility in psychiatric terms. If aged senile persons were cared for in state institutions rather than local or county almshouses, the burden of support would be transferred to the state level. From an economic point of view, of course, it made little difference whether the care of the insane was paid for by local or state funds; public expenditures remained public expenditures, irrespective of the level on which they were incurred. From a political point of view, on the other hand, localities benefited if responsibility was shifted elsewhere. Slowly but surely the mental hospital assumed the almshouse function of caring for elderly persons.

That mental hospitals were beginning to serve as surrogate old age homes did not go unnoticed. The New York State Commission in Lunacy in 1900 called attention to the presence of increasing numbers of aged persons, even though it refused to endorse legislation that precluded the admission of "dotards" to state mental hospitals. Whether or not senility should be defined in psychiatric terms was in some respects irrelevant; the necessity of caring for such persons was obvious to all. Public financing and growing hostility to almshouses combined to shift responsibility for the welfare of elderly senile and dependent persons to mental hospitals.[33]

Psychiatrists were neither insensitive to nor unaware of the implications of this new development for their specialty and their institutions. After the turn of the century articles on senile dementia and arteriosclerosis which attempted to distinguish between pathological and aging processes appeared in increasing numbers. By World War II discussions of mental hospitals always included elderly patients. Indeed, in 1941 the U.S. Public Health Service convened a conference on "Mental Health in Later Maturity," and five years later the distinguished British psychiatrist Aubrey Lewis called attention to aging and senility, which he described as "A Major Problem of Psychiatry."[34]

Ambivalence if not confusion, however, was characteristic of psychiatric thinking. By training and socialization psychiatrists were concerned with pathology, whereas senility involved at least in part natural and inevitable physiological processes. Pathology, at least in theory, was reversible by appropriate hospital-based therapies. Senility, by contrast, was inevitable and suggested the need for general care rather than for strictly medical interventions. But if hospitals treated an elderly population requiring mostly custodial care, what role remained for psychiatry? Trained as physicians, most psychiatrists were not prepared to emphasize custodial care to the exclusion of their therapeutic role. In their view society had to develop alternative strategies to deal with the elderly. "We are receiving every year," Dr. Charles G. Wagner (superintendent of the Binghamton State Hospital) noted in 1900,

> a large number of old people, some of them very old, who are simply suffering from the mental decay incident to extreme old age. A little mental confusion, forgetfulness and garrulity are sometimes the only symptoms

exhibited, but the patient is duly certified to us as insane and has no one at home capable or possessed of means to care for him. We are unable to refuse these patients without creating ill-feeling in the community where they reside, nor are we able to assert that they are not insane within the meaning of the statute, for many of them, judged by the ordinary standards of sanity, cannot be regarded as entirely sane.[35]

Wagner's remarks were by no means idiosyncratic and were repeated by others in subsequent decades. A study of Illinois state hospitals three decades later emphasized that "social revolutions, radical changes in housing and living problems, the growth of urban life" and similar elements had combined to force elderly men and women from their homes. At the same time, the study concluded, the government had failed in its responsibilities toward the elderly. "The state mental hospital, organized for quite other purposes, has become their only haven." Thus Chicago State Hospital was "converted into a huge infirmary, with nearly seventy percent of its 4,000 patients aged or infirm, suffering from no psychoses which would be beyond the capacity of the old-fashioned detached city cottage or rural home or of a well-managed county home."[36]

Sympathetic with the plight of the elderly, most psychiatrists were not persuaded that confinement in mental hospitals was the appropriate response. Such individuals could be cared for more cheaply and as effectively in alternative facilities, thereby permitting hospitals to emphasize their therapeutic functions. Lawrence Kolb, a prominent psychiatrist affiliated with the U.S. Public Health Service, noted in 1941 that mental hospitals "were increasingly overburdened by aged persons for whom nothing can be done" and that it was "economically unwise and therapeutically unsound to take care of all dementing old people in hospitals." Yet the question raised more than three decades earlier by a New York State psychiatrist remained pertinent even if unresolved. Were not the elderly "entitled to the State's bounty" along with other mentally disordered persons? "If they are not to be received by the State Hospitals, what shall be done with them?"[37]

The steadily increasing proportion of elderly patients in public hospitals after 1900, however, was not due solely to rising admission rates. High death rates among the aged, as a matter of fact, ensured that their length-of-stay would be limited. At Warren State Hospital in Pennsylvania, for example, 72 percent of such patients died within five years of admission in the decade following 1936. A comparable study in Maryland indicated that 47 percent died within twelve months and only 10 percent ever left the hospital. The ranks of the elderly, however, were augmented by the admission of young schizophrenics whose length-of-stay was measured in decades and who grew old in institutions. The presence of this group accounted for the fact that by the early 1960s the median stay for schizophrenics in twenty-three selected states was 12.8 years, whereas the comparable figure for those admitted with mental diseases of the senium was only 3 years.[38]

The rapid increase in the number of elderly patients altered the character and functions of mental hospitals. Many became surrogate old age homes for elderly persons whose severe behavioral symptoms were related to an underlying somatic pathology. The consequences of this development were mixed. Mental hospitals clearly met an important social need by providing custodial care for such elderly dependent individuals. In so doing, however, hospitals implicitly subordinated their therapeutic ideals. Custodial care often conflicted with professional perceptions and goals, and increasingly the legitimacy of hospitals as medical institutions was eroded.

The chronic institutionalized population was by no means composed solely of the elderly. On the contrary, heterogeneity rather than homogeneity was characteristic. To be sure, the absence of accurate data and a psychiatric classification nosology based largely on symptoms rather than etiology renders it virtually impossible to describe the hundreds of thousands of mental hospital residents with any degree of precision. Surviving data, nevertheless, suggest that the large institutional system, in addition to the elderly, cared for substantial numbers of patients whose behavioral peculiarities were related to an underlying somatic pathology that often resulted in chronicity because of the absence of effective therapies.

Syphilis was a case in point. Before the introduction of such antibiotic drugs as penicillin after World War II, insanity resulting from venereal disease accounted for substantial numbers of long-stay admissions to asylums. By the nineteenth century syphilis had emerged as a three-stage disease. The first or acute stage was marked by a chancre (or sore) in the genital region. The second stage was asymptomatic, although the spirochete remained present in the body. Although many infected persons never progressed beyond this stage, a proportion entered the tertiary stage. This phase—known as general paralysis of the insane or paresis—involved massive damage to the central nervous system and brain and was characterized by dramatic behavioral symptoms, neurological deterioration, paralysis, and eventually death. During the tertiary stage total care was often unavoidable.

Paretics (those in the tertiary stage) often presented difficult problems. In an important study of the disease at the Boston Psychopathic Hospital, E. E. Southard and Harry C. Solomon described and analyzed more than a hundred cases of neurosyphilis. In a typical case, a salesman underwent a personality change during a two- or three-year period that began to interfere with his work. He began to manifest "unreasonable aversions to people, had become irritable and emotionally depressed, and often fell to weeping without cause." He began to tire easily; his gait and speech were impaired; and his memory began to fail. Subsequent convulsive attacks followed that resulted in loss of consciousness for as long as two days; restlessness, irritability, and irrational talk followed. Convulsive attacks were often followed by improvement; yet each attack left him "at a lower terrace of capacity than had been before shown." The patient died four years after manifesting symptoms of a general asthenia. General paresis, Southard and Solomon pointed out, had dramatic and protean physical and mental symptoms, including amnesia, shifting emotions, delusions, character change, speech impairment, nervous disorders, impaired judgment, seizures, headaches, visual disorder, loss of manual dexterity, and paralysis.[39]

By the early twentieth century, the number of paretic admissions began to increase dramatically. Between 1911 and 1920, for example, about 20 percent of all first admissions to New York State mental hospitals fell into this category (the comparable rate for females was about one-third that of males). By the 1930s slightly over 9 percent of all first admissions to all mental hospitals were cases of general paralysis. Given the nature of the disease, few households were prepared to cope with paretic members. Nor could general hospitals pick up the slack; their concern with acute illnesses and short patient stays rendered them unsuitable for the care for paretic patients capable of surviving for as long as five years.[40]

Consequently, responsibility for syphilitics in the tertiary stage devolved upon mental hospitals. Paretic patients presented quite different problems from elderly inmates. The former tended to be younger; about two-thirds were under the age of fifty. For most the mental hospital represented a final stop. Between 1913 and 1922, 87.7 percent of all first admission paretics in the Empire State died during their confinement. About half died in the twelve months following admission; the remainder within one to four years. By the 1930s death rates among this group declined sharply, but the trend toward greater longevity only enhanced the custodial function of mental hospitals.[41]

Paresis was by no means the only chronic disease with a somatic etiology. Generally speaking, perhaps a third to a half of all first admissions to state mental hospitals represented individuals whose abnormal behavior was related to an underlying physiological causes. Of 49,116 first admissions to mental hospitals in 1922, 16,407 suffered from a variety of identifiable somatic conditions, including senility, cerebral arteriosclerosis, paresis, Huntington's disease, pellagra, and brain tumors. Indeed, during the 1920s and 1930s the proportion of individuals admitted for the first time with such diagnoses increased from 33.4 to 42.4 percent, a figure that prevailed through the 1940s.[42]

Not surprisingly, the institutionalized mentally ill had far higher mortality rates than the general population. In 1930, their mortality rate was approximately five times that of the general population. Oddly enough, the disparity was greatest among younger persons. The chance of an institutionalized patient dying between the age of twenty and twenty-four, as compared with the same age group in the general population, was 15.6 times as great. The leading causes of death in rank order included heart disease, pneumonia, paresis, tuberculosis, arterial diseases, and nephritis. Such high death rates reflected admission policies rather than institutional environments. Many patients, according to Benjamin Malzberg, were admitted "almost at the point of death." Treatment in such cases was "without effect," and admissions served "the purpose of merely relieving relatives or friends of onerous duties." That death rates tended to be highest among recently admitted cases only confirmed the validity of these observations.[43]

The growing significance of chronic mental illnesses was mirrored in other data. For much of the nineteenth century, the bulk of patients remained in the institution for less than a year. By the turn of the century a different situation prevailed. In 1904, for example, only 27.8 percent of all patients had been hospitalized for less than a year, 26 percent from one to four years, 16.4 for five to nine years, and the remainder (29.8 percent) for a decade or longer. By 1923 the proportion of recent cases had fallen to 17.4 percent, and the trend toward increasing length-of-stays was evident. The result was a further strengthening of the mental hospital's custodial character and a corresponding decline in its therapeutic functions.[44]

The large numbers of chronic and aged patients led to a fundamental transformation in the character of mental hospitals. To be sure, their therapeutic functions were by no means obliterated. But the presence of large numbers of chronic long-term patients had dramatic consequences. Internally it resulted in a more depressing environment. To cure and discharge patients was associated with an aura of optimism and achievement; to care for those who rarely manifested improvement and would ultimately die was hardly consistent with twentieth-century images of medical and scientific progress. For psychiatrists the rise of custodialism created negative images of themselves, their work, and their institutions. Ultimately this situation led them to reexamine their position and to become receptive to new roles that shattered their hitherto inseparable links with mental hospitals, which then lost much of their social legitimacy.

Nor was the impact on the lay staff fundamentally dissimilar. Nurses and attendants spent a good part of their working days with patients who behaved in bizarre ways and whose deteriorated physical condition mandated careful monitoring and total care. Given such tragic circumstances, few staff members could maintain any degree of enthusiasm or demonstrate consistently high morale. Indeed, the character of the patient population strengthened the centrifugal forces that had always been present in asylums; conflict and disorganization remained perennial problems.

Equally important, chronic mental illnesses altered public perceptions as well. Slowly the positive images of hospitals that had prevailed in the mid-nineteenth century gave way to far more negative ones associated with hopelessness, abuse, and ultimately death. Indeed, by World War II mental hospitals were identified as "snakepits," to use the title of Mary Jane Ward's famous and influential novel. Such images created a receptivity on the part of both the public and their elected representatives to find alternative policies that promised far better outcomes then an allegedly cruel and obsolete institutional system.

That the inability of institutions to alleviate chronic mental illnesses had a powerful negative impact was indisputable. But the conclusion that traditional mental hospitals were obsolete did not necessarily follow. Admittedly, many of their patients suffered from irreversible chronic diseases or from diseases for which no effective therapies were available. For such individuals, mental hospitals—whatever their shortcomings and faults—were the only facilities then available to provide, at public expense, access to such necessities as food, clothing, and shelter. The traditional caring functions of mental hospitals during and after the 1960s, as a matter of fact, were simply assumed by chronic care facilities because of changes in funding. Patients suffering from Alzheimer's disease and other irreversible conditions often characteristic of an aged population still required access to care, which during the first half of the twentieth century had been provided in state hospitals. This is not to suggest that alternative ways of providing care for severely and chronically mentally ill persons could not have been developed. It is only to insist that specific historical circumstances led to the creation of an institution that was able to adapt to a changing constituency. The subsequent decline of traditional mental hospitals would force the American people to deal with severely and chronically mentally ill persons in the community who were unable to work, lacked access to the basic necessities of life, and had to live without well-established social relationships.

6

A New Psychiatry

In its origins in the early nineteenth century the specialty of psychiatry was indistinguishable from the mental hospital. The links between them were most eloquently described by Thomas Kirkbride in the second edition of his classic work on mental hospitals in 1880.

> As the insane generally cannot be treated successfully nor be properly cared for in private houses, very clearly they cannot be in ordinary hospitals, almshouses, nor in penal institutions. The only mode, then, of taking proper care of this class in a community . . . is to provide in every State just as many special hospitals as may be necessary, to give prompt and proper accommodations for *all* its insane, to cure those that are curable, to give every reasonable comfort to those that are not curable, and to prevent their becoming worse—and, what is of very great importance, hardly to be over-estimated—to protect their families and the community from the acts and influences of irresponsible and often dangerous persons.

Under the guidance of wise and beneficent physicians, appropriate care and treatment could cure a large proportion of the insane. "These institutions," Kirkbride concluded, "can never be dispensed with,—no matter how persistently ignorance, prejudice, or sophistry may declare to the contrary—without retrograding to a greater or less extent to the conditions of a past period, with all the inhumanity and barbarity connected with it."[1]

129

Yet even as Kirkbride was defending traditional modes of care and treatment, the identification of psychiatrists and mental hospitals was beginning to weaken. By then both came under sharp attack from a variety of sources. The rise of "scientific" medicine—perhaps best symbolized by the specific germ theory of disease and the efforts to apply laboratory findings and new technologies to clinical practice—seemed to accentuate the seeming backwardness of asylum medicine. To younger physicians trained in the precepts of scientific medicine, their asylum brethren appeared a vestigial remnant of the past. Whereas the former were exploring the biological roots of disease, the latter remained preoccupied with administrative and managerial functions associated with the care of large numbers of dependent chronic mentally ill persons. Additional criticism came from public officials concerned with the mounting costs of welfare, the growth of mental hospitals, the increase in the chronic inpatient population, and alleged abuse of patients.

Between 1880 and 1940 psychiatrists responded to their critics by altering the basic foundation of their specialty. They identified new careers outside of institutions; articulated novel theories and therapies; expanded jurisdictional boundaries to include not only mental disorders but the problems of everyday life; and defined a preventive role. Their goal was nothing less than the reintegration of psychiatry into medicine, which would permit them to share in the status and prestige enjoyed by the latter.

The focus on inner professional needs and issues, however, inadvertently weakened and ultimately shattered the links between psychiatrists and mental hospitals. In shifting their concerns elsewhere, psychiatrists called into doubt the caring function that had defined the essential character of their nineteenth-century institutional predecessors. Like their counterparts in general medical practice, the new generation of psychiatrists that reached maturity around the turn of the century were increasingly disillusioned with mental hospital practice and the emphasis on overseeing the care of severely and chronically mentally ill persons. They were hostile to the managerial and administrative nature of asylum practice, and preferred instead a wider and more expansive role outside of institutions. They hoped to emulate their medical colleagues who had created a laboratory-based profession that sought to identify the causes of disease and to develop appropriate interventions for acute illnesses. In dissolving the links between themselves and mental hospitals, psychiatrists implicitly began to abandon responsibility for severely and chronically mentally ill persons in hospitals. Ultimately the issue of providing care for individuals whose dependent status was a function of their illness would become a matter of public concern and heated debate.

Asylum physicians found themselves under mounting criticism in the closing decades of the nineteenth century. To be sure, they had been attacked in the past by former patients who demanded more effective legal safeguards to limit the authority of hospital officials. "There is no dispute," wrote Elizabeth T. Stone, a former patient at the McLean Asylum who felt that she had been wrongfully committed,

> but what there should be such an institution as an Insane Assylum [*sic*], but let it come under the jurisdiction of the Legislature, and not have all the power consigned into the hands of a few individuals, over a distressed class of beings, a money-making system, at the expense of happiness, in a great measure. If it was thought best to have all power put into the hands of one individual, then we should have a King in this country, but it is not thought best. . . . Would it not be well to have it a law that no person should be carried into an Insane Hospital without the advice of a council of physicians, and not have it left to the judgment of one person, for it is not an uncommon thing for persons to be put in there who are not insane, and they cannot help themselves.

Stone and other disaffected patients had at most a limited impact, if only because they questioned neither the necessity nor legitimacy of institutional care and treatment. Even Elizabeth Packard, who launched her crusade against arbitrary commitment procedures, wanted to strengthen the legal rights of patients rather than abolish mental hospitals.[2]

Far more serious were the criticisms of a broad and loose coalition composed of charity reformers, public welfare officials and agencies, and urban neurologists. The first two groups were concerned with such social problems as dependency, poverty, and crime, and committed increasingly to administrative and bureaucratic solutions. Social policy, they averred, had to be placed on a "scientific" foundation—a view that implied the imposition of controls upon previously autonomous institutions. Initially their activities led to the creation of state boards of charity. In the events leading to the establishment of the first of such boards in Massachusetts, a legislative committee concerned with retrenchment condemned the state's "hospital palaces." In recommending the creation of a central state agency to ensure greater efficiency in public welfare, board members insisted that "no one desires of course to deal with any harshness towards the unfortunate poor of the Commonwealth; no one wishes or expects to be relieved from the burden of their support; but the errors, inconsistencies and unnecessary expenses of a *wrong system* should be pointed out and corrected."[3]

In 1874 a group of individuals associated with several state boards and the American Social Science Association founded the National Conference of Charities and Corrections. The Conference subsequently evolved into a major professional association involved with social work. Concerned with larger policy issues relating to dependency, the organization could hardly ignore mental hospitals, which represented the single largest social welfare investment of states in the nineteenth century. Admittedly, neither state officials nor Conference members directly challenged institutional psychiatry. Yet the very issues they considered—the structure and organization of mental hospitals, alternatives to traditional institutional care, public supervision—all implied the need for change and thus constituted an implicit criticism of asylum psychiatry.[4]

A far more serious challenge came from physicians who identified themselves with the new specialty of neurology. At that time the term neurology had a quite different meaning. Neurology had developed in Europe when investigators began to deal with psychopathology in terms of the relationship between structure and function. In the United States physicians who dealt with nervous tissue wounds during the Civil War subsequently identified themselves as neurologists. By the 1870s they had broadened their interests to include a wide range of "nervous conditions" involving emotional and stress-related problems. Virtually all were in private practice in large urban areas, and their clients were drawn overwhelmingly from affluent middle- and upper-class groups.[5]

Unlike asylum physicians whose outlook was shaped by a pietistic Protestantism, neurologists identified with the newly emerging scientific medicine. Their outlook, derived from European medicine, blurred the distinction between neurology and psychiatry. Their preoccupation with the brain and central nervous system, moreover, inevitably directed them toward the mental illnesses. But the professional world in which they lived and their affluent clientele led them to reject institutional psychiatry—a specialty they deemed hopelessly obsolete. Edward C. Spitzka, for example, insisted that the study of insanity—a disease that involved lesions—was simply "a subdivision of neurology." In a speech before the New York Neurological Society in 1874 and published shortly thereafter, he castigated institutional psychiatrists for their scientific ignorance and general lack of knowledge of cerebral anatomy. Superintendents, he wrote in disdainful language, were

> experts in gardening and farming (although the farm account frequently comes out on the wrong side of the ledger), tin roofing (although the roof and cupola is usually leaky), drain-pipe laying (although the grounds are often moist and unhealthy), engineering (though the wards are either too hot or too cold), history (though their facts are incorrect, and their inferences beyond all measure so); in short, experts at everything except the diagnosis, pathology and treatment of insanity.

In describing the members of the AMSAII, he employed such terms as "ignorance, charlatanism, insincerity, and neglect" because "no other words could characterize so aptly the conditions to which I found it necessary to allude in the course of this inquiry."[6]

Spitzka's vituperative attack aroused a sympathetic response. Within a month the Society endorsed a crusade on behalf of "asylum reform" and the abolition of mechanical restraint. When a committee of the Medico-Legal Society of New York—which included Spitzka and William A. Hammond—demanded a legislative investigation of the state's mental hospitals, the conflict became even more bitter. Hammond, a former Civil War Surgeon-General and the most prominent figure in American neurology, harshly criticized his institutional brethren and attacked the very legitimacy of asylums. Rejecting the necessity of institutionalization, he suggested that there was "nothing surprisingly difficult, obscure or mysterious about diseases of the brain which can only be learned within the walls of an asylum." For the remainder of the decade the two medical groups traded charges in public. Despite the fact that most neurologists were uncomfortable with these extremist views, the two men continued their crusade by portraying asylum medicine as hopelessly unscientific and obsolete. Members of the AMSAII responded publicly to the allegations. Indeed, one superintendent charged that Hammond was motivated by a desire for high fees rather than intellectual consistency, and that his views were atheistic.[7]

The attack on asylum medicine and the demands by such figures as Packard for patient rights led to the founding of the National Association for the Protection of the Insane and the Prevention of Insanity in 1880. A broad umbrella organization, its founders hoped to forge a coalition that included professional and lay groups united around an inclusive program that would benefit physicians and patients and also inform a larger public constituency. Nevertheless, its very creation rested on two beliefs that undercut its conciliatory efforts: namely, that asylum medicine impeded constructive progress, and that medical science had already created the means for effective changes in the treatment of insanity. Neither of these beliefs had a basis in fact. The character of asylums, for example, was shaped less by their medical staff than by the nature of their patients and interaction among patients and staffs as well as the resources supplied by state and local governments. Similarly, the growing faith in the efficacy of medical therapeutics for the insane was based largely on illusory rhetoric rather than a body of supportive evidence.[8]

The National Association proved ephemeral; by 1884 it had disappeared from the scene. Yet its very creation and appeal to a broad constituency had the effect of opening the debate into a public arena. Indeed, in 1881 Dorman B. Eaton—an advocate of change in the structure of urban governments—used the pages of the influential *North American Review* to launch a blistering attack. Entitled "Despotism in Lunatic Asylums," his article charged asylum managers with exercising arbitrary power and a dedication to secrecy.[9]

That same year Charles J. Guiteau was brought to trial for the assassination of President James A. Garfield. The proceedings, which received national attention, revolved around the sanity of the defendant. The two major protagonists included Spitzka for the defense and John P. Gray for the prosecution. Their testimony again revealed deep divisions within psychiatry that went even beyond the attack on asylum physicians by their neurological opponents to include divergent views on the fundamental nature of human beings.

The redoubtable Spitzka insisted that Guiteau had a history of hereditary insanity, and that any expert "who would pronounce this man sane, positively, is either not an expert or not an honest one." Guiteau was nothing but a "congenital moral monster." By this, Spitzka explained,

> I mean a person who is born with so defective a nervous organization that he is altogether deprived of that moral sense which is an integral and essential constituent of the normal human mind, he being analogous in that respect to the congenital cripple who is born speechless, or with one leg shorter than the other, or with any other monstrous development, that we now and again see.

In arguing in this vein, Spitzka was following other late nineteenth-century thinkers who were prone to emphasize that such conditions as insanity, criminality, imbecility, alcoholism, and other ills were the products of evolutionary degeneration in which constitutional weaknesses manifested themselves in successive generations of a particular family.

Gray, on the other hand, represented both institutional psychiatry and traditional Protestant morality. For three decades he had served as superintendent of the Utica State Hospital and edited the *American Journal of Insanity*. He rejected the deterministic arguments that lay at the heart of Spitzka's testimony. There was, he averred, a fundamental distinction between insanity and criminality. Insanity was a disease of the brain that involved changes in behavior and thought. Guiteau's entire life, by contrast, had been normal, even if his behavior was reprehensible and evil. The defendant displayed reason and judgment. Gray was adamantly opposed to hereditarian explanations because they negated free will and undermined individual responsibility. The idea that an individual could inherit a cerebral lesion was as ludicrous as the idea "that your ancestor could give you a cough or a pain in your side." Although Guiteau was found guilty and subsequently executed, his trial symbolized the split between asylum psychiatrists concerned with defending traditional morality and younger neurologists committed to more materialist and reductionist explanations of human behavior.[10]

Asylum physicians did not remain silent, and they often used the meetings of the AMSAII to respond to their critics. The slow but steady accumulation of chronic cases (a consequence of the fact that the total number of admissions always exceeded the total number of deaths, recoveries, and discharges) tended to enhance a negative public image, conceded Dr. Orpheus Everts (who had also testified for the prosecution during the Guiteau trial). But what alternative to hospitalization would be better? "More insane persons," he insisted, "are ill-treated, injudiciously restrained, neglected and otherwise abused while among friends in the family relation, than suffer from similar treatment in the least reputable insane hospital in America, proportionately considered."[11]

The neurological onslaught and internecine warfare that commenced in the late 1870s threatened not only to undermine the legitimacy of asylum physicians, but that of the medical profession in general. The harsh language inadvertently jeopardized efforts to strengthen medical legitimacy and autonomy by granting laypersons greater authority. As the perceived dangers of unrestrained debate mounted, all participants began to retreat from their immoderate positions. In 1883 John B. Chapin, superintendent of Willard and a figure who often disagreed with his asylum colleagues, observed that public confidence in mental hospitals was being undermined. The appeal by critics to public opinion, he added, distressed families of hospitalized relatives, deterred younger physicians from entering the specialty, and subverted professional "comity and courtesy." More importantly, mental hospitals were increasingly perceived "as objects of suspicion; as convenient places for the 'incarceration' of persons by designing relatives, and lunatic prisons, proper only for the detention of the criminal and dangerous insane." Chapin was not a foe of state supervision, but preferred a cooperative rather than an adversarial relationship. He was particularly critical of the appeal of physicians to "outside . . . tribunals illy prepared by technical training to render judgment."[12]

Fear of discrediting asylum and general medicine was not the only element that contributed to the decline in confrontational debates. Equally significant was the fact that few participants—whatever their affiliation—suggested that mental hospitals were either obsolete or unnecessary. Consequently, all parties recognized that it was not in their interest to undermine public confidence to the point where the legitimacy of asylums was called into question. The muted reaction to S. Weir Mitchell's address to the American Medico-Psychological Association (formerly the AMSAII) in 1894 was illustrative. Mitchell, a prominent neurologist associated with the "rest cure" for neurotic patients, used his address to chastise his asylum colleagues. "You were the first of the specialists," he stated

> and you have never come back into line. It is easy to see how this came about. You soon began to live apart, and you still do so. Your hospitals are not our hospitals; your ways are not our ways. You live out of range of critical shot; you are not preceded and followed in your ward by clever rivals, or watched by able residents fresh with the learning of the schools.

Mitchell decried the absence of research; the distrust of asylum therapeutics; the failure to educate the public; and the intrusion of politics into hospital management and administration. Yet when he finished his address, the delegates elected him an honorary member. Indeed, those who responded stressed that he had expressed nothing that asylum physicians themselves had not said during the past decade.[13]

The imposition of bureaucratic controls by regulatory agencies eager to rationalize and streamline social welfare policies represented an implied criticism of asylum physicians and a rejection of their faith that medical expertise justified full independence and autonomy. From a psychiatric perspective, efforts to regulate the specialty reflected an undesirable intrusion of politics into the management of hospitals. "Partisan politics," charged Dr. Henry Smith Williams in the *North American Review*, had "become influential in the conduct of the asylums in which the dependent insane are cared for. The baleful effects of this custom are as yet fully understood only by those persons who have had opportunity to view the subject as it were from the inside." At the Philadelphia municipal hospital, physicians remained subordinate to a lay superintendent. "The present system," Williams quoted a knowledgeable individual, "consigns the insane to wretched, crowded dark buildings, that have been odious and odorous for half a century, with no facilities for suitable out-of-door exercise or occupation. The plans and grounds of the asylum belong to a period long passed, and within the buildings the allowance of fresh air equals but a few square feet per patient. All in all, the condition of the insane here is one of the saddest spectacles to be seen in this country." Attempts to improve conditions were doomed to failure because of the desire of politicians to maintain their lucrative control over patronage.[14]

Asylum physicians were not free agents. Their institutions were supported by public funds and therefore were accountable to public officials and susceptible to political considerations. Officials at the Kankakee hospital in Cook County (Illinois), for example, were enmeshed in local and state politics and faced unremitting pressure to make staff appointments on the basis of political party affiliation and friendship. Yet, it was difficult to untangle the claims by asylum officials that politics represented an undesirable intrusion into their institutions from their own desire for autonomy and independence. Williams's charges, for example, were rejected by a group of eminent Philadelphia physicians, who insisted that his harsh portrayal of political interference in the insane department of the Philadelphia Hospital was grossly inaccurate.[15]

Asylum physicians also faced internal pressures that made it increasingly difficult for them to speak with a unified voice. In its origins the specialty of psychiatry had been exclusively male. During the last quarter of the nineteenth century some asylums began to employ female physicians to care for female patients; by 1900 as many as two hundred women had occupied staff positions. Their recruitment in part grew out of the mid-nineteenth century concept of a semiautonomous "women's sphere," which presupposed a separate world in which females could find the kinds of intimate friendships that were unavailable in a male-dominated society. Out of this came the belief that female patients might be more effectively treated by physicians of their own sex.[16]

Within hospitals female physicians occupied distinctly subordinate roles, and therefore did not offer undivided loyalty. The dilemmas faced by women were graphically portrayed by Dr. Mary M. Wolfe of the Department for Women at the Norristown State Hospital in Pennsylvania. She emphasized the marginal status of female physicians in mental hospitals. A woman, she observed in a paper delivered before her peers, had to have "a tremendous amount of native ambition before she can be ambitious for the reason that there are no material rewards for her" in terms of professional advancement. "The whole matter," she concluded in ambiguous terms susceptible to a variety of interpretations, "resolves itself into a question of individual ability, attainment and character and not a question of sex." Other women were less guarded in their feelings. Louise G. Rabinovitch, a European-born and trained physician and the first woman to publish a psychiatric journal, was a militant critic of American asylum psychiatry.[17]

———————

As they came under increasing criticism from both within and without, asylum physicians began a slow and arduous process of redefining the character of their specialty. The ever-increasing number of chronic patients in mental hospitals reinforced the need for change. At a time when the innovations in scientific and laboratory-based medicine held out the alluring promise of a new age of health, asylum psychiatry seemed out of step. Fearful of being left behind, younger psychiatrists began to abandon the principles of the founding patriarchs of asylum medicine. They changed the requirements for membership in their professional association by admitting assistant physicians, and began to shift the focus from their empirical observation of patients to a more abstract and theoretical concern with mental diseases. Defining new roles, responsibilities, and institutional forms, they definitively broke the previously inseparable links of psychiatry with asylums. In undertaking a radical reorientation of their specialty, they set the stage for fundamental changes that would have major consequences for the institutionalized mentally ill. In brief, they would increasingly turn away from the caring function that had been an intrinsic element of mid-nineteenth-century asylum medicine.

An early indication of change came in the mid-1880s when the AMSAII began to consider the possibility of opening its membership to assistant physicians rather then limiting it only to superintendents. Since its founding four decades earlier, the AMSAII had been preoccupied with managerial and administrative concerns. To open membership to a cadre of younger assistant physicians suggested the growing importance of the medical and scientific aspects of mental diseases. During the debate on the requirements for membership, the issue of changing the name of the Association to a "medico-psychological society" arose—a further clue that asylum psychiatry was entering a period of transition. To the majority both suggestions appeared too radical. In the end the delegates simply adopted a motion granting assistant physicians the status of ex-officio membership.[18]

The debate, however modest, was a precursor of things to come. Two years later a committee considering the authoritative "Propositions" adopted in 1851 and 1853 dealing with the construction, organization, and management of hospitals paid homage to Ray and Kirkbride. Yet committee members declined to endorse the views associated with the two patriarchs. Instead they distinguished between mental hospitals (which should resemble modern general hospitals) and chronic care facilities. The former ideally emphasized "individual treatment" and their superintendents had to be educated in the precepts of scientific medicine. After a lengthy discussion the full Association refused to reaffirm the propositions or to endorse new principles. The failure to act suggested that the traditional commitment to management and administration was all but defunct even though a new course had yet to be charted.[19]

Within several years the AMSAII went much further in rejecting its administrative and managerial legacy. In 1892 it changed its name to the American Medico-Psychological Association (AMPA). A revised constitution stipulated that its goal was "the study of all subjects pertaining to mental disease, including the care, treatment, and promotion of the best interests of the insane." Full membership remained with superintendents, but assistant physicians were granted associate status; full membership followed three years of hospital experience. The altered definition of membership mirrored other changes as well. The papers delivered at the annual meetings indicated a new concern with pathology, physiology, and pharmacology, as well as a receptivity toward experimentation with surgical and endocrinological treatments. All of these subjects were somewhat removed from mid-nineteenth century psychiatric theory, which had emphasized the importance of care as well as psychological and somatic treatment. In his presidential address in 1895 Dr. Edward Cowles, superintendent of McLean and a driving force for change, defined the attributes of the new psychiatry in language that indicated how far the specialty had come since the days of Ray and Kirkbride.

> The alienist, as a psychologist, is a general physician who is a student of neurology, and uses its anatomy and physiology; but he does a great deal more, for he must include all the bodily organs. . . . He is being aided by the more promising contributions from organic chemistry, and bacteriology. . . . Thus it is that psychiatry is shown, more than ever before, to be dependent upon general medicine.[20]

The effort to reintegrate psychiatry into medicine was indicative of the former's declining image and status in an age that elevated the laboratory to a central position. In their efforts to rejoin their medical colleagues, however, psychiatrists overlooked some significant differences between them. In the late nineteenth and early twentieth centuries medicine was preoccupied with acute infectious diseases of relatively brief duration. The impressive advances in bacteriology had shed light on the etiology of diseases that resulted in high mortality rates among infants and children. Psychiatry, on the other hand, dealt for the most part with chronic illnesses of long duration. Such illnesses, unlike their acute counterparts, required managed care whether within or without institutions. Concerned with strengthening their medical credentials, many psychiatrists tended to overlook the fact that the needs of their patients were not always similar to those seen by their colleagues in general practice. By emphasizing more impersonal disease processes, they ignored in part the distinctive needs of the mentally ill. The founding generation, by way of contrast, had emphasized managerial and administrative techniques precisely because the care of patients in institutions, not the origins or dynamics of their disease, was their primary concern.

By the beginning of the twentieth century American psychiatrists began to expand their horizons and slowly dissolve their hitherto inseparable affiliations with mental hospitals. Regardless of their orientation, they shared a faith in the progress of their specialty. Bernard Sachs, a distinguished New York neurologist, noted in 1897 that psychiatry's past was discouraging, its present uncertain, "but the future is full of hope." Members of the specialty shared with other early twentieth-century Progressive activists a belief in the possibility of creating a new rational social and moral order that would eliminate existing flaws and alleviate human suffering. Some Progressives emphasized the environmental roots of evil and injustice and urged broad social and economic reforms to destroy them. Other Progressives insisted upon the need for coercive measures, including the exclusion of "undesirable" immigrants, a ban on intoxicating liquors, an end to sexual licentiousness, and in extreme cases the involuntary sterilization of defective individuals to rid society of "evils." Whatever their ideological persuasion, all were driven by the belief that human destiny could be altered by conscious and purposive action.[21]

The dreams of social redemption through progressive reform led psychiatrists to look beyond the walls of mental hospitals. Some explored the somatic roots of mental diseases in laboratories; some developed a psychogenic psychiatry that incorporated Freudian insights; some attempted to unify psychological and physiological phenomena in hope of illuminating disordered thinking; some experimented with novel therapies; and others expanded the boundaries of the specialty by creating a mental hygiene movement. Whatever their orientation, psychiatrists began to distance their specialty from asylums. They not only defined new concepts of mental illnesses and treatment, but altered the very context of practice. In so doing they began to abandon the mental hospital and thus to diminish the importance of the caring responsibilities of their specialty.

The prevailing belief that psychiatry stood on the threshold of a golden age of rehabilitation, however, did not indicate a consensus about the nature of mental illnesses. Like virtually every other medical specialty, psychiatrists were divided into groups, each with its own assumptions and beliefs. Conflict, not harmony, was characteristic. Those who believed that mental diseases were physiological in character found themselves under siege. Critics pointed to the absence of evidence demonstrating a causal relationship between lesions and behavior; a protean and ever-changing classification system; an etiology based on personal ideological presuppositions; and an absence of any systematic research tradition. Yet those who disparaged somaticism—few of whom were employed in mental hospitals—were open to similar criticisms.

Internal conflicts notwithstanding, a new vision of psychiatry began to take shape after 1900. "Dynamic psychiatry" (the name by which it was known) involved a sharp modification in the traditional model of disease. Generally speaking, nineteenth-century asylum psychiatrists made a fundamental distinction between health and disease. The presence of mental illnesses was indicated by dramatic behavioral and somatic signs that fundamentally deviated from the prior "normal" behavior of that individual. The new model of psychic distress, by contrast, suggested that behavior occurred along a continuum that commenced with the normal and spanned to the abnormal. Such an approach elevated the significance of the life history and prior experiences of the individual, thereby blurring the clear demarcation between health and disease. Indeed, psychiatric intervention began to emerge as a distinct option well short of the acute stage of the mental illness. From here it was but a short step to suggest that early outpatient treatment either in offices or clinics might prevent the onset of the severe mental disorders that up to that time had required institutionalization.

Dynamic psychiatry expanded the jurisdiction and boundaries of psychiatric practice to include psychologically troubled individuals as well as allegedly dysfunctional social structures and relationships. Correspondingly, the severely and chronically mentally ill—heretofore the sole focus of an institutionally oriented policy—began to lose their central position within the mental health system. The difficulty of treating the severe mental disorders made psychiatrists receptive to new clients and to careers outside the ubiquitous walls of mental hospitals. Although the consequences of this shift would not become evident until after World War II, its foundations were laid in the opening decades of the twentieth century.

The career of Adolf Meyer—a key figure in American psychiatry from the 1890s until his retirement on the eve of World War II—illustrates both the promise of the specialty as well as its problems. Born in Switzerland in 1866, he was originally trained in neurology. After his arrival in the United States in 1892, he worked for nearly eight years in two state hospitals in Illinois and Massachusetts before becoming Director of the Pathological Institute of the New York state hospitals, which had been created in 1895 to foster research and to educate asylum physicians. When Henry Phipps in 1908 offered to endow a psychiatric clinic at Johns Hopkins—the most influential medical school in the United States—Meyer was chosen as its first head. For more than three decades he played a leading role in American psychiatry. He contributed to the emergence of dynamic psychiatry and helped to train future leaders of the specialty.

Initially Meyer's interests lay more in neurology than psychiatry. During his brief sojourn in Illinois, however, he was introduced to the philosophy of pragmatism and became familiar with the writings of Charles S. Pierce, John Dewey, and William James. He quickly moved toward a biological and pluralistic view of human beings and rejected any kind of dualism that distinguished between mind and body. Psychiatry, he wrote in the mid-1890s, had to rest on a "biological conception" of human beings. "We must . . . accept the statement," he insisted, "that all mental activity must have its physiological side and its anatomical substratum." All mental reactions had their physiological counterparts; conversely, purely psychical (i.e., functional) disorders were also disorders of the brain.[22]

Meyer developed a genetic-dynamic or developmental approach to mental illnesses, which he named "psychobiology." Stressing the interaction of organism and environment, he defined mental disorders in behavioral terms and traced their origins to defective habits. Hostile to classical psychoanalysis, he nevertheless concurred with Freud that certain early experiences shaped subsequent maladaptive traits. A knowledge of disease patterns, therefore, depended on a full understanding of an individual's life history. Although seeking to integrate somatic, constitutional, and genetic influences, he tended to emphasize psychogenic factors.

Yet Meyer was unable to integrate facts and theory in any systematic manner. In his relationships with colleagues and students at Hopkins, he always resisted efforts to arrive at definitive conclusions. "Our New World environment," he wrote to William Healy in 1917, "has been too readily overawed by the formulations of Kraepelin, Freud and others, much to the detriment of the fresh and courageous pragmatism which is the sanest product of our best leaders." Decrying the search for dogma, he expressed a desire to "swear allegiance to the rich harvest of fact" and to recognize that "the systematizers . . . are always a side product." Meyer incorporated virtually every intellectual and scientific current within his framework. A source of both strength and weakness, his eclecticism and dense prose offered relatively little to mental hospital psychiatry.[23]

Meyer, whose influence was in part transmitted through his prestigious institutional affiliation, was by no means alone in helping to reshape psychiatric thinking. Such figures as William Alanson White and Smith Ely Jelliffe also contributed to the emergence of dynamic psychiatry. Both had come to psychiatry and psychoanalysis through neurology. Like Meyer, they were committed to an evolutionary point of view that emphasized development from the simple to the complex as well as the importance of adaptation. Medicine, the two averred in a later edition of their famous *Diseases of the Nervous System: A Text-Book of Neurology and Psychiatry* (first published in 1915), must look "toward a more psychological conception . . . if its understanding of disease processes is to [be] better founded." White's expansive and eclectic approach to psychiatry was reflected in his career. As the head of Saint Elizabeths—a federal hospital in the District of Columbia and one of the largest in the nation—he always insisted upon the legitimacy and importance of the mental hospital. At the same time he was a proponent of psychoanalysis and took an active role in both forensic psychiatry and the mental hygiene movement, both of which were somewhat removed from the needs of the severely and chronically mentally ill.[24]

The process of change that would ultimately transform the nature of psychiatric practice was not immediately apparent prior to 1940; eclecticism and controversy were characteristic. Some psychiatrists emphasized brain pathology; some stressed that bacterial infections in any part of the body could lead to mental illness; and some centered their attention on the role of the endocrine system. Those who demonstrated an affinity for somatic explanations could point to paresis and pellagra as proof of their approach. The former was the tertiary stage of syphilis in which massive damage to the central nervous system and brain resulted in insanity; the latter, a disease of dietary origins, in many cases caused bizarre and abnormal behavior. Whether paresis and pellagra were appropriate models for schizophrenia remained problematic, if only because knowledge of causal mechanisms was virtually nil. Much the same was true of hereditarian theories of insanity; its proponents were never able to identify specific mechanisms involved in the intergenerational transfer of disease. Similarly, psychoanalytic concepts, which grew in popularity, had a far greater influence on culture and thought than on medicine in general or psychiatry in particular. Indeed, Jelliffe as late as 1940 noted that psychoanalysis "in a mental hospital is practically useless. One has not the time, nor are the patients in the main of the type for whom it can be used."[25] The clients of practicing psychoanalysts, as a matter of fact, were drawn from the ranks of well-educated and relatively affluent individuals experiencing personal problems.

The rise of dynamic psychiatry in the early twentieth century was accompanied by a shift from the asylum as a place to practice to the research institute and psychopathic hospital. These new institutions suggested a growing dissatisfaction with traditional mental hospitals and their large chronic inpatient population.

The ferment of these decades was not simply a consequence of theoretical shifts, but rather resulted from the sense that the chasm between psychiatry and the larger medical community was widening. Medical science appeared to be standing on the threshold of a new age. The specific germ theory of disease and the growing importance of bacteriology gave rise to a faith that understanding the etiology and course of disease was both possible and empirically verifiable, and that effective therapies would surely follow. The creation of the modern general hospital—an institution that unified medical authority, faith in technology, and a spirit of social altruism—reflected the belief that the conquest of disease was within reach. Aware of their declining status within medicine and cognizant of the seeming obsolescence of their custodial hospitals, psychiatrists were receptive to the kinds of scientific and institutional innovation that would presumably bring them closer to their medical colleagues.[26]

The first center devoted exclusively to research in psychiatry was the Pathological Institute of the New York State Hospital system. Founded in 1895, it had two mandates: to study mental diseases "from the standpoint of cellular biology;"and to offer instruction in brain pathology to state hospital physicians. Ira Van Giesen, its first director, hoped to liberate psychiatry "from the confines of the asylum walls." Scientists, not asylum physicians, had to define problems worthy of investigation. Although including psychology and psychopathology as legitimate subjects of inquiry, Van Giesen clearly preferred physiological and somatic research. Within a short time he was embroiled in heated disputes with hospital superintendents. The basic issue, he wrote to Meyer, was between the freedom of psychiatry as a science versus bondage "to the rock of asylum superintendency which is general[ly] ignorant of genius and future expansion of scientific psychiatry." Van Giesen's biting words illustrated the chasm between the managerial and administrative concerns of asylum psychiatrists responsible for thousands of severely and chronically mentally ill persons and a younger generation committed to research that would presumably illuminate the physiological and psychological causes of mental disorders.[27]

The fratricidal conflict diminished when Meyer succeeded Van Giesen as director in 1901. Meyer's clinical concerns and focus on the individual proved somewhat more congenial to asylum psychiatrists. Patients within the New York state hospital system—by far the largest in the nation—probably benefitted from the new emphasis on individuals rather than the group. To deal with more than five hundred male patients without restraint or drugs, wrote one physician to Meyer, "was entirely due to the methods you instituted in showing me how to find out all there was to know about patients: my judgment was then clear to know what to do for them." The taking of life histories, for example, may have had indirect benefits because it conveyed a message that staff was concerned with patient problems and needs. Yet C. P. Oberndorf, who worked at the Institute in his early career, was critical of Meyer's preoccupation with assembling "all the facts" relating to the life history of a patient. "Where Dr. Meyer's grasp seemed wanting was in the correlation of a wealth of laboriously ascertained facts with the meaning of the clinical picture that the patient presented. Facts without theory, just as theory without facts, are not enough."[28]

The Pathological Institute (subsequently renamed the Psychiatric Institute) never lived up to its promise. The ideal of pure research on the causes and nature of mental diseases was remote from the clinical concerns of a large state hospital system whose administrators were immersed with the daily problems of the behavioral disorders of thousands of patients. Nor were the experiences of New York unique. Other states, including Massachusetts, Illinois, Wisconsin, and Michigan, created somewhat comparable research organizations, but the results were similar. Tensions with clinicians who worked directly with the insane and the absence of a tradition of public support for theoretical research undoubtedly inhibited the work of the Psychiatric Institute. "Isn't it rather a commentary on the American manner of doing things that we go enthusiastically and busily about matters of hospital organization and bringing up recalcitrant states into line," observed E. E. Southard, "and do not so eagerly push the fundamental basis of progress?"[29]

Southard's assumption that pathological research was not the American way of dealing with the insane did not go to the heart of the problem. The barriers that impeded research were far more formidable. Simon Flexner, director of the Rockefeller Institute for Medical Research (now Rockefeller University), expressed doubts about the feasibility of undertaking neuropsychiatric research. He virtually claimed "that there were no problems in a fit state to work." Flexner's characterization was not without merit. It is possible to identify significant problems that are not yet at an appropriate stage for study because of the inability to meet specific prerequisites (e.g., lack of a particular technology). The development of an effective vaccine for polio, for example, had to await the development of the subdisciplines of virology and serology (with their appropriate technologies). To suggest—as many medical researchers did—that psychiatry was backward was merely to underestimate the formidable problems of relating pathology and behavior. In the early twentieth century it was extraordinarily difficult, if not impossible, to study the physiology and functions of the human brain, undoubtedly the most complex organ in the body. At best psychiatrists could describe behavior and symptoms, but were unable to delineate the mechanisms involved in such severe disorders as schizophrenia.[30]

The psychopathic (or reception) hospital represented another innovation. Before 1900 traditional mental hospitals served two functions; providing acute and custodial care and treatment. Although divided over the wisdom of differentiating between chronic and therapeutic institutions, psychiatrists never considered alternatives to hospitalization of the mentally ill. Between 1890 and 1920, however, members of the specialty began to consider possibilities that represented at least a partial break with conventional wisdom. Their receptivity toward institutional innovation was in part a defensive reaction to the perceived fear that the boundary separating medicine and psychiatry was widening rather than narrowing.

The psychopathic hospital had its origins in the closing years of the nineteenth century. Urban areas in particular faced some unique problems pertaining to the treatment of mentally ill persons during the commitment process and prior to their actual institutionalization. As early as 1879 New York City had established a pavilion for the insane at Bellevue Hospital, which served as a short-term reception center pending an evaluation and final disposition of a patient. To move from a reception facility to a psychopathic hospital was but a logical step. Just as acute

diseases were treated in general hospitals, why could not acute cases of
insanity be treated in general hospital special wards or in psychopathic
hospitals modeled along general hospital lines?

One of the earliest such facilities was Pavilion F (Department of
Mental Diseases) at the Albany Hospital in New York—a private facility that served the community. During its first five years over a thousand
patients were admitted to Pavilion F. The hospital claimed that nearly 58
percent either improved or recovered and were sent home, and only
about 24 percent were transferred to mental hospitals. Without such a
facility, according to J. Montgomery Mosher, the attending physician,
most of these patients "would either have had to be improperly treated
at home, or would have been committed after a probably harmful development of the disease."[31]

Although interest in psychopathic hospitals and wards grew apace,
only three new ones were actually established before 1920. In 1901 the
Michigan legislature appropriated funds for the Psychopathic Hospital
at the University of Michigan Medical School in Ann Arbor. More than
a decade would pass, however, before Massachusetts opened the Boston
Psychopathic Hospital in 1912 and Johns Hopkins the Phipps Psychiatric Clinic the following year. The subsequent history of the Baltimore
and Boston institutions, precisely because of their visibility and reputation, is revealing and suggests that alternatives to traditional mental hospitalization would face formidable difficulties.

Under the leadership of Meyer and affiliated with the nation's most
prestigious medical school, the Phipps Clinic acquired an envious reputation. During the first eight years of its existence the staff published
nearly a hundred papers in journals and books. Nevertheless, the Clinic did not become a vehicle for change. Its funding levels remained
modest, a fact that Meyer attributed to the inability of the Hopkins
administration and philanthropic foundations to understand the nature
and needs of dynamic psychiatry. The prevailing emphasis at Hopkins
on laboratory research divorced from living patients also tended to give
Phipps a somewhat remote character. Consequently, the relationship
between psychiatry and other medical and scientific departments was
never close. Meyer's affinity for dense and obscure terminology further
hampered cross-departmental collaboration. The atypical character of
Phipps's patients—few of whom were in the severely mentally ill categories—ensured that it would remain isolated from public mental hospitals. The Clinic's reputation, therefore, was largely a reflection of its

institutional affiliation and role as a training center; its achievements as a psychiatric research institution seemed to pale by comparison.[32]

Boston Psychopathic Hospital had quite different origins. In 1908 L. Vernon Briggs, a young physician embarking on a career as a psychiatric activist, persuaded the legislature to transfer the Boston Insane Hospital from city to state jurisdiction and to establish an observation hospital as part of the renamed Boston State Hospital. Boston Psychopathic Hospital opened in 1912 as a department of Boston State Hospital, but was located adjacent to the Harvard Medical School. Under the leadership of E. E. Southard, who also held the Bullard professorship at Harvard, the hospital quickly acquired national visibility because of its identification with a prominent medical school. Southard's interests were extraordinarily broad, and he contributed to the emergence of social psychiatry, psychiatric social work, and the concept of the psychiatric team. Yet he remained a committed somaticist, and spent considerable energy on studies dealing with the relationship between brain structure and insanity as well as such diseases as syphilis. Southard was concerned more with abstract disease processes, and he urged younger physicians to "look beyond the individual patient. Not to see the woods for the trees, not to observe disease principles in the rush of individual patients, is the fallacy."[33]

Like Phipps, the experience of Boston Psychopathic suggested that new organizations did not necessarily lead to novel solutions in caring for the insane. Relations with Boston State were not ideal, if only because a preoccupation with patient care was not always congenial to research. Nor did research necessarily lead to changes in either therapy or care. Southard's orientation, observed one of his successors, "was in many respects away from the patient, especially his immediate living problems. Enthusiasm was primarily for hydrotherapy, chemicals to control distraught behavior, and studies of metabolism, neuropathology, and syphilis of the nervous system with its dramatic neurological signs."[34] Such concerns diminished interest in the provision of care for individuals whose mental disorders fostered dependency.

More importantly, the kinds of patients seen at Boston Psychopathic differed in important ways from those found in traditional mental hospitals. To be sure, Boston Psychopathic admitted substantial numbers of paretic patients, a group well represented in asylum populations. But the medical and social work staff also dealt with what was termed "psychopathic" personalities. The category of psychopath first appeared in late-nineteenth-century Europe, and generally was applied to criminals with normal mentalities who exhibited abnormal behavior. By the 1930s this classification referred largely to male criminals and particularly those charged with sexual offenses. At Boston Psychopathic the designation of psychopath generally referred to a variety of deviant types, including prostitutes and juvenile delinquents engaging in allegedly immoral behavior. The use of such a designation was consistent with the effort to broaden the relevance and jurisdiction of psychiatry and allied disciplines to include more than the severe mental disorders. Although confined in the early twentieth century to a relatively small group of practitioners and institutions, the effort to expand boundaries was but a portent of future developments.

The new concern with conduct disorder was an indication that the traditional psychiatric preoccupation with the severely and chronically mentally ill was diminishing, and that behavior perceived to be outside acceptable social norms was coming under psychiatric jurisdiction. Confronting new patterns of sexual behavior—particularly among working class women—the hospital's staff began to break with an older Victorian image that emphasized female sexual passivity. In this respect they were engaging in an ongoing debate dealing with changes in gender roles occasioned by the appearance of independent women who insisted upon their right to define for themselves appropriate sexual behavioral norms. Fearful that standards of sexual behavior were eroding, staff members—psychiatrists and others—focused on the role of presumably shameless females who were exploiting their hypersexual nature. In medicalizing so-called deviant sexual behavior, they implicitly employed a double standard. Young males could "sow their oats," after which they were transformed into upright and respectable citizens. But what was normal and acceptable behavior for males became evidence of pathology in females and led to a diagnosis of psychopathic personality.

The example of Lillian Thomas, age twenty-two, was instructive. She had been cared for at public expense since the age of ten. After becoming independent, she fell in love and agreed to "illicit relations" with a man and subsequently became pregnant. She rejected his proposal of marriage because she "preferred the alternative of living single and fighting out her own battle rather than being the wife of a drunkard." After giving birth at a home for expectant unmarried females, she was committed to Boston Psychopathic for a determination of her ability to care for the child. Investigation by social workers found that she entertained men in her rooms in the evening, and "went often to dances and came home very late." Staff disapproval of such behavior did not extend to African-American females. Hypersexual activity in white females was taken as evidence of psychopathy to the staff; similar behavior by black women was regarded as an expression of an ingrained natural immorality of that race. In dealing with the deviant behavior of presumably normal individuals, psychiatrists at Boston Psychopathic Hospital were slowly moving away from the traditional focus on the severely mentally ill. Southard was quite aware of this shift, and on one occasion complained that the hospital's "essential function of caring for the non-insane is not understood."[35]

The intellectual and institutional ferment within early twentieth-century psychiatry also prepared the way for the emergence of a mental hygiene movement, which was based on the belief that it was possible and easier to prevent mental disorders that it was to treat and cure them. Mental hygiene was an attractive concept, partly because its diffuse and protean character gave it multiple meanings. Whatever the significance of its message, however, its emergence was consistent with the effort to expand the role and authority of psychiatry in American life. Equally important, the mental hygiene movement reflected the growing separation between psychiatry and mental hospitals.

Outwardly the concern with mental hygiene was but a continuation of a venerable religious tradition that stressed natural law, free will, and individual responsibility. Within this older synthesis, disease in some way was a consequence of the willful disregard of a divine moral code, while health was a consequence of a morally responsible life. The nineteenth-century concept of prevention, therefore, emphasized the importance of living a moral and God-fearing life. The modern concept of mental hygiene represented a break with the past in that it grew out of a radical new faith in the redemptive authority of science, not religion. Disease was less a consequence of willful and immoral behavior than a product of environmental and hereditarian deficiencies; its control and eradication required a fusion of scientific knowledge and administrative and organizational action.

Like a variety of other newly emerging professional groups, psychiatrists believed that they had an important role to play in the creation of a new society that would maximize health and minimize the possibility of disease. In an address on the eve of World War I, Thomas W. Salmon, a psychiatrist destined to play an important role in the mental hygiene movement, outlined an agenda for the future. In the past the segregation of patients in mental hospitals had isolated the physicians responsible for their care and treatment as well. The new psychiatry, he proclaimed, would reach beyond the walls of the asylum and play a crucial role "in the great movements for social betterment." Psychiatric jurisdiction transcended the severe and chronic mental illnesses. On the contrary, psychiatrists had to lay out a new research and policy agenda. Psychiatry, Salmon insisted, had responsibilities that included mental hygiene, care of the feebleminded, eugenics, control of alcoholism, management of abnormal children, treatment of criminals, and the prevention of crime, prostitution, and dependency.[36]

Oddly enough, the creation of a mental hygiene movement began with Clifford W. Beers, a former mental patient. A graduate of Yale, he was unsuccessful in business in his early career. Following a suicide attempt, he was hospitalized and spent several years in the Hartford Retreat and the Connecticut Hospital for the Insane. Disillusioned by his experiences at both institutions, he decided to write a book that would do for the mentally ill what he believed *Uncle Tom's Cabin* had done for the antebellum abolitionists, namely, to popularize a cause. In 1907 he completed his classic work *A Mind That Found Itself*, which was published the following year by the respected firm of Longmans, Green and Company.

Beers accepted the fact that he had been mentally ill. He had experienced grandiose delusions, and his behavior had alternated between clinical depression and extreme excitement, His psychiatrists had diagnosed him as a manic-depressive. What was at issue, therefore, was not his illness. In both his extensive correspondence as a patient and in his book, Beers was critical of the psychiatrists who had treated him. They were neither cruel nor brutal, but were sometimes ignorant and incompetent and too prone to adopt punitive measures, including the use of restraints such as straitjackets or seclusion. Above all, they tolerated a "lax system of supervision." Beers reserved his harshest words for attendants, who were generally ignorant, untrained, and frequently brutal in their treatment of patients. The low pay ensured that only unqualified individuals would be hired as attendants. "The two who were first put in charge of me," wrote Beers, did not strike me with their fists or even threaten to do so; but their unconscious lack of consideration for my comfort and peace of mind was torture. They were typical eighteen-dollar-a-month attendants. Another of the same sort, on one occasion, cursed me with a degree of brutality which I prefer not to recall, much less record. And a few days later the climax was appropriately capped when still another attendant perpetrated an outrage which a sane man would have resented to the point of homicide. He was a man of the coarsest type. . . . Because I refused to obey a peremptory command, and this at a time when I habitually refused even on pain of imagined torture to obey or speak, this brute not only cursed me with abandon, he deliberately spat on me. I was a mental incompetent, but like many others in a similar position I was both by antecedents and by training a gentleman. Vitriol could not have seared my flesh more deeply than the venom of this human viper stung my soul! Yet, as I was rendered speechless by delusions, I could not offer so much as a word of protest. I trust that it is not now too late, however, to protest in behalf of the thousands of outraged patients in private and state hospitals whose mute submission to such indignities has never been recorded.[37]

Although exposés of institutional life were not uncommon, none had the impact of Beers's classic work. The book combined passion and information; its author freely conceded that he had been mentally ill. Nor did Beers reject the legitimacy or necessity of institutions; he focused rather upon the sometimes insensitive and occasionally brutal treatment of patients by staff concerned with the maintenance of order. In submitting his work to eminent psychiatrists before publication, Beers also managed to endow it with reliability and sensitivity. Couched in elegant and passionate language, *A Mind That Found Itself* was a clarion call for action to eliminate existing evils and inaugurate a new beginning in the institutional care and treatment of the mentally ill.[38]

To Beers, the writing of the book was but a prelude to the creation of a national movement. In 1905 he wanted to establish an organization dedicated to the improvement of conditions within hospitals, but one that rejected "yellow journalism or other sensational means." He hoped to secure financial support from prominent philanthropists. By 1907 his vision had broadened; he hoped that a "National Society for the Improvement of Conditions Among the Insane" could represent both institutionalized and noninstitutionalized insane persons. Beers undoubtedly agreed with William James—the eminent philosopher and psychologist who was his staunchest supporter—that a national organization could mediate between "officials, patients, and the public conscience."[39]

Even before the publication of his book, Beers had corresponded with and met Meyer—a person who could help to confer legitimacy upon his goals. Despite some misgivings, Meyer wrote a favorable review of the book in the prestigious *North American Review*. But privately he expressed the hope that Beers's strong convictions could be channeled by figures like himself who had "wide experience" in the field. These early contacts between two determined men inaugurated a fruitful but troubled relationship. Meyer was concerned that a national movement had to be under psychiatric guidance and leadership. Beers was by no means opposed, but believed that laypersons like himself had an equally prominent and important part to play; his views could not be cavalierly ignored or dismissed by professionals whose claim to authority rested on their presumed superior training and knowledge.[40]

In advising Beers, Meyer proposed the formation of a Society for Mental Hygiene "to show our people better ways of healthy living, prevention of trouble, and efficient handling of what is not prevented." This suggestion introduced a novel element; it deflected Beers's original emphasis on institutional improvement and directed it toward the more amorphous goal of promoting mental hygiene. To psychiatrists like Meyer hygienic concepts opened entirely new vistas and suggested roles outside of isolated mental institutions with chronic populations. Prevention might also hasten the reintegration of psychiatry into medicine and assist the former in efforts to join with other medical prevention movements. To the budding specialty of social work, the movement provided an opportunity of affiliating on a more equal basis with physicians and assisting in the effort to promote behavioral patterns within families and larger social groups that were conducive to sound health. An organizational effort was consistent with a faith that unified science and rational administrative structures. Above all, hygienic goals seemed certain to attract broad support from a public increasingly fearful of the seeming rise in venereal diseases, alcoholism, and a variety of other aberrant behaviors that fostered illness, dependency, and crime.

Initially Meyer urged Beers to confine his activities to a single state. A successful demonstration project, Meyer noted, would open the door to innovations elsewhere. Although not fully persuaded, Beers agreed to focus his activities and in the spring of 1908 formed the Connecticut Society for Mental Hygiene. Relations between the two strong-willed men, however, deteriorated rapidly. Beers was not content to follow the lead of another person, and his attempts to tap wealthy philanthropists brought him into direct competition with Meyer's efforts to enlarge his clinic's endowment. If hospital officials refused to cooperate in a plan of organization that included both public and professional representatives, Beers warned Meyer, then "the laymen identified with the Mental Hygiene movement would be well within their rights if they finally undertook an aggressive campaign which would force hospital officials in all States to measure up to the highest standard attained in the admittedly best hospital in any State."[41]

Beers ultimately prevailed when the National Committee for Mental Hygiene (NCMH) was officially founded in early 1909. The stated goals of the new organization indicated how far Beers's views had evolved since 1905. The NCMH would protect the public's mental health; promote research into and disseminate materials dealing with etiology, treatment, and prevention; seek federal funds and assistance; and promote the establishment of state societies for mental hygiene. To make mental hygiene an explicit organizational goal, however, was to break with the prevailing emphasis on the care and treatment of those already insane. To be sure, mental hygiene—in the words of a knowledgeable observer—was a "flabby and evasive" if not "misleading" term; the "real subject" was "*Insanity.*" However amorphous, the concept became a key element in the subsequent drive to diminish the central role of mental hospitals, to create alternative policies for the care of the insane, and to expand mental health boundaries.[42]

By the end of 1910 Meyer had come to the conclusion that Beers was out of touch with reality and had also engaged in irresponsible fiscal practices, and consequently resigned from the NCMH. Beers, on the other hand, insisted that he—not Meyer—was the central figure. In William James's inimitable words, it was a case of "the ox and the 'Wild Ass' not working well in double harness." Meyer had been brought up "scientifically" and believed "in work accreting bit by bit in finished form." Beers on the other hand, was an advocate of a "big movement." "Psychiatrists," Beers wrote in an obvious allusion to Meyer, "have an aversion to direct statement. Instead of saying that 'work will begin,' they say 'it seems about on the point of beginning.' Thus they play safe. If the world should come to an end before the actual beginning of the work, they can tell the angel Gabriel that they left no unfinished task on earth."[43]

The struggle between Beers and Meyer had deflected attention from a series of major organizational concerns in the mental hygiene movement: the formulation of a program; recruitment of a staff; and the development of sources of financial support. The NCMH after Meyer's departure assumed a more permanent form. By 1912 it had opened headquarters in New York City. Beers was selected as its salaried secretary and Dr. Thomas W. Salmon as its medical director. Initial support came from Henry Phipps; subsequent funding came from Mrs. William K. Vanderbilt, Elizabeth Milbank Anderson, and the Rockefeller Foundation.

From the very beginning the fledgling organization faced a serious dilemma. Knowledge about the nature and etiology of psychiatric diseases was at best rudimentary, and therapy tended to be empirical and problematic. Under such circumstances it was virtually impossible to define effective prophylactic strategies even though the concept of prevention had taken on an almost messianic quality. The emphasis on "healthy living" and "prevention of trouble," however appealing, had little if any substance, if only because virtually nothing was known about the causes of severe mental disorders. Ultimately the NCMH adopted a typical Progressive era strategy; its supporters and staff decided to undertake systematic surveys of conditions among the mentally ill. By this time the social survey had become one of the major weapons in the Progressive armamentarium. The presumption was that investigations by trained and knowledgeable professionals would facilitate the collection of objective data that would serve as a prescription for action. An intelligent and enlightened public, in turn, would accept the guidance of a rational scientific intelligentsia.

The first surveys conducted under the Committee's auspices focused on the institutionalized insane in South Carolina, Texas, Tennessee, and Pennsylvania. That three of the four were Southern states was understandable; the poverty of that region created particularly troublesome problems insofar as expenditures for illness and dependency were concerned. In South Carolina, for example, J. W. Babcock, superintendent of the state hospital in Columbia, had persistently called attention to deficiencies in his own institution, including an obsolete physical plant and inadequate operating funds. His conflicts with the governor led to his eventual resignation. A new governor conceded the accuracy of his criticisms, and called upon the NCMH to investigate conditions. The result was a large appropriation to rebuild the hospital. Other surveys in

the South had more mixed results. In Pennsylvania Dr. C. Floyd Haviland used the survey to heap praise upon state hospitals and to discredit county asylums under the control of local officials utterly ignorant of
modern psychiatry.[44]

Under Salmon's direction, the NCMH began to redirect its efforts.
His vision of psychiatry transcended the institutional care and treatment
of the mentally ill. Like many younger psychiatrists who were disillusioned with mental hospitals and unresponsive chronic patients, Salmon
wanted to expand professional boundaries in the belief that preventive
measures could change those behaviors that created social problems and
eventually led to insanity. The early emphasis on the institutionalized
insane, Salmon noted in 1917, "is not of our choosing," and he urged his
psychiatric colleagues to broaden their horizons in order to make
"schools and prisons . . . the chief fields of efforts and not the institutions
for the so-called insane." Nor was his call for change mere rhetoric; the
focus of the organization had already begun to shift. Increasingly its surveys dealt with alcoholism, retardation, crime, juvenile delinquency, and
deviant behavior. With the support of the Commonwealth Fund, the
NCMH created a Division on the Prevention of Delinquency, which in
turn sponsored child-guidance demonstration clinics. Salmon identified
crime and delinquency as medical rather than social problems; delinquency in his eyes was but a symptom and prelude to mental illness.
Frankwood E. Williams, Salmon's successor as Medical Director, promoted similar policies. In 1925 he applied to the Rockefeller Foundation
for funding of a study dealing with the "psychopathology of dependency." Dependency, according to the application, did not grow out of misfortune or lack of opportunity, but rather out of the inability of the
individual to respond to environmental challenges because of "intellectual inadequacy in himself, to a mental or nervous disease that has taken
away what adequacy he may once have had, or to personality, psychopathological in type, that would make adequate adjustment to situations . . . impossible."[45]

The NCMH, to be sure, in theory never abandoned its commitment
to work for improved hospital conditions. Nevertheless, its broadened
focus implicitly relegated the problems faced by severely and chronically mentally ill persons to a far less important position. The shift in organizational activities was even reflected in Beers's career. At the outset he
was preoccupied with improving conditions in mental hospitals.
Between 1910 and 1920 he concentrated on fund raising. In the 1920s

he became involved in efforts to form an international association dedicated to the cause of mental hygiene. During the depression of the 1930s the NCMH encountered serious financial problems that were compounded by a professional staff increasingly uncertain about their organization's raison d'être. Although Beers attempted to assist in fundraising and even persuaded Meyer to take an active role in the NCMH, he was already experiencing another major emotional crisis. Once again he became depressed and delusional. In 1939 he was admitted to the Butler Hospital under the care of Arthur H. Ruggles, its superintendent and an old friend. He remained there until his death in 1943 at the age of sixty-seven.[46]

Although the concept of mental hygiene struck a responsive chord among large segments of the general public, its practical consequences for the mentally ill were problematic at best. The fact of the matter was that the prevailing understanding of the nature and etiology of mental illnesses was so rudimentary that preventive strategies and interventions were simply not available. "I hope," Meyer wrote in 1930, "we shall before long have a mental hygiene division which shall be in a position to give an honest account of its actual work without having to swell the unfortunate noise and propaganda that has become necessary to maintain the salaries and professionalism of so many half-doctors and new 'professions' under the name of mental hygiene, and under the praise of unattainable panaceas." Others questioned the very legitimacy of the concept and movement. "Its capacity for creating a need has developed far in advance of its capacity for meeting the developed need," Maxwell Gitelson, a future president of the American Psychoanalytic Association, noted in 1939. "My own clinical experience," he added, "has been replete with the present necessity to tone down expectations in terms of what we were actually in a position to offer, both in child psychiatry and adult psychiatry."[47]

That the NCMH would gradually shift its focus away from the severely and chronically mentally ill was understandable. The growing custodial image of mental hospitals and their seeming remoteness from modern medicine had begun to exact a heavy toll. Just as some psychiatrists were in the process of disengaging from institutions and defining new career patterns, so the NCMH and its constituent state societies sought wider horizons. Prevention was an attractive alternative, particularly since it emphasized the problems related to childhood. Severely and chronically mentally ill persons often aroused hostility and rejec-

tion, whereas children—even those engaging in disruptive behavior—
were perceived with compassion and sympathy. To prevent or to alleviate incipient pathology and thus halt the development of more severe
problems in adult life provided an attractive alternative for those in the
mental health field. Prevention offered to psychiatrists an important
social role. By the 1930s some psychiatrists had identified careers for
themselves in education and industry, and the American Psychiatric
Association even organized a Social Problems Section.[48] As psychiatrists
and others embraced a more comprehensive if illusory mental hygiene
movement, they implicitly distanced themselves from the intractable
problems associated with the severely and chronically mentally ill.

Mental hygiene incorporated a variety of beliefs; it implied a pessimistic attitude insofar as curability was concerned while simultaneously affirming an optimistic faith in the possibility of prevention. But
the concept of prevention had other implications. When attached to
racial and ethnic stereotypes, it had the potential to shape social policies
with less benign consequences. In the late nineteenth and early twentieth century a preoccupation with an alleged increase in degeneracy in
general and mental illnesses in particular aroused fears that the biological well-being of the American people was being undermined. More
than two decades of economic depression that began with the Panic of
1873 had fostered class and social conflicts, rising levels of violence, and
a generalized loss of confidence. Under these circumstances receptivity
toward hereditarian ideologies increased. Pessimistic about the future,
some individuals and groups began to endorse such measures as marriage regulation, immigration restriction, and involuntary sterilization of
the mentally ill.

In 1896 Connecticut became the first state to enact legislation regulating marriage for eugenic purposes, and other states followed. Many of
these early laws forbade, among other things, marriage involving insane
persons. Cognizant that such laws had only limited effects, eugenicists
turned as well to immigration restriction. A precedent already existed;
a federal statute enacted in 1882 prohibited the entrance of convicts,
insane persons, idiots, and dependent persons without visible means of
support. Deficient enforcement procedures, however, weakened the
intent of the statute. Between 1921 and 1927 restrictionists succeeded
in persuading the federal government to enact legislation that sharply
diminished the number of individuals entering the United States from
eastern and southern Europe.

In general, psychiatrists provided little support for the restrictionist movement. The development of more sophisticated statistical techniques after 1900 had begun to call into question the oft-repeated allegation that immigrants were more susceptible to insanity than foreign-born Americans. The census of 1910, for example, noted that unadjusted mental hospital admission rates for native-born white Americans was 57.9 per 100,000, as compared with 116.3 for foreign-born whites. But if the respective age distribution for each group was taken into account, the corrected figures was 91.2 for the former and 123.3 for the latter; by the second and third generation the figures had narrowed still further if not altogether disappearing. Relatively few psychiatrists were involved with the restrictionists. Meyer was an exception; he permitted his name to be used by the Eugenics Committee of the United States of America, an organization chaired by economist Irving Fisher and including such prominent racist ideologues as Madison Grant. But when asked to comment on a committee report urging the adoption of restrictionist legislation, Meyer responded in negative terms. Would it not be wiser, he noted, for such a report "to put forth a rather modest acknowledgement that a great deal of the trouble may lie in our actual unpreparedness in this country to assimilate the unusual?" He rejected the idea of discriminating against Catholics, Jews, Greeks, and Turks for personal reasons.[49]

Immigration restriction was directed mainly against Catholics and Jews from southern and eastern Europe; the mentally ill were only of marginal concern. Those who promoted involuntary sterilization, on the other hand, were determined to prevent the propagation of individuals with allegedly undesirable traits, including the mentally ill, the feebleminded, and criminals. The development of salpingectomy (cutting and tying the fallopian tubes) and vasectomy in the 1890s provided a relatively simple and safe technology. Influenced by eugenical concepts imported from England, advocates of involuntary sterilization hoped to persuade their fellow citizens to act decisively to rid themselves of a variety of supposedly defective individuals. In their eyes mental illnesses were less a function of individual experiences, social environment, or chance, and more a consequence of heredity. But if insanity was a genetic disorder, treatment would be futile. The implication was self-evident; the expenditure of large sums of money to provide care and treatment of severely mentally ill persons in public institutions was misplaced. The only sound policy was to sterilize such individuals and thus prevent them from transmitting their illness to future generations.[50]

In 1907 Indiana enacted the first law that provided for mandatory sterilization of confirmed criminals, idiots, imbeciles, and rapists when recommended by a board of experts. Other states quickly followed suit; by World War II no less than thirty states had adopted similar laws, many of which included the mentally ill. Between 1907 and 1940 about 18,500 mentally ill patients in public hospitals were surgically sterilized. The number, however, was not equally distributed. More than half of all sterilizations were performed in California; another quarter in Virginia and Kansas. The presence of determined public officials and the absence of opposition were major factors; population size, age, race, and sex were not key variables in the unequal distribution of sterilization procedures.[51]

Among psychiatrists there was no clear consensus about the wisdom or desirability of using an invasive surgical technique on institutionalized patients. They did not dispute the idea that heredity played a role in the etiology of mental illnesses. Yet the absence of confirming evidence inhibited the adoption of radical interventionist strategies; few psychiatrists supported sterilization, and some were even vocal opponents. When asked to address a conference dealing with prevention and sterilization, William A. White—a figure whose influence equaled that of Meyer—expressed his views in no uncertain terms. "I do not believe," he responded, "that there is the slightest particle of justification for the mutilating operations that are being advocated . . . and if I should happen to talk in Baltimore at your meeting I should unhesitatingly denounce the sterilization propaganda." Other leading figures held similar views. J. K. Hall, the eminent Southern psychiatrist who served as president of the American Psychiatric Association in the early 1940s, ridiculed the procedure. "Some better method of preventing human diseases will have to be thought of than human sterilization," he wrote in *Southern Medicine and Surgery* in 1937. "There could never be another flood—if all the water were dried up; nor another sun-stroke—if the sun were blotted out. Sterilization of the human being primarily prevents begetting or conceiving children. The prevention of disease in an unconceived child—is almost inconceivable." A lengthy investigation by the American Neurological Association (an organization that included prominent psychiatrists) led to the publication of a report in 1936 that emphasized the lack of "scientifically valid work,"condemned involuntary sterilization on scientific and moral grounds, and endorsed voluntary sterilization for selected patients "with the consent of the patient or those responsible for him."[52]

––––––––––

The interest in mental hygiene and institutional innovation suggested that psychiatrists were acutely aware that careers in traditional mental hospitals were a professional dead end. They recognized their inferior status within the medical profession. When Richard Dewey sought a candidate for the position of first assistant at his institution in 1906, White declined to recommend anyone. "Men who have the sort of ability that you desire either do not want to go into institution work or else are already well provided for." The ambiguous status of the specialty even led to a symbolic change in the name of its professional organization and journal; in 1921 the American Medico-Psychological Association became the American Psychiatric Association (APA) and the *American Journal of Insanity* became the *American Journal of Psychiatry*. In his presidential address four years later White paid homage to the "old-fashioned hospital superintendent," but went on to urge his colleagues to reshape the Association along the lines of the successful and powerful American Medical Association.[53] White's call for organizational change was premature and would have to await the transforming impact of World War II. Nevertheless, his endorsement of the need for reform was indicative of a pervasive feeling that the foundations of psychiatric practice had to change.

In the 1920s and 1930s psychiatry continued to turn inward and to loosen its ties with mental hospitals. Concern with psychiatric education and credentialing became increasingly prominent as its members attempted to elevate the status of their specialty. In the half century following 1870 American medical schools had undergone significant changes. Together with the modern hospital, they symbolized the dominance of a scientific and laboratory based medicine. Yet psychiatry—precisely because of its location in public mental hospitals—had found no secure place within the structure of medicine. "I wish at the outset to make several confessions," observed Dr. Charles W. Burr in the *Journal of the American Medical Association* in 1913.

First, I have never personally known a genius who devoted himself to teaching psychiatry. Second, psychiatry is the most backward of all the sciences fundamental to the art of medicine. Third, the time devoted to mental diseases in medical schools is too short to teach anything beyond the alphabet.[54]

Nor did the situation appreciably change in the ensuing two decades. A study of the role of psychiatry in medical schools by the Division on Psychiatric Education of the NCMH found that medical school deans, although sympathetic toward the specialty, tended to be critical of psychiatry because of its "lack of integration, isolation; inadequate personnel; varying terminology; inexactness; therapeutic inefficiency."[55]

In the 1920s the APA finally began to consider its marginal status within medical education. Ultimately it narrowed its concerns to several central issues: the integration of psychiatry into the general medical curriculum; the establishment of departments of psychiatry in medical schools; and the creation of a specialty board to certify practitioners. For a variety of reasons psychiatry was unable to gain a foothold in medical schools until after World War II. Yet it was among the early specialties to succeed in providing for board certification. Ironically, the founding of the American Board of Psychiatry and Neurology in 1934 was a reflection of weakness rather than strength. The Board grew out of a compromise that merged psychiatry and neurology and thus limited the role of the American Medical Association, which had been involved in a protracted dispute with the APA. During the complex maneuvering that preceded the creation of the Board, James V. May warned his colleagues in his APA presidential address in 1933 that it was quite obvious

that measures of some kind will eventually be adopted either by the American Medical Association, the state medical societies, the National Board of Medical Examiners, or all of these organizations, for the qualification of specialists in the various branches of medicine, including our own, unless this Association decides to qualify candidates for specialization in the field of psychiatry, and insists upon a recognition of its authority to take such action. . . .

It will at least be conceded, I think, that if we are to maintain a position of supremacy in our own field we must establish standards fully equivalent to those already erected by [other medical specialties].[56]

The compromise that brought the American Board of Psychiatry and Neurology into existence resolved few issues. At the first meeting differences between psychiatrists and neurologists surfaced; the two, in the words of one observer, "got along like a couple of strange bulldogs," and even fought over which specialty would come first in the organization's title. Differences notwithstanding, it was evident that the APA conceived of the Board not only in terms of its right to certify credentials, but also as a vehicle for change. In 1938 the Association's Committee on Psychiatric Standards and Policies expressed the hope that in the future hospital psychiatrists would be board certified. They also called attention in approving terms to the development of "extra-mural psychiatry" and the "introduction of psychiatric concepts and techniques into general medicine," and urged mental hospitals to make a major commitment to "community work." The committee's comments implied that psychiatry's natural clientele included individuals not found in traditional mental hospitals.[57]

Such pronouncements were revealing of the changes within psychiatry. Conceived in an institutional setting in the early nineteenth century, the founding fathers had defined their functions and roles in terms that assumed unbreakable links with hospitals. In this sense psychiatry—given its base in public institutions—differed in fundamental respects from the rest of medicine, which was organized along private and entrepreneurial lines. Psychiatry and mental hospitals, by contrast, represented public or state medicine, and practitioners dealt exclusively with severely and chronically mentally ill persons.

Between 1880 and 1940 the commitment to mental hospital care and treatment began to erode. Whether advocating new institutional forms, new social and medical roles, or new kinds of patients, the psychiatrists who reached maturity during these decades no longer insisted that the links between themselves and mental hospitals were sacrosanct. Their new vision emphasized the reintegration of psychiatry into medicine in ways that called into doubt the caring function that had defined the essential character of the founding generation. To be sure, the majority of psychiatrists continued to be employed in institutional settings until World War II. Yet they were already moving in a direction that called into doubt the wisdom and legitimacy of an institutionally based policy.

7

Depression, War, and the Crisis of Care

The transformation of psychiatry and creation of a mental hygiene movement in the early twentieth century did not, at least in the short run, lead states to abandon their large mental hospital systems. In spite of the widening chasm between the specialty of psychiatry and asylums, inpatient populations and expenditures continued their steady rise. The resiliency and persistence of hospitals was largely a function of their ability to provide care for large numbers of individuals whose mental illnesses rendered them dependent upon others. The absence of community systems to meet the needs of this disabled population further magnified the importance of the caring and custodial functions of mental hospitals.

The apparent stability of mental institutions, nevertheless, concealed a variety of problems and tensions. The depression of the 1930s and ensuing global conflict discouraged investment in the public sector as a whole. A decade and a half of fiscal neglect would lead to a deterioration of a mental hospital system responsible for an inpatient population that by 1940 approached nearly half a million, the majority of whom were in the chronic category. Institutional decline had the paradoxical effect of both stimulating the rapid introduction of radical somatic therapies and magnifying friction between psychiatrists who administered mental hospitals and state legislators and officials concerned with economy and accountability. In the interwar years the contradictions within the mental health system were for the most part ignored, if only because Americans were preoccupied with the problems of depression and war.

———————

Despite mounting problems, mental hospitals continued their steady growth during the first half of the twentieth century. In 1910 more than 60,000 persons entered hospitals, which had an inpatient population of 187,791. By 1939 these institutions cared for nearly 425,000 persons or about 92 percent of the total number of inpatients; the remainder were in private facilities (2.8 percent) and veterans hospitals (5.6 percent). New York, which had the largest asylum system in the nation and accounted for about a fifth of all institutionalized patients, was an extreme example of the commitment to a hospital-based policy. Between 1913 and 1917 an average of 8,122 persons were admitted to its hospitals; the inpatient population was 33,124. Fifteen years later the respective figures were 11,557 and 47,775. By the mid-1950s its inpatient population had risen to over 93,000.[1]

Although national data on diagnostic categories prior to 1940 are imprecise or nonexistent, it was clear that the asylum population was composed overwhelmingly of individuals with a diagnosis of severe mental illness. The experiences of Warren State Hospital in Pennsylvania are illustrative. Between 1916 and 1925 about 90 percent of all first admissions were in the psychotic (or severely mentally ill) category, which included mental disorders of the senium (14.8 percent), syphilitic (13.1 percent), alcoholic (5.3 percent), schizophrenic (18.6 percent), and manic-depressive (9.4 percent).[2]

There were important demographic differences between the severely mentally ill and the general population, of which marital status and age were among the most significant. When the U. S. Bureau of the Census gathered data in 1910, it found that 63.5 percent of the male inpatient population was single, 6.6 percent widowed or divorced, and 26.4 percent married; the comparable figures among women were 41.7 percent, 15.7 percent, and 40.4. In the general population, by contrast, 55.8 percent of males and 58.9 percent of females were married. Moreover, about 69 percent of the inpatient population was age forty or older.[3] The significance of these data is obvious; the majority of mentally ill persons in hospitals had neither spouses nor parents capable of providing care. When the absence of community support programs is taken into consideration, the persistence of mental hospitals becomes understandable.

The economic costs to the public of maintaining an extensive hospital system were substantial. Yet there was little or no disposition to question the historic commitment to provide care and treatment for the mentally disordered. Mental health remained an important component in the operating budgets of most states. Shortly before World War II the annual cost of providing care for hospitalized patients was over $100 million; overhead and charges in capital investment brought the total to over $200 million. By 1951 about 8 percent of the current operations budget of states (a figure that excluded debt servicing and capital outlays) was devoted to mental illnesses. Some states spent as little as 2 percent, while New York spent about a third. The most striking fact was the variability between states. In 1940 the average per capita expenditure per patient for the United States as a whole was $301. New England, by way of contrast, spent $388, whereas the East South Central states (Kentucky, Tennessee, Alabama, and Mississippi) spent only $172.[4]

So pervasive was the faith in an institutional policy that alternatives were rarely considered before World War II. A few states experimented with programs designed to facilitate the boarding of harmless and chronic insane patients in households willing to assume responsibility for their care. In turn, these households received state subsidies. Massachusetts led the way when it enacted legislation in 1885. Its boarding-out program persisted, but the number of patients placed rarely exceeded 2 percent of the total. Rural households and households presided over by widows—both of which were attracted by the prospect of additional income—constituted the largest group of participants. Female patients far outnumbered male patients—a reflection of the belief that males were more difficult to control. Overall the cost of home care was less expensive than institutional care. Maintenance costs were approximately equal, but when patients were boarded out the state avoided the high costs associated with the construction and upkeep of hospital physical plants. As late as World War II only eight other states had followed the Massachusetts model, and the number of patients involved was never large.

The obstacles to an expansion of home care were formidable. Hospital officials were reluctant to assume additional supervisory responsibilities that would have added to their burdens. The obvious candidates for the program were quiet and harmless individuals, and these were the kinds of patients hospitals preferred to retain. Although families in more remote rural and farming areas expressed the greatest willingness to participate, the bulk of patients came from distant urban areas. Finally, many patients suffered from a variety of physical impairments associated with senility and disease, and therefore required comprehensive institutional care.

Family care proved feasible whenever patients demonstrated an ability to live in the community. Yet many households were reluctant to accept members even when they were deemed capable of leaving the hospital: the fact that the state provided an institutional home may have encouraged families not to take back their own. In other cases internal problems precluded family placement; and some patients simply had no families. Most patients responded favorably to placement; family care was clearly preferable to hospital life. One sixteen year old male suffering from hypopituitary syndrome (a deficient production of growth hormones in the pituitary gland that also affected behavior) had a mother who had vented her hatred of an unfaithful husband on the son who resembled his father. The boy had attempted suicide during a period of depression. In view of the mother's attitude, placement in a family other than his own was essential, and the boy adjusted well in his new surroundings. Another woman who had sat listlessly in an asylum ward for several decades became involved in household duties and ultimately supported herself by doing domestic work when placed in a home presided by a "busy, jolly woman who dashed energetically about her house."Upon visiting family care homes, Edith M. Stern, a social worker, was deeply moved by patients' "pathetic joy at being released from regimentation, [and] their delight in the simple normalities of family life."[5]

Despite some positive results from community placement, many families remained unwilling or unable to accept discharged members. In evaluating a program of family care at the Worcester hospital between 1934 and 1938, two physicians found that 23.4 percent of those deemed ready for community placement had been rejected by their own families, and an additional 46.7 percent were not accepted because of "family problems."[6] Even with promising beginnings, family care remained a marginal activity. The difficulties in administration and supervision of the mentally ill were formidable, and community resistance to the presence of former patients—particularly in urban areas—remained significant. Indeed, the experience of placement in the interwar years demonstrated that the most formidable problem was to find appropriate living facilities—to say nothing about social relations and work—for discharge-ready patients. As the consequences of the boarding-out experiment suggested, it was unrealistic to base any policy on the expectation that families would be able to care for their discharged relations or tolerate others.

The weaknesses of community placement programs did not lead to efforts to strengthen mental hospitals. Indeed, the depression of the 1930s and World War II had a devastating impact upon these institutions. In the short run mental hospitals suffered no more than other institutions, for their patients were shielded from the catastrophic impact of unemployment that threatened millions of American families with starvation and homelessness. Similarly, the decline in per capita expenditure after 1929 was in part compensated by deflation. By the close of the 1930s spending for mentally ill patient maintenance had reached pre-1929 levels. An NCMH study in 1934 concluded that declining funding levels had only a modest impact. Faced with budgetary reductions, superintendents made rational decisions to maintain the budget for food and other necessities and reduce expenditures for such less essential functions as libraries and other services; some even reduced salaries rather than medical staff.[7]

National aggregate data, however, concealed sharp variations. In New York the decline in appropriations was roughly equal to the decline in the purchasing power of the dollar, thus permitting its hospitals to maintain their level of service. But elsewhere budgetary shortfalls had more dramatic consequences. In one north central state crowded conditions resulted in a waiting list that exceeded 2,500. The pressure of admissions may have been even higher, since many judges were reluctant to use their authority to commit in light of overcrowded conditions. On occasion the inability to send patients to the hospital had fatal repercussions. One young man whose refusal to eat was related to an underlying mental pathology became so emaciated that he had to be carried to the hospital when room became available. He died within one day of admission. Another individual who lacked proper care died shortly after entering the hospital after a long wait for admission. Such cases were symptomatic of the precarious status of many public institutions and their limited ability to care for the mentally ill.[8]

The physical plants of hospitals were perhaps hardest hit during and after the depression. A virtual halt to new construction and deferred maintenance boded ill for the future even though their immediate effects were not always apparent. Modest funding for construction was provided through the Public Works Administration of the federal government, but 90 percent of the $12 million available for asylums went to four states (Massachusetts, New York, New Jersey, and Illinois) whose officials proved politically adept in taking advantage of new funding opportunities. A federal study found persistent rates of overcrowding virtually everywhere. In 1938, the average daily population of state hospitals exceeded capacity by 10.6 percent. In three states corresponding rates exceeded 40 percent, and in ten others the range was from 22 to 33 percent. As early as 1941 Albert Deutsch, whose journalistic writings catapulted him to national prominence after World War II, called attention to the "smashing blow" dealt to mental hospitals by the depression.[9]

The end of the depression did little to reverse the deterioration of state hospital systems. Concern with poverty and unemployment gave way to the military preoccupation with defeating Germany and Japan. Wartime neglect caused overcrowding in mental hospitals to rise from about 10 to 16 percent. More significantly, the induction of physicians and staff into the military created acute personnel problems. By the end of 1943 New York found that 31 percent of its medical positions and 32 percent of ward employee slots were vacant. Patient care, reported the superintendent of Pilgrim State Hospital in 1942, had declined markedly. "Inferior grade" persons replaced those inducted into the military, and he was forced to hire "from the Welfare roles in New York City and you can imagine that these people are not the type to make good employees." A survey by a nurse employed by the American Public Health Association found comparable conditions in other states. One hospital with 6,000 patients had 168 attendants on duty, as compared with a normal complement of 538. The number of elderly patients had increased as military service and defense-related jobs emptied homes of caregivers. As ward supervision declined, personal hygiene deteriorated, restraint increased, and recreation was curtailed. Some hospitals were forced to discontinue treatment programs because of personnel shortages.[10]

An independent survey by the Group for the Advancement of Psychiatry (GAP) shortly after the end of the war suggested an even bleaker picture. It found rates of overcrowding ranging from 20 to 74 percent in its ten-state survey. Shortages of doctors and nurses were "serious." In one area the doctor-patient ratio was 1 to 500, and a hospital that reported the lowest proportion of doctors described them as "retired general practitioners." In the same area the nurse-patient ratio was an absurd 1 to 1,320. "The functioning of the state hospital is inadequate," it reported. "It operates below humanitarian and good professional standards."[11]

Most contemporary observers were critical of the internal environment of mental hospitals. "In the ward rooms of one of our state psychiatric hospitals," John M. Gessell wrote in angry words,

> the beginning of each day is marked by the resurgence of a giant throbbing tempo of life, as much felt as heard. . . . One notices, among others, a middle-aged man whose teeth are falling out because of a severe gum infection. There has been no dentist at the institution for some years. Several patients' legs are covered with suppurating ulcers, sometimes dressed, often left raw by the restlessly fidgeting patients themselves. One old man's arm is a crooked, useless appendage. It was broken by an attendant years ago and was never set.
>
> A lad, slight of stature, stands all day on the same foot in a corner of the room, never moving. He must be fed and all his wants must be anticipated and cared for by the overworked, underpaid attendant. . . . He was brought to the hospital by his despairing parents in the hope that something could be done for him. Something might have been done, had it been undertaken in time, but no attempt at cure was made. Now he has been assigned to a ward to which small attention is given by the doctor, who has in his care 436 other patients, many of whom are much more demanding and quite violent. A lovable old man who has become a child again is crawling about the floor or sitting in his own filth, since there is seldom anyone to help him keep himself clean.
>
> Violent patients are kept on the floor above. The silence of the night is often rent by their cries of insane rage. . . .
>
> All too often one finds every sort and condition of patients locked together in the same ward, milling about and bruising one another. The noise and filth, the crying, swearing, laughter and inarticulate mumbling drive the depressed into deeper chasms of oblivion and the maniacs up ever more dizzy precipices of exaltation. Few are ever helped to break out of the fog of illusion that envelops them and to grasp some little part of reality which might lead toward mental health again.[12]

The slow erosion in the qualitative and quantitative aspects of mental hospital life during the depression and war years exacerbated friction between psychiatrists critical of inadequate funding and state officials whose concerns involved more than mental illnesses. Admittedly of paramount significance, financial issues were not the only source of conflict. To be sure, the daily management of hundreds of thousands of institutionalized patients remained under psychiatric jurisdiction. Yet mental hospitals and their psychiatric staffs had to be accountable to elected legislatures and executives. The problem was how to find mechanisms that could assure accountability. How were indices of success and failure to be defined and measured? What were the limits of professional autonomy? How could public officials evaluate a professional group whose claims to authority rested upon their mastery of a body of technical and specialized knowledge presumably beyond the comprehension of nonspecialists? Although such issues had been debated in the nineteenth century, they assumed a more prominent role in a society where traditional and decentralized decision-making mechanisms had been weakened by a commitment to the ideals of efficiency, rationalization, and centralization, and where professional groups played increasingly important roles. In such a society the ideals associated with science and technology were not always compatible with those of representative government.

The demand for professional autonomy and the insistence upon public accountability from legislatures would sometimes clash. Indeed, the creation of the first boards of state charities in the 1860s had led to the adoption of a series of resolutions in 1875 by the AMSAII reaffirming the necessity for medical independence. Nineteenth-century provisions for supervision, however, were rudimentary, and overt conflict was muted. State boards of charity could in theory investigate, collect data, and offer policy recommendations. Nevertheless, their budgetary and administrative authority was virtually nil, and the absence of a permanent staff vitiated efforts to enhance their role. The diversity of the American political structure meant that regulatory structures varied from state to state and region to region, which discouraged efforts to evaluate the efficacy of different organizational patterns governing mental hospitals.

After 1900 state governments expanded their regulatory activities in the hope of achieving greater efficiency and economy. On the eve of World War I, twenty-one states had boards of charity and/or corrections. Several of these states, notably New York and Massachusetts, had boards whose jurisdiction was limited to the mentally ill. Twelve states had boards of control, which—by virtue of their fiscal authority—tended to be more powerful than boards of charity. Seven states had no central agencies whatsoever, and the pattern in the remaining states was mixed.[13] If there was little agreement on what constituted the most appropriate model, there was a broad consensus that centralized control held the key to more effective policies.

During the interwar years states experimented with a variety of regulatory systems. New York and Massachusetts—the two most innovative and influential states—retained the structures they had created in the 1890s: namely, a board whose jurisdiction was limited to the mentally ill. This model was favored by psychiatrists, since its head was generally a physician with broad mental hospital experience. The examples of New York and Massachusetts were widely praised but little emulated. By 1939 nine states had public welfare departments with authority over all dependent groups, including the mentally ill. Five others with comparable agencies made provision for a subdepartment having responsibility for the mentally ill. Ten states adhered to the board of control model, and the pattern elsewhere was mixed.[14]

The prevailing administrative eclecticism was symbolic of a deeper ambivalence about the nature of medical and welfare institutions. Sickness generally aroused sympathetic attitudes, since all individuals were at risk. Dependency, on the other hand, provoked more equivocal responses, if only because of a widespread perception that it was the product of laziness and character deficiencies. Unlike general hospitals, asylums providing therapy and care were the object of both sympathy and hostility. Therapy suggested illness, whereas care was identified with dependency. The marginalized character of mental hospitals, therefore, made it possible for them to be subsumed under either the medical care or welfare systems (and sometimes under both).

The debate over appropriate structures to administer the expanding network of mental hospitals engendered controversy. Yet the degree of centralization of administration, at least in the mental health arena, had only a limited impact. Centralized agencies had authority to promulgate uniform rules and regulations that in theory applied to all hospitals under their jurisdiction. Whether or not institutions complied with bureaucratic regulations was more questionable. In many instances behavioral adaptations by both patients and staff circumvented or even negated the intent of new rules. Nor were state regulatory agencies in a position to monitor in a careful and sustained manner the activities of individual institutions. Despite the rhetoric of its supporters, central-ized management and administration proved attractive in theory, but less effective in practice.

Centralized administration facilitated certain kinds of policies. The exclusion or removal of nonresident or immigrant insane persons from public hospitals was more easily accomplished by central boards than by individual institutions, as was the adoption of uniform salary schedules for all hospital employees. The overall relationship between structure and policy, however, was at best obscure. The examples of New York and Massachusetts are again instructive. Both had highly regarded depart-ments whose jurisdiction encompassed only the mentally ill and whose commissioners were psychiatrists; both developed uniform statistical reporting systems that played major roles in the development of psy-chiatric epidemiology (a discipline that attempted to shed light on those social and environmental variables that affected the etiology and out-comes of mental disorders); both had mental health budgets well above the national average; and both created programs to facilitate research, train staff, and disseminate information. Correspondingly, states that lacked effective central structures appeared to have lower standards of care. In 1931 the national average per capita expenditure for mainte-nance at state hospitals was $291. Massachusetts spent $366 and New York $392. Southern states, which lacked strong central departments, allocated far less; the comparable figures for Virginia, North Carolina, Mississippi, and Alabama were $177, $163, $183, and $193, respective-ly. J. K. Hall, the most prominent Southern psychiatrist in the 1920s and 1930s, expended considerable time and effort to induce his state to cre-ate a department comparable to those in Massachusetts and New York. Virginia, he insisted, "needs a Commissioner of Mental Hygiene to deal with the problem as a state problem, and to activate, direct, and coordi-nate such work." "So long as psychiatric administration remains so thor-oughly laymanized," he wrote subsequently, "just so long, in my opinion, will psychiatry remain static."[15]

Qualitative and quantitative differences among states, however, were not necessarily due to different administrative systems. Tradition rather than structure was often the most important determinant of public poli-cy. During the first half of the nineteenth century—well before the emergence of centralized administrative systems—New York and Mass-achusetts already had a long history of using the state as an instrument to promote social innovations designed to liberate individuals from conditions and circumstances that inhibited their self-development.[16] But other states with quite dissimilar administrative structures acted similarly. Wisconsin, which had a board of control, had still higher average per capita expenditures ($466 in 1931) than either New York or Massachusetts.

Organizational forms often provoked friction if not conflict between public officials and institutional psychiatrists. The former were preoccupied with financial issues, the latter with professional autonomy. Since two-thirds of all psychiatrists were employed in mental hospitals as late as 1940, it was understandable that relations with state authorities were of major concern.

Recognizing that some form of accountability was inevitable, most psychiatrists favored the Massachusetts and New York model of a mental health commission whose director was a qualified psychiatrist. Nevertheless, demographic factors precluded widespread adoption of this model. The two states had the highest concentration of psychiatrists in the nation, accounting for slightly over a third of the total in 1940. By contrast, thirty-one of the forty-eight states had fewer than twenty-five psychiatrists within their borders. Desirable though the New York and Massachusetts model was in theory, it was largely irrelevant in practice. The desire to find an acceptable modus vivendi, therefore, took other forms.

As the professional representative of the specialty, the APA took up the issue of state regulation in the 1920s when it created a Committee on Standards and Policies modeled along the line of the AMA's powerful Council on Medical Education and Hospitals. Its members attempted to develop a set of minimum standards for mental hospitals that included a stipulation that "positions and the administration of the institution must be free from control by partisan politics." The context in which the Committee functioned implied that the demand for freedom from political control was equivalent to an organizational structure in which both key decisions and evaluation mechanisms would remain in psychiatric hands. This early effort to define hospital standards and appropriate organizational structures apart from political intervention, however, did not succeed.[17]

The issue did not disappear, and in the mid-1930s the Committee proposed a modest survey of state regulatory agencies. Its members reiterated their belief that the highest standard of care existed in states where central agencies were "free from political interference" and reserved the harshest criticism for boards of control whose members lacked "specialized knowledge in the prevention and treatment of mental disability."[18]

The existence of a mental health agency headed by a psychiatrist was no guarantee of professional autonomy. Massachusetts is a case in point. Long held up as a model, the Bay State had a Department of Mental Diseases that for two decades had been headed by two prominent figures, both of whom had served as APA presidents. With a large concentration of psychiatrists and distinguished medical and teaching institutions, the large state hospital system appeared to be well insulated from political strife. Yet between 1936 and 1938 both the Department of Mental Diseases and the state hospitals became enmeshed in a conflict that revealed the limits of autonomy and independence of psychiatry and its institutions within the state.

The conflict began when James Michael Curley was inaugurated as the state's governor in 1935. One of the most colorful and controversial urban politicians of his era, Curley had a checkered career that included four terms as mayor of Boston, one as Governor, and a subsequent term in a federal prison for influence peddling. In many ways he was the last of a vanishing species of urban political bosses whose political strength derived from his links to a working- and lower-class constituency for whom he provided both jobs and services. In mid-1936 Curley, who was then running for the United States Senate, visited a Boston State Hospital ward occupied by elderly women who appeared untidy. At that time James V. May was the superintendent of the hospital and Winfred Overholser was Commissioner of the Department of Mental Diseases (his term was about to expire). In a bid for votes, Curley denounced conditions at the hospital, which included a shortage of food, clothing, and linens, and suggested that both May and Overholser resign.

A heated controversy that drew the attention of the press followed. The real object, according to one psychiatrist, was to discredit Overholser and thus not reappoint him. Overholser conceded that some of Curley's allegations were accurate, but attributed them to a prior cut in appropriations. Defeated in his run for the Senate, Curley then proceeded to nominate as Overholser's successor a VA physician without any experience in psychiatry. Curley also took advantage of an obscure law to confer upon the Department of Mental Diseases the functions previously exercised by the trustees of Boston State. May was quickly removed from office and replaced by Harold Norton.

When Charles Hurley succeeded Curley as governor in 1937, he immediately restored authority to the trustees of the hospital, who in turn removed Norton. The latter promptly issued a public statement describing "shocking conditions" at the institution. Hurley then proposed that the legislature authorize an investigation. The Commonwealth, he noted, had begun to extend its obligations "into fields where we cannot sensibly assume responsibility. There is in the public mind an ever-growing tendency, which has been deliberately fostered and directed, to throw upon the care of the Commonwealth many who should and could be cared for at home." Given the budgetary crisis of the depression and the fact that the Department of Mental Diseases already absorbed about a quarter of the state's income, the legislature concurred with the governor's recommendation.

At the end of 1937 the Commission issued its report. Its members absolved the state's mental hospitals of wrongdoing, but were critical of the Department of Mental Diseases, which "had become a one-man affair." Their report recommended the creation of a Department of Mental Health headed by a commissioner who could appoint and discharge hospital superintendents. Bay State psychiatrists were not enthusiastic. "With a politically minded, unsympathetic and ruthless Governor and a subservient commissioner," noted one prominent psychiatrist, "the effectiveness of the state hospitals could be destroyed almost overnight." "The whole affair," insisted Overholser (who by this time had succeeded the recently deceased White as head of St. Elizabeths Hospital), "is a dirty mess and the reputation of Massachusetts, or such little as it has left, is being blasted in grand shape." The controversy did not completely disappear until the legislature passed a new law giving hospital trustees the right to appoint the superintendent, but subject to the approval of the commissioner. A further requirement that the commissioner, assistant commissioner, and superintendents be diplomates of the American Board of Psychiatry and Neurology assured psychiatric support.[19]

Though it received national publicity, the internecine warfare in Massachusetts was by no means unique. Efforts to resolve the tensions between professional autonomy and public accountability proved elusive and difficult. Beneath the surface lay perhaps certain unresolvable contradictions. If psychiatrists gained independence from public supervision, by what standards and by whom would they be judged? Psychiatric autonomy, for example, could very well promote an emphasis on therapy, but diminish the significance and importance of the caring or custodial function of mental hospitals. Professional aspirations might be served by such an outcome, but the needs of patients and families might very well suffer.

The difficulty of resolving the competing demands of psychiatry and government was evident in a paper given by Overholser at the meetings of the APA in 1939. He favored the New York and Massachusetts model of an independent department headed by a qualified psychiatrist, but conceded that in smaller states such a structure was impractical. At the same time he quoted in approving terms the AMSAII resolutions adopted nearly three-quarters of a century earlier rejecting the idea of oversight by laypersons. Overholser's paper was enthusiastically received by his colleagues even in the absence of evidence that independent departments led to better care. The success of centralized control, observed Nolan D. C. Lewis, was dependent on the personality of the individual in charge. "An absolute monarchy isn't a bad type of government," he added in a revealing comment. "If you have a good king who lives long enough it will be successful. If physicians . . . are in the hands of spoilsmen, then your central system fails."[20]

———

Deterioration in the quality of life at many mental hospitals during the depression was paradoxically accompanied by the introduction of a series of radical therapeutic innovations that seemed to hold out the prospect of recovery for tens of thousands of severely and chronically mentally ill persons. First developed in Europe, these new therapies quickly found enthusiastic and widespread acceptance in the United States. Based upon a somatic model of mental disorders, they appealed to psychiatrists who practiced in an institutional setting that precluded extensive labor-intensive individual psychotherapies. Equally important, the introduction of the new somatic therapies suggested that mental hospitals could shift their focus and become therapeutic rather than custodial institutions. Even before 1940, fever therapy, insulin, metrazol and electric shock therapy, and lobotomy had begun to transform institutional practice and foster a long-absent spirit of optimism.

American psychiatrists eagerly accepted European innovations into their therapeutic armamentarium. They had traditionally used drugs to control the behavioral symptoms of the mentally ill, and had employed as well a variety of nonspecific interventions, including hydrotherapy and occupational therapy. The prevailing image, nevertheless, was that psychiatric therapies were distinctly inferior to those employed in general practice. That therapeutics in general medical practice were no different from those in psychiatry was all but ignored.

The first of the therapeutic innovations was associated with the work of Julius Wagner-Jauregg. Trained at the University of Vienna, Wagner-Jauregg early in his career observed that mental symptoms occasionally disappeared in patients ill with typhoid fever. His observation led him to undertake studies of the effects of fever on psychoses. During World War I he obtained blood from a soldier infected with malaria and inoculated a number of soldiers. The results appeared promising; four of his eight cases achieved what appeared to be a complete remission, and two others improved.

During the 1920s and 1930s Wagner-Jauregg's work received an enthusiastic reception, and he was awarded a Nobel Prize in 1927 for his work in developing fever therapy. His popularity in the United States was derived in part from the widespread preoccupation with the problems associated with neurosyphilis. At that time about a fifth of all male first admissions to mental hospitals fell into the paretic category. Syphilis, moreover, was a disease that simultaneously engaged medical, moral, and behavioral concerns, and had been a subject of public concern since the turn of the century. Wagner-Jauregg's fever therapy seemed to hold out the promise of recovery for paretic and psychotic patients.[21]

American mental hospitals were quick to employ Wagner-Jauregg's new therapy. Malaria therapy, along with the use of arsphenamine drugs, became the dominant treatment of paresis. Both were capable of being administered to large numbers of patients in institutions with only modest medical staffs, and both could be justified in theoretical terms. In the case of drug therapy a specific chemical killed the spirochete; in the other a general reaction of the immunological system produced comparable results. Malaria therapy, therefore, introduced an element of optimism in psychiatry. Indeed, White employed the new therapy not because of "any tremendous optimism" about results, but because he believed it "exceedingly important to prevent such problems as that of paresis from getting into the discard because of a general feeling of hopelessness about it."[22]

Variations on malarial fever therapy followed quickly, and in 1937 an International Conference on Fever Therapy was held in New York City. Fever therapy was even used in the treatment of schizophrenia. Despite its seeming popularity, many recognized that this novel therapy posed risks. Since the malarial plasmodium could not be cultivated or preserved for any length of time outside the human body, blood drawn from a malarial patient was used. Once introduced into mental hospitals, the obvious source of blood was the patients. The procedure thus raised the possibility of spreading syphilis from infected donors to susceptible individuals. White refused to authorize the use of syphilitic donors at St. Elizabeths, but few shared his concern.[23]

Aside from the obvious risks, the evidence to support the efficacy of fever therapy was extraordinarily weak. The criteria employed to judge remission or improvement were vague, and the results were dubious since those administering the therapy were also the evaluators. The absence of control groups and follow-up studies further vitiated any conclusions. Malarial fever therapy, conceded a partisan, had been "greatly abused as a method of treatment and . . . has too easily taken this country by storm." In spite of excellent reported results, A. E. Bennett was concerned about the "inherent dangers of engrafting one serious disease on another." In 1939 Oskar Diethelm expressed dismay at the spirit of empiricism that guided the new somatic therapies, and called for the imposition of experimental controls. His article was an implicit condemnation of the enthusiasm for novel but untested therapies, and he raised a series of ethical questions about the burgeoning psychiatric armamentarium.[24]

Diethelm's warnings were not issued in a medical or scientific vacuum. The decade of the 1930s was particularly notable for the proliferation of new radical somatic therapies. The most famous was undoubtedly the "shock" treatments. The technique was originally developed by Manfred Sakel, a Viennese physician who had observed mental changes in diabetic drug addicts whom he had treated with insulin in 1928. By the mid-1930s Sakel was using the procedure on psychotics, especially schizophrenics. The administration of insulin lowered the sugar content of the blood, thus inducing a hypoglycemic state. In this state of "shock" the patient fell into a deep coma that was relieved by the administration of sugar. Sakel claimed that the procedure was highly effective in the treatment of mental illnesses.[25]

Insulin therapy created a significant theoretical problem, since it had no relationship to prevailing biological and physiological principles and knowledge. Even Sakel conceded that his therapy lacked a rational explanation, but insisted that its effectiveness justified its use. He provided a possible working (although admittedly speculative) hypothesis. The products of the adrenal system, he noted, sensitized cells excessively, and consequently normal stimuli produced pathological effects. Insulin neutralized the products of the adrenal system and kept cells quiescent, thus reducing pathological behavioral effects. Sakel's claims, of course, presented psychiatrists with a series of ethical and medical dilemmas. Should physicians deploy experimental therapies on patients whose illness often impaired their mental faculties? Should therapies be used if their utility and long-range consequences had yet to be established?

Such theoretical and ethical questions, however relevant, were highly abstract and distant from the arena in which existential choices were made. Sakel's therapy was introduced at a time when many mental hospitals had a high proportion of chronic patients seemingly destined to spend their lives within institutions. If there was even a remote chance that an experimental therapy would aid them, should they be deprived of its use until more conclusive evidence was available?

Within the ranks of psychiatrists no clear consensus emerged; many remained profoundly troubled and ambivalent. Oriented toward psychodynamic and psychoanalytic approaches, White was skeptical. "I have a suspicion," he wrote to a colleague, "that some of these schizophrenic patients get well with insulin shock treatment and other similar methods that are exceedingly painful and disagreeable in order to get out of the sanitarium where they use such methods or at least to escape their repetition." Abraham Brill—Freud's disciple and popularizer in the United States—and Meyer were more sympathetic; they evinced willingness to try experimental therapies that might aid the thousands who languished in hospitals. Overholser feared that a promising therapy had become overly "popularized and prematurely hailed as a panacea." J. K. Hall expressed the hope of finding an adequate explanation for the way in which such treatments brought improvement, but conceded that "we may never know in truth how treatment brings about either improvement or recovery."[26]

At about the same time that insulin therapy came into use, Ladislas von Meduna, a Hungarian physician, developed a similar intervention. Noting that epileptics rarely became schizophrenic, Meduna employed metrazol to induce convulsions. He postulated a "biological antagonism" between the two diseases, thus providing a theoretical justification.[27] The widespread use of "shock" therapies quickly brought to the fore another concern. Both Sakel's and Meduna's therapies posed some risk for patients. Insulin enhanced the possibility of comas that were occasionally fatal, as well as pulmonary edema, epileptic seizures, and respiratory distress; the mortality rate ranged between 1 and 5 percent. Metrazol had a lower mortality level, but ensuing convulsions led to various fractures and respiratory problems. As risks became evident, some psychiatrists were attracted to electroshock therapy. First developed by two Italian physicians, electroshock quickly replaced metrazol. The new procedure reduced the risk of injury, but did not eliminate it entirely.

By 1940 virtually every mental hospital had introduced one of the new shock therapies. Lawrence C. Kolb and Victor H. Vogel estimated that between 1935 and 1941 more than 75,000 patients had received some form of shock therapy. Indeed, the new therapies had a transforming effect; institutional psychiatry seemed once again to be on the threshold of a new era in which therapeutic optimism was the norm rather than the exception. "All reasonable steps should be taken by the State Department of Mental Hygiene," concluded an investigation by the New York Temporary Commission on State Hospital Problems in mid-1944, "to make insulin shock therapy available to all Dementia Praecox patients in its hospitals who are not ineligible therefor by reason of physical ailments or other factors." The new shock treatments were described in a new textbook published in 1946 as the "indispensable tools of psychiatric therapy." "All the available evidence," added the two authors, "indicates that they are effective weapons in the treatment of certain types of mental diseases."[28]

Undoubtedly the most striking innovation of the 1930s was lobotomy—a relatively simple surgical procedure that involved severing the nerve fibers of the frontal lobes of the brain. The procedure was developed by Egas Moniz in Portugal in 1935 and introduced into the United States a year later by Walter Freeman and James W. Watts of the George Washington University Hospital in Washington, D.C. Psychosurgery (a generic term that included prefrontal and transorbital lobotomy) was undoubtedly the most radical therapeutic procedure ever developed in psychiatry; its effects were irreversible and the outcome not always predictable. Yet lobotomy had a firmer theoretical justification than the shock therapies. During the 1930s John F. Fulton, chair of Yale's Department of Physiology, had undertaken investigations of the nervous system in general and the frontal lobes in particular. His surgical experiments on chimpanzees confirmed his faith in a neurophysiological theory of localization of brain function. Fulton's work suggested that surgical intervention in humans held out the hope of altering abnormal neuron pathways and thus facilitating the reeducation of patients.

Deteriorated and overcrowded state hospitals and the presence of tens of thousands of chronic schizophrenic institutionalized individuals for whom the shock therapies were ineffective created an environment in which psychosurgery could be perceived as an important addition to hospital-based therapies. World War II inhibited the widespread use of lobotomy; between 1940 and 1945 only 924 psychosurgical procedures were reported. After 1945, however, the crusading efforts of Freeman in particular led to a dramatic increase in the numbers of patients undergoing psychosurgery. In the peak year of 1949 there were slightly over 5,000 operations. Between 1936 and 1951 no less than 18,608 individuals had undergone psychosurgery.[29]

New somatic therapies were quickly absorbed into the psychiatric armamentarium. They offered to psychiatrists what appeared to be a tangible cure. These treatments could also be understood by their medical colleagues, thus hastening the integration of psychiatry into medicine, and could facilitate the behavioral adjustment of the mentally ill. For patients and their families the obvious gain was the possibility of leaving the mental hospital and living in the community. Hospital officials were equally enthusiastic; successful interventions would both relieve overcrowding and restore their therapeutic role, which had been eclipsed because of the presence of large numbers of chronic mentally ill persons requiring custodial care. The rapid acceptance of these therapies was also facilitated by the vast publicity accorded them in the popular media. Newspapers and magazines as well as radio disseminated information about these therapies and created the impression that they represented major breakthroughs.

The introduction of novel somatic therapies, however eagerly received, posed a variety of theoretical and practical difficulties. Shock treatments, for example, lacked any theoretical foundation, a fact that Kalinowsky and Hoch freely conceded in their influential textbook. "At present we can only say that we are treating empirically disorders whose etiology is unknown with shock treatments whose action is also shrouded in mystery."[30] The absence of a rationale for a therapy, on the other hand, rarely precluded its use. Aspirin, for example, found its way into general medical practice long before its physiological action was understood. The overwhelming majority of medical therapies, as a matter of fact, tended to be empirical in origins.

The absence of a theoretical foundation, however, was overshadowed by a far more serious problem relating to efficacy. What kinds of studies could ensure that empirical therapies were truly effective? To be sure, some of the principles of clinical trials were understood. Yet their application in psychiatry (as well as other medical specialties) remained highly problematic. Psychiatrists—like all physicians—were trained as clinicians; they had little exposure to or knowledge about methodology, statistics, or scientific method. Consequently, claims of therapeutic efficacy often reflected individual opinions rather than conclusions drawn from a systematic body of data. Stanley Cobb, the eminent Harvard neuropsychiatrist, was especially critical of the crude nature of the psychiatric literature dealing with electroshock. The diagnoses of the diseases treated were vague; the courses of the diseases were not reliably predictable; there were inadequate controls; and animal experimentation was deficient. Much evaluation, he added, relied on "clinical impression," thus vitiating the claims of favorable outcomes.[31]

Yet at the individual level shock therapy often had a beneficial outcome. The case of a young college student was revealing. Subject to mild episodes of elation and depression, he left college in his senior year after becoming severely depressed. A period of hyperactivity followed, and he spent most of the succeeding three years in a state hospital. His condition deteriorated; he heard voices and his behavior became violent. At that point the physician decided to try electroshock therapy. Despite a temporary memory loss, the young man eventually recovered. In an autobiographical account written shortly after his hospitalization, he insisted that electroshock therapy had given him "a new chance."

> I was able to start over fresh. With no memory, no delusions, no fears. Or at least I had no memory of them for that period of days before I could again remember the details of my life. I was on the right track for the first time in some years. I had been offered a job on a silver platter. In fact it

had been forced upon me. That was a very smart move on Dr. S 's part. And I was discharged as sane . . . [and] returned to college . . . [and] graduated.[32]

Perhaps the most extensive studies of shock therapies were undertaken in New York. Aggregate results of metrazol and insulin therapy were kept on standard forms by each state hospital and then forwarded to a central agency. There they were analyzed by either Benjamin Malzberg or Horatio M. Pollock, the two leading psychiatric statisticians in the nation. Malzberg's study, which included over a thousand patients, compared those treated with insulin with untreated cases. He also conducted a follow-up study in order to ascertain whether the benefits were lasting. Both studies found that even if the mechanisms of the therapy remained unknown, insulin-treated patients had better and more lasting outcomes. Pollock's studies attempted to determine the effectiveness of metrazol treatment and to compare it with insulin. His overall findings suggested that metrazol was far less effective than insulin, and should only be used when the latter was ineffective.[33]

Perhaps the greatest problem with electroshock therapy was its indiscriminate utilization. "The promiscuous use of E.C.T. [electroshock therapy] without other adequate psychiatric therapies," charged one authority in 1949, "has become a medical scandal. Many institutions use it wholesale for all forms of mental illnesses without any other therapy— no proper nursing supervision, no occupational therapy, no psychotherapy—simply a pure physiotherapeutic procedure." Electroshock, he insisted, was merely a treatment to alleviate the disabling symptoms of affective disorders and was to be used only as one element in a total psychiatric program.[34]

Aside from the work of Malzberg and Pollock, studies dealing with the efficacy of the shock therapies were extraordinarily crude. Many lacked any control group; others had far too small a sample. More serious was the absence of any standardized criteria for such general categories as "recovered," "much improved," "improved," or "unimproved." Above all, the evaluation of outcomes was made by the very same physician responsible for administering the therapy, thus calling into doubt the entire study. Solomon Katzenelbogen of Johns Hopkins emphasized the flaws and weaknesses in the very design of most studies. "The enthusiasm aroused by a new, dramatic and—according to numerous reports—almost universally successful method of treatment, and the active interest of the therapist in getting results after spending so much time and effort," he wrote, "are factors which may account for some unintentional leniency in the estimation of the condition of patients who had received treatment; these factors obviously would not be present in the evaluation of the control group." Even demonstrably favorable outcomes could not by themselves be regarded as conclusive evidence; there was a distinct possibility that the administration of insulin created a sympathetic rapport with patients that itself had therapeutic effects. Although raising important issues, Katzenelbogen was unwilling to recommend discontinuation of a therapy that might benefit patients who otherwise might remain hospitalized for most of their adult lives.[35]

Psychosurgery presented even more formidable problems. To be sure, some of the studies reported that perhaps one-third of patients undergoing psychosurgery had been discharged and were living at home. Moreover, lobotomized patients, previously regarded as highly disruptive or intractable, became more manageable and were able to adapt better to institutional life. On the other hand, the dramatic changes in personality that often followed lobotomy—which were irreversible—hardly augured well for a wider deployment. In a detailed study of thirty-two lobotomies, Swedish psychiatrist Gosta Rylander found that the emotional lives of lobotomized patients were dulled. They were subject to paroxysms of rage; they became tactless and distractible; intellectually they could neither synthesize nor think abstractly; they showed poor judgment and impaired retention; their ability to work was diminished; and they manifested exaggerated emotional responses.[36]

Psychosurgery magnified the significance of psychiatric decision making. What were the criteria for selecting patients? Which of several procedures was best suited in individual cases? How were outcomes to be evaluated? These were difficult questions, and there were no easy answers. Indeed, psychosurgery demonstrated that clinical judgment rested on slippery foundations. Three annual conferences on psychosurgery sponsored by the National Institute of Mental Health between 1949 and 1951 brought together more than two dozen distinguished figures from psychiatry and the social and behavioral sciences At the initial meeting Fred Mettler, organizer and chair, specified five canons that governed therapeutic evaluation, and then noted that the most pressing need was to identify and collect basic data that were lacking. At the third meeting he conceded "that the state of psychiatric information is not sufficiently evolved nor clear to allow one to meet the above criteria." Diagnoses were imprecise; statistics "inadequate, incomplete, and unreliable"; and there was little evidence that "any form" of psychiatric therapy altered five-year outcomes. "Lacking facts," he added, "we must be content to remain in the realm of opinion, for the present at least." Mettler's conclusions recalled Carney Landis's comments on evaluating psychotherapy a decade and a half before. Landis found gross inconsistencies; dissimilar techniques gave rise to comparable results. He then repeated Pierre Janet's observation that the psychotherapist who understood the patient and who was adept at psychological stimulation could succeed "with any method that he cares to use."[37]

The obstacles impeding the evaluation of the efficacy of the new somatic therapies remained formidable. Yet aggregate data lend some credence to the claims that recovery and improvement rates were rising even though the reasons were obscure. In 1935 Pollock compared the period from 1926 to 1931 with the preceding five years; he found a marked increase in recovery and improvement rates and a decline in mortality for general paresis. A census official noted a modest upward trend in discharge rates in the ten years between 1933 and 1942. In 1933 57.1 out of every 100 patients separated from state hospitals had been discharged and the remainder had died. By 1942 the number had risen to 61.0. Similarly, Malzberg called attention to improving outcomes of schizophrenic and paretic patients.[38]

Perhaps the most detailed and sophisticated study of patient outcomes was undertaken by a group led by Morton Kramer. Shortly after becoming the first head of the Biometrics Branch of the National Institute of Mental Health (NIMH), Kramer and his colleagues decided to conduct a systematic investigation of the history of all first admissions to Warren State Hospital in Pennsylvania from 1916 to 1950. Because of the imprecision of such terms as "recovered," "improved," and "unimproved," the study simply focused on release—the point in time when the staff agreed that the patient was ready to return to the community. First admissions (which during the entire period totalled 15,472) were divided into four chronological periods: 1916–1925, 1926–1935, 1936–1945, and 1946–1950. In the first period the hospital had not initiated any major treatment program. During the second heavy stress had been placed on industrial and occupational therapy. Between 1936 and 1945 malarial therapy for paresis and shock therapies for functional psychotics were introduced, even though World War II had decimated the medical and nursing staff. In the immediate postwar period the number of psychiatrists increased dramatically, and the use of electroshock plus individual and group psychotherapies intensified.

Kramer's longitudinal data yielded some surprising findings. The probability of release of functional psychotics within the first twelve months increased from 42 to 62 percent between 1926–1935 and 1946–1950; death rates also declined from 6 to 4 percent. The early two cohorts showed little change; release rates rose markedly in the two other groups and the greatest increase occurred between 1946 and 1950. Indeed, the study undermined at least in part some popular perceptions about the presumed custodial character of mental hospitals. The data revealed that the patient population included a high proportion of chronic patients composed of two distinct groups: individuals admitted at a young age but who remained hospitalized for the rest of their lives; and elderly admissions who remained for a relatively short period before dying. The large chronic population, however, tended to shield from sight a much larger group of patients who were admitted, treated, and discharged after relatively short length-of-stays. No less than 61 percent of patients admitted between 1916 and 1925 were discharged within twelve months; the figures for the subsequent three chronological periods were 64, 67, and 72 percent, respectively.

Kramer and his colleagues were extremely cautious in rendering any firm conclusions. They conceded it was impossible to attribute improving outcomes, particularly from 1946 to 1950, to improved therapies. But other variables had to be taken into account. It was entirely possible, for example, that better risks were being admitted; that new administrative practices within hospitals were involved; and that changes in familial and community practices enhanced the possibility of release. Nor did they have any data on discharged patients never readmitted to the Warren Hospital. Moreover, Kramer was particularly sensitive to the need for more adequate clinical trials.

> Obviously, because of the large number of variables involved, what is needed before statements can be made about the effect of specific therapies or therapeutic programs on the release rates of mental hospital patients are well-designed experimental studies to evaluate the various therapies (shock, group, psychosurgery, and so on) singly and in combination with each other and with various ancillary programs. In such studies, there should be carefully defined diagnostic groups of patients, comparable control groups, carefully specified therapeutic plans, and

staffing patterns and specific objective criteria for evaluating results of treatment and for determining condition at time of release.

Although expressed in cautious terms, the study pointed to more hopeful outcomes even if it was impossible to specify the causal factors responsible for the changes.[39]

Psychiatrists faced formidable and perhaps insurmountable problems in measuring therapeutic efficacy with any degree of precision. Aside from the fact that etiology remained shrouded in mystery and diagnostic categories were protean in character, it was extraordinarily difficult to sort out the multiplicity of variables, including the important but intangible interactions between patients, physicians, and staff. To emphasize the inherent complexities of evaluation is not to suggest that the problems faced by psychiatrists were unique. Although generally skeptical of psychiatric therapies, colleagues in other specialties and general medical practice were rarely able to offer evidence that their pre-World War II interventions were demonstrably effective. Such was the case of the continued use of tonsillectomy—a procedure that lacked an empirical foundation. Indeed, the Tuskegee Study of untreated syphilis in black males by the Public Health Service between the 1940s and 1960s drew little or no criticism from the medical profession despite the fact that the entire evaluation rested on racial assumptions and was lacking in any understanding of methodological rigor.[40] With these qualifications in mind, there seems little reason to reject the finding that release rates were gradually improving during the 1930s and 1940s.

As late as 1945 the commitment to an institutional policy appeared stable. The Mental Hospital Survey Committee (created in 1936 and jointly supported by the APA and U.S. Public Health Service) admittedly identified severe shortcomings. Nevertheless, the prevailing faith in the need for institutional care and treatment remained pervasive. The introduction of the new somatic therapies reinforced an optimistic attitude for the future. "I can envisage a time arriving when we in the field of Psychiatry will entirely forsake our ancestry, forgetting that we had our beginnings in the poorhouse, the workhouse and the jail," noted Charles C. Burlingame, director of the Institute of Living (formerly the Hartford Retreat) and an ardent advocate of psychosurgery. "I can envisage a time when we will be doctors, think as doctors, and run our psychiatric institutions in much the same way and with much the same relationships as obtain in the best medical and surgical institutions." If mental hospitals "can be provided with adequate funds and can be kept free from the slimy hands of spoilsman politics," observed Overholser, "the psychiatrists of this country may be trusted to raise the standards of the mental hospitals even higher than they are at present."[41]

Yet within a few short years after World War II Americans would find themselves entertaining radical new policies for caring and treating the mentally ill. The eventual adoption of these new approaches would lead to a sharp break with the institutional legacy of the nineteenth century. Postwar innovations would alter in unexpected and unintended ways the lives of hundreds of thousands of severely and persistently mentally ill persons.

8

World War II and New Models of Mental Illnesses

"We are in the midst of a revolution in the status of psychiatry," wrote Karl A. Menninger, the *enfant terrible* of American psychiatry at the end of World War II. Psychiatry "today has gone far beyond the institutional phase. . . . Outpatient psychiatry now dominates the field and its emphasis upon treatment has already begun to revolutionize in-patient psychiatry."[1] Menninger's words were to prove prophetic. After 1945 there was a concerted attempt to shift the care and treatment of the mentally ill from the asylum to the community. In many respects this development represented a radical departure, for it was intended to diminish the significance of the asylum, which had been the centerpiece of public policy for more than a century.

More than any other event, World War II was the catalyst of change. During that conflict military psychiatrists found that neuropsychiatric disorders were far more pervasive and serious than had been previously recognized, that environmental stress associated with combat contributed to mental maladjustment, and that early and purposeful treatment in noninstitutional settings produced favorable outcomes. These beliefs, which were brought to civilian life by a new generation of psychiatrists who had served in the military, became the basis for claims after 1945 that early identification of symptoms and treatment in community settings could prevent the onset of more serious mental disor-

191

ders and thus obviate the need for prolonged institutionalization. War-related experiences, therefore, led to innovative models of psychiatric practice that subsequently became the basis of postwar efforts to create a new mental health system.

The initial involvement of psychiatrists in the war was with the Selective Service System. Their role was to assist in identifying individuals unqualified for military service because of neuropsychiatric problems. The military feared in particular that the inadvertent recruitment of homosexual males would have a devastating effect on the armed forces, and supported any measures that might exclude them. The assumption underlying the screening process was that knowledge of the personality and background of the individual could be used to predict combat behavior and disposition to mental disorders.

The mechanics of screening proved both elusive and difficult. In 1941 there were perhaps fewer than three thousand psychiatrists in the entire nation. At the outset the initial psychiatric evaluation was conducted by a physician serving as medical examiner to a local draft board. These physicians were provided with some rudimentary directions to assist them in identifying those who were psychiatrically unfit for military service. This was followed by a second examination at the induction center by a qualified psychiatrist. By early 1942 the double-screening process had been dropped and replaced by a single examination at the induction center. But the number of men involved was staggering, and the psychiatric interview was limited to about two minutes. At some centers a psychiatrist examined as many as two hundred men in a single day. Moreover, personal histories were all but absent. One draftee was hospitalized as a psychotic five weeks after being drafted. Further investigation determined that he had been a schizophrenic patient for a decade, during which time he was confined in four different mental hospitals, and had been discharged from the Naval Academy at Annapolis following a mental breakdown. Under such conditions, wrote one psychiatrist, "hunch," "intuition," and "guess[work]" determined whether or not an individual was mentally fit. "It is ridiculous to assume that in two or three minutes it is possible to detect any but the most gross nervous or mental disorders."[2]

In practice mass screening proved ineffective. Available techniques—personal interviews, tests, social histories—fell far short of predictive reliability. Psychiatric examinations were at best cursory. Opponents of psychiatric screening provided devastating critiques of the process. Screening, they noted, was arbitrary and capricious: racial and ethnic considerations intruded into the process; rejectees faced discrimination in civilian life; personal histories were often inaccurate and misleading; and personality tests were biased and unreliable. Moreover, military authorities were themselves ambivalent about the practice; the rejection of more than 1,750,000 individuals for neuropsychiatric reasons (including mental deficiency) ran directly contrary to their goal of maximizing manpower.[3]

The difficulties of screening, however, were soon eclipsed by the problems arising out of nervous breakdowns occurring among military personnel. The high battlefield neuropsychiatric casualty rates beginning in 1942 called into question the assumptions and effectiveness underlying the screening effort. The bulk of those identified as psychiatrically "unfit" had supposedly been weeded out from the draft. Yet some soldiers exhibited psychological symptoms after a brief encounter with the rigors of military life; some when experiencing the potential threat of danger upon arrival in a war zone; and some broke down after prolonged exposure to life-threatening combat situations. As early as 1942 evidence mounted that prolonged stress associated with warfare led to breakdowns even among those who manifested no prior symptomatology. The case of J. S., a hardworking and efficient platoon staff sergeant, was typical. In the Tunisian campaign he was on nightly patrol duty for two months. After launching an attack with his unit, he reached a hill. Before being able to dig in, he came under a heavy mortar barrage that stunned but did not wound him. He managed to continue fighting and held the hill for an hour, but then began to experience tremors and was unable to hold his rifle. After spending two days at the aid station, many of his symptoms disappeared, but he was left with a tic in the form of eyeblinking and head twitching. Yet he continued in active combat for three months with a high degree of efficiency.[4]

The results of the Guadalcanal and North African campaigns seemed to confirm the belief that environmental stress, that is, the actual conditions of combat, played a major etiological role; predisposition was not a significant factor. In the Southwest Pacific the tropical climate, tropical diseases, an unfamiliar jungle habitat, and the absence of a rotation policy proved decisive variables; in the North African campaign veteran soldiers in continuous combat had a higher incidence of psychiatric symptoms than newer and inexperienced soldiers. William C. Menninger, chief of the army's Neuropsychiatric Division and the first psy-

chiatrist to hold the rank of Brigadier General, drew the obvious conclusion. The "history or the personality make-up or the internal psychodynamic stresses" were less important than "the force of factors in the
environment which supported or disrupted the individual."[5]

If the rigors of military life and the stress of combat—not the structure of personality—fostered mental breakdown, then it followed that
careful and intelligent planning could reduce the number of psychological casualties. All individuals, after all, were at risk. "The realities of
war," the peculiarities of military life, and "traumatic stimuli" could
"produce a potential war neurosis in every soldier," noted Roy R.
Grinker and John P. Spiegel. In a series of classic studies they, along
with John W. Appel and Herbert X. Spiegel, promoted the view that the
dangers of "combat exhaustion" (a term that presumably avoided stigmatization) could be minimized. Limitations of the time soldiers were kept
in actual combat (i.e., fixed tours of duty), measures to promote group
cohesion, and regular rest periods proved effective preventive measures. Neurotic symptoms could be managed by brief psychotherapy.
Narcosynthesis—the intravenous administration of sodium pentothal—
enabled patients to recall repressed traumatic battlefield experiences
and thus to deal with them in a rational manner rather than with "catastrophic defensive devices" that ultimately ended in serious psychological crippling.[6]

Under a plan developed by Colonel Frederick Hanson (psychiatric
consultant for the Mediterranean theater), battalion aid station surgeons
were given instruction in "first-aid" psychiatry. Many of the soldiers sent
to the station displayed a variety of symptoms that included sleep disturbances and nightmares, anxiety states, sudden mild shocks, subtle
behavioral changes such as abstracted manners, modification in voice
and simple daily habits, and irritability. The typical course of treatment
for such individuals was mild sedation, a night of sound sleep, and warm
food. More seriously troubled soldiers were sent to the rear, where they
received brief psychotherapy, rest, and relaxation under psychiatric
guidance. Such relatively simple interventions produced almost instan-
taneous results. With prompt treatment nearly two-thirds of all neuropsychiatric casualties were returned to duty in less than a week. Rear
base hospitals salvaged about a third of the patients sent to them for
noncombat duties. The remainder were returned to the United States
for further treatment in military and VA hospitals.[7]

The psychiatric lessons gleaned from wartime experiences had significant policy implications. The greatest successes in treating soldiers with psychological symptoms occurred at the company aid station level; the therapeutic success rate declined in rear echelon units. "Treatment in the battle zone," a military psychiatrist noted, "was of crucial importance in providing the atmosphere of expectancy for recovery and return to combat duty. Forward, brief simplified treatment clearly communicated to patients, treatment personnel, and the combat reference group that psychiatric casualties were only temporarily unable to function. Conversely, evacuation of psychiatric casualties to distant medical facilities weakened relationships with the combat group and implied failure in battle for which continuation of the sick role was the only honorable explanation."[8] A logical conclusion followed; treatment in civilian life, as in the military, had to be provided in a family and community setting rather than in a remote, isolated, and impersonal institution. The implications for psychiatrists were clear; community and private practice should replace employment in mental hospitals.

Psychiatrists knew from their wartime experiences that the debilitating effects of stress, if alleviated, could have significant influence upon mental stability. If such innovations as rest periods, rotation policies, and measures encouraging group cohesion and social relationships had reduced psychoneurotic episodes in the military, might not corresponding social and environmental changes in civilian life optimize mental as well as physical health? Conceding that environmental stresses were more diverse and less amenable to centralized control in civilian life than in the military, John W. Appel expressed the belief that institutions of government, industry, education, religion, and communication possessed sufficient means to undertake efforts to remove or ameliorate "some of the situation stresses which adversely affect mental health."[9]

Appel's expansive themes were echoed by many of his colleagues who maintained that their specialty possessed the knowledge and techniques to identify appropriate social and environmental changes that presumably could optimize mental as well as physical health. "Good mental health or well-being," wrote Henry W. Brosin in spelling out the implications of the military experience for American society, "is a commodity which *can be created* under favorable circumstances." In the immediate postwar years psychiatrists—like virtually all professionals, medical and other—attempted to expand their jurisdictional boundaries and authority; they went beyond their clinical role of treating individual patients and assumed a professional authority to speak and act on behalf of the public's mental health. The invocation of professional expertise included medical and ideological prescriptions to deal with a myriad of social problems. Mental hygiene, insisted Robert H. Felix and R. V. Bowers in 1948, had to be concerned "with more than the psychoses and with more than hospitalized mental illness." Personality was shaped by socioenvironmental influences, and psychiatry had to emphasize as well the problems of the "ambulatory ill and the preambulatory ill (those whose probability of breakdown is high)." The community, not the hospital, they added, should be psychiatry's natural habitat. Nor was Felix speaking in abstract terms. Serving as the visible and influential director of the National Institute of Mental Health from its creation in the late 1940s until 1964, he worked assiduously to reshape postwar mental health policy along community and preventive lines.[10]

The significance of wartime experiences could hardly be exaggerated, implied two influential psychiatrists in a work published shortly after the return of peace. World War II had confirmed the importance of environmental factors in mental health, and psychiatric practice had to take them into account. In a similar vein, Nolan D. C. Lewis observed that the war demonstrated the desirability of treating people before they required hospitalization. Thus if potential schizophrenics could be identified before the onset of the acute stage, treatment in a community setting (as in the military) might preclude institutionalization. "We as civilians," he added, "should insist (not merely request) on the establishment of more child guidance centers and treatment clinics in the cities and towns over the country, that corrective measures may be available to those who seek aid."[11]

The war not only created a new therapeutic model, but also transformed the specialty of psychiatry. In 1940 the APA had only 2,295 members, perhaps two-thirds of whom were employed in mental hospitals and were associated with an older somatic tradition. Under Brigadier General Menninger about 2,400 physicians (most without specialty training) were assigned to psychiatry.[12] Their wartime experiences in successfully treating neuropsychiatric symptoms in noninstitutional settings (and allegedly preventing the onset of more serious psychotic symptoms) created an alluring model. The concept that there was a smooth continuum from health to disease appeared to justify the claim that early treatment in noninstitutional settings represented an effective strategy. From the 1940s through the 1960s psychodynamic and psychoanalytic psychiatrists—few of whom opted for careers in traditional public mental hospitals—worked assiduously to apply wartime lessons and move the locus of practice from the asylum to the community.

————

Many psychiatrists left military life convinced of the need for fundamental changes in the ways in which the needs of mentally ill and psychologically troubled individuals were addressed. Social and medical innovation, however, required an effective organization capable of translating concepts into practice. The APA, which was the oldest medical specialty association and had just celebrated its centenary, was the obvious choice. Yet in 1945 the APA still represented the interests of hospital psychiatry and an older more somatically oriented tradition. More importantly, it was relatively inactive; its two main functions were to hold an annual convention and to publish the *American Journal of Psychiatry*. It lacked a salaried leader, an efficient staff, and a secure financial foundation, and its elected officers rarely devoted much time to its affairs.

Dissatisfaction surfaced in early 1944 when a committee recommended that the APA modernize its structure and establish a central headquarters under the direction of a qualified psychiatrist. The APA Council (the highest governing board) then created a Special Committee on Reorganization chaired by Karl A. Menninger. Born in 1893 in Topeka, Kansas, Karl received his M.D. from the Harvard Medical School and subsequently studied with E. E. Southard at Boston Psychopathic Hospital. He returned to Topeka and entered a partnership with his father that within a few years had been transformed into the Menninger Clinic. Joined by his brother William, the two soon made Topeka into one of the nation's premier psychiatric centers; in the two decades following the end of World War II it became the leading training center of psychodynamic psychiatrists. Karl's interests were extraordinarily broad. He became the popularizer of psychoanalytic psychiatry through such best-selling books as *The Human Mind* (1929), *Man Against Himself* (1938), and *Love Against Hate* (1942). Possessed of a domineering and charismatic personality, he was a source of controversy until his death in 1990. By contrast, his younger brother William was generally beloved by his colleagues and became the acknowledged national spokesperson of American psychiatry until his death in 1966. Most of those who worked for and with Karl developed a love-hate relationship. Indeed, his fellow psychiatrists never elected him to the presidency of the APA (a post held by many lesser figures), largely because they feared the consequences of his unpredictable behavior. His selection as chair was thus somewhat surprising.[13]

Although the Special Committee on Reorganization operated in an open and democratic manner, it was clear that the majority of its members were sympathetic to a psychodynamic point of view. Rumors began to circulate that the Special Committee was dominated by a small group bent on seizing control of the Association. Clarence B. Farrar, the respected editor of the *American Journal of Psychiatry*, feared that the appointment of a permanent medical director—as contrasted with an elected president—created the possibility of a "dictatorship" and development of a "potential bureaucracy." The goal of reorganization, he added, was "domination by this radical sectarian group." William L. Russell, long associated with the New York Hospital, expressed the view that reorganization was "a movement towards control of the Association by the psychoanalytical group."[14]

Surprised by mounting rumors and innuendoes, the Special Committee decided to solicit opinions by polling the entire membership. Following a lackadaisical response to its questionnaire, the committee proposed an open debate at the 1946 convention, thus defusing much of the excitement. Shortly before the APA meeting in the spring of 1946, William C. Menninger and thirteen colleagues met and founded the Group for the Advancement of Psychiatry (GAP), an organization dedicated to psychodynamic principles and social activism. Its goal was not to replace the APA, but to modernize and invigorate an old association in order to make it into a vehicle for change. Controversy followed when GAP members offered their own nominations for Council on the floor of the convention, thus setting the stage for the first contested election in the APA's long history. The establishment of GAP immediately aroused fears that a minority was seeking to seize control and use the APA for its own purposes.[15]

GAP also began to issue position papers and reports that reflected its commitment to psychodynamic and social psychiatry. The specialty, its members insisted, possessed expertise that was relevant to a variety of social and economic problems. One report called into question— although it did not reject—the indiscriminate use of such somatic therapies as electroshock; another emphasized the absence of any empirical data evaluating the outcome of lobotomy. In a document delineating the social responsibility of psychiatry, GAP went on record as favoring the application of psychiatric principles to all those problems which have to do with family welfare, child rearing, child and adult education, social and economic factors which influence the community status of individuals and families, inter-group tensions, civil rights and personal liberty.

This, in a true sense, carries psychiatry out of the hospitals and clinics and into the community.[16]

More traditionally-minded members of the APA, feeling threatened by a fledgling group that seemed bent on revolutionizing an old and venerable organization, responded with scathing sarcasm. Within six months of the founding of GAP and even before that organization had begun to issue position papers, Farrar humorously proposed the formation of an alternative organization—"The Group of Unknowns in Psychiatry" (GUP). Individual members, Farrar wrote, were to be known as "Guppies." Since GUP would be "a very select outfit," members "should be required to grow long beards and wear dark green spectacles; and . . . at meetings . . . wear their coats and vests buttoned up behind." As its slogan, GUP would adopt the cry "Back to Hippocrates"—an obvious allusion to the belief that GAP and its psychoanalytic orientation was not part of medicine. One requirement for membership in GUP would be an "acceptable thesis" on a prescribed subject, including "Psychiatric Observations on the Passengers in Noah's Ark," "Group Psychotherapy during Passage in the Ark which Permitted all Passengers to Land with Sound Minds," or "The Malign Influence of Grandpopism, a Menace to the Future of the Human Race." If a candidate did not prefer "too scientific a subject, he might be let off by writing a good 'Topeka-boo story'" (an obvious allusion to the Menningers).[17] Such a humorous characterization of psychodynamic and psychoanalytic psychiatry suggested that a fundamental schism was developing with the specialty. Opponents of GAP were determined to keep psychiatry rooted within a more somatic and presumably medical tradition and were less inclined to elevate psychological and environmental phenomena to a position of paramount significance.

For several years such prominent figures as Farrar, Winfred Overholser (superintendent of Saint Elizabeths Hospital), Samuel Hamilton, and a few others enjoyed corresponding among themselves about GUP and GAP. Indeed, a "constitution" gave preferred membership status to those "who have accepted standpat dogmas." Officers of GUP included the following; a "Grand Bazooka, three Grand Trombones, a Great Dictaphone who shall keep records, and as many Grand Trumpets as there are members." Officers would be "elected casually by attrition." On a more serious note, Farrar was willing to publish GAP material in the *American Journal of Psychiatry* despite his dislike of the organization.[18]

Between 1946 and 1949 the issues raised by both reorganization and the founding of GAP became so controversial that they threatened the very unity if not the very existence of the APA. In 1947 a three-way race resulted in the election of William C. Menninger as president, and a number of other GAP members were elected to important organizational positions. The appointment of Daniel Blain (Chief of the Veterans Administration Neuropsychiatry Division) to the newly created office of Medical Director in early 1948 only added to fears that GAP was bent on imposing its ideological views on the APA.

At the convention in 1948 long-simmering differences erupted into an open clash. Opponents of GAP succeeded in persuading the Nominating Committee to recommend C. C. Burlingame, head of the Institute of Living and a strong proponent of psychosurgery, as Menninger's successor. Dexter Bullard then offered from the floor the name of George S. Stevenson, head of the NCMH. Bullard, a well-known psychoanalyst who was a staunch opponent of virtually all somatic therapies, shocked many members when he attacked Burlingame's therapeutic views on the floor of the convention. In a polarized election Stevenson won by a margin of 47 out of 731 total votes cast.[19]

The election revealed a deep division within the ranks of American psychiatrists. Perhaps the most incisive analysis came from Albert Deutsch, the knowledgeable and perceptive medical journalist whose sympathies clearly resided with GAP. There were, according to Deutsch, three divisions within the APA. The first pitted "neurologically oriented" psychiatrists who stressed somatic factors and therapies against those committed to a more psychoanalytic and psychotherapeutic approach. The second reflected a division between those who believed that psychiatrists should confine themselves to the care and treatment of the mentally ill versus those who believed that the specialty had an important role to play in social change. Finally, there was a schism between "old-line psychiatrists" and a new and more progressive group.[20] Deutsch may have overstated the case, but it was evident that the specialty was divided into two warring factions. On the one side were the heirs of institutional psychiatry committed to a somatic pathology and organic and directive therapies. On the other were those who believed that institutional psychiatry was obsolete, favored psychodynamic and psychoanalytic concepts, and endorsed community treatment and social activism.

Although both sides attempted to reconcile their differences, the mutual suspicions, hostilities, and mistrust precluded any amicable resolution. Even minor issues were elevated to major conflicts. By early 1949 opponents of GAP had formed the Committee for the Preservation of Medical Standards in Psychiatry. They urged APA members to defeat all reorganization proposals; demanded an amendment to the APA constitution mandating a mail ballot on all important issues; and urged that greater emphasis be placed on "biological investigation and study, and less emphasis on teaching a patchwork of philosophical theories that the public has already rejected as bearing the imprint of neither science nor sense." The best thing that could be said about GAP, the Committee's *Newsletter* stated in one of its early issues, "is that it was conceived on the emotional level of high school days and is reminiscent of the gappa gappa clubs."[21]

The language and allegations made by the Committee for the Preservation of Medical Standards in Psychiatry against GAP and its sympathizers came like a bolt out of the blue. The open airing of ideological and personal differences had the potential of undermining public confidence and thus discrediting a specialty that was seeking to expand its authority and jurisdiction. In the months preceding the 1949 meetings in Montreal, some leading protagonists on both sides made efforts "to prevent reports of dissension [from] reaching the press." As president of the APA William C. Menninger issued a number of moderate and low-keyed statements. The Committee on Reorganization agreed to recommend that the vote on a new constitution be deferred until mutually satisfactory changes were made. A middle group led by some senior figures undertook efforts to conciliate the warring factions. At the meetings moderation seemingly carried the day and the threat of disunity rapidly receded. GAP became an independent entity that served as an organizational vehicle for those in favor of a socially active stance. By 1954 the Committee for the Preservation of Medical Standards in Psychiatry had disappeared from the scene.[22]

In a superficial sense the transformation of GAP after 1950 and the failure of the original reorganization plan suggested that the effort to reshape American psychiatry had failed. In a deeper sense, however, William Menninger and his allies may have lost the battle, but they surely won the war. During and after the 1950s the APA, through a revamped structure and a medical director who helped provide focus and leadership, became a visible and active organization. Its agenda reflected the views of the psychodynamic and psychoanalytic figures who were rapidly assuming a dominant position. Psychodynamic psychiatrists, moreover, not only reshaped the APA, but also took control of virtually all university departments of psychiatry, thus assuring that an entire generation that matured in the 1950s and 1960s would share their views.

The significance of the conflict within American psychiatry in the immediate postwar years, however, went well beyond individual or organizational differences. Protagonists, perhaps unknowingly, were debating fundamental issues dealing with the foundations of personality and sources of behavior. On the one side were psychiatrists who were involved with institutionalized patients with severe psychoses or somatic illnesses with accompanying behavioral signs. Both their etiological concepts and therapies remained in an older somatic tradition; they rejected for the most part the claim that their specialty had particular competence to resolve broad social issues. Their psychodynamic opponents, by contrast, were more environmentally oriented; they believed that the community and society—not the mental hospital—should be the logical habitat of psychiatry. Such activists wanted to make the APA the vehicle for altering the location and manner in which mentally ill and psychologically distressed persons were treated, and also for resolving a wide variety of social problems. By the mid-1950s they had largely succeeded in breaking the hitherto inseparable links between the specialty and mental hospitals. In 1957, for example, only about 17 percent of the ten thousand or so members of the APA were employed in state mental hospitals or Veterans Administration facilities; the remainder were either in private practice or employed in government, educational agencies, community clinics, and medical schools.[23] Having created a national specialty medical organization with both visibility and influence, the new psychiatry that had grown out of the crucible of war was in a strategic position to help reshape public policies and social attitudes toward the psychologically troubled and severely mentally ill.

To alter mental health policy required that the public and their elected representatives be sensitized to the need for change. That many hospitals faced a crisis of unprecedented proportions because of nearly two decades of neglect during depression and war was obvious to those in positions of administrative authority. These officials, however, were not in a position to generate sufficient pressure for major changes. But even between 1941 and 1945—a period in which war-related concerns dominated the domestic scene—a number of states were unable to evade mounting institutional problems. New York State, for example, created a Temporary Commission on State Hospital Problems, and a subsequent outbreak of amoebic dysentery at Creedmoor State Hospital in Queens led to the immediate resignation of the Commissioner of the Department of Mental Hygiene. Others states faced equally compelling problems and created comparable investigatory commissions. "Deplorable conditions" in mental hospitals, a Macy Foundation official warned the American Hospital Association in 1946, posed a serious social threat and could result in "disaster for our patients and dynamite for the politicians."[24]

To rivet public attention on mental illnesses was a daunting task. The goal of creating a new political agenda, however, received critical assistance in the mass media from a number of journalists and others concerned with the problem. The most prominent was Albert Deutsch, a liberal crusading journalist whose early life in an impoverished Jewish immigrant household led him to identify with the poor, sick, and disabled. Although he never attended college, Deutsch was a voracious reader and a self-taught individual. His introduction to psychiatry came when he was commissioned by the NCMH to prepare a study detailing the history of the care and treatment of the mentally ill in America. Published in 1937, the book became an instant classic. In 1941 Deutsch began to write a daily column for *PM*, one of the most liberal newspapers of the time. He quickly became the preeminent medical journalist of the postwar era, earning the enmity of Morris Fishbein and the American Medical Association because of his advocacy for universal health care.[25]

Deutsch began to examine psychiatric facilities in 1944, and in 1946 and 1947 published several dozen graphic articles exposing severe deficiencies in the nation's mental hospitals. The city of Detroit, he wrote in anguished terms "pays less attention to its humans, sick in mind, than it does to its machines. I have seen animals better treated and more comfortably housed in zoos than are the mentally sick inmates of Detroit's institution, which is not even an asylum much less a hospital." What struck him above all else—

above the occasional shriek, the hysterical crying and senseless laughter, the moaning and the muttered soliloquies—was the oppressive crowding of the nervously sleeping inmates of the depressing, dirty, dim-lit wards.

Cots and beds were strewn all over the place to accommodate the 289 mental patients packed into wards intended for 126. Cots lined the corridors, with restless patients often strapped into them. (It appeared that about one-third of all patients in the psycho wards were under mechanical restraint that night—tied down to their beds by leather thongs, muffs or handcuffs linked to chains.) . . .

I had noticed, during the day, an unusually large number of women patients abed. An attendant, when I asked about this, replied that there wasn't enough clothing to go around . . . and it was necessary to keep many in bed to preserve some semblance of decency.

Deutsch's anger was not directed against the hospital's physicians or staff. The chief psychiatrist, he noted, was "humane and enlightened," and the staff "kindly and competent." But all were "struggling desperately to overcome the twin disease that affects most institutions for the mentally sick throughout the land—overcrowding and understaffing." Deutsch's portraits of dozens of other institutions were basically similar. The emotional force of his articles was strengthened by dramatic photographs that revealed tragedy and degradation. Ultimately he used his journalistic accounts as the basis for his well-received book, *The Shame of the States*, published in 1948 with a warm and supportive introduction by Karl Menninger.[26]

The Shame of the States, which received generally laudatory reviews, was intended neither to discredit mental hospitals nor impair their legitimacy. On the contrary, it was a clarion call for reform. The "Ideal State Hospital," Deutsch insisted, was an achievable dream. Such an institution would have no more than one thousand patients; it would be funded on a par with general hospitals; have a competent and well-paid staff; operate as a "therapeutic community" that utilized psychological and somatic therapies; reject mechanical restraint and have more open wards; make provision for aged patients in satellite colonies; affiliate with adjoining medical schools; and retain links with all mental hygiene agencies, including family counseling services, child guidance centers, and psychiatric wards in general hospitals. Deutsch's faith in hospital reform, however, was less than total, for he urged the creation of a parallel system of community psychiatric clinics.[27]

At about the same time, *Life* published a lengthy piece by Albert Q. Maisel entitled "Bedlam 1946." Maisel, author of several popular books on military medicine, had also played a role in instigating improvements in VA mental hospitals. His decision to publish his article in *Life* was significant, for the magazine reached an extraordinarily large and varied audience. Equally significant, it employed visual materials in imaginative ways that often had a far greater emotional impact than the accompanying text. His text and accompanying photographs compared institutions with Nazi concentration camps and found few differences. Most mental hospitals, he insisted, were "a shame and a disgrace." They were "dreary, dilapidated excuses for hospitals, costly monuments to the states' betrayal of the duty they have assumed to their most helpless wards." Yet Maisel, like Deutsch, was confident that if the public were given the facts, they would act "to put an end to concentration camps that masquerade as hospitals and . . . make cure rather than incarceration the goal." More importantly, the vivid photographs that accompanied the text undoubtedly aroused indignation among readers. The impact of *Life's* vivid feature was evident in the pages of such influential religious periodicals as *Commonweal* and *Christian Century*, each of which published editorials endorsing a reform agenda.[28]

Many of Maisel's informants were conscientious objectors from Quaker and Mennonite backgrounds who had served as mental hospital attendants as substitutes for military service. Their religious sensibilities had been shocked and offended by their experiences, and after the war they were determined to change asylum conditions. Mainstream mental health organizations kept their distance from these individuals because, as Alan Gregg of the Rockefeller Foundation observed, they were "unmanageably determined and perhaps even reckless in obtaining their objectives." These conscientious objectors formed their own organization, which in 1947 sponsored the publication of Frank L. Wright's *Out of Sight Out of Mind*, which also was a stentorian call for reform.[29]

Mike Gorman, by contrast, had no contacts with mental hospitals or psychiatrists before 1946. While serving in the army, he became enamored with Oklahoma; following his discharge he went to work for the *Daily Oklahoman*. In mid-1946 he was sent by his editor to investigate conditions at the state hospital in Norman. The assignment had a dramatic effect upon his life. His investigations catapulted him to national prominence, and between the 1950s and 1970s he became, with the financial backing of Mary Lasker, one of the most powerful mental health lobbyists of his generation.

In mid-1946 Gorman wrote a series of articles that described the sad state of Oklahoma's state hospitals and contrasted them unfavorably with such institutions as the Menninger Foundation and Colorado Psychopathic. Unlike Deutsch and Maisel, he tended to place less emphasis on institutional reform, and expressed a clear preference for early treatment in community settings. Although a planned book never materialized, Gorman published an abbreviated version under the title "Oklahoma Attacks Its Snakepits" in the widely read and influential *Reader's Digest*. His writings caught the attention of Mary Lasker, then beginning her career as the nation's most important health lobbyist, and she was probably responsible for designating him as the winner of the Lasker award in mental hygiene (formally conferred by the NCMH).[30]

Yet, the most vivid and influential portrait of mental hospitals came from the hand of Mary Jane Ward. Her famous novel, *The Snake Pit*, was published in 1946, condensed in the *Reader's Digest*, and made into a motion picture in 1948. The theme of both the novel and motion picture was simple. The heroine (played by Olivia de Haviland, who was nominated for an Academy Award) confronts a severe marital crisis. Unable to accept love from a devoted husband, she ends up in a mental hospital where the wards are akin to a snakepit. Anatole Litvak, the director, had the ward photographed from the top down, thus creating the image of a human snakepit. The theme of the movie, however, is more ambiguous. A warm and concerned psychiatrist, by employing a blend of psychotherapy and narcosynthesis, enables the patient to develop personal insights. The film (which ranked among the top five for 1949) thus depicted severe institutional defects, but at the same time conveyed a message of faith in psychodynamic and psychoanalytic psychiatry. The psychiatric reception of the book and film was highly laudatory, for Ward had placed primary responsibility for existing problems upon parsimonious governments that did not adequately support their mental hospitals.[31]

Professional groups, including the APA and GAP, added to the efforts designed to arouse a positive governmental response. The APA Council frequently issued releases emphasizing institutional deficiencies as well as "public . . . [and] legislative indifference." In 1945 it adopted a set of standards and policies for all hospitals and clinics, and three years later created the Central Inspection Board to assume the American College of Surgeon's responsibility for inspecting hospitals. GAP published several reports on the shortcomings of many public hospitals. The NCMH was also active, although its traditional emphasis on prevention made it an advocate of services for individuals not sufficiently ill so as to require hospitalization. Professional advocacy, however, played a distinctly subordinate role, if only because of the suspicion that self-interest was involved.[32]

The impact of the exposés of institutional defects—printed and visual—was substantial. To be sure, most of the figures involved (with the possible exception of Deutsch) were better at portraying problems than offering concrete and workable solutions. But if prescriptions for the future were vague, the cumulative effect of their work was to give mental health a more prominent position on the political agenda. In the two decades that followed the end of war, all levels of government were forced to confront—as they had not in the preceding decades—the issue of how best to care for and treat their severely and chronically mentally ill citizens.

———————

The experiences of war, the reorganization of American psychiatry, and the exposés of severe institutional deficiencies, however important, were but preconditions for change. Yet major structural impediments remained. Traditionally the care and treatment of the mentally ill was the responsibility of state governments. A century and a half earlier the authors of the Constitution had recognized their countrymen's fear of centralized power by limiting federal authority. The divided nature of the American constitutional system in turn placed seemingly insuperable obstacles in the way of those who wanted to deal with social problems on a regional or national basis. One alternative was to create a coalition to persuade state legislatures and governors of the necessity for new policy initiatives. In individual states such a strategy proved successful. In the postwar years the Menninger brothers played decisive roles in Kansas because of their charismatic personalities and national visibility. By cultivating close relationships with state and federal officials, they made the Menninger Foundation a potent force for change.[33] But what was possible in Kansas was not easily emulated in other states. Generally speaking, the diversity within and between states made it difficult to pursue a strategy of change that relied on forty-eight governments.

A more plausible alternative was to expand the role of the federal government, which hitherto had been remote from the mental health arena. The prospects for such a development were mixed. The U.S. Public Health Service's Division of Mental Hygiene, created in 1930, dealt only with narcotic addiction. And an effort by Lawrence C. Kolb, the Division's head, in the late 1930s to persuade Congress to establish a National Neuropsychiatric Institute modeled somewhat after the National Cancer Institute (established by law in 1937) failed when war-related concerns quickly overwhelmed domestic issues. Nevertheless, as a result of the New Deal and World War II the scope of federal authority had dramatically broadened. The recruitment of scientists and intellectuals to deal with major policy issues, moreover, had strengthened the conviction that national problems required national solutions. At the same time, hereditarian thinking, identified with the horrors of Nazism, fell into disrepute, and environmental ideologies conducive to social activism gained in popularity.[34]

At the end of the war conditions appeared propitious for dramatic changes in the nation's entire health care system. By then the Public Health Service under Thomas Parran had laid the foundations for a major extramural research program in the National Institute of Health. The passage of the Hill-Burton Act in 1946, which provided generous subsidies for hospital construction, was another symbol of an expanded federal role. Moreover, the emergence of a major lobby promoting massive federal support for biomedical research ensured that the agenda for health policy changes would increasingly be centered in Washington. The overwhelming faith in medical science was reflected in President Harry S. Truman's Scientific Research Board, which not only reaffirmed faith in medical progress, but insisted on the necessity of a "national policy."[35]

After 1945 the nation's health care system underwent major changes as a result of three developments: new federal initiatives, the development of third-party health insurance, and a commitment to medical technology and specialization. Within such a context it was not surprising that an effort would be made to assure that the benefits of new policies would be distributed to the mentally ill. Moreover, the growing preoccupation with chronic illness—as compared with the older concern with acute infectious diseases—seemed to move the general health care system closer to the mental health system, which had always been involved with severe and persistent psychiatric illnesses.

More than any other individual, Robert H. Felix played the key role in ending the long-standing tradition of federal passiveness in mental health policy. Trained at the University of Colorado, he had been influenced by both Franklin G. Ebaugh (a proponent of psychiatric wards in general hospitals[36]), and his early experiences in a problem-plagued mental hospital. After joining the Public Health Service, he studied at Johns Hopkins and became familiar with the public health approach to mental illnesses. Felix was also a master of bureaucratic and organizational politics. Possessed of a charismatic, gregarious, humorous, and outgoing personality, he cultivated close relationships with key congressional figures—relationships that were only strengthened by his willingness to provided them with psychiatric assistance in coping with mentally ill relatives.

Toward the end of the war Felix succeeded Kolb as head of the Division of Mental Hygiene and immediately set out to create a new federal bureaucratic structure that would alter the entrenched tradition of state responsibility and employ the prestige and resources of the national government to redirect policy. He began by drafting legislation in late 1944 that provided for the creation of a National Neuropsychiatric Institute whose functions included but were not limited to the support of research. Mary E. Switzer (a federal official who played a key role in federal rehabilitation policies) and Mary Lasker (a layperson with considerable resources who had just launched a career that would make her, along with Florence Mahoney, major figures in the emerging biomedical lobby) provided indispensable assistance in moving the project along. Felix also enlisted the aid of Representative J. Percy Priest, an obscure Tennessee congressman interested in mental illnesses, and subsequently received further assistance from Senator Claude Pepper, a leading New Deal Democrat. Although denying that he was lobbying (and perhaps violating the provisions of the Hatch Act), Felix orchestrated the movement of the bill through Congress.

Priest and Pepper each presided over House and Senate subcommittees that held public hearings. The purpose was not to investigate the problems posed by mental illnesses, but rather to mobilize support for the then radical concept that the federal government could be a significant participant in mental health policy. A number of prominent figures appeared before both subcommittees. Major General Louis B. Hershey, the director of the Selective Service System, described high rates of rejections for military service because of neuropsychiatric problems. Surgeon General Parran emphasized that "mental diseases equal all physical diseases in subtracting from the total vigor, the total fitness of our population," and that half of all hospital beds were occupied by psychiatric patients. Despite this situation, psychiatry remained a marginal and understaffed specialty, and expenditures for research on mental disorders were inconsequential. William C. Menninger and others stressed the applicability of the lessons of war to civilian society. Francis Braceland (chief of the Navy's Neuropsychiatric Branch) emphasized the need for broad preventive programs. "In the same manner in which medicine has overcome such diseases as lockjaw and smallpox by prophylaxis," he observed, "psychiatry can do likewise by providing information and a public understanding which will prevent much unnecessary unhappiness."[37]

Both congressional subcommittees were sympathetic toward the legislation. Concern with health care was pervasive at the time, and there seemed little reason to exclude mental illnesses from impending federal initiatives. A tone of deference pervaded the hearings, and there was virtually no disposition to probe or challenge claims made by psychiatrists. Only Senator Robert H. Taft and Congressman Clarence J. Brown raised questions about federal funding, but they were assured that the intent of the legislation would exclude support for patient care and treatment in state institutions. After favorable reports by both committees, the bill moved easily through both houses. Support by such conservative Republicans as Taft and Brown depoliticized the proceedings, and following the reconciliation of minor differences the legislation passed Congress by overwhelming votes and was signed into law by President Truman on July 3, 1946.[38]

The National Mental Health Act incorporated three basic goals: first, to support research relating to the cause, diagnosis, and treatment of psychiatric disorders; second, to train mental health personnel by providing individual fellowships and institutional grants; and third, to award grants to states to assist in the establishment of clinics and treatment centers and to fund demonstration studies dealing with the prevention, diagnosis, and treatment of neuropsychiatric disorders. The Act provided for the creation of a National Mental Health Advisory Council to provide advice and to recommend grants, and also established the National Institute of Mental Health with an intramural research program. The initial authorization was modest; $30 million per annum for state programs and research, and $7.5 million for a physical plant for the NIMH. Although the act was silent on the use of federal funds for institutional care and treatment, Felix insisted that such expenditures were forbidden, and his interpretation prevailed.[39]

The significance of the National Mental Health Act, however, lay not in its specific provisions, but rather in its general goals and the manner in which they were implemented. The breadth and generalities of its provisions posed more a vision of the future than a specific agenda or policy. Indeed, the Act was largely the creation of Felix; its passage helped to create an organized mental health lobby that played an important role in subsequent policy deliberations. Federal policy was thus shaped not only by legislation and appropriations, but by the outlook of officials responsible for creating and administering programs as well as by sympathetic allies.

No individual played a more prominent role than Felix, who led the NIMH from its formal creation in 1949 until his retirement from federal service a decade and a half later. His political sagacity, charismatic and outgoing personality, congressional ties, and ability to define agendas made him the most effective and influential figure in the mental health arena during the postwar decades. Adroitly employing his authority and influence, he and his agency played key roles in redirecting mental health policy.[40]

Mental disorders, Felix proclaimed, represented "a true public health problem," the resolution of which required more knowledge about the etiology and nature of mental diseases, more effective methods of prevention and treatment, and better trained personnel. Public health was concerned with the "collective health" of the community, he argued. Unlike clinicians who dealt with individuals, public health workers emphasized "the application and development of methods of mass approach to health problems," including mental disorders. The NIMH's mental health program was designed "to help the individual by helping the community; to make mental health a part of the community's total health program, to the end that all individuals will have greater assurance of an emotionally and physically healthy and satisfying life for themselves and their families."[41] Such an approach implied that the role of psychiatry was not limited to the treatment of the severe and chronic mental disorders, but included assistance to individuals and groups that enabled them to achieve a happier and more satisfying life. The boundaries of psychiatry, therefore, included all of human society.

From the beginning Felix demonstrated his mastery of seemingly minor concerns. A case in point involved the placement of the NIMH within the Public Health Service. Beneath what appeared to be a strictly organizational problem lay more substantive issues. Organizational location, after all, could play a crucial role in shaping the function and significance of the Institute. One likely alternative was to attach the NIMH to the Bureau of State Services, which administered the Hill-Burton Act that provided federal funding for the construction of general hospitals throughout the nation. The obvious effect would have been to make the NIMH a service-oriented agency whose function was to process and disburse federal funds. Placement within the Bureau of State Services hardly meshed with Felix's more ambitious agenda. Instead he persuaded the Surgeon General to place the NIMH within the National Institutes of Health, thus linking his organization with other research-oriented entities such as the National Cancer Institute. This decision proved of considerable importance; it enabled the NIMH to exploit the extraordinarily favorable congressional sentiment in the 1950s that led to higher and higher appropriations each year. That the NIMH (unlike other institutes) was indirectly funding services as well as research and training was largely ignored outside of the Public Health Service. Indeed, funding for demonstration clinics was rationalized by placing it under the rubric of research. Consequently, Felix was able to exploit the identification of mental health with biomedical science during the 1950s.[42]

In the three years following the passage of the National Mental Health Act, Felix and his associates began to create an organizational structure that culminated with the formal establishment of the NIMH in the spring of 1949 (although operations were under way as early as 1947). In its early days the NIMH had several components, including Professional Services, Publications and Reports, and Biometrics. The Professional Services Branch dealt with long-range program planning and advised other departments. Biometrics was responsible for data gathering and analysis, and in 1947 it took over the task of compiling mental hospital data from the Bureau of the Census, which had begun annual surveys in 1923. Slowly but surely the responsibilities of the Biometrics Branch grew in scope and sophistication as quantitative analysis became a distinguishing characteristic of the social sciences. Publications and Reports was charged with the dissemination of information about mental illness and its prevention. Three extramural branches (Research, Community Services, and Training) were responsible for implementing the grants programs (which ultimately accounted for more than three-quarters of the total NIMH annual appropriation). The National Advisory Mental Health Council, composed of external medical, scientific, and lay members, had responsibility for developing policy proposals and reviewing and recommending support of research and training grants. Finally, the NIMH developed a relatively small but significant intramural research program.[43]

Organizational structures are merely skeletons, even though particular forms may help to shape certain kinds of policies. More significant are the strategy, tactics, and ideology of the individuals who staff and administer the organization. The NIMH is a case in point of an organization whose activities to a large extent were shaped by its leadership. This is not to imply that legislation, federal executive policies, or appropriations played minor roles, for such was not the case. It is only to insist that policy cannot be understood without reference to strong-minded leaders determined to push policy in particular directions.

The innovative aspects of the NIMH policy under Felix took several forms: assistance to state governments; the inclusion of the behavioral sciences and nonmedical mental health professionals in mental health activities; and the awarding of research grants in the field of mental health. The National Mental Health Act of 1946 had included provision for grants-in-aid to states to assist them in establishing and improving their mental health services. Each state was asked to designate a mental health authority to prepare a plan detailing how federal funds would be used and to maintain liaison with the NIMH. By 1947 every state and territory had acted: thirty-two designated their health department; the remainder selected departments of welfare, institutions, mental hygiene, or some other agency. The Community Services Branch of the NIMH in turn sent representatives to meet with each state mental health authority, thus beginning the process of creating a sympathetic national constituency that only enhanced the growing significance of this federal agency.

Although federal funds could be used for a variety of purposes, it was evident that NIMH officials were determined to use their resources to persuade states to develop additions, if not alternatives, to traditional mental hospitals. In effect, the policy of the leaders of the NIMH was to broaden dramatically the scope of mental health services, thus implicitly diminishing the central position occupied by the severely and chronically mentally ill under the older institutional policy. Community institutions assumed a more important position. They became the institutional embodiment of the continuum and psychodynamic model of mental illnesses, which presumed that early diagnosis and treatment of mental disorders and personal problems in a community setting would obviate the need for subsequent institutionalization. The ultimate goal of federal officials was to make available services for a broad range of individuals: emotionally disturbed children, adults not in need of hospitalization, and patients in the early stages of mental illness when prospects for cure appeared greatest. In addition, clinics would provide follow-up treatment of institutionalized patients on furlough, supervise boarded-out cases, and assume responsibility for mental health education in their respective communities. Although appropriations remained modest, the program's impact was substantial.[44]

During the 1950s community-oriented and preventive programs existed in virtually every state, and some states even began to enact legislation providing matching funds to local communities to establish outpatient mental health clinics. Moreover, state matching funds far outpaced federal allocations; by 1954 states were voluntarily providing $2.70 for each federal dollar (as compared with the fifty cents required under federal regulations). When the NIMH conducted its first survey of outpatient psychiatric clinics in the mid-1950s, it found nearly 1,300 in existence. Of these, 277 were associated with state hospitals and 500 others were operated or subsidized by states.[45] State officials in general were enthusiastic about clinics. The claim that early identification and treatment in outpatient community facilities would minimize the need for institutionalization was attractive to public officials who were faced with constant increases in the size of the hospitalized population. In its efforts to assist states in developing community programs, the NIMH also established a few demonstration clinics.

The establishment of community clinics was also accompanied by the development of close relationships between the NIMH and mental health professionals employed in community institutions. In the late 1940s the NIMH began to cultivate close relationships with such individuals by providing advice and assistance. By 1950 it had ten regional offices with seventeen mental health consultants in psychiatry, clinical psychology, psychiatric social work, and mental health nursing. The result was the appearance of a new professional constituency with links to the national government as well as to state officials. In subsequent decades its members would contribute to the effort to shift mental health services from traditional state hospitals to community institutions by drawing on the seemingly inexhaustible resources of the federal government. Indeed, the rapid expansion in the number of nonmedical mental health professionals further strengthened community activities, since many of them were not employed in traditional mental hospitals. The result, noted the National Advisory Mental Health Council in 1954, involved divisions "between agencies administering institutions and those conducting community programs." Although their regional consultants remained neutral, it was evident that the NIMH policies had the potential for fostering friction between community institutions and state hospitals, if only because the former had a higher priority than the latter.[46]

The NIMH was committed to the development of new and innovative community programs. The agency, nevertheless, devoted relatively little attention to program evaluation; claims of accomplishments and program effectiveness were rarely, if ever, accompanied by supporting empirical data. As early as 1950 the National Advisory Mental Health Council received from one of its committees a recommendation that funds be allocated to investigate methods and encourage research "for determining the effectiveness of community mental health programs." Guidelines and information about the kind of training required for community mental health personnel were all but nonexistent. By 1955 the members of the Council expressed concern over "the vagueness surrounding the whole problem of community mental health, the unclearness surrounding the function and role of the personnel working in this area, and the kinds of preparation these people needed." A study by one subcommittee came to the conclusion that mental health evaluation was "necessarily difficult." A "baffling" problem, noted its members, "is how to ascertain the validity of results in the face of elusive variables, both known and unknown, which either influence results or present themselves for their relatedness with undue emphasis." After a survey of the literature, they conceded that there was a "thinness of the efforts at evaluation . . . [and] a confusion of levels of conceptualization."[47]

The inattention paid to evaluation of community programs was but a reflection of the rhetoric that was characteristic not only of psychiatry, but of medicine in general in the postwar era. Like other professionals, psychiatrists were prone to exaggerate their ability to resolve difficult problems. Yet claims of professional omniscience were enthusiastically accepted by both elected government officials and a larger public, all of whom shared a pervasive faith that the conquest of disease was within reach.

Besides laying the foundations for a community system, the NIMH also played an important role in furthering behavioral and social science research on mental health. To be sure, before World War II members from these disciplines had published important studies. Nevertheless, the NIMH, for understandable reasons, proved to be a potent catalyst. In the late 1940s and 1950s the barriers that impeded fundamental biological research into the etiology and physiology of the mental illnesses were formidable. It is entirely possible, after all, to identify significant problems that are not yet at an appropriate stage for study because of the inability to meet specific prerequisites (e.g., lack of a specific technology). This generalization was particularly applicable to psychiatry in the immediate postwar years. Unlike infectious diseases (a classification based on etiology rather than symptomatology), psychiatric diagnostic categories remained for the most part descriptive in character. Symptomatic descriptions, however, were often protean, vague, and shifting, a fact that complicated efforts to design or undertake basic biological or physiological research. The category of schizophrenia, for example, was generally defined in terms of an inability to relate to the external world or to other human beings. The symptoms—depending on the form— were equally broad, and there were a variety of operational definitions that employed different criteria. Theoretical explanations of schizophrenia were equally varied: some emphasized genetic factors; others focused on environmental or chemical determinants; and some attributed the disease to certain forms of interpersonal and familial relationships. The inability to agree on the very definition of schizophrenia made biological research a formidable and extraordinarily difficult undertaking.

Yet in many ways the psychiatric categories of these years resembled the medical categories of the previous century. Lacking any other basis for classification, mid-nineteenth century physicians had expended much energy in an often futile effort to distinguish between various "fevers" (e.g., scarlet fever, yellow fever, rheumatic fever, typhoid fever, etc.). Not until the development of modern bacteriology in the late nineteenth century made possible a shift to an etiologically based classification system did some of the confusion dissipate. To compare psychiatric with earlier medical classifications is not to imply that psychiatry was "backward." It is only to state that the problems of undertaking research on the mental illnesses were extraordinarily complex because of the inability to relate pathology with behavior. General medicine, interestingly enough, faced similar kinds of problems when its focus shifted from infectious to chronic and degenerative diseases where knowledge of specific etiological elements was minimal.[48]

Behavioral and to a lesser extent social science research on the mental illnesses (which emphasized broad social, cultural, and demographic elements) did not face, at least superficially, the same kinds of barriers as biological research. Moreover, by the 1940s such disciplines as psychology and sociology claimed to have amassed significant data and derived explanatory theories relevant to the study of normal and abnormal behavior in both individual and social settings. Psychodynamic psychiatrists were sympathetic to these related disciplines that emphasized the social and cultural elements that presumably shaped behavior. As clinicians, however, they had relatively little training in evaluating such factors, and were even less prepared to judge the efficacy of therapeutic interventions or preventive activities in any kind of systematic or scientific manner. At that time psychiatric training (not unlike medical training) included little or no attention to research design, controlled studies, or statistical methods, all of which played a major role in behavioral and social science training. The conclusion seemed inescapable; research on the mental illnesses had to involve a multidisciplinary effort.

The broad and innovative nature of the NIMH was illustrated in its extramural programs, which involved allocation of funds for training and research. By the end of World War II, there was a clear recognition that if psychiatry was to play a more prominent and effective role, there would have to be a dramatic increase in the number of qualified medical and nonmedical mental health personnel. In the hearings preceding passage of the National Mental Health Act, as well as in annual testimony before congressional appropriation committees, Felix and other prominent leaders reiterated over and over again their belief in the necessity of increasing both the quality and quantity of mental health personnel. Congress proved extraordinarily sympathetic, and slowly but surely funding for training increased.

From the very outset Felix and others, both within and without NIMH, insisted that funds be used to further both interdisciplinary and psychodynamically oriented training. A Subcommittee on Integrative Training, appointed in late 1947 and chaired by John C. Whitehorn of

Johns Hopkins, recommended that training programs emphasize the necessity for close collaboration between psychiatrists, clinical psychologists, psychiatric social workers, and psychiatric nurses (irrespective of the setting where treatment was provided). Since psychiatrists "had to carry the ultimate responsibility," it followed that their training had to involve the development of collaborative skills. Felix was supportive of such recommendations. Indeed, he wanted to ensure that "the concept of extramural psychiatry, or to term it better, preventive psychiatry . . . be pushed energetically," and that funding be employed to produce a corps of well-trained psychiatrists to work in medical schools that lacked qualified faculty.[49] Such a program would ensure that new psychiatric concepts would be disseminated among future practitioners.

There is little doubt that training grants furthered some of the broader goals of the NIMH. The bulk of trainees, irrespective of disciplinary affiliation, elected not to work in traditional mental hospital settings. The data on initial employment following completion of training—though admittedly incomplete—suggests as much. Between 1948 and 1951, 27 percent of the NIMH trainees from psychiatry, neurology, and public health mental hygiene entered teaching and 33 percent were employed in psychiatric clinics; the remainder were in government employment or private practice. As time passed more and more psychiatrists elected to enter private practice. By the 1960s, about half had chosen this option. Similar patterns persisted in clinical psychology, psychiatric social work, and psychiatric nursing. Employment in mental hospitals was clearly not a preferred choice. Following passage of the National Mental Health Act, therefore, federal funds helped to train an entire generation of mental health professionals whose career interests and activities lay outside of mental hospitals.[50] The implications of this development were of major significance; it strengthened the resolve of those who were determined to shift policy away from traditional mental institutions.

Following passage of the landmark legislation of 1946, the role and activities of the federal government slowly but surely expanded. In its early years the NIMH budget grew at a slow pace. When it came into formal existence in 1949, its appropriation was nine million dollars; six years later it had only reached 14 million. From this point on, however, the rise was dramatic. By 1959 its appropriation was 50 million, and within five years had tripled to 189 million.

Curiously enough, neither the executive nor legislative branch played a decisive role in shaping policy, although budgetary recommendations and appropriations set boundaries and limitations. The key figures instead were Felix and his associates. As the director of the NIMH, Felix developed close contacts with important congressional leaders concerned with health-related issues. Year after year he appeared before congressional committees, and his testimony implied that rapid progress was being made in understanding the etiology of the mental disorders and developing effective therapies. Rarely was his testimony challenged or subjected to careful scrutiny. As laypersons, legislators were not inclined to probe the extent to which the validity of claims could be substantiated by empirical data. Felix's enthusiasm at times proved disconcerting even to such close colleagues as Morton Kramer, the head of the NIMH Biometrics Branch. Under Felix, the NIMH became an important component of the biomedical lobby that was so successful in persuading the federal government and the American people that the key to health and longevity lay in the discovery and application of new scientific knowledge. Indeed, the most important contribution of the NIMH was its role in helping to legitimate the importance of psychiatric and psychological services and to develop support for community-based mental health policies. In this sense Felix and his agency symbolized the faith of that era in the ability of medical science to uncover the etiology of disease and to develop effective interventions. The development of antibiotics had seemingly rendered innocuous bacterial infections. Why then could not comparable therapies be found for other chronic and degenerative diseases, given an appropriate investment in clinical facilities and research?

The political sagacity of Felix and his staff only added to their influence. In public they assumed a neutral stance, and rarely criticized or offended those with whom they disagreed. They were particularly adept in building a variety of constituencies. NIMH's support for training brought into the mental health professions thousands of sympathetic supporters; funding of demonstration clinics and research enhanced its influence and visibility; and its message to the American people was one of hope and optimism. The organization was also cognizant of the value of public relations. By the early 1950s the Publications and Reports Section actively disseminated materials among the general public, press, radio, and television.[51]

The influence of the federal initiative, of course, can easily be exaggerated. By the 1950s, as a matter of fact, the expansion of health services was largely consumer-driven. To many Americans physical and psychological health appeared within reach, and support for an expansion of funding and services became all but irresistible. A favorable environment, therefore, provided the foundation for a remarkable expansion of funding for both research and services, and the leadership of the NIMH was quick to exploit the situation.

Because of its national character, the NIMH was in a strategic position to promote alternatives to the prevailing institutional policy. The possibility that severely and chronically mentally ill persons might not benefit from new community institutions offering services to a broad clientele was never seriously considered. Nor were those who administered state hospital systems in a position to challenge the NIMH policies and officials. The latter had a national forum and access to a sympathetic Congress; the former were responsible to forty-eight jurisdictions. Under such circumstances it was not surprising that responsibility for mental health policy slowly began to tilt from state capitals to Washington.

––––––––

During the 1940s the foundation for innovative policies for the care and treatment of the mentally ill slowly took shape. Wartime experiences had helped to create a model that emphasized the superiority of community-based over mental hospital systems. Moreover, substantial numbers of young physicians had been recruited into psychiatry and trained in psychodynamic concepts during the war. After 1945 they began to transform their specialty. A series of exposés of conditions in mental hospitals reinforced the belief that new approaches were both necessary and inevitable. With the passage of the National Mental Health Act of 1946, the federal government became the obvious vehicle to promote change. Postwar optimism reinforced the belief that science and technology—which had contributed heavily to the war effort—could be mobilized to deal with social and medical problems as well.

Yet beneath the heady atmosphere of these years lurked unresolved issues. To be sure, there had been impressive advances in science, medicine, and technology. Antibiotics had reduced the risk from bacterial infectious diseases, and surgical techniques had become increasingly sophisticated. Whether therapies for chronic and degenerative diseases could be developed remained an open question. Similarly, the belief that community care and treatment of the severely and chronically mentally ill was effective had yet to be tested. Despite lingering questions, there was a pervasive faith that American society stood on the threshold of a new era that would end the segregation of the mentally ill in remote custodial institutions, bring them the benefits of psychiatric advances, and integrate them into the mainstream of community life.

9

The Foundations of Change in Postwar America

During the 1940s the foundation for fundamental changes in the care and treatment of the mentally ill was laid. Yet the factors that created expectations of a brighter future—the triumph of psychodynamic and psychoanalytic psychiatry, the lessons drawn from wartime experiences, the exposés of institutional shortcomings, the entry of the federal government into the mental health arena—were but a beginning. The remaining task was to translate ideals, visions, and aspirations into concrete policies and programs.

The initial step came with the development and introduction of a series of innovative therapies. During the 1950s these new therapies created a sense of euphoria among psychiatrists not unlike the optimism that had accompanied early nineteenth-century moral treatment. The simultaneous development of the psychotropic drugs and milieu therapy—in addition to electroshock, psychosurgery, and psychotherapy—seemed to hold out the promise that severely mentally ill institutionalized patients, with appropriate treatment, might be able to be released and live in the community. Moreover, these new therapies also weakened the traditional distinction between psychological and biological interventions. To be sure, biological therapies embodied the orientation of institutional psychiatry. Psychologically oriented therapies, in contrast, were associated with psychodynamic practitioners, many of whom tended to be concentrated in medical schools and in private and community practice. The line of demarcation between the two groups, however, blurred, and the ensuing eclecticism reinforced a belief that those internal differences that had threatened the unity of psychiatry were fast disappearing.

Psychotherapy became one of the most widely acclaimed interventions of the postwar era. The concept of psychotherapy, of course, was not of recent origin, but wartime experiences seemed to confirm its efficacy in dealing with stress-related symptoms. Whether or not such experiences were an analogue for its deployment in noncombat situations or with other kinds of patients—particularly the seriously and chronically mentally ill—was problematical. Moreover, there was neither agreement on the method and technique of psychotherapy nor data confirming its effectiveness. Nevertheless, psychotherapy was offered by a wide range of professional groups: psychiatrists, nonpsychiatric physicians, irregular practitioners such as chiropractors and naturopaths, clinical psychologists, social workers, marriage counselors, rehabilitation and vocational counselors, parole officers, and clergymen, among others. Its popularity grew out of a fortuitous combination of circumstances: the rise of private and community practice in psychiatry; the general receptivity toward psychological explanations; an economic prosperity that created a middle-class clientele able to pay for and eager to use psychological services; seemingly favorable clinical results; and the general popularization of Freudian theories. Although psychotherapy was widely used in a few select private institutions—notably at the Menninger Foundation and Chestnut Lodge in Maryland[1]—it was more often employed in the treatment of noninstitutionalized psychoneurotic individuals capable of functioning independently. "The pattern of psychotherapeutic practice in America," wrote Jerome D. Frank, an eminent psychiatrist at Johns Hopkins, "is seriously imbalanced in that too many of the ablest, most experienced psychiatrists spend most of their time with patients who need them least." Affluent and well-educated persons were the most numerous candidates for psychotherapy, whereas "lower class, seriously ill patients" received the least attention even though they constituted "by far the greater challenge."[2] Psychotherapy was at best of marginal use for institutionalized seriously disordered patients.

Despite its popularity, psychotherapy, noted APA president Leo Bartemeier in 1952, was "a rather vague concept." Jules H. Masserman, a distinguished psychoanalyst and psychiatrist, even suggested that it was little more than a defense mechanism that sheltered human beings from "harsh reality." In a tongue-in-cheek lecture on "The Psychosomatic Profile of an Ingrown Toe Nail," he expressed his disdain for the popularization of psychotherapy. The toenail, he told an audience of internists,

> is the most protuberant part of the body, hard and rounded; in locomotion it describes a most suggestive to-and-fro movement—obviously, then, it is a basic penile symbol displaced, for a change, downward. But let us also remember the anatomic origin of this important little phallus, namely the *nail-bed* . . . a region consummately feminine in its conformation, physiology, and import. . . . But now consider what happens when this normal functioning is disrupted by frustration and conflict: when, specifically, the erect nail is stubbed and traumatized, or is too long opposed by unyielding reality in the form of a repressive shoe. Clinically and perhaps personally we know the effects all too well: the nail, particularly at the peripheral portions of its individuality (or more technically, its "ego boundaries") turns about and digs its way back into the flesh of its origin.

Masserman was chagrined when he was congratulated for his "clinical and analytic perspicacity" for illuminating "the etiology and possible therapy of that hitherto unexplored psychosomatic disorder—onychocryptosis, or ingrown toenail." Nor were doubts absent among psychologists. At the Conference on Graduate Education in Clinical Psychology in 1949 one participant offered a facetious but revealing comment: "Psychotherapy is an undefined technique applied to unspecified problems with unpredictable outcome. For this technique we recommend rigorous training." The protean nature of the term was evident in its myriad forms, which included brief, depth, multiple, social, and group psychotherapy.[3]

Such humorous characterizations notwithstanding, psychotherapy presented formidable intellectual and philosophical problems. At its most fundamental level it involved complex human relationships that could not be easily disaggregated into smaller and presumably more manageable components. It was possible to describe such emotions as love and hate in purely physiological terms (e.g., blood pressure), but to do so in all probability vitiated, if not destroyed, their holistic meaning. Equally significant, psychotherapy brought together a subject and a therapist, and their interaction introduced a new variable. Psychotherapy, therefore, involved more than technique. To distinguish between its different forms and to measure their respective effectiveness posed a difficult, if not insoluble, challenge.

The psychodynamic orientation of the specialty, however, aroused interest in other forms of environmental therapies capable of being applied in institutional settings. Of these, "milieu therapy" (or therapeutic community) had the greatest potential to alter the lives of patients in mental hospitals. Milieu therapy had much in common with early nineteenth-century moral treatment, namely, the belief that the environment of the asylum could assist in the treatment of mentally ill persons and thus facilitate their release into the community. The origins of milieu therapy, however, were secular rather than moral or religious. The concept of the therapeutic community had part of its roots in psychodynamic psychiatry, which emphasized an environmental etiology. An equally significant contribution came from the social and behavioral sciences, which had traditionally been preoccupied with the role and function of institutions and the mediating influence of culture and social structure on personality.

The idea that the mental hospital could act as a therapeutic community was given concrete meaning by Maxwell Jones, a British psychiatrist who had worked with psychologically impaired servicemen and repatriated prisoners of war. After the war Jones created a specialized unit within a traditional mental hospital in which staff and patients held daily meetings. The result was the creation of a "therapeutic culture"; patients gained insights about themselves and psychiatrists were taught to speak the patient's language. It was possible, Jones reported in an influential volume that spelled out his experiences, "to change social attitudes in relatively desocialized patients with severe character disorders, provided they are treated together in a therapeutic community." The work of Jones and his colleagues fostered an awareness of the impact of the hospital environment on individual patients and the possibility of employing the hospital community "as an active force in treatment."[4]

Even as Jones was popularizing the therapeutic community concept, multidisciplinary teams in the United States were already analyzing the mental hospital as a social system and the implications for care and treatment. Many of the studies represented collaborative efforts between psychiatrists familiar with the behavior and outlook of patients, and social and behavioral scientists sensitive to the complexities of social organization and personality structure, and better trained in research design and methodology. An early postwar investigation by a psychiatrist and sociologist, for example, found that staff-patient relationships in a traditional mental hospital created an institutional culture that only aggravated the "existing personality conflicts" of inmates.[5]

During the 1950s multidisciplinary team efforts resulted in the publication of a series of influential studies that popularized the concept of the therapeutic community. Alfred H. Stanton and Morris S. Schwartz found that patient-staff interaction shaped outcomes, and that an authoritarian hospital structure was incompatible with a therapeutic environment. The implication was clear; mental hospitals had to be more democratically structured and patients had to take an active role in organizing their lives. Similarly, Milton Greenblatt and his colleagues emphasized that traditional biological and psychological treatments together with "the therapeutic use of the social environment" made possible the return of "a large proportion" of hospitalized patients "to the community within a relatively brief period." Other studies seemed to confirm these optimistic findings. "One of brightest stars in the social psychiatric firmament," Robert N. Rapoport wrote in 1960,

> is the "therapeutic community" idea. According to this approach, the hospital is not seen as a place where patients are classified and stored, nor a place where one group of individuals (the medical staff) gives treatment to another group of individuals (the patients) according to the model of general medical hospitals; but as a place which is organized as a community in which everyone is expected to make some contribution towards the shared goals of creating a social organization that will have healing properties.[6]

Whatever its specifics, it is clear that the concept of the therapeutic community rested on two beliefs. First, that authoritarian hospitals fostered dependency and reinforced the pathological symptoms characteristic of mental disorders. Second, that active patient participation in the therapeutic process had beneficial outcomes. The faith in the therapeutic community idea in many ways reflected the post World War II proclivity to interpret social reality in terms of a perennial struggle of democracy and freedom on the one hand (the United States and its allies) and authoritarianism on the other (the Soviet Union). The former was identified with responsible and mature behavior; the latter with apathy and dependency.

Those who advocated milieu therapy were cognizant of the fact that their efforts would be in vain if discharged patients were stigmatized and rejected when returned to the communities from which they came.

They therefore moved to blur still further the distinction between hospital and community by creating the open-door hospital—an institution that abolished locked doors and fences. Moreover, they believed that psychiatric services had to be integrated along an unbroken continuum to ease the release of patients. They experimented therefore with the day hospital where patients returned to their homes in the evening as well as with the night hospital. In effect, these novel institutional forms represented the fusion of the concept of community care with the principles of milieu therapy.[7]

Psychodynamic and environmental therapies represented the cutting edge of postwar psychiatry. Yet biological interventions never disappeared entirely. Indeed, the eclectic character of the specialty ensured that any therapy would be assimilated into the psychiatric armamentarium if there was evidence of efficacy. Boston Psychopathic Hospital (affiliated with the prestigious Harvard Medical School) was an example of such eclecticism. In the postwar years it sponsored a large lobotomy project while simultaneously pioneering the development of milieu therapy. The presumption was that the inseparable unity of mind and matter made possible both biological and psychological approaches.

The most striking therapeutic development of the 1950s was the introduction of the psychotropic drugs, which made it possible to modify and to alleviate the symptoms associated with schizophrenia, manic-depressive psychosis, and other severe disorders. As late as 1945 it would have been impossible to predict the development of such drugs. Yet the discovery that chlorpromazine (CPZ)—the first of the psychoactive drugs—had therapeutic qualities was not the product of serendipity or pure accident, even though fortuitous circumstances played a large part. Louis Pasteur's famous observation that "chance favors the prepared mind" perhaps more accurately describes the events that inaugurated a new era in psychiatric therapy.[8]

In attempting to apply the tools of organic chemistry to the synthetic dye industry in the late nineteenth century, German scientists had synthesized phenothiazine in 1883 (the parent compound of CPZ). After 1900 an entirely separate line of inquiry centered on the pharmacological actions of histamine, which, when administered intravenously to anesthetized animals, caused vasodilatation (or widening of the systemic arterioles) and a steep decline in systemic blood pressure. The action of histamine resembled anaphylactic shock—the often severe and occasionally fatal reaction of an organism to a foreign substance (e.g., wasp venom or penicillin). During the 1930s a number of scientists were working on synthetic antihistamines, which they believed might have potential use in managing surgical trauma. Clinical interest in trauma was further stimulated by the experiences in dealing with battlefield casualties during World War II. By 1949 Henri Laborit had found that promethazine induced a "euphoric quietude" in surgical patients. When CPZ was synthesized a year later in the French laboratory of Rhone-Poulenc, a decision followed to launch a broad clinical study of its possible therapeutic effects.[9]

Initially French scientists believed that CPZ might have broad applications in surgery, obstetrics, neurology, dermatology, and might even modify the hyperactive behavior of maniacal patients. In 1951 clinical testing expanded rapidly, and included a variety of patients with neuropsychiatric symptoms. The following year two French psychiatrists published the results of their clinical trials at a Parisian mental hospital. CPZ, they reported, not only calmed excited states, but had a direct and positive impact on a variety of mental disorders. Indeed, CPZ even "brought about a transformation of the atmosphere of the locked wards and definitively relegated the old means of restraint."[10]

Between 1952 and 1954 Smith Kline and French, under license from Rhone-Poulenc, began extensive laboratory and clinical evaluations before marketing CPZ under the name Thorazine. The initial reception of the new drug in the United States was cautious and restrained, an understandable response by psychiatrists committed to psychodynamic concepts. Early results, however, suggested that Thorazine had dramatic beneficial consequences, especially upon schizophrenic patients resistant to all other treatments. At about the same time, a second class of "tranquilizers"—the rauwolfia alkaloids (or reserpine, which was marketed as Serpasil by Ciba Pharmaceutical) entered practice, and they were followed by the development of such antidepressants as iproniazid and imipramine. In the succeeding decade dozens of new drugs were developed. As a result, such dramatic and irreversible treatments as psychosurgery—a procedure intended to diminish symptomatology—virtually disappeared from psychiatric practice. The simultaneous development of milieu and drug therapies also helped to blur further the traditional schism between biological and psychodynamic psychiatry, and thus appeared to anticipate the reintegration of psychiatry into medicine.[11]

Taken as a group, these drugs appeared to be the harbinger of a new era in psychiatry. Yet an element of caution was present, and most psychiatrists were realistic in their appraisal of the efficacy of the new drugs. They recognized that unanswered questions persisted about the precise pharmacological effects, risks of long-term usage, and potential adverse side effects. The APA was also concerned about their indiscriminate use and about the casual application of the new drugs to alleviate "the routine tensions of everyday living." On the whole, the reception of the new drugs was favorable. As Winfred Overholser noted, CPZ improved the behavior and outlook of severely ill patients, "revolutionized" the atmosphere of disturbed wards, improved staff morale, gave the hospital an entirely new character, and created optimism among family members.[12]

The development of psychoactive drugs brought into prominence the thorny issue of evaluation. Few of the mental hospitals that tested drugs did so with any degree of methodological sophistication; they failed to use control groups or to distinguish between the characteristics of different kinds of patients. Larger aggregate studies of release rates suffered from comparable shortcomings. Morton Kramer, head of the NIMH Biometrics Branch, was particularly concerned with the quality of many of the efficacy studies. Yet the preoccupation with the miracle antibiotic drugs of the postwar decades had raised expectations about drug therapy in general; the result was to increase consumer demand. Indeed, Mike Gorman, the most important mental health lobbyist of these years, was extremely critical of psychiatric caution. In a public address in 1957, he openly excoriated Felix and described Kramer's work on drug evaluation as "drivel." Deutsch, in turn, was critical of Gorman's excessive zeal, and called attention to past therapies—insulin, metrazol, electroshock, and lobotomy—each of which had been initially heralded as a new miracle, but which in time revealed its limitations. The NIMH moved slowly, largely because of the concern of Felix and other staff members that any evaluation study be undertaken with care and discrimination. Its Psychopharmacology Service Center was unable to begin a careful collaborative effort involving nine institutions until 1961. The results, although not published until 1964, affirmed the effectiveness of the newer phenothiazines and their importance for treating acute schizophrenic psychoses and preventing chronic disability.[13]

By the close of the 1950s therapeutic optimism reigned supreme on the psychiatric scene. Biological psychiatrists could take satisfaction from the efficacy of drug therapy; their psychodynamic counterparts could envisage the deployment of psychological, psychosocial, and environmental therapies with hitherto chronic and intractable patients. For many the specialty of psychiatry seemed poised to cross a threshold on which it had been standing for more than a century and to bring the benefits of new therapies to large numbers of severely and chronically mentally disordered persons who had previously been confined in custodial asylums for extended lengths of time. Such spectacular therapeutic innovations also suggested the outlines of a new public policy. Drug therapy would make hitherto isolated and withdrawn patients amenable to milieu therapy; a more humane and effective institutional environment would facilitate the recovery of patients and their subsequent release into the community; and an extensive network of local services would assist such individuals to reintegrate themselves into society and oversee their varied psychiatric, social, and economic needs in the community.

Psychiatric optimism was accompanied by hopeful policy innovations at both the state and local levels. In the years following the end of World War II, governors and other state officials expressed a determination to upgrade their badly deteriorated mental hospital system. A report in 1950 by the Council of State Governments (an organization representing the nation's governors) urged the rebuilding of public mental hospitals and the construction of facilities that would alleviate overcrowding and meet the needs of alcoholics, drug addicts, sex deviants, and children. Cognizant of the interest in community care and treatment, the study also recommended an expansion of clinics and aftercare programs.[14]

The Council's report received the firm backing of the nation's governors, most of whom supported the rebuilding of their mental hospital systems. But they also accepted the claims of mental health professionals that community and preventive programs had the potential to reduce the seemingly ever-increasing need for long-term institutional care. Hence during the 1950s states pursued two distinct but related strategies; the improvement of mental hospitals and expansion of community services. The presumption was that an effective system required both kinds of facilities.[15]

Public mental hospitals benefited from the generally favorable disposition to improve the care of the mentally ill during the 1950s. Large bond issues provided substantial funding for capital construction and renovation. Even in the South—a region whose poverty had caused it to lag behind in all social welfare responsibilities—mental health became an important priority. The effort to improve institutional care and treatment also received assistance from the APA. Its Central Inspection Board provided a yardstick by which states could evaluate the quality and effectiveness of their hospitals. The annual Mental Hospital Institutes sponsored by the Association offered hospital officials an opportunity to become familiar with recent developments in psychiatric care and treatment. The APA also provided direct assistance to states by sponsoring comprehensive surveys. Upon receiving a gubernatorial invitation, the APA created a broadly based committee that prepared an extensive report evaluating institutional efficacy, identifying needs, and providing specific recommendations.[16]

Slowly but surely the quality of patient care in mental hospitals improved. During World War II the patient-employee ratio had worsened, rising from 5.7 to 1 to 6.8 to 1. After the war it improved dramatically, and within a decade had fallen to 3.8 to 1. Similarly, average per capita expenditures for patient maintenance rose 284 percent between 1946 and 1960 (even if adjusted for inflation the increase was still a substantial 153.5 percent). To be sure, there were sharp variations. Kansas, which ranked first, had a patient-staff ratio of 2.1 to 1 and an average per capita expenditure of $2,840 in 1955; Tennessee, ranked last, had a 6.9 to 1 ratio and spent only $562.[17]

Despite the substantial progress evident in these figures, the improvement in the quality of institutional care was often overlooked by both the public and mental health professionals. A reason perhaps was that a high proportion of aged patients (in 1958 about a third were sixty-five years or older) reinforced the prevailing image of the mental institution as a chronic-care hospital from which there was no exit. Even the APA—despite its efforts on behalf of mental hospitals—tended to be removed from them and associated with noninstitutional programs and policies—a direct reflection of the composition of its psychodynamically oriented membership. In his APA presidential address in 1958, Harry C. Solomon described the large mental hospital as "antiquated, outmoded, and rapidly becoming obsolete," thus ignoring the improvements made during the preceding decade. Angered by Solomon's remarks, Robert Hunt, director of a New York state hospital, insisted that the APA had not played a constructive role in countering the negative attributes of "the state hospital stereotype." The majority of APA members had neither knowledge about nor contacts with hospitalized patients, and hence accepted prevailing stereotypes. "No serious young professional knowing only this stereotype is willing to acquire or practice his skills in a state hospital setting if he can possibly get anything else."[18]

Hunt's observations about the growing isolation of hospital psychiatrists was accurate but incomplete. To be sure, most psychiatrists rationalized their rejection of a career in mental hospitals by employing professional rhetoric that emphasized a commitment to treatment and a rejection of caring responsibilities. In making such a choice, they had, perhaps unconsciously, embraced a particular concept of medical science that made objective knowledge and biological reductionism its defining elements. The older and more traditional concept, by contrast, had been based on a holistic definition of disease that made sympathy and care central elements of medical practice. By the late nineteenth century objectivity had come to be identified as a masculine attribute and sympathy and care as feminine qualities. The psychiatric rejection of an older tradition that emphasized care, therefore, reflected in part the stratification of occupations along gender lines and the ensuing devaluation of careers that were identified as female in nature.[19]

The rebuilding of the public hospital system was accompanied by an expansion in community services, which prior to 1940 tended to be limited to a small number of child guidance clinics created under the auspices of the Commonwealth Fund and the NCMH. The initial impetus to provide other noninstitutional alternatives came initially from the federal government. The National Mental Health Act of 1946 provided modest grants to states to establish outpatient facilities that would offer mental health services in the community. In addition, the Hill-Burton Act, passed that same year, provided substantial federal funds for general hospital expansion, which ultimately facilitated the admission of psychiatric patients. Within fifteen years more than 15 percent of all patient care episodes* were treated in general hospital psychiatric units. The availability of psychiatric services in general hospitals was fueled by several interrelated developments: the movement of psychiatrists into

---

*The *term patient care episode* represents the sum of two numbers: resident hospitalized patients at the beginning of the year or those on the active role of outpatient clinics; and admissions during the year. The first is an unduplicated account; the second includes duplications, since some individuals had multiple admissions.

private practice; their need to use some sort of hospital facilities for their patients; and the growth of third-party health insurance.[20]

Faith in the effectiveness of community programs and institutions was characteristic of the postwar years. Psychological and environmental explanations of normal and abnormal behavior strengthened the belief that early intervention could prevent the onset of serious mental illnesses and thus prevent hospitalization. Albert Deutsch, a figure whose journalistic writings captured the essence of the postwar psychiatric scene with remarkable acumen, often emphasized that "many emotional disorders have their origin in early childhood" or grow out of family and marital problems. Thus a modest investment in outpatient facilities would diminish the far higher costs of institutionalization. Similarly, the Milbank Memorial Fund—a foundation long active in health affairs since its formal creation in 1918—sponsored a series of important conferences during the 1950s that attempted to translate psychodynamic concepts into community programs. Bringing together virtually every important figure from psychiatry and the academic world, these conferences served to stimulate interest in a community oriented policy, which assumed the community's ability to care for the mentally ill and its responsibility to do so. They provided as well a forum for a new kind of psychiatric epidemiology whose goal was the study of the incidence and prevalence of mental disorders in the community and the isolation of a range of socioenvironmental variables. Epidemiological findings would presumably enhance the ability to predict who was at risk and to specify environmental factors that promoted or retarded the onset of serious symptoms, thus creating the possibility of early intervention in the community.[21]

During the 1950s the rhetoric and enthusiasm for community-oriented programs far exceeded any specific achievements. Rhetoric and expectations, nevertheless, fueled the desire for innovations. Once again New York—whose hospitals cared for about a fifth of the nation's entire institutionalized population and whose officials were eager to act—was a catalyst for change. To be sure, Governor Thomas E. Dewey was initially reluctant to commit additional resources for community programs. Nevertheless, a rising mental hospital budget and an annual average increase of three thousand new resident patients led him to support a new approach. In early 1954 the Community Mental Health Services Act became law. Under its provisions any county or city with fifty thousand or more residents was empowered to create a local mental health board, which, in turn, appointed a psychiatrist as director. Four services were eligible for reimbursement: outpatient psychiatric clinics, inpatient general hospital psychiatric services, psychiatric rehabilitation for those suffering from mental disorders, and consultant and educational services. Half of all expenditures incurred by local governments were eligible for state reimbursement up to a maximum of one dollar per resident per year.

The New York law rested on the presumption that serious and persistent mental illnesses could be prevented by early intervention in the community. But the protean nature of the concept of prevention and lack of a clearly defined target population proved troublesome. The State Department of Mental Hygiene (which had responsibility for implementing the act's provisions) decided to define a mental health service by the kind of professional providing the service. This decision, however, did not provide for links between community services and mental hospitals, nor did it identify any particular target population. Such problems notwithstanding, the law had an immediate impact. The overwhelming majority of counties and urban areas elected to participate; by 1958–1959 state subsidies totaled nearly $11 million.[22]

The experiences of California somewhat paralleled those of New York. Under Governor Earl Warren interest in community programs increased in the late 1940s, and the introduction of the new psychotropic drugs acted as a further catalyst. In mid-1957 the legislature passed the Short-Doyle Act. It provided that the costs of local mental health services would be shared equally between the state and participating counties. Under this and subsequent acts California slowly shifted the focus of state policy away from institutional care and treatment. In 1959 the state appropriated $69 million for hospitals and $1.6 million for community services; within a decade the figures were $112 and $23.9 million, respectively. The relationship between Short-Doyle and changes in mental hospital populations, however, was less than clear. Those under treatment at Short-Doyle facilities came from higher socioeconomic groups and had less serious mental disorders. Moreover, the decline of state hospital resident populations between 1959 and 1966 from 37,592 to 26,567 did not necessarily occur because of the establishment of local clinics. Indeed, during this same period mental hospital admissions increased from 20,015 to 25,300.[23]

New York and California were by no means alone in seeking to shift the focus from hospital to community care, treatment, and prevention;

other states acted in similar ways. Even in states that did not follow suit, officials, accepting the claim that untreated mental disorders led to more serious mental illnesses, began to place greater emphasis on preventive programs. During the 1950s, therefore, outpatient clinics and mental hygiene services in schools, courts, and social agencies grew rapidly. In 1954 there were 1,234 clinics; five years later there had been a 16 percent increase. Regional differences admittedly persisted. The highest concentration of clinics was in the Northeast and North Central states; the lowest was in the South; local mental health services were also more prevalent in urban than rural areas. Nevertheless, there was a growing consensus on the importance of outpatient and community services.[24]

In the 1950s the concept of prevention and the belief in the superiority of community care and treatment found a receptive audience among political, professional, and lay audiences. That these beliefs rested on somewhat tenuous foundations did not go completely unnoticed. Deutsch, for example, was critical of many mental health advocates for expending their zeal "in promoting ambiguous and often fleeting concepts about 'mental health,' along with confusing and mutually contradictory theories unsupported by solid scientific knowledge." The result was "a virtual abandonment of mental hospital patients."[25]

Rhetoric, as a matter of fact, often overwhelmed data. In the mid-1950s, for example, a group of California researchers undertook a study of the effectiveness of hospital and clinic treatment for comparable psychiatric patients. From a sample of mental hospital admissions, they screened 504 patients in the hope that half could be referred to clinics. But they could identify only fifty-seven as candidates for clinic referral. Of this number, twenty were referred and six were accepted, of whom only two kept appointments and improved. The study concluded that there were "marked discontinuities in functions" of hospitals and clinics. Those who required an extensive social support network were not candidates for clinics, which provided no assistance in finding living quarters or employment. In another classic epidemiological study some years later, Benjamin Pasamanick and associates began with three groups: a hospital control group; a placebo home care group; and a home care group provided with drug therapy. They found a clear advantage for the latter. But Pasamanick noted that psychiatrists in private practice emphasized psychotherapy for nonpsychotic patients, and hence paid little attention to the severely and chronically mentally ill. The greatest need was for supportive, continuous, coordinated, and comprehensive services for the severely and persistently mentally ill. Yet he noted that most of these services were absent despite the theoretical commitment to community care and treatment.[26]

The triumph of psychodynamic and social psychiatry and the shift from institutional to community practice, however welcomed, inadvertently began to alter professional boundaries and set the stage for a rapid expansion of such mental health occupations as clinical psychology, psychiatric social work, and psychiatric nursing. This development fueled the proliferation and growth of services offered by these mental health professionals to individuals and groups who believed that personal problems could be alleviated by professional intervention. At the same time the multiplicity of training and outlook enhanced the potential of professional intergroup conflict. Occupational growth had another unanticipated consequence. The expansion of the pool of qualified personnel increased the range of services to a broader clientele. However, the recruitment of new kinds of clients tended to distract from the traditional focus on the severely and persistently mentally ill, the very group that posed the greatest problem to themselves, their families, and the community.

The growth in the mental health professions was given impetus by World War II. Psychologists, for example, found that the exigencies of war created new opportunities for practical and applied services. They assisted in the mobilization and training of military personnel, prepared propaganda and motivational materials, conducted research on human adaptability, and developed standardized diagnostic and evaluation tools. The American Psychological Association, hitherto the representative of academic psychologists, underwent a significant postwar reorganization (not unlike that of the APA) that recognized the growing significance of clinical and applied psychologists. The relative shortage of trained psychiatrists and presence of thousands of neuropsychiatric cases among war returning servicemen, moreover, led the Veterans Administration to create joint doctoral training programs with a number of universities in order to increase dramatically the number of clinical psychologists and thus alleviate professional staff shortages. The cumulative impact of the increasing numbers of trained psychologists and their enhanced responsibilities in VA hospitals, outpatient and other public facilities, and the private sector all hastened the development of a self-conscious and confident specialty ready and eager to provide services. The popularity of psychological explanations of human behavior during these years only enhanced the public image of psychology.

Psychiatrists recognized that the growth of clinical psychology offered benefits as well as risks. They were aware that psychologists were better trained in testing, research design and statistical analysis, vocational and educational counseling, speech and group therapy, and hence were willing to integrate these functions into a team effort. The assertion by psychologists that they were qualified to offer individual psychotherapy, on the other hand, was a quite different matter, and set the stage for decades of protracted conflict. Even GAP—whose members tended to be politically liberal, socially active, and supportive of multidisciplinary collaboration—believed that clinical psychologists could offer psychotherapy only under the supervision of a psychiatrist—a position similar to that taken by the APA. In an address before the American Psychological Association, William C. Menninger—who had supported clinical psychology in the military during the war—emphasized that certain kinds of clinical knowledge were "prerequisites to carrying on psychotherapy," and that psychiatrists had to be the "chief teachers" of psychologists. Psychiatrists, he added, had to be the "quarterback of a team that works together"—a position that reaffirmed psychiatric leadership.[27]

Legal issues tended to exacerbate intergroup tensions. In the postwar years psychologists pushed for the passage of state certification and even licensing laws. Such efforts did not necessarily grow out of jealousy of or rivalry with psychiatry. On the contrary, psychologists were eager to exclude quacks, charlatans, and others ostensibly lacking appropriate training. The potential market for services was large and expanding, and psychologists, like many other groups, hoped to meet existing needs. Bureaucratic and organizational imperatives promoted the concept of adjustment, while cultural norms incorporated a preoccupation with the self.

Although psychiatrists were not opposed to certification by the American Board of Examiners in Professional Psychology, they had more reservations about formal statutory licensing, and conflict in the political arena was common. Both the APA and the American Psychological Association attempted to resolve differences through private negotiations, but the former's insistence that psychotherapy was "a form of medical treatment" posed a formidable obstacle. Indeed, the APA position, noted the executive secretary of the American Psychological Association, left psychology with only two alternatives, namely, "to submit quietly to the medical profession" or "to oppose openly and vigorously . . . the move to establish medical hegemony over the field of mental health."[28]

During the 1950s and 1960s continued negotiations between the two associations failed to resolve jurisdictional issues. In the end psychiatrists found it virtually impossible to maintain hegemonic control over psychotherapy and certain other mental health services (excluding medication). Curiously enough, the rhetoric, countercharges, and claims of both groups were conducted in a partial intellectual vacuum. The debate over psychotherapy was largely symbolic. Neither psychiatrists nor psychologists had ever defined its distinctive attributes or justified their claims to overarching competence. Many groups, as a matter of fact—medical and nonmedical—were providing psychotherapeutic services to troubled individuals. Above all, there were virtually no adequate evaluations of efficacy, and those that existed generally violated most principles of research design. Neither group considered the possibility of submitting their respective claims to disinterested parties; to do so would be to call into question the very foundations of professional authority and autonomy. A profession that permitted its claims to be adjudicated, William J. Goode observed, "would be comparable to a nation permitting a world court to adjudicate its right to existence." The failure to engage in meaningful evaluation, however, was hardly surprising. An emerging profession, added Goode, "typically survives by faith, not by proof of works." His observation caught the essence of the dispute. Differences could not be resolved by reference to empirical data, if only because the struggle had all the attributes of a confrontation between two religious groups, each persuaded that it had a monopoly on eternal truth and virtue.[29]

Unlike clinical psychology, relationships between psychiatry and such nonmedical mental health professions as psychiatric social work and psychiatric nursing were, at least outwardly, relatively tranquil. This is not in any way to suggest that social workers and nurses did not harbor resentments, for such was not the case. But whatever their underlying feelings, they did not directly challenge psychiatric authority by seeking to create an autonomous sphere through legislation. Moreover, the fact that neither required a doctoral degree tended to minimize friction; they stood to gain, as a matter of fact, from their membership on

the "psychiatric team." Finally, social work and nursing were traditionally female professions whose members did not at that time challenge
the more male-dominated specialty of psychiatry.

Psychiatric social work was a case in point. During the war social
workers in the military accepted such traditional tasks as taking case histories and assisting servicemen in utilizing available services. The shortages of psychiatric services even gave them expanded therapeutic
opportunities. Nevertheless, social workers never questioned the necessity for psychiatric supervision. Indeed, casework—the defining characteristic of social work—was impregnated with the language and insights
of psychodynamic and psychoanalytic psychiatry. Though concerned
with creating a separate identity within the mental health system, psychiatric social workers met with little success. Casework in a hospital
or clinic setting was hardly a firm foundation for the creation of professional autonomy, and its intellectual foundations were unclear and shifted continuously between psychological and sociological extremes.
Moreover, the M.S. was the terminal degree, and training in research
and research methods was absent. Consequently, social work offered little or no threat to psychiatry. On the contrary, its members had much to
gain and little to lose by its identification with a medical specialty.[30]

The growth and elaboration of the various mental health specialties
after World War II had mixed results. Troubled but functional individuals undoubtedly benefited from the expansion of community-based therapeutic services. The severely mentally and chronically mentally ill, on
the other hand, gained far less. Perhaps the major benefit to them
derived from the growing sensitivity to the importance of the internal
institutional environment, which in turn contributed to efforts to elevate
the quality of the nursing and attendant staff. Overall, the search for professional self-identity and the internecine struggle among some of the
mental health specialties were often irrelevant to severely and persistently mentally ill persons, most of whom required comprehensive and
continuous care. In this sense, therefore, the debate over boundaries
reflected the internal concerns of professional groups rather than the
interests of hospitalized patients.

The pace of change in the decade following the end of the war, however rapid, seemed cumbersome and slow to those involved with mental
health issues. The decentralized nature of the American political system

meant that the struggle to transform public policy had to be fought in each individual state. Under these circumstances a unified campaign was extraordinarily difficult. The experiences of the New Deal, World War II, the passage of the National Mental Health Act of 1946, and the growing federal role in health and welfare suggested an alternative strategy, namely, to transfer a large share of responsibility for mental health policy from the states to the federal government. The advantages were obvious. The federal government had far greater financial resources, and its leaders had easy access to professional elites. The existence of a powerful and flourishing biomedical lobby with close congressional ties and public receptivity toward psychological explanations and services, augured well for the creation of a national, as contrasted with a state, agenda.

In 1953 Kenneth E. Appel, then APA president and professor of psychiatry at the University of Pennsylvania School of Medicine, proposed "a sociological study of the breakdown crisis in the administration of state mental hospital functions," and subsequently expressed concern about the intrusion of politics in mental health policy. "Planning on a nationwide, long-term scale is essential," he remarked in 1954. Appel's words found a receptive audience, and in early 1955 psychiatrists representing the APA and AMA met to discuss concrete steps. There was strong sentiment in favor of establishing a joint commission with two overriding objectives: first, to inventory all resources and methods employed in the diagnosis, care, and treatment of the mentally ill and mentally retarded; and second, to formulate "a *feasible program*" of improvement. There was agreement that the commission should be sponsored by the APA and AMA rather than the federal government (although financial assistance from a grant-making agency would be desirable).[31]

Shortly thereafter a drive was launched to secure federal approval and support. Representative J. Percy Priest, the sponsor of the National Mental Health Act, and Senator Lister Hill arranged for congressional hearings in their respective chambers. The goal was not to mobilize Congress, which during the 1950s was extraordinarily receptive to health-related initiatives. The objective was rather to focus public attention on mental health problems, and thus to strengthen the case for an enhanced federal role. In late July the Mental Health Study Act passed the Congress and was signed into law by President Dwight D. Eisenhower. Under its provisions the Joint Commission on Mental Illness and

Health (JCMIH), although a nongovernmental body, received the endorsement of the federal government and was deemed eligible for a modest level of funding.[32]

The structure of the JCMIH was designed both to insure medical dominance and to mobilize a wide constituency. Thirty-six organizations ultimately joined, and Jack R. Ewalt, then Commissioner of Mental Health in Massachusetts, was selected as director. Yet its creation was but a modest beginning. Much remained to be done, including the recruitment of a staff and, most importantly, defining goals and adopting a plan of action. Given diverse and often competing beliefs, ideologies, and interests, it was clear that the forging of an acceptable consensus was not an easy task. At some of the early planning sessions differences emerged. There was general agreement that national planning was required. But on many substantive questions differences existed. Should the Commission focus on the problems of the severely and persistently mentally ill, or should it emphasize prevention and the promotion of mental health? Was it possible to study mental illness without an explicit concept of mental health? If the mental illnesses were to be the primary target of the investigation, what specific issues merited analysis? What kinds of studies were feasible, in light of the imprecision of psychiatric etiology and nosology? Given the temporary nature of the Commission, how could its members be expected to provide answers to problems that had resisted solutions for decades if not centuries? Above all, were there significant and important questions that could not even be answered because of the lack of knowledge or the absence of appropriate technologies?

The official goals, adopted formally in September 1955, were rhetorical in character and global in scope. First, to study mental illness and health and the various "medical, psychological, social, economic, cultural and other factors that relate to etiology." Second, to discover, develop, and apply appropriate methods for the diagnosis, treatment, care, and rehabilitation of the mentally ill and mentally retarded.[33] Third, to evaluate and to improve the recruitment and training of personnel. Fourth, to conduct a national survey and to develop a comprehensive program. Finally, to issue a report on its deliberations.[34]

Ewalt and his colleagues began their work with a commitment to psychodynamic concepts and the continuum theory. Individuals were subject to health-promoting and illness-producing elements that led to effective, borderline, and ineffective "bio-psycho-social functioning."

The study of these categories, they averred hopefully, would illuminate those causal factors—including "family, community institutions, cultural values, and peer and reference group relationships"—that molded personality. To be sure, a "biological substratum of organic and chemical factors" underlay human behavior. Nevertheless, the barriers that impeded research into physiological mechanisms at that time were so formidable that they directed their inquiry toward the study of social and environmental factors, thus becoming largely a social and behavioral science operation.[35]

Ewalt and his staff initially decided to sponsor a series of studies that would serve as the basis for a final report. By mid-1957 they had commissioned a number of individuals to investigate a variety of topics: mental health personnel; patterns of patient care; the role of schools in the production of mental health; community resources in mental health; epidemiology; research; popular attitudes; economics; and concepts of mental health. The original blueprint included other topics, but an inability to raise sufficient funds forced Ewalt to curtail the number of commissioned studies.[36]

The selection of topics mirrored a basic ambivalence within the JCMIH. "By far the larger part of our total study," Ewalt observed in 1956, "will concern itself, inescapably, with the mentally ill who need definitive care in a psychiatrist's office, a mental health clinic or a mental hospital, private or public." Yet this statement concealed an inner ambiguity, for it rested on the undemonstrated presumption that individuals utilizing community clinics or private practitioners were similar to the patients found in mental hospitals. By resting their inquiry on the continuum model of mental illness and mental health, the Commission vacillated between two kinds of policies. The first was concerned with the needs of the seriously and persistently mentally ill; the second with the delivery of services to a broader clientele in the hope that early identification and treatment would prevent a progression toward more serious mental disorders.[37]

In the end the Commission sponsored ten individual studies, nine of which were published.[38] Their cumulative impact was striking. Most of the authors shared the belief that the pervasiveness of psychological and environmental stress mandated an expansion of therapeutic services in both institutions and communities; that early interventions would prevent the onset of more serious disorders; that the efficacy of social and psychological therapies was a matter of fact rather than an object of study; and that a concerted attack on the prevalence of psychological disturbances and mental illnesses required the creation of a broad-based coalition of professional and lay groups. Most significant—though little understood at the time—the reports tended to blur the distinction between individuals experiencing personal problems and those who were severely and persistently mentally ill. In ensuing years, the focus shifted inexorably from the latter to the former. This is not to imply that the JCMIH deliberately downplayed or ignored the mentally ill. It is only to suggest that the consequences of its activities were sometimes at variance with its original goals.

Not all members of the JCMIH embraced the views embodied in the reports. Walter E. Barton—a prominent psychiatrist who also played an important role within the APA—was particularly dismayed at the omission of any biochemical or biopsychiatric elements in Marie Jahoda's work on concepts of mental health. He was even more critical of Morris and Charlotte Schwartz's Task Force on Patterns of Patient Care for asserting that mental illnesses were not illnesses but social disorders, and that physicians had no business treating them. Together with M. Ralph Kaufman, he filed a dissent that began with a list of mental disorders of somatic origin. Many psychoses, they wrote,

> frequently require management in a mental hospital. The chronically ill may require prolonged care. Research offers hope that additional disorders, now classified as functional, may be understood and more effectively treated. . . .
>
> The authors of the volume attack the assumption that psychoses are illnesses and occur in persons called sick . . . [and] challenge the assumption that the physician is the appropriate individual to carry out treatment of the psychotic. Presumably the writers were not thinking of psychoses in the broad context of patients who require hospital care, when they suggested that milieu therapy was the principal tool effective in changing social behavior. It might be easier to teach psychiatrists the social dynamics necessary for group work than it would be [to] teach social scientists the medical knowledge essential to total treatment of hospitalized patients.
>
> We recognize the desirability of experimentation by social scientists in a more active therapeutic role to test in the field their belief that they can cure more patients than have those with a medical clinical orientation. We know of no proof that social scientists have been more effective than psychiatrists in curing mental disease.[39]

By the summer of 1960 the final report of the Joint Commission—
Action for Mental Health—was largely complete. It was not released to
federal and state officials or the general public until the following
March. The delay was probably the result of a calculated political judgment. Specifically, there was some sentiment that the Eisenhower
administration would not be overly sympathetic to the far-reaching recommendations and fiscal implications of the report. The hope of a more
receptive administration was realized when John F. Kennedy defeated
Richard M. Nixon in the election. The release of the report was probably timed to coincide with the inauguration of a president whose youth
and vision seemed to inspire many individuals and groups seeking basic
changes in some of the nation's social policies.[40]

Written in lay rather than medical or technical language, *Action for
Mental Health* portrayed the shortcomings of the mental health system
while emphasizing its potentialities. Mental health programs admittedly lagged behind programs for individuals suffering from other acute
and chronic diseases. The problem, therefore, revolved around "the
unmet need—those who are untreated and inadequately cared for."
Therapeutic failures were not responsible; the prognosis for treated
functional psychoses was considerably better than that of many forms
of malignancies. The lag in providing services, the report insisted, was
rather due to the failure to recognize psychological illness as illness.
Moreover, the often bizarre behavior of mentally ill persons aroused
hostility rather than sympathy. Unlike other illnesses, madness shattered
the bonds that defined humanity and isolated the mentally ill as a group.
Consequently, state mental hospitals, founded to provide therapy, often
became dumping grounds for individuals outside the pale of normal
society.[41]

Nearly half of *Action for Mental Health* was devoted to a summary of
the ten commissioned studies, which—taken as a group—provided evidence that negative attitudes could be overcome. The report, however,
evaded some significant differences. The basic objective of the Joint
Commission was to develop a program to meet the "individual needs of
the mentally ill people of America." Yet most of the studies had clouded
the distinction between the seriously and persistently mentally ill, on
the one hand, and psychologically troubled individuals, on the other
hand; they implied a redirection of policy and shifting of funding patterns to accommodate the needs of the latter. The JCMIH's report tend-

ed to gloss if not vacillate over the implications of such a shift. It criticized the mental hygiene movement for diverting attention "from the
core problem of major mental illness" by emphasizing "primary prevention" (eliminating the causes of disease) and instead endorsed "secondary prevention" (early treatment to ward off more serious illness).
But the document also emphasized the need "to provide every person
with the chance to develop a personality or character of sufficient
strength to cope with the stresses life imposes upon him, or, to provide
those persons who find the stress too great with the benefits of proper
diagnosis, adequate treatment, and rehabilitation."[42]

After identifying basic issues and problems, Action for Mental Health
offered a comprehensive national program that included four distinct
but interrelated elements. First, it called for much larger investments
in basic research, venture and risk capital to support individuals and
concepts; an expansion in the educational and research activities of the
NIMH; and federal support for geographically dispersed research centers. Moreover, research had to be eclectic and deal with biological, psychological, and social factors. Effective policies, after all, required that
"the large gaps in our scientific knowledge about the fundamentals of
mental illness and mental health" be diminished.[43]

Second, Action for Mental health proposed a series of recommendations relating to personnel and services. A national recruitment and
training program and "a broad liberal philosophy" of treatment would
both alleviate staff shortages and minimize jurisdictional conflict. Nevertheless, somatic interventions required medical training, whereas psychoanalysis and "depth psychotherapy" could be provided by
physicians, psychologists, or others with appropriate training. Nonmedical mental health workers, if qualified, could offer short-term psychotherapy "under the auspices of recognized mental health agencies."
Moreover, existing needs could be met if teachers, clergy, social workers, family physicians, nurses, and others assumed the role of mental
health counselors.[44]

In dealing with services, the JCMIH offered a program that grew out
of postwar mental health ideology. Acutely ill patients required access to
emergency care and treatment in general and mental hospitals as well as
community clinics. Community clinics in particular occupied a crucial
position because of their ability to reduce the need for prolonged and
repeated hospitalization. Hence the report recommended one clinic for
each 50,000 of population. General hospital psychiatric units and

regional psychiatric treatment centers (limited to no more than 1,000 acutely ill patients) would supplement community clinics.[45]

The logic of the report also led to a radical and controversial recommendation, namely, that no state mental hospital with more than 1,000 beds be constructed, and that existing institutions with more than 1,000 beds "be gradually and progressively converted into centers for the long-term and combined care of chronic diseases, including mental illness." Such institutions would require fewer psychiatrists and more nurses, occupational therapists, and attendants to work with patients and "create a stimulating day-to-day life for the patient." The Commission also insisted that aftercare and rehabilitation be integrated with all other services in order to limit the need for either hospitalization or rehospitalization.[46]

Third, *Action for Mental Health* identified a need to disseminate information about mental illnesses among the public. The goal was to reduce stigmatization and the presence of a pervasive defeatism that impeded the deployment of effective therapies. The need to modify attitudes and beliefs was equally applicable to psychiatry. Professional legitimacy rested on public trust, which could be threatened if the specialty overvalued, overreached, and oversold itself and assumed "attitudes of omniscience or superiority."[47]

Having sketched out a broad national program, the Joint Commission faced its final and most sensitive task, namely, to estimate costs and to suggest how funds would be raised. The issue, it insisted, was not economic but moral. It quoted Rashi Fein, author of the study dealing with the economics of mental illness. Fein had openly asked the question, "What *can* society afford to spend on mental illness?" His answer was succinct.

> An economy can afford to spend whatever it desires to spend. All that is necessary in order to spend more on one thing is that we spend less on something else. . . .
>
> What society can spend (and ultimately what society should spend) depends on the value system that society holds to. It is obvious that society *can* spend much more on mental illness (or an anything) than it presently is doing. Whether or not it chooses to do so is another question.

What was required, according to *Action for Mental Health*, was a doubling of expenditures for public mental patients services in five years and a tripling in ten. Such an investment could only be met by a massive increase in federal funding. The Commission proposed a gradual yearly increase in the federal share; at the end of ten years the national government would pay for 58 percent of all mental health expenditures, states and localities 33 and 8 per cent, respectively, "*We believe*," the report concluded, "*that the time is at hand and their courage is such that modern legislators may make history by adopting a new policy of action for mental health.*"[48]

———————

By the close of the 1950s the foundation for a new policy appeared to have been laid. The introduction of the psychotropic drugs and rediscovery of milieu therapy held out the hope that large numbers of mentally ill persons might be able to live more or less normal lives in the community. Slowly but surely states moved away from their longstanding reliance on hospitals and began to explore community alternatives. The time seemed ripe for the adoption of radical new policies. Indeed, the press release accompanying *Action for Mental Health* embodied a perhaps exaggerated but not entirely unrealistic feeling when it suggested that the Joint Commission's recommendations, if enacted into law, would "revolutionize public care of persons with major mental illness—the nearly 1,000,000 patients who pass through State hospitals and community mental health clinics each year."[49] The stage was now set for a fundamental policy debate that would ultimately have a profound impact upon the lives of hundreds of thousands of mentally ill persons.

10

The New Frontier and the Promise
of Community Mental Health

When *Action for Mental Health* was released to the public in early 1961, the political climate for the introduction of major changes in mental health policy seemed extraordinarily favorable. The inauguration of John F. Kennedy had given the White House an energetic, youthful, and activist image. Change came even more rapidly under Lyndon B. Johnson, whose Great Society agenda stimulated an extraordinarily growth of federal social programs. Before the Vietnam War overshadowed domestic concerns, Congress—prodded by a shrewd and domineering president—enacted in rapid succession a series of laws designed to diminish economic inequalities, address divisive racial issues, and ensure that all Americans would have access to medical care. Much of the legislation enacted in the early and mid-1960s reflected the pervasive faith that state governments were reactionary and were best bypassed in favor of a federal-community partnership.

In the optimistic atmosphere of the early and mid-1960s mental health rhetoric and ideology paralleled newly enacted federal programs. Both grew out of the belief that the origins of most social problems could be traced to a deficient environment. The emphasis on community mental health services responded to that belief by stressing the empowerment of individuals and small groups at the local level whose involvement in all decisions that impacted on the lives of the mentally ill should greatly improve their condition. Their claim that mental hospitals were obsolete reflected the growing anti-institutionalist sentiment that idealized individuals as caring while condemning arbitrary bureaucratic organizations as controlling.

Community psychiatry became the term that best defined some of the distinguishing characteristics of these years. Faith in the redemptive qualities of modern psychiatry was fused with other goals: a demand for social justice; an end to structural barriers that impeded the realization of the full potentiality of individuals; and the realignment of mental health services at the community level where a professional-public partnership could function more effectively.

To one individual community psychiatry constituted no less than a fourth psychiatric revolution that was directed toward "the saturation of a given geographical area with medical services aimed at all levels of prevention and treatment for the families who reside therein." Such a restructuring of services rested on "effective symptom" controls developed after 1945. Community psychiatry, noted an NIMH official, was concerned "with optimizing the adaptive potential and psychosocial life skills, as well as lessening the amount of pathology, in population groups . . . by population-wide programs of prevention, case finding, care, treatment and rehabilitation."[1]

Community psychiatry in fact often defied precise definition. Perhaps the most global definition was offered by Gerald Caplan of the Harvard Medical School. The community psychiatrist, he wrote,

> needs a chart which emphasizes not the individual peculiarities of a single patient, but broad issues of mental disorder and its causation which apply to populations of patients. His task is to investigate widely occurring harmful factors and their pathological consequences, and also to plan programs of intervention which will significantly affect many people not only by his direct interaction with them, but also indirectly through the mediation of other caregivers and by altering social and cultural influences which affect them.

Critical of the rehabilitative emphasis of the JCMIH, Caplan insisted that prevention held the key to future progress. His popular and influential *Principles of Preventive Psychiatry* embodied many of the intellectual and social currents of these years.[2]

Community psychiatry was identified with social and political activism. To conflate the two, however, raised serious intellectual problems. How could a medical specialty such as psychiatry reconcile its claims to professional autonomy and legitimacy with a commitment to democratic politics in which partisanship and competing ideologies played a vital role? H. Warren Dunham, a distinguished sociologist and coauthor of a classic work on mental disorders in urban areas, was skeptical of the claim that community psychiatrists had unique skills "in the techniques of social action"; such claims rested entirely on faith. Nor was Dunham impressed with the concept of prevention. "How are we going to take the first preventive actions if we are still uncertain about the causes of mental disorders?" he asked. Dunham was equally critical about the rush to treat individuals with mild emotional disorders, which followed the rise of office psychiatry and frustration with the difficulties of dealing with severely mentally ill persons. Community psychiatry, he insisted, mirrored the cherished American belief that all problems were solvable "if we can just discover the key by means of the scientific methodology at our disposal."[3]

Despite these criticisms, community psychiatry assumed the character of a social movement during the 1960s. In this sense it paralleled the adoption of the melioristic social policies that helped to reshape the welfare and health systems, diminish poverty, and end discrimination. The pervasive social activism associated with community psychiatry even led the APA to reorganize its structure in order to become a more effective vehicle for social change.[4] Within such a context it was understandable that the sustained effort to reshape the mental health system would meet with some successes.

When *Action for Mental Health* became public, the JCMIH assumed that a broad coalition would be mobilized in support of its program, and that the passage of appropriate legislation would follow. Realization of such expectations, however, faced formidable obstacles. The Commission's recommendations had yet to be translated into concrete legislative programs. Moreover, the reception of its final report, though generally favorable, was by no means uncritical. Proponents of change, therefore, had to reconcile views that were not always compatible. Some questioned the use of nonmedical personnel as "Mental Health Counsellors"; others expressed doubt about the wisdom of abandoning a strictly medical definition of psychotherapy; still others were distressed that pharmacological and other somatic therapies had not been given due credit. The recommendation to change the functions of mental hospitals proved controversial, and there was concern about implementing a national program while taking into account regional and local differences. The harshest criticism came from individuals identified with traditional public mental hospitals. Newton Bigelow, a figure long associated with the New York State mental health system and editor of the *Psychiatric Quarterly*, disliked the recommendation dealing with the segregation of chronic mental patients and the disregard of the elderly. He maintained that there was widespread ignorance about the functions of traditional mental hospitals. The APA Council's position paper was supportive, but also dissented from several statements dealing with mental institutions. Other organizations, including the AMA and American Psychological Association, were somewhat guarded in their approval.[5]

The persistence of disagreements, however, did not dampen enthusiasm for positive action by the federal government. The experiences of the New Deal and acceptance of the concept of the welfare state had persuaded many that the federal government was better equipped than its state counterparts to resolve pressing social problems. The belief that many state governments had failed to meet their social welfare responsibilities and were opposed to civil rights legislation reinforced the conviction that the federal government, in collaboration with local communities, should assume political leadership on social policy issues.

Critics of state social policy-making received support from federal agencies, notably the NIMH, where key personnel did not believe that states possessed either the knowledge or capacity to oversee meaningful change, and for this reason remained committed to the large but increasingly obsolete mental hospital system. Hence NIMH officials were supportive of legislative initiatives that favored community services and alternatives to mental hospital care. Committed to a public health approach, they were eager to create a new system capable of providing a wide range of mental health services to an entire population within a defined geographical area. Seeking to improve the care and treatment of the mentally ill and to expand psychological services for nonmentally ill persons, they foresaw no negative consequences that might follow a diminution in the mental health activities of the states.

The inauguration of John F. Kennedy in early 1961 augured well for those seeking change. His party's platform included a pledge of federal support for research, training, and community programs. Yet Kennedy and his family were primarily concerned with mental retardation. His younger sister Rosemary had been diagnosed as mildly retarded and had undergone a lobotomy that had appreciably worsened her condition. Eunice Shriver, the president's sister, had emerged as a crucial figure within the administration and as an outspoken advocate of action in the field of retardation. Shriver was also hostile toward psychiatrists because of their alleged disregard of the retarded. The result was growing political tensions between those seeking changes in the mental health system and those favoring greater emphasis on the needs of the retarded.[6]

Faced with such divisive internal pressures, the administration moved with caution. Kennedy and his staff had already decided to create a number of "task forces" to develop policy recommendations. When the President's Panel on Mental Retardation was formally organized in the autumn of 1961, pressures mounted to take commensurate action on mental health. In December the president created an Interagency Task Force on Mental Health. Chaired nominally by Abraham Ribicoff (Secretary of Health, Education and Welfare), the group included representatives from several other agencies. The real work, however, was done by a smaller group that included Boisfeuillet Jones, Robert Felix and his deputy Stanley Yolles, Daniel Patrick Moynihan, and several others. Felix, as a leading figure in the mental health arena, was strategically situated to create a legislative agenda that reflected his views and that of his staff.[7]

As the Task Force was deliberating, the NIMH created two internal groups to formulate its own policy recommendations. The first was critical of state hospitals on the grounds that they fostered dependency and were governed by archaic administrative systems. It recommended that new approaches be devised and that federal funds be used to assist states in formulating new policies. The second group, headed by Yolles, developed a comprehensive program that reflected its own preference for a community-oriented public health approach. Its members began with the presumption that progress in prevention and a growing acceptance of community responsibility for the mentally ill would lead to an inescapable conclusion, namely, that a comprehensive community mental health programs would make it possible *"for the mental hospital as it is now known to disappear from the scene within the next twenty-five years."* Yolles and his colleagues also conceptualized a new kind of institution. The JCMIH had spoken about clinics; the NIMH group spoke about *centers*. Such an institution, they insisted, "is a multi-service community facility designed to provide early diagnosis and treatment of mental illness, both on an inpatient and outpatient basis, and serve as a locus for aftercare of discharged hospital patients." Ultimately all services within communities and regions—preventive, therapeutic, educational—would be absorbed into these comprehensive centers, which would serve a designated population within a specific geographical area.[8]

In April, 1962, the presidential task force began to consider the NIMH proposals. In general, members were enthusiastic, for the NIMH—unlike the JCMIH—had defined an institution that seemed to offer an attractive alternative. The group readily accepted the assertion that new knowledge about diagnosis, treatment, and prevention offered the potential for an exciting new policy departure that could "really make a difference in length and severity of illness, in prevention of illness, and in eliminating the necessity for the institutionalization of individuals." During their deliberations several task force members were receptive to a strategy of diminishing the role of states in providing mental health services. Felix, Moynihan, and Jones, however, hoped that informal persuasion and education might convince state officials to alter their policies. In the end the task force agreed that the comprehensive community mental health center should become the basis of a presidential recommendation. Specifically, they proposed that federal grants assist in the construction of such centers and that a decreasing federal subsidy cover initial operating costs. The goal was to have five hundred centers in operation by 1970 and an additional fifteen hundred a decade later.[9]

It was clear that the interagency task force had partly ignored—if not rejected—the recommendations of the JCMIH. Moreover, the presidential group had made a series of striking assertions. Yet empirical data to support these claims were all but lacking. There was little or no evidence, for example, that comprehensive centers would obviate the need for mental hospital care. Moreover, the recommendations ignored certain realities. Was there a sufficient supply of trained personnel to staff two thousand centers? Projections by the Bureau of the Budget indicated that the goal of increasing dramatically the number of psychiatrists might have the inadvertent effect of reducing the supply of general practitioners and specialties providing services to the nonmentally ill, and thereby exacerbate other health problems. Finally, enthusiasm for a community-oriented policy concealed striking ambiguities. Federal beneficence and wisdom presumably would combine with community enlightenment to create a new institutional form that would overcome the myopic inability of states to formulate and implement effective mental health policies. In effect, the task force had developed a paradoxical synthesis that rationalized centralized control and local autonomy while implicitly weakening the mediating role of state governments.[10]

In the late autumn of 1962 Anthony Celebrezze (Ribicoff's successor) submitted the recommendations of the task force to the White House. He rejected the emphasis placed by the JCMIH on the need to increase services to the severely mentally ill within the state hospital system. Celebrezze insisted instead that the "primary interest in future mental health programs should be improvement of the mental health of the people of the community through a continuum of local services." Public policy had to incorporate two overriding objectives. The first was the development of measures "to promote mental health and prevent mental illness." The second was an emphasis on cure rather than incarceration. Recent progress in therapy had rendered traditional arrangements for patient care "outmoded, unnecessary and inefficient." Hence the time had come "when almost all the mentally ill could be cared for in treatment centers in their own communities."[11]

Celebrezze therefore endorsed the creation of a "comprehensive community mental health center—a comparatively new concept which offers exciting possibilities for upgrading mental health services."

> Such centers, replacing the traditional institutions, should be the foci of future mental health activities. They would be close to the patient's home, and would provide preventive, early diagnostic, and outpatient and inpatient treatment, and transitional and rehabilitation services. They would include psychiatric units in general hospitals, thereby providing the patient with the opportunity of being treated within his community environment. These facilities would be conveniently located in population centers and could provide patients with a continuity of care not now available. As his needs change, the patient in such a center could move quickly to appropriate services such as those for diagnosis, treatment, and rehabilitation; inpatient, outpatient, day or night programs; foster care, sheltered workshop, and industry.

Construction of such centers was to follow the cost-sharing arrangements of the Hill-Burton program, which had led to a rapid expansion in the postwar years of general hospitals. Although operating costs of community mental health centers would be borne by state and local governments and the private sector, Celebrezze recommended that the federal government provide financial support for staffing (50 percent in the first year and a decreasing amount for two additional years). Such assistance would stimulate communities "to undertake reasonably comprehensive programs quickly, and, at the same time, will afford them opportunity to find long-term, non-Federal sources of operating support." Conceding that the transition from hospital to community care would take time, the Secretary also supported modest funding for upgrading institutional care and treatment and for training the additional personnel required by the new policy initiatives.[12]

When the Panel on Retardation offered its own proposals in the autumn of 1962, the stage was set for some form of presidential decision. The White House staff recognized that they were entering a political mine field because of the mutual hostility of the mental health and mental retardation advocates. Ultimately Kennedy agreed with Myer Feldman, the presidential assistant responsible for mental health and retardation, that a single message would be appropriate. Such a tactic, Feldman recalled, would result in a "more salable" program. When Kennedy was shown a draft of his message to Congress, he uncharacteristically accepted it with few comments and made no changes. On retardation he deferred to his sister; on mental health he relied on the recommendations of his advisers.[13]

On February 5, 1963, Kennedy forwarded his mental illness and mental retardation message to Congress. He began by providing a brief review of the dimensions of the problem and the cost to the nation. In spite of the nationwide impact of mental illnesses, the federal government had "largely left the solutions up to the States." The states, in turn, "have depended on custodial hospitals and homes. Many such hospitals and homes have been shamefully understaffed, overcrowded, unpleasant institutions from which death too often provided the only firm hope of release." Kennedy then called for a "bold new approach" based upon "new knowledge and new drugs" that made it possible "for most of the mentally ill to be successfully and quickly treated in their own communities and returned to a useful place in society." The centerpiece of his new policy was to be the comprehensive community mental health center. It would integrate "diagnostic and evaluation services, emergency psychiatric units, outpatient services, inpatient services, day and night care, foster home care, rehabilitation, consultive services to other community agencies, and mental health information and education." The role of the federal government was to stimulate "State, local, and private action." The President urged Congress to authorize construction grants and short-term subsidies for staffing as well as $4 million for state planning. Since it would take more than a decade to implement fully the new policy, he also endorsed a modest appropriation of $10 million for demonstration projects to improve patient care and staff training in mental hospitals. Kennedy noted that the shortage of professional personnel could be alleviated by an increase in funds for training. His proposals dealing with retardation followed similar lines of thought.[14]

The president's message received national publicity and aroused relatively little overt opposition. Identical bills were introduced in the Senate by Lister Hill and in the House by Oren Harris. Hill arranged for public hearings, which were orchestrated by organizations and individuals long active in the mental health field. In many respects the most striking testimony was offered by Jack Ewalt, who now claimed that the bill had grown out of the recommendations of the JCMIH. In point of fact, *Action for Mental Health* had been largely directed at the improvement of care and treatment for the severely mentally ill, although it did not rule out additional services for nonmentally ill but troubled individuals. The bill, by contrast, was designed to create a novel institution with a less clearly defined but comprehensive service. The members of Harris's committee were not as inclined to accept the statements by prominent figures. Paul Rogers, for example, questioned the feasibility of staffing the centers with adequate personnel, and another member expressed doubt whether temporary financial support for staffing could actually be phased out in the future. Nevertheless, the hearings before both committees were largely exercises in rhetoric rather than attempts to evaluate competing claims.[15]

During the deliberations Hill persuaded the administration to support the merger of mental health and retardation into a single bill. This strategy forced partisans on both sides to compromise for fear that a protracted conflict would end any hope of favorable action. In the late spring of 1963 the legislation passed the Senate by an overwhelming vote of 72 to 1. At this point the AMA came out in opposition to the provision authorizing federal funding for staffing centers, which it regarded as a step toward "socialized medicine." Divisions in the House led Harris to delete the staffing authorization for fear that its inclusion might imperil the entire legislation. A revised bill passed the House and ultimately the Senate, and was signed into law by President Kennedy on October 31.[16]

The mental health provisions of the Mental Retardation and Community Mental Health Centers Construction Act of 1963 were relatively simple. It provided a three-year authorization for grants totalling $150 million for fiscal years 1965 through 1967 for construction; the federal share ranged between one-third and two-thirds. To be eligible, states had to submit a comprehensive plan; designate an agency to administer the plan as well as an advisory council with broad representation; and establish a construction program based on a statewide inventory of existing facilities and needs. The designated state agency would forward individual construction applications to Washington for final approval. The legislation, proclaimed Felix,

> reflects the concept that many forms and degrees of mental illness can be prevented or ameliorated more effectively through community oriented preventive, diagnostic, treatment, and rehabilitation services than through care in the traditional—and traditionally isolated—state mental hospital. The act is designed to stimulate state, local, and private action. It is based on the belief that it will be possible to reduce substantially, within a decade or two, the numbers of patients who receive only custodial care—or no care at all—when they could be helped by the application of one or more of the modern methods of dealing with emotional disturbances and the mental illnesses.[17]

The context of policy-making in the early 1960s reflected a faith that a community-oriented policy could overcome the intrinsic and unchanging defects of mental hospitals. Yet this faith was not always compatible with a large body of empirical data. Under Morton Kramer, the Biometrics Division of the NIMH had collected and analyzed a large mass of data on the institutionalized population that raised serious questions about prevailing beliefs. Between 1914 and 1948, for example, discharge rates for schizophrenics—the core of the seriously mentally ill—had risen dramatically, whereas patients with mental diseases associated with aging had increased. Such data suggested that the oft-repeated claims about the warehousing functions of mental hospitals were somewhat inaccurate, and that policy had to take into account a diverse patient population with a variety of disorders, each with its own specific prognosis.

Other data raised even more serious questions. A community policy was based on the expectation that patients could be treated outside of institutions. Underlying this belief were four assumptions: that patients had a home; that they had a sympathetic family or other person willing and able to assume responsibility for their care; that the organization of the household would not impede rehabilitation; and that the patient's presence would not cause undue hardships for other family members. In 1960, however, 48 percent of the mental hospital population was unmarried, 12 percent were widowed, and 13 percent were divorced or separated. A large proportion of patients, in other words, may have had no families to care for them. The assumption that patients could reside in the community with their families while undergoing rehabilitation was hardly supported by such findings. Indeed, a community-based policy had to incorporate supportive services that included, but were not limited to, housing. Such data (which were obviously known to Felix and others who set the agenda and developed a rationale for the community mental health center concept) were barely considered during the political and legislative deliberations between 1961 and 1963 even though they were crucial to the implementation of the new policy departure.[18]

The establishment of the JCMIH in 1955 reflected a concern with seriously and persistently mentally ill persons both within and without hospitals. Eight years later federal legislation created a new kind of institution that represented a radical break with the past. The new departure had major implications for the pattern of intergovernmental relations. In effect, the federal government undertook to reshape policy by forging more direct links with local communities, which inadvertently tended to diminish the authority and policy role of state governments. Aside from the consequences for intergovernmental relationships, the act of 1963 created an institution whose nature and functions were unclear. Moreover, their potential clientele was protean and not limited to the severely and persistently mentally ill. Finally, no effort was made to spell out the relationships between community mental health centers and traditional mental hospitals, nor was serious consideration given to the ways in which centers would or could assume the caring role of hospitals. The consequences of the new departure only became clear in succeeding years.

The passage of legislation is often only a beginning. Laws require administrative regulations, standards, and procedures, and the task of writing them gives government officials extraordinary scope to create and reshape policy. The act of 1963 offers dramatic evidence of the validity of this generalization. Its provisions were relatively vague, although the alleged goal was to replace custodial institutions with local therapeutic centers. The act did not define the essential services that community mental health centers were required to provide, but left that responsibility to the Department of Health, Education and Welfare.

At the outset an internal bureaucratic struggle took place within the Public Health Service. The Bureau of Medical Services, which administered the award of hospital construction funds under Hill-Burton, claimed jurisdiction. Felix, on the other hand, interpreted the act as mandating a service system, and insisted that the program more properly belonged in the NIMH. In the ensuing struggle Felix easily prevailed. By early 1964 NIMH officials had issued regulations that defined five essential services that each community mental health center was required to provide: inpatient services; outpatient services; partial hospitalization services; twenty-four hour emergency services within the previous three services; and consultation and educational services for community agencies and professional personnel. A variety of other services were encouraged but not mandated. Control of the clinical program was placed under psychiatric jurisdiction. Finally, the legislation also employed the term *community*, but did not define its meaning. Ultimately the regulations fell back on sheer numbers and stipulated a population range of 75,000 to 200,000. These figures had been arbitrarily developed by Felix and his colleagues and represented a compromise designed to avoid the high costs associated with a large number of small units or the chaos that might accompany organizations serving more than 200,000 persons.[19]

Perhaps the most curious aspect of the new regulations was the omission of any mention of state hospitals. In one sense this was understandable, given the claim that centers would replace hospitals. Nevertheless, the absence of linkages in many states between centers and hospitals was striking. If centers were designed to offer comprehensive services and continuity of care, how could they function in isolation from state hospital systems with an inpatient population of half a million? Indeed, the absence of specific linkages facilitated the development of a system of centers that ultimately catered to a quite different clientele and largely ignored the severely and persistently mentally ill.

The final element in the new community-oriented system—legislation providing for federal support for staffing centers—followed. The assassination of Kennedy brought to the White House an individual extraordinarily skilled in the intricacies of congressional politics. Unlike his more popular predecessor (whose legislative program was largely languishing), Lyndon B. Johnson used his talents and authority in shrewd, determined, forceful, and sometimes ruthless ways to push Congress to enact the elements that made up his Great Society program. The nomination and subsequent defeat of Senator Barry Goldwater in the election of 1964 strengthened Johnson's hand. It gave his program the aura of moderation when placed alongside the militant antigovernment ideology of his opponent.

Johnson's elevation to the presidency mobilized the NIMH, which began to push for federal support for staffing. To be sure, dissatisfaction within the mental health constituency was present. State officials such as Dr. David Vail of Minnesota insisted that centers could not alleviate "social ills," and he called for measures that strengthened state hospital systems and filled in the gaps at the community level. Others were critical of the effort to bypass state authority, and insisted that the center concept was poorly conceived. Nevertheless, those who favored the new policy proved too strong. The weakness of the AMA (which was preoccupied by the impending Medicare bill) only spurred them to push the staffing law. In the summer of 1965 legislation easily passed that authorized federal grants for staffing community mental health centers and new services. The regulations promulgated by the NIMH retained their broad and ambiguous character; centers retained responsibility for the "mental health of the community, . . . the prevention of mental illness and the more rapid and complete recovery of persons affected with mental illness in the community, . . . [and] the development of improved methods of treating and rehabilitating the mentally ill."[20]

By 1965 the final elements of a *national* program were in place. The acts of 1963 and 1965, together with accompanying regulations, had created a new institution that represented a repudiation of an institutional policy that had been in place for more than a century. The enactment of formal legislation, however, does not imply that desired results will automatically follow. Indeed, laws assume a static universe; a legal mandate supposedly alters individual and group behavior to produce the stipulated end. But reality is much more complex, for individuals often adjust their behavior to new realities. In so doing they transform laws in unforeseen and unpredictable ways. The actual evolution of community mental health centers after 1965 was a case in point.

Initially the creation and construction of centers moved at a slow pace. A significant element was the shortage of professional personnel.

Equally important, the funds for construction and staffing, as well as for a variety of other Great Society programs, declined as the Vietnam War escalated. The gap between authorization and actual funding widened rapidly. Between 1966 and 1970, 274 centers were funded; in the succeeding decade an additional 480 were the beneficiaries of federal subsidies. By 1980 the total number of centers receiving grants was 754, a figure that fell far short of the original goal of 2,000. The program, however, did help to bring services to new areas. At the outset about a quarter of all centers funded were located in urban areas with populations of half a million or more. During the 1970s, however, cities with populations of 10,000 to 50,000 accounted for 40 percent of the total, and a large proportion were in more remote areas in the South and Southwest with large minority populations. Although the largest states received the most federal funds, the program was mildly redistributive in that poorer states and states with minimal mental health services received a proportionately larger share of the total allocation.[21]

Two decades later Senator Daniel Patrick Moynihan, who had been involved with Kennedy's interagency task force, charged that the failure to construct and staff the projected 2,000 centers by 1980 was responsible for the creation of a large population of "homeless, deranged people."[22] Moynihan's observations, however informed, were only partly true. The fact of the matter is that the euphoria and rhetoric surrounding the acts of 1963 and 1965 concealed an inner ambiguity about the precise nature and functions of community mental health centers. Such terms as *mental illness*, *mental health*, and *community mental health* were hardly clear concepts; they meant different things even to professionals. To some the terms implied community care and treatment of the mentally ill; others interpreted them in terms of prevention, and still others emphasized changes in those environmental conditions that presumably promoted mental disorders. Each of these meanings in turn implied quite different organizational functions and structures. Nor was a body of evidence measuring efficacy available. "The community mental health movement," noted a member of GAP,

> is at present handicapped by overenthusiasm, partly because of much childishly gullible fascination with the new and adolescent rejection of the old. We have been through these phases many times before—remember! In the beginning, two-thirds of schizophrenic patients were "cured" by insulin coma; sixty percent of paranoid schizophrenics were improved by convulsive therapy; and similarly rosy results were initially attributed

to psychoanalysis, lobotomy, tranquilizers, and the therapeutic community. This enthusiasm is not necessarily all bad: the new must be tested, applied with mild indiscrimination; sustain a shakedown cruise, be pushed to the limits that inform what it can and cannot accomplish, where it fits and where it rattles. Furor therapeutics has its value if one does not lose perspective and indulge in chauvinistic adherence to an innovation.[23]

More important, there was no consensus on the kind of clientele that would be served by centers. The widely accepted continuum theory of mental illnesses was a source of confusion. The theory assumed the feasibility of identifying individuals who—if untreated—would be at high risk to become mentally ill. Yet the data confirming the ability to identify such individuals was all but absent. Moreover, little or no consideration was given to the behavior of consumers. In the postwar decades Americans became enthusiastic users of medical services of all kinds; their faith in the efficacy of medical science and development of third-party insurance plans combined to alter traditional usage patterns. Community mental health centers from their origins began to deal with new categories of individuals with emotional disturbances rather than severe mental disorders. In 1970 about 20 percent of all patients seen in centers had diagnoses of depressive disorders and 19 percent fell into the schizophrenic category. By 1974 these figures had fallen to 13 and 11 percent, respectively, whereas patients with diagnoses of "social maladjustments" rose from 4.6 to 20 percent. Most centers made little effort to provide coordinated aftercare services and continuing assistance to severely and persistently mentally ill persons. They preferred to emphasize psychotherapy, an intervention especially adapted to individuals with emotional and personal problems as well as to professional staff. Even psychiatrists in community settings tended to deal with more affluent neurotic patients.[24]

Community mental health centers were also shaped by the weaknesses of intergovernmental linkages and the increasing diversity and complexity of the mental health field. If the frailty of state regulation left them with the autonomy to experiment, it also left them free to move in directions not always conducive to the needs of the severely mentally ill. Many centers, for reasons that are understandable, ultimately serviced a very different population. The severely and chronically mentally ill, after all, presented daunting problems. They were not always easy to manage; they often required comprehensive care; and many were poor candidates for psychotherapies, the approach most favored by center staffs. Needs that in mental hospitals were minimally satisfied were not easily met in community settings. Who would ensure that mentally ill persons would have access to housing, food, support systems, and jobs? To provide for the mentally ill in the community, in other words, was arduous and time-consuming, and the available means of administration—despite the confident rhetoric of these years—were not always adequate. Under such circumstances centers tended to respond to local pressures for services to nonmentally ill constituencies. To be sure, some states—notably California—attempted to integrate state hospitals and community institutions. At best the results were mixed; variations among counties was striking.[25]

As the federal role in mental health policy grew, friction with states became more evident. At a conference convened by the NIMH in 1966, representatives from a number of states expressed their concerns about the growing "dichotomy between state hospital[s] and community programs." Public mental hospitals could not be ignored; many provided "comprehensive services of high quality to a community." Centers, most participants concluded, should not be freestanding, but rather part of an integrated service system. Such advice notwithstanding, community mental health centers during and after the 1970s by and large followed an independent path. Admittedly, mental hospital populations declined in the 1960s and 1970s. Yet the decline had little to do with centers, which generally serviced a quite different clientele that included large numbers of substance abusers (alcoholics and drug addicts). However important their contributions, centers did not provide an alternative to mental hospital care. Moreover, there was a steady decline in the number of psychiatrists who either directed or worked in centers. Between 1970 and 1981 the number of average full-time equivalent psychiatrists declined from 6.8 to 3.8, whereas the comparable figure for psychologists rose from 4.9 to 9.4. All of these elements vitiated still further the already marginal involvement of community mental health centers with the severely and persistently mentally ill.[26]

Centers were sometimes caught up in the social and political conflicts of the Vietnam era. Influenced by antiorganizational and community empowerment ideologies, some urban centers shifted their emphasis toward the improvement of social conditions. Dr. Bertram Brown, the NIMH official who administered the centers program, and a colleague put the issue quite succinctly in 1967 at the meetings of the American

Psychopathological Association. "The success of a mental health program is no longer simply a function of the clinical skills of the program staff; the success of a program is equally dependent on skills in coping with, and adapting to, and sometimes even changing the local political, social, and economic environment."[27]

The most publicized example of political activism occurred at the Lincoln Hospital Mental Health Services in the southeast Bronx, a neighborhood that seemed to symbolize all of the problems of urban America. Organized in 1963 under a contract between New York City and Albert Einstein College of Medicine of Yeshiva University, the new organization (with a three-year grant from the Office of Economic Opportunity in 1965) launched an experiment. With the use of neighborhood service centers staffed by trained indigenous nonprofessionals to stimulate social and community action programs, the hospital attempted to deal with the chronic problems of urban ghettos. In early 1969 nonprofessional staff workers went on strike, occupied administrative offices, and demanded that power be transferred from professionals associated with a predominantly white and Jewish university power structure to the poor, blacks, and disenfranchised persons. The confrontation at Lincoln Hospital was perhaps an extreme example. Nevertheless, internecine conflict in other urban areas was common, given the ideology of community control and demand for actions that would transform an environment that allegedly produced high rates of psychiatric pathologies.[28]

The federal role in mental health policy, however, was not restricted simply to the creation of centers. Equally significant was the passage of amendments to the Social Security Act of 1935. In 1965 Congress, with presidential prodding and encouragement, passed a series of far-reaching amendments. Two programs in particular—Medicare and Medicaid—were designed to provide medical care for the aged and poor. Title 18, Part A (Medicare) dealt with hospital insurance for the aged; Part B with insurance for physicians' services. Title 19 (Medicaid) involved grants to states for medical assistance programs for indigent persons. The most surprising feature of these amendments was the inclusion of psychiatric benefits.

The developments that followed the enactment of Titles 18 and 19 were both profound and paradoxical. Medicaid in particular became an important source of funding for the care of elderly patients in mental hospitals, even though payments were limited. More importantly, the limitation on the use of Medicare and Medicaid funds for aged patients in state hospitals tacitly encouraged states to send such individuals to nursing homes because of the far more generous federal payments. The result was a shift in the nature of mental hospital populations. In 1962 153,309 of 504,604 resident patients were sixty-five or older; in 1969 the comparable figures were 111,420 and 369,969. By 1972 the number of such patients had fallen to 78,479 out of a total of 274,837. This is not to suggest that aged persons were no longer being institutionalized, for such was not the case. The decline in the number of aged patients in state hospitals was accompanied by a sharp increase in the number of aged mentally ill in nursing homes. In 1963 nursing homes cared for 221,721 individuals with mental disorders, of whom 187,675 were sixty-five or older. Six years later the comparable figures were 426,712 and 367,586. What had occurred was not a deinstitutionalization movement, but rather a lateral shift of patients among institutions. Aged (as well as younger) persons diagnosed as mentally disordered were now being sent to nursing homes rather than state hospitals simply because the passage of Titles 18 and 19 made possible a substitution of federal for state funds.[29]

The reduced admissions of elderly long-term patients into public mental hospitals had a major impact. Relieved of the task of providing long-term care of elderly patients, many were able to focus more attention on treating acute cases. To be sure, state appropriations did not necessarily increase. Nevertheless, the decline in the resident population meant that more resources were available for the remaining patients. The result was a significant change in the quality of care and treatment in mental hospitals. Virtually every indicator after 1970 showed a marked improvement in this regard.

Although the shape of the mental health system changed dramatically during the 1960s, ambiguities and inconsistencies were ever present. During these years the traditionally sharp line of demarcation between mental health and mental illnesses grew vaguer. The appearance of centers and the completion of the transfer of the specialty of psychiatry from mental hospitals to the community greatly facilitated the expansion of services for a broader and more diverse population that did not have diagnoses of severe mental disorders.

Nowhere were such changes more visible than in the aggregate data dealing with patient care episodes. In 1955 77.4 percent of all patient care episodes were treated in inpatient facilities, and 22.6 percent in outpatient settings. Thirteen years later the respective figures were 47.3 and 52.7 percent. This change, however, did not mean that care and treatment in mental hospitals were on the road to extinction. It merely signified that new groups who were for the most part not mentally ill were increasingly using mental health services. Indeed, the decline in the institutionalized population that began slowly in the 1950s and accelerated sharply after 1965 was accompanied by sharply rising numbers of admissions. Between 1955 and 1970 the resident patient population at public mental institutions fell from 558,922 to 337,619; during this same period admissions rose from 178,003 to 384,511. Other data revealed that public institutions continued to treat and care for more severely and chronically ill persons than any other type of facility. As late as 1975 public hospitals accounted for more than two-thirds of all days of inpatient psychiatric care.[30]

To be sure, the number of patient care episodes in general hospitals and CMHCs increased as well, although there were sharp variations from place to place. Yet even the imperfect data that is available suggests that these facilities did not generally treat individuals previously admitted or likely to be admitted to mental hospitals. Moreover, length-of stays were considerably shorter in general hospitals than in mental hospitals, suggesting that the most seriously impaired were not being treated in community inpatient (or outpatient) facilities. Nor were community mental health centers geared toward meeting the long-term needs of chronically mentally ill patients; comprehensive aftercare programs were all but absent.[31]

Interestingly enough, there were sporadic efforts to create aftercare programs. Led by Massachusetts, some states had programs for placing released patients with families. In 1960 thirteen states and the VA had placed 9,610 patients in family households. Yet the difficulties in administering and supervising such programs—to say nothing about community resistance—ensured that home care would not be of major importance. Others efforts to assist discharged patients in making the transition from hospital to community included "halfway houses." The best known was Fountain House in New York City, which evolved out of an informal organization of former Rockland State Hospital patients. By 1970 such facilities cared for between six and nine thousand residents. Despite high hopes, halfway houses never became a significant force. The system for financing mental health services made few provisions for them, and private contributions remained their primary source of funding. Most importantly, halfway houses were not designed to offer long term assistance for persistently mentally ill persons. "Many mental health professionals," noted the authors of an APA study, "do not have much knowledge of, interest in, or commitment to the importance of rehabilitative and supporting resources that must be made available on an intermediate or long-term basis to the seriously ill people that they seek to retain in the community."[32]

The relative weaknesses of aftercare services and deficiencies in mechanisms designed to ensure linked and coordinated services thus pointed up the sharp contradictions within the mental health system. In theory the increase in the number of centers and general hospital psychiatric services should have been matched by a decline in the numbers and sizes of state hospitals. In practice the situation was quite different. Centers treated new categories of individuals for a variety of problems ranging from substance addiction to personal and marital problems. General hospital inpatient units dealt with more severely and persistently mentally ill patients, but did not resolve the issue of how to provide supportive care and services after discharge. The broadening of the boundaries of the mental health system characteristic of the 1960s and later was thus accompanied by a diffusion of responsibility toward the most severely impaired persons. The increase in admissions at mental hospitals implied that these institutions would continue to be the primary provider of services for these individuals. But the declining length-of-stay characteristic of these years also meant that their role as a provider of such care would diminish. Consequently, severely and persistently mentally ill persons would be scattered through society, but no single organization accepted longitudinal responsibility for their basic human needs. Hence for many individuals some of the changes in the mental health system that began during the 1960s only exacerbated their plight.[33]

———————

By the mid-1960s the prestige of both psychiatry and the mental health system had reached unprecedented heights. One indication was the manner in which psychiatrists were depicted in motion pictures. Between 1957 and 1963 Hollywood produced more than twenty films that presented psychiatrists—the purveyors of reason, knowledge, and well-being—in glowing and idealized terms. One of the best known was Nunnally Johnson's *The Three Faces of Eve*, which was released in 1957.

Joanne Woodward—who won an Academy Award for her performance—plays a woman with two distinctly different personalities. Eve White is a withdrawn housewife; Eve Black is a seductive histrionic female. Her caring and sympathetic psychiatrist (played by Lee J. Cobb) searches in her past for the origins of her condition. Under hypnosis, Eve recovers a repressed traumatic experience, and Jane—a third and healthy woman—emerges as the individual that integrates the two dysfunctional personalities of Eve White and Eve Black. The film ends on as happy note as Jane is reunited with her husband and daughter. Other films—including Elia Kazan's *Splendor in the Grass* (1961), Hubert Cornfield's *Pressure Point* (1962), and John Huston's *Freud* (1962)—presented psychiatry in a positive and sympathetic light.[34]

Yet at precisely the time the social legitimacy of psychiatry was peaking, a series of disquieting developments were already eroding its very foundation. Within the specialty the hegemony of psychodynamic and psychoanalytic psychiatrists was beginning to come under attack from more biologically oriented colleagues. To internal controversies were added sharp criticisms of both the theory and practice of psychiatry by individuals and groups from without. Equally significant, psychiatry was unable to remain above the strains and tensions of the larger society. The willingness of members to offer prescriptions for broad social problems raised troubling dilemmas. The invocation of professional authority based on training and expertise was not always compatible with the principles of representative government and citizenship. Finally, the growing challenges to constituted authority so characteristic of the late 1960s and early 1970s, combined with an active civil rights movement that focused part of its attention on the mentally ill, posed new problems for all of the mental health professions.

In the two decades following the end of World War II, American psychiatry was led by individuals whose outlook had been shaped by psychodynamic and psychoanalytic concepts and who had an affinity for a liberal and activist political agenda. Such varied organizations as GAP, the APA, and the NIMH were all involved with issues whose direct relationships to mental illnesses were often tenuous or problematic. Stanley Yolles, Felix's successor as director of NIMH and staunch proponent of community activism to improve the physical and social environment, decried "professional isolation." He endorsed the involvement of younger figures in "social action," and applauded the use of their expertise "to effect changes to improve the communities in which they live and work." Seymour Halleck of the University of Wisconsin's Department of Psychiatry went even further when he insisted that the search for political neutrality was illusory. "As long as mental illness is even partially related to social processes," he insisted, "the physician must involve himself in preserving or changing the status quo." Nowhere was the ethos of the 1960s better portrayed than in the writings of Robert L. Coles of Harvard, a figure who attempted to spell out the impact of poverty, racism, and other social ills on behavior and personality. "A dirty, ugly environment," he wrote in *Wages of Neglect* in 1969,

> reinforces the ghetto child's sense of worthlessness, which he has already acquired through his parent's overly desperate moralism and plaintively rigid lecturing.
>
> Thus the once rural, now urbanized and rapidly disintegrating family combines with an ugly, unsafe environment to prepare the child of poverty for a life without hope and without self-esteem, a life which he may well help to perpetuate, alas, a "world without end"—unless, that is, we all care enough to make all sorts of changes in our society.[35]

Psychiatric activism, of course, had provocative and potentially divisive consequences, for it blurred the distinction between professional authority and citizenship. Joseph Wortis, a more biologically oriented figure, warned his colleagues about the dangers of rationalizing social action in professional terms. The record of psychiatric activism, he observed, was mixed.

> Jung defended the Nazis, [Wilhelm] Reich regarded the plough as a phallic symbol and tried to found a new science of sexoeconomics, Freud ascribed war to aggressive instincts and took sides with the Germans in World War I; psychiatry has been invoked to support individualism and collectivism, progress and reaction, and to smear or incarcerate political opponents. In a democracy, the general population should be the final judge and main instigator of social action. Psychiatrists can make an important contribution by directing attention to the basic social factors that can cause or aggravate mental disorder, and by treating their patients in accordance with these insights, but it is presumptuous for psychiatrists to base their claims for leadership in the broader arena of social action on their technical credentials.[36]

Indeed, even before 1960s psychiatry had come under attack from a variety of groups who believed that its members had gone beyond its medical boundaries. In 1947 Monsignor Fulton J. Sheen, a prominent

Catholic publicist, described psychiatry as "irreligious," an allegation echoed by some of his co-religionists. In the 1950s and 1960s the extreme anticommunist right—including the John Birch Society, the D.A.R., and Gerald L. K. Smith's antisemitic Christian Nationalist Crusade—viciously attacked psychiatry for its alleged support of the Soviet Union and the fact that it was dominated by a Zionist conspiracy seeking the triumph of communism.[37]

Extremist attacks had little impact upon psychiatry or public policy. Of far greater significance was the appearance of a critical literature that attacked the very foundations of psychiatry. The best known internal critic was Thomas S. Szasz. Committed to a puristic libertarian ideology that defined individual liberty as the highest good and denigrated the role of government, Szasz denied the very existence of "mental" illness. In his eyes the very concept of mental illness was a form of social labeling designed to serve as a facade for the suppression of nonconformist behavior. Thus psychiatry was a pseudoscience that served the needs of what he called the "Therapeutic State." In a series of books and articles he bitterly attacked psychiatry and mental hospitals during the 1960s and 1970s. "To maintain that a social institution suffers from certain 'abuses,'" he wrote in an ostensibly historical work, "is to imply that it has certain other desirable or good uses. This, in my opinion, has been the fatal weakness of the countless exposés—old and recent, literary and professional—of private and public mental hospitals. My thesis is quite different: Simply put, it is that there are, and can be, no abuses *of* Institutional Psychiatry, because Institutional Psychiatry *is*, itself, an abuse."[38]

The attack on psychiatry from the libertarian right was matched by an equally vituperative assault from a small group of radical psychiatrists sympathetic to the New Left counterculture during the 1960s and early 1970s. The emergence of a dissenting tradition was not an isolated or even indigenous development, but crossed national boundaries and defied clear ideological categorization. In England R. D. Laing developed a powerful critique that was compatible with the social activism and political radicalism of the 1960s. Laing agreed with Szasz that concepts of sanity and insanity often reflected moral rather than medical and scientific judgments. In a vivid analogy he described a formation of planes observed from the ground. One plane could be out of formation, and hence perceived as "abnormal, bad or 'mad' from the point of view of the formation." There was a distinct possibility, on the other hand, that the formation was "bad or mad," and that the errant plane was actually on a truer course than all the others. By insisting that madness might be a rational response to an irrational world, Laing and his colleagues aligned themselves with a radical politics and thus became part of the antipsychiatry movement of that decade.[39]

Equally if not more significant were external challenges to psychiatric legitimacy. The most prominent came from the social and behavioral sciences, whose prestige reached unprecedented heights in the three decades following World War II. The most famous and influential work of this kind was Erving Goffman's *Asylums*. Based on fieldwork at St. Elizabeths Hospital in the District of Columbia, *Asylums* was rapidly absorbed into counterculture thinking even though its author was far removed from the social and political radicalism of that era. Goffman's work focused on the impact of institutions such as mental hospitals on the personality and behavior of patients. His portrait of mental institutions was devastating; he described the ways in which a humiliating institutionalization stripped individuals of their self-identity and esteem and induced deviant responses. "Mental patients," Goffman wrote at the end of his book,

> can find themselves in a special bind. To get out of the hospital, or to ease their life within it, they must show acceptance of the place accorded them, and the place accorded them is to support the occupational role of those [psychiatrists and staff] who appear to force this bargain. This self-alienating moral servitude, which perhaps helps to account for some inmates becoming mentally confused, is achieved by invoking the great tradition of the expert servicing relation, especially its medical variety. Mental patients can find themselves crushed by the weight of a service ideal that eases life for the rest of us.[40]

The literary and intellectual characteristics of *Asylums* were striking, and often overshadowed the methodological difficulties inherent in relying—as Goffman had done—solely on personal observations. The book proved immensely popular among social activists, intellectuals, academics, and counterculture figures, many of whom believed that established institutions served only the rich and powerful. Curiously, Goffman's commitment to individual autonomy and a kind of eccentricity kept him at a distance and uninvolved in the controversies of the 1960s. Nor did he offer any prescriptions for better or more effective ways of dealing with individuals designated as mental patients. He even conceded that the closing of all hospitals would "raise a clamor for new ones" by relatives and public authorities. His work, nevertheless, was absorbed into both popular and professional thought and strengthened the growing antipathy toward established institutions.[41]

At about the same time that Goffman's critique was being popularized, sociologists were developing "labeling" (or societal reaction) theory. Popularized by Thomas J. Scheff, this theory insisted that psychiatric diagnoses were merely convenient labels attached to individuals who violated conventional behavioral norms. The stigmatizing of individuals as mentally ill in turn produced disturbed behavior. The implications of labeling theory were obvious. Concepts of mental illness, insisted Scheff, were "the leading edge of an ideology embedded in the historical and cultural present of the white middle class of Western societies"; the function of psychiatric labels was to reify and legitimate the existing social order. Labeling theory was especially useful to critics of psychiatry and to political radicals, both of whom employed its insights to buttress their insistence on the long-overdue need for fundamental social change.[42]

The attack on psychiatric legitimacy was not limited to academic figures, but came from some directly involved in the delivery of mental health services but who lacked medical training. Psychologists in particular were irritated by a medical model that in their view was deficient. During the 1950s they had already come into conflict with psychiatry on the issue of licensing and certification. Psychologists also believed that they were equally, if not more, qualified to offer psychotherapy. By the 1960s they were challenging psychiatric hegemony in clear terms. In a debate with Roy R. Grinker, Sr.—a distinguished psychiatrist—George W. Albee (a psychologist who had prepared one of the monographs for the JCMIH) rejected the illness model. In its place he substituted one based on the presumption that disturbed behavior reflected "the results of social-developmental learning in pathological environments." The destruction of the "emotional integrity of the family," for example, had a negative impact on mental health. Effective interventions, he added, had to be social and educational in nature; one-to-one therapeutic relationships were essentially futile. Albee's analysis—which dismissed the intellectual and scientific foundations of psychiatry—left little room for compromise or even debate.[43]

Foes of psychiatric orthodoxy also relied on the work of Michel Foucault, the seminal French thinker who helped to break down disciplinary barriers by synthesizing insights from Marx and Freud. In a variety of books, Foucault insisted that the creation of asylums represented an effort to impose a new rationalized system of order on the mad that was designed to enforce conformity. Moral treatment was merely an effort to force insane persons to develop an understanding of their own moral transgressions and to alter their behavior by having them internalize the values of their keepers. The authority of the asylum physician, therefore, was not derived from science, but rather from the moral and social order associated with bourgeois society and its values. Similarly, the appeal of and importance of psychiatry had little to do with its contribution to an understanding of human behavior, but rather stemmed from its relationships to the sources of power and domination. Ever changing and often obscure, Foucault's writings became the inspiration for dissenting and counterculture figures who emphasized the social control functions of psychiatry and mental hospitals, the abuses inherent in institutionalization, and the demands generated by a capitalist social order that insisted on conformity to a unitary standard of citizenship and behavior.[44]

A more subtle but equally significant critique of psychiatry came from civil rights advocates and members of the legal profession. Concerned initially with racial inequality, the postwar civil rights movement rapidly broadened its scope to include gender and class as well as the rights of the mentally ill. The new concern with patient rights was related in part to the perceived crisis of mental hospitals after 1945. If society had authority to enforce involuntary commitment, did it not have a commensurate responsibility to provide treatment, as contrasted with custodial care? In 1960 Morton Birnbaum, an individual trained in law and medicine, argued that courts should be prepared to rule that a hospital "that involuntarily institutionalizes the mentally ill without giving them adequate medical treatment for their mental illness" was a "prison." Substantive due process of law, he added, "does not allow a mentally ill person who has committed no crime to be deprived of his liberty by indefinitely institutionalizing him in a mental prison." Six years later Judge David Bazelon, speaking for the District of Columbia Circuit Court of Appeals in *Rouse v. Cameron*, stated that mental patients committed by criminal courts had a right to adequate treatment. Since such persons had been found not guilty by reason of insanity, they could neither be punished nor incarcerated. Commitment to a high-security hospital was appropriate, but only if accompanied by an adequate treatment program. Bazelon did not demand that patients be given the best possible treatment or even cured, but he did insist that the hospital make a

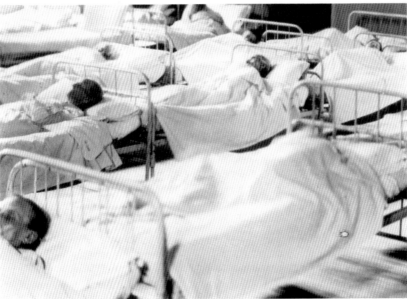

By the early twentieth century mental hospitals were serving as chronic care facilities for young schizophrenics who grew old in the institution and elderly senile persons committed by families unable to care for them. The growing numbers of long-term chronic patients magnified the need for custodial care and subverted therapeutic goals. At the Buffalo State Hospital in the early twentieth century, hallways assumed the function of a dayroom for idle patients, while whole wards were devoted to the care of elderly senile persons.

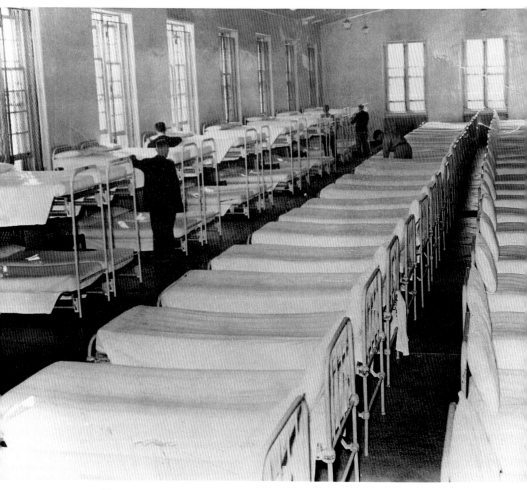

Mental hospitals during the first half of the twentieth century became homes for aged persons requiring custodial care. By World War II they were one of the major providers of custodial care for elderly dependent persons. The growth of population and disproportionate increase in the numbers of elderly persons in mental hospitals created novel problems. The depression of the 1930s and World War II only exacerbated crowding and neglect. By the 1940s Philadelphia State Hospital (Byberry) officials were forced to confine as many as eighty male patients in a single dormitory room.

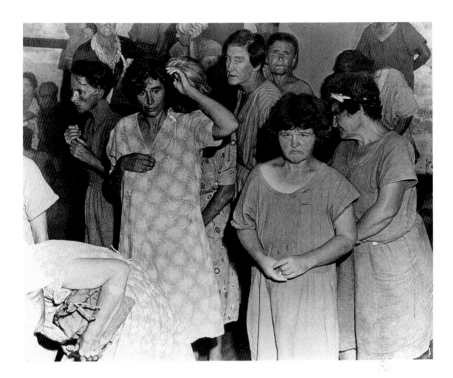

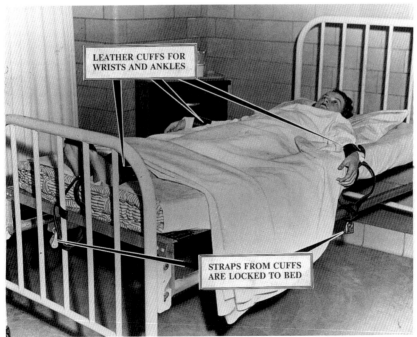

Crowding was so severe at Byberry in 1946 that female patients wandered about aimlessly in a ward that lacked adequate seating facilities. Traditional means of restraining violent patients were also employed at Byberry as late as 1950.

By the mid-twentieth century many hospitals had become large self-contained communities providing care for thousands of disabled persons. St. Elizabeth's Hospital—a federal institution that served the residents of the District of Columbia—had an inpatient population that exceeded 7,000. With a staff of thousands and a physical plant that covered several hundred acres, it embodied the caring functions of hospitals and the separation of the mentally ill from the community.

A Scene from the 20th Century-Fox Production
"THE SNAKE PIT"

In the 1948 film of Mary Jane Ward's novel *The Snake Pit* (Twentieth-Century-Fox), the heroine—played by Olivia de Haviland—is sent to a mental hospital where life on the wards was horrendous. Helped by a warm and concerned psychiatrist, the heroine develops insight into her behavior and emerges cured. The film thus depicted severe institutional shortcomings, but emphasized both the possibility of improvement and the psychiatric ability to cure severely disordered patients.

A scene from the Twentieth Century-Fox production
"THE THREE FACES OF EVE"
in CinemaScope CinemaScope – Reg. Trademark of 20th Century-Fox Film Corp.
Printed in U.S.A. Printed in U.S.A.

During the 1950s Hollywood glorified psychiatry and psychological explanations of human behavior. In *The Three Faces of Eve*, a Twentieth-Century-Fox film (1957), Joanne Woodward played the role of a woman with a multiple personality. With the assistance of psychodynamic psychiatrists, she emerges with a healthy integrated personality, reflecting the general high regard for psychiatrists in the postwar decades.

In the postwar era psychiatric activists like William C. Menninger (with President John F. Kennedy in 1962 above) had two related but sometimes opposing goals: to rebuild the state hospital system and to create a new system of providing care and treatment for the mentally ill in the community. The passage of the Community Mental Health Centers Act in 1963 (President Kennedy below signing the bill into law with Representative Paul Rogers [center] and Senator George Smathers [left]) seemed to inaugurate a new era. Federal authority and funds would ensure that severely mentally ill persons would receive care and treatment in the community and ultimately make mental hospitals obsolete.

In the late 1960s psychodynamic psychiatrists and mental hospitals came under attack by critics who argued that both were designed to control the behavior of persons who refused to conform. In *One Flew Over the Cuckoo's Nest*, a United Artists film (1975), Jack Nicholson plays a patient whose free and spirited behavior disrupts the institutional regimen. Hospital authorities perform a lobotomy on him as a punishment for his independence.

The presence of a new subgroup of homeless individuals with a dual diagnosis of mental illness and substance abuse on the streets of communities throughout the United States in the last decades of the twentieth century posed troubling dilemmas. Joyce Brown (right), who referred to herself as Billy Boggs, lived on the streets of Manhattan and exhibited behavior commonly associated with severe mental disorders. She was picked up when city authorities began to remove mentally ill persons whose lives might be endangered by inclement weather. The ACLU and its attorney Norman Siegel (left) came to Brown's defense. The ensuing case dramatized the clash of two moral principles: individual autonomy and freedom on the one hand versus the obligation of the community to protect residents and to ensure that the mentally disabled would not be abandoned.

Since the 1970s large numbers of homeless people, such as these men in Los Angeles in 1989, have lived on the streets of virtually every American city. It has been estimated that perhaps 25 percent of this homeless population have a diagnosis of severe mental illness. The twin problems of homelessness and mental disorder pose major challenges to a society that accepts a moral obligation to provide assistance to individuals who are either disabled or unable to achieve independence.

bona fide effort to provide an individualized treatment plan and periodic evaluation.[45]

The major challenges to the procedures governing commitment, hospitalization, and treatment came from lower federal and state courts during the 1970s. During that decade public-interest lawyers, representing clients previously without access to traditional legal services, challenged many long-standing doctrines that had governed the process of mental hospitalization. They argued that commitment statutes were vague and arbitrary; that courts and legislatures be required to follow a least restrictive alternative approach to civil commitment; that all persons facing the prospect of involuntary hospitalization be provided with maximum due process of law to ensure that they would not be deprived in arbitrary ways of their liberties; and that hospitalized patients should also retain certain basic rights, including a right to treatment, a right to refuse (within certain limits) some controversial or undesirable treatments, and confidentiality of their records.[46] In a series of landmark decisions, the courts accepted many of these arguments, thereby limiting the discretionary authority of psychiatrists, public officials, and other mental health professionals. Although the precise impact of changing legal doctrine was not always clear, there is little doubt that judicial decisions tended to weaken the authority of both psychiatrists and mental hospital officials.

The multifaceted attack on psychiatry was also mirrored in new public images in the press and media. By the mid-1960s the postwar favorable image of psychiatry had all but vanished; psychiatrists were now portrayed either as malevolent or comedy-like figures. In *Shock Treatment* (1964), Lauren Bacall played an immoral psychiatrist who administered an institution for illicit financial gain. At the end she became psychotic. Similarly, such popular novels as Ken Kesey's *One Flew Over the Cuckoo's Nest* (1962) and Elliot Baker's *A Fine Madness* (1964) used fiction to describe psychiatrists as evil egomaniacs. The former was made into a popular motion picture starring Jack Nicholson in 1975. In this film patients were depicted as weak rather than mentally disordered, and electroshock and lobotomy as instruments of repression rather than bona fide medical treatments.[47]

The attack on psychiatry and mental hospitals from without was also accompanied by internal fragmentation. In the two decades following the end of World War II psychodynamic figures dominated the specialty. But even before the close of the 1960s their dominant position had begun to erode. As other mental health professions advanced jurisdictional claims, psychiatric hegemony over the psychotherapies became tenuous at best. Moreover, psychotherapy—whatever its form—was time-consuming and labor intensive; its efficacy in treating serious and persistent mental illnesses was questionable. The introduction of the psychotropic drugs in the 1950s, in addition, had provided somatic therapies that had efficacious results. Finally, the rise of private office practice meant that most psychodynamic psychiatrists were preoccupied with the neuroses (especially depression) and other personality disorders, and thus had relatively few contacts with individuals suffering from schizophrenia and other serious mental disorders.

As the psychodynamic consensus unraveled, biological psychiatry assumed a more prominent position. To be sure, the somatic tradition had never completely disappeared even when psychodynamic thinking dominated the scene. The development of the psychotropic drugs in the early 1950s in particular helped to maintain interest in biological therapies. In 1959 the members of the Society of Biological Psychiatry began publishing the proceedings of their annual meetings, and within a decade had created a new journal (*Biological Psychiatry*). Yet it was clear that those committed to physiological explanations and therapies remained a distinct minority.

During and after the 1970s, however, psychodynamic and psychoanalytic psychiatry was eclipsed by biological psychiatry. The loss of jurisdiction over the psychotherapies undoubtedly hastened the return to a more biologically oriented psychiatry, which was more congenial to orthodox medical thinking. But the disillusionment with liberal, psychological, and environmental explanations of human behavior characteristic of these years played an important role as well. Biological psychiatry in many ways mirrored the ever-increasing fascination with the life sciences and the growing tendency to explain human behavior in physiological and genetic terms. By contrast, the psychodynamic tradition had seemingly failed to live up to its promise. In a textbook published in 1966, two prominent psychiatrists conceded that

> the important questions of diagnosis, prognosis, etiology, and therapy are still unanswered and constitute psychiatry's greatest challenge. Can the behavioral processes and changes be described with any precision and order? Is schizophrenia a group of ill-defined syndromes, or is it a true nosological entity? Is it a disease? A maladjustment? A way of life? Is the

irrationality of schizophrenia transmitted by genes or by interpersonal relations? What are the best methods of treatment?

That such issues were raised suggested the growing disillusionment with purely psychosocial and psychodynamic explanations. Consequently, psychiatrists and other medical specialists began to focus on the role of genetic factors, neurotransmitters, and aberrant metabolism. At the same time somatic therapies assumed even greater prominence.[48]

The growing strength of biological psychiatry did not necessarily lead to a new unified consensus. The absence of conclusive evidence to support competing theories—biological as well as psychodynamic—created constant controversy. A case in point involved the emergence of what became known as orthomolecular psychiatry, which was based on the belief that brain function was dependent upon the internal molecular environment. A low concentration of certain vitamins, for example, could influence mental function and behavior. During the 1950s Humphrey Osmond and Abram Hoffer began to employ a model of mental disorders based on pellagra—a disease caused by a vitamin deficiency that often included psychotic behavioral symptoms. They claimed to have striking successes in treating disturbed patients with megavitamin therapy. When Linus Pauling—the distinguished Nobel laureate in chemistry—threw his influence behind their work in 1968, a heated public debate followed. Although orthomolecular psychiatry quickly disappeared, its short-lived popularity offered testimony to the growing receptivity toward biological explanations and the growing disillusionment with psychotherapy.[49]

The gulf between psychodynamic and biological psychiatrists was never absolute. Therapy was often eclectic; most practitioners employed a blend of drug and psychotherapeutic techniques. One survey revealed that about 60 percent of psychoanalysts prescribed medication for some of their patients. Nevertheless, the trend was clearly in the direction of a biologically oriented specialty. By the mid-1970s few departments of psychiatry were chaired by psychodynamic or psychoanalytic figures, and biological psychiatry seemed to represent the wave of the future.[50]

The internal changes within psychiatry and the growing dominance of a biological model of mental disorders had significant consequences. Less concerned with the role of broad environmental and psychological factors, biological psychiatrists stressed the importance of exploiting new technologies that might illuminate the pathology of mental disorders and reintegrate themselves with other medical specialties. Paradoxically, a preoccupation with pathology and diagnosis shifted psychiatric interest toward such severe mental illnesses as schizophrenia while simultaneously separating the medical and social aspects of mental disorders. Preoccupied with the former, biological psychiatrists tended to be less involved and concerned with psychosocial rehabilitation or community support systems.

In the nineteenth century psychiatry's inseparable links with mental asylums were the defining characteristic of public policy. In effect, care and treatment was integrated within a comprehensive system of institutions. That many hospitals failed to live up to their ideals was obvious. Yet one of the basic goals of public policy—to assure that the most severely disordered would have access to comprehensive care—was at least minimally met.

During the 1960s the mental health system underwent a series of dramatic changes. The postwar claim that community care and treatment of the mentally ill was superior to confinement in remote custodial mental hospitals became an article of faith that shaped the political agenda. The presumption that shaped the legislation passed in 1963 was that a national system of community mental health centers would meet the needs of the most severely mentally ill and provide a range of psychological services for those seeking assistance in dealing with personal problems.

The expansion of community institutions and services in the halcyon atmosphere of the early and mid-1960s, however, failed to usher in a golden age. The new community mental health policy often overlooked the need for supportive services to ensure that severely mentally ill persons would have access to housing, food, social networks, and recreation; it also created a bifurcated system with weak or nonexistent linkages between centers and mental hospitals. Similarly, the shift from psychodynamic to biological psychiatry diminished still further the specialty's historic preoccupation with care. The unmet needs of severely and persistently mentally ill would force a fundamental reevaluation of mental health policy after 1970 when new demographic factors and a different social and political environment combined to transform both the nature of the problem and the context in which policy was formulated.

11

Confronting the Mad Among Us in Contemporary America

In the 1960s a virtual revolution in social programs transformed American welfare. To be sure, most middle-class Americans still retained stereotyped images of the poor and of minority groups and often continued to express opposition to programs that provided benefits to presumably lazy and improvident individuals. Yet the expansion of Social Security, including Medicare and Medicaid, and similar federal programs had broad-based support. As a whole, these programs contributed to a dramatic reduction in the incidence of poverty as well as an expansion in benefits for a variety of more affluent groups, particularly the elderly.[1] The mentally ill also benefited, since federal funding assisted in improving their lives in a variety of ways.

This massive increase in social welfare and medical expenditures, however, came at precisely the time that America became enmeshed in the long, divisive, and costly war in Vietnam. The conflict had a decidedly negative effect on many of the domestic initiatives of the 1960s. Lyndon B. Johnson was forced from office in 1968. Domestic programs were scrapped to meet war-related needs. The stage was set for a political reaction that gave a more conservative Republican party control of the White House for twenty out of the next twenty-four years.

But even before any new administration took office, it was clear that the Community Mental Health Centers Act of 1963 had not met many of the varied needs of the severely mentally ill. Appropriations during the first five years of the program, according to Mike Gorman, amounted to about 40 percent of the sum originally authorized. "At night sometimes when I am dispirited and think up all kinds of bills," he testified in 1969, "I think we ought to go to the Pentagon—mental health as an amendment to the Pentagon authorization." More importantly, community mental health centers (CMHCs) served a different population.[2]

Outwardly the mental health initiatives of the Kennedy and Johnson administrations had an aura of success. The increase in the number of CMHCs and the decrease in the inpatient population of mental hospitals appeared to confirm the claim that CMHCs would indeed ultimately replace obsolete mental hospitals. At a series of congressional hearings prominent individuals expressed gratification that the legislation of 1963 had achieved a virtual revolution in the ways mentally ill persons received care and treatment. In describing the changes that had occurred, Wilbur Cohen, Acting Secretary of the Department of Health, Education and Welfare, told a congressional committee in early 1968 that mental illnesses had been brought "out in the open" because of the presence of community mental health services. Many mentally ill persons, he added, "can be put back to work, can be given their rightful place in society and they are not a drain on either their families or the taxpayer." Robert Finch, Cohen's successor, was equally sanguine. "One of the real successes of recent years has been the program of community mental health centers."[3]

Rhetoric aside, there was little or no evidence to prove such optimistic assertions. The decline in the inpatient mental hospital population had little to do with the slow expansion in the number of centers, many of which had only tenuous relationships with seriously mentally ill persons. Centers, charged APA president Donald G. Langsley, had "drifted away from their original purpose" and featured "counseling and crisis intervention for predictable problems of living." This type of counseling tended to reduce proportionately services for the severely mentally ill. At the same time the number of psychiatrists affiliated with centers fell sharply; their places were taken by psychologists and social workers. This development further vitiated the original mandate of centers, since psychiatrists were more likely to work with severely disordered persons than other staff.[4]

Federal pressure could have been used to force centers to emphasize services for the most impaired part of the population. But the federal government was in no position to provide oversight of the large numbers of CMHCs. State authorities might have assumed a supervisory role, but much of the legislation enacted during the 1960s was based on the assumption that states were both too conservative and obsolete, and that a federal-local partnership would prove more effective. Precisely because of the remoteness of federal authority, community institutions became vulnerable to constituent pressures to deal with personal problems and substance abuse. Under such circumstances the severely and persistently mentally ill tended to suffer; they lacked an effective lobby capable of protecting their interests.

More importantly, the focus of federal policy shifted dramatically because of a growing perception that substance abuse (particularly drugs and, to a lesser extent, alcohol) represented major threats to the public at large. Beginning in 1968 Congress enacted legislation that sharply altered the role of centers by adding new services for substance abusers, children, and elderly persons. The Congress believed that the act of 1963 had resolved most of the major problems of the mentally ill and that greater attention should be paid to other groups in need of mental health services. As the services provided by centers proliferated, the interests of the severely and persistently mentally ill—clearly the group with the most formidable problems—slowly receded into the background.

Changes in the presidency in 1969 added yet another discordant element. Between 1946 and 1969 those who occupied the White House tended to follow the lead of a powerful bipartisan health lobby determined to expand federal biomedical research and then to disseminate the benefits of modern medicine to the entire population. The biomedical lobby's agenda included support for strong programs for mental health. By the late 1960s, however, its power had begun to ebb. The pressures of war, alleged financial mismanagement by National Institutes of Health officials, internal differences over priorities, and the death of John Fogarty in the House and retirement of Lister Hill in the Senate sapped the lobby's strength. When Richard M. Nixon took office in early 1969, friction inevitably followed.

Unlike his predecessors, Nixon had an uneasy relationship with the specialty of psychiatry. Psychodynamic practitioners, who still dominated the specialty, were generally associated with a liberal political ideology and committed to a variety of social programs. Moreover, some community mental health centers—particularly those in urban areas—

were associated with a radical political agenda. Given Nixon's conservative political base and outlook, it was perhaps inevitable that conflict over both the proper shape of mental health policy and the role of the federal government would follow.

Nixon's attention during his first year in office was focused on the Vietnam War. Hence domestic legislation to provide continuing funding for construction and staffing passed without a great deal of controversy. In 1970, however, an open conflict erupted. Stanley Yolles was forced out as Director of the NIMH because of basic policy differences with members of the administration who either opposed many of the social programs of the 1960s or believed that categorical grants were ineffective. Between 1970 and 1972 the administration worked assiduously to cut NIMH programs, many of which survived only because of a sympathetic Congress. Differences came to a head in 1973 when the administration recommended that the community mental health centers program be terminated forthwith. Moreover, funds already appropriated under the legislation were impounded. In his testimony before a congressional committee, Casper W. Weinberger (Secretary of Health, Education, and Welfare) insisted that the centers program had always been designed only as a demonstration project. He urged that the federal role in this area be ended, and that the program be administered and funded by the states. His interpretation that the act of 1963 was intended as a demonstration was emphatically rejected by committee members. Their position was upheld by Judge Gerhard Gesell of the U.S. District Court for the District of Columbia, who ordered the impounded funds released. The act of 1963, he added, "was never viewed by Congress as a demonstration program . . . but rather a national effort to redress the present wholly inadequate measures being taken to meet increasing mental health treatment needs."[5]

The conflict between the administration and Congress produced more heat than light; the claims of both protagonists rested on slippery grounds. Defenders insisted that there was a direct relationship between centers and the decline in the censuses of mental hospitals even though data to support such a contention were largely absent. The administration's claim that the intent of the original legislation was to create a demonstration project was equally without foundation; its position reflected the dominance of ideology over evidence. The partisan nature of the conflict had the inadvertent result of deflecting attention from the basic problem, namely, growing numbers of mentally ill persons living in communities and lacking access to services that would meet their needs for food, housing, and social support networks.

While Congress was considering legislation to extend the CMHCs program, continuing revelations about the Watergate scandal increasingly began to preoccupy the attention of the White House. Nixon's resignation in the summer of 1974 was welcomed by those concerned with mental health policy issues, if only because the administration was perceived as an opponent of any significant federal role in shaping and financing services. In the months preceding and following Nixon's resignation, Congress undertook a reassessment of the program. By this time it was evident that centers had serious shortcomings. The General Accounting Office (which provides studies and evaluations for Congress) had come to the same conclusion. In 1974 it noted that a system "for the coordinated delivery of mental-health services has not been fully developed." The report also emphasized the lack of working relationships between mental hospitals and centers.[6]

In mid-1975 Congress finally passed a mental health law, overriding President Gerald Ford's veto. Cognizant of the patchwork nature of the existing system, the legislation substantially altered the definition of a center. Under the regulations governing the original act of 1963, CMHCs were required to deliver five essential services. The new law mandated no less than twelve. These included screening, follow-up care and therapy for released patients, as well as specialized services for children, the elderly, and alcohol and drug abusers. A two-year grant program offered temporary assistance to enable centers to institute these services. In 1977 and 1978 Congress extended the program's authorization for one and two years, respectively. By then there were about 650 CMHCs, a total far below the original goal of 2,000 centers by 1980. Nevertheless, the program had managed to survive through four presidential administrations, and the 1975 legislation expressly endorsed the goals that had been written into law in 1963. Community mental health care, noted the preamble to the act,

> is the most effective and humane form of care for a majority of mentally ill individuals; the federally funded community mental health centers have had a major impact on the improvement of mental health by (a) fostering coordination and cooperation between agencies responsible for mental health care, which in turn has resulted in a decrease of overlapping services and more efficient utilization of available resources, (b) bringing comprehensive community mental health care to all who need care with-

in a specific geographic area regardless of ability to pay, and (c) developing a system of care which insures continuity of care for all patients and thus our national resource to which all Americans should enjoy access.[7]

CMHCs were officially recognized to be an important component within the mental health system. Yet as limited federal resources were diverted to new centers, older ones were left in an increasingly precarious condition. More importantly, centers were not serving the needs of severely and persistently mentally ill persons being released in ever-growing numbers from state hospitals. The counterproductive friction between Congress and the White House had prevented both sides from asking whether or not the basic human needs of a severely disabled population were being met. By the mid-1970s, the failure to address that issue was becoming apparent as deinstitutionalized patients were becoming more visible.

By 1976 most of the individuals who had played a prominent role in shifting policy away from mental hospitals during the postwar decades had largely passed from the scene. No one of stature had replaced Robert Felix, who had skillfully presided over the creation of a powerful federal presence and orchestrated the passage of the legislation of 1963. Hope arrived with the inauguration of Jimmy Carter in 1977. His wife, Rosalynn, had been active in efforts to transform the mental health system in Georgia and to create community alternatives to the traditional asylum system. In one of his first acts, Carter signed an executive order creating the President's Commission on Mental Health to review national needs and to make necessary recommendations. His wife served as honorary chairperson and played an important role in the ensuing deliberations as well as providing direct access to the White House staff.

During its year-long existence the Commission held public meetings and reviewed a large number of panel reports. Although its members had taken on a task similar to that of the JCMIH some twenty years before, the environment in which they operated was quite different. By the mid-1970s mental health services had proliferated; the clientele was far larger and variegated in character; and the groups involved often had different interests. The largely uncoordinated nature of the mental health system precluded any agreement on a single agenda. Moreover, the economic climate was hardly propitious for new and costly initiatives. The raging inflation, escalation in federal expenditures following the start of the Medicare and Medicaid programs, and other problems virtually ensured that substantial new resources would not be forthcoming. The Commission also functioned in a difficult political environment. The severely and persistently mentally ill represented but one constituency, and had to compete with others in need of mental health care. Nor were the mental health professions united around any single course of action; diverse interests and ideologies were characteristic.

To be sure, Commission members recognized that there were

> people with chronic mental disabilities who have been released from hospitals but who do not have the basic necessities of life. They lack adequate food, clothing, or shelter. We have heard of woefully inadequate follow-up mental health and general medical care. And we have seen evidence that half the people released from large mental hospitals are being readmitted within a year of discharge. While not every individual can be treated within the community, many of the readmissions to State hospitals could have been avoided if comprehensive assistance had existed within their communities.

Similarly, the task panel on assessing CMHCs noted that "the total program is moving away from caring for the most severely mentally disabled, the type most likely to spend time in a State hospital." This view was confirmed by an influential General Accounting Office report in 1977.[8]

The Commission's final report offered at best a potpourri of diverse and sometimes conflicting recommendations that touched on virtually every aspect of the mental health system. It supported linkages between family and community networks, on the one hand, and mental health agencies on the other. It called for a more responsive service system; a national plan to meet the needs of the chronic mentally ill; more effective ways of financing care and treatment; and an expansion in the number of mental health personnel and greater diversity in recruitment. The report urged greater protection of patient rights; more resources for research; an expansion of preventive activities; and heightened sensitivity toward the needs of special populations, including minorities, children, and the elderly. In brief, the report offered something to virtually every constituency. But its generalized nature, unwillingness to face fiscal realities, and inability to set priorities gave the massive document a diffuse character that offered no coherent policy guidelines. Indeed, the Commission's failure to provide clear recommendations set the stage for subsequent conflicts both within the administration and in Congress.[9]

After receiving the report, Carter directed Joseph Califano (Secretary of Heath, Education and Welfare) to draft necessary legislation. The process, however, moved with glacial slowness. The NIMH was in a transitional stage because of a change in leadership, and its involvement was delayed. Moreover, the existence of numerous constituencies proved a major impediment. State officials wanted greater regulatory authority; CHMC leaders wanted to preserve their autonomy; the American Federation of State and County Municipal Employees was fearful that the process of change would threaten the livelihoods of state hospital employees; representatives of specialized populations wanted to protect the interests of their constituencies; and various professional groups and organizations had their own agendas. The process of drafting a law took about a year, and in the spring of 1979 President Carter finally submitted a bill to Congress.[10]

The draft legislation aroused immediate opposition in both branches of Congress as well as from the various mental health constituencies. After complex maneuvering (in which Rosalynn Carter played an important role), a quite different bill emerged. The Mental Health Systems Act was passed by Congress and signed into law in October, 1980, just weeks before the presidential election. Its provisions were complex and in some respects contradictory. It assumed continued federal leadership in improving community services, even though the CMHC program would eventually lose federal funding. The law emphasized support services for vulnerable groups, including individuals with chronic mental illnesses, children, and the elderly. It called for planning, accountability, and "performance contracts"; linkages between mental health and general medical care; and the protection of patient rights. Although authorizing somewhat larger funding levels, the act did not mandate any clear priorities. Nevertheless, the law suggested at the very least the outlines of a national system that would ensure the availability of both care and treatment in community settings.[11]

The Mental Health Systems Act had hardly become law when its provisions became moot. The accession of Ronald Reagan to the presidency led to an immediate reversal of policy. Preoccupied with reducing both taxes and federal expenditures, the new administration proposed a 25 percent cut in federal funding. More importantly, it called for a conversion of federal mental health programs into a single block grant to the states carrying few restrictions and without policy guidelines. The presidential juggernaut proved irresistible, and in the summer of 1981 the Omnibus Budget Reconciliation Act was signed into law. Among other things, it provided a block grant to states for mental health services and substance abuse. At the same time, it repealed most of the provisions of the Mental Health Systems Act. The new legislation did more than reduce federal funding; it reversed nearly three decades of federal involvement and leadership. In the ensuing decade the focus of policy and funding shifted back to the states and local communities, thus restoring in part the tradition that had prevailed until World War II. The transfer and decentralization of authority, however, exacerbated existing tensions; federal support was reduced at precisely the same time that states were confronted with monumental social and economic problems that increased their fiscal burdens.

———————

Disagreement over national mental health policy was but one development that had major repercussions on the mentally ill. Equally significant, states in the 1970s accelerated the discharge of large numbers of severely and persistently mentally ill persons from public mental hospitals. Before 1965 many patients spent years, if not decades, in asylums. After 1970 length-of-stays began to be measured in days or weeks. As more and more mentally ill persons began living in the community rather than in state hospitals, issues of treatment and care became more complex and problematic, since no single authority had overall responsibility to provide them with services.

The extraordinary difficulties sometimes faced by mentally ill persons in the community were graphically portrayed by Susan Sheehan. In a series of dramatic articles in the *New Yorker* that gained national attention and were subsequently published as a book in 1982 entitled *Is There No Place on Earth for Me?* she vividly portrayed the life of Sylvia Frumkin (a pseudonym), a thirty-two-year-old chronic mental patient. As an adolescent living at home, Sylvia had begun to experience difficulty relating to her family and peers. Her parents initially dismissed their daughter's fears of having a nervous breakdown, but sent her to a psychiatric social worker after she made a suicidal gesture. Sylvia was referred for further treatment to a psychiatric clinic, and was subsequently institutionalized in a private psychiatric hospital. Since her hospitalization was not covered by her family's health insurance, she was transferred to a general hospital and began a course of psychiatric medication. When her condition continued to deteriorate, she was sent to Creedmoor State Hospital. Over the next seventeen years she experienced periodic episodes of mental illness. Her symptomatology varied in the extreme. At times she was delusional, hallucinatory, hostile, violent, and posed a threat to her own well-being; at other times she was lucid and aware. During these years she underwent no less than forty-five changes in treatment, and moved between family and various hospital and community residential facilities. She was hospitalized on no less than twenty-seven different occasions. Sheehan's dramatic and heart-wrenching portrayal of the travails of one person illustrated both the human and social costs of mental illness and some of the problems in providing care and treatment outside of asylums.[12]

Prior to World War II, by contrast, responsibility for care and treatment had been centralized in public mental hospitals. Under the policies adopted during and after the 1960s, however, responsibility was diffused among a number of different programs and systems. The failure of CMHCs to assume the burdens previously shouldered by state hospitals, for example, magnified the significance of the medical care and entitlement systems. General hospitals with and without psychiatric wards began to play an increasingly important role in treating the mentally ill. Because such persons tended to be unemployed and thus lacked either private resources or health insurance, their psychiatric treatment was often financed by Medicaid. Similarly, responsibility for care (i.e., food, clothing, and shelter) was slowly subsumed under the jurisdiction of federal entitlement programs. A paradoxical result followed. The fragmentation of what had once been a unified approach to mental illnesses was accompanied by an expansion of resources to enable seriously mentally ill persons to reside in the community.

During and after the 1960s deinstitutionalization was indirectly sanctioned by the judiciary when federal and state courts began to take up longstanding legal issues relating to the mentally ill. In a series of notable cases, courts raised a variety of questions. Under what circumstances could states deprive mentally ill persons of their liberties by involuntarily confining them in mental hospitals? Did states have the authority to institutionalize mentally disordered persons who posed neither a threat to others nor to themselves? If institutionalization was justified, were patients entitled to minimum levels of treatment and care?

The identification of these new legal issues had significant consequences for psychiatrists and the mentally ill. Discussions about the
ethics of therapeutic experimentation, informed consent, and patient
rights were rare before World War II. By the 1960s, however, the traditional preoccupation with professional needs was supplemented by a
new concern with patient rights. Courts defined a right to treatment in
the least restrictive environment; shortened the duration of all forms of
commitment and placed restraints on its application; undermined the
sole right of psychiatrists to make purely medical judgments about the
necessity of commitment; accepted the right of patients to litigate both
before and after admission to a mental institution; and even defined a
right of a patient to refuse treatment under certain circumstances. The
emergence of mental health law advocates tended to weaken the authority of both psychiatrists and mental hospitals, and conferred added legitimacy to the belief that protracted hospitalization was somehow
counterproductive and that community care and treatment represented
a more desirable policy choice.[13]

Judicial decisions, however significant, merely confirmed existing
trends by providing a legal sanction for deinstitutionalization. Some
experts recognized the danger and voiced concern.[14] Nevertheless, the
pattern of discharging patients from mental hospitals after relatively brief
length-of-stays accelerated after 1970 because of the expansion of federal entitlement programs having no direct relationship with mental health
policy. States began to take advantage of a series of relatively new federal initiatives that were designed to provide assistance for a variety of disabled groups and thus facilitate their maintenance in the community.

The elderly were among the first to be affected by new federal policies. Immediately following the passage of Medicaid in 1965, states
began to shift the care of elderly persons with behavioral symptoms
from mental hospitals to chronic care nursing facilities. Such a move was
hardly the result of altruism or a belief that the interests of aged persons
would be better served in such institutions. On the contrary, state officials were predisposed to the use of nursing homes because a large part
of the costs were assumed by the federal government. The quality of
care in such facilities (which varied in the extreme) was not an important
consideration in transferring patients. Indeed, the relocation of elderly
patients from mental hospitals to extended care facilities was often
marked by increases in the death rate. Moreover, many nursing homes

provided no psychiatric care. When Bruce C. Vladeck published his study of nursing homes in 1980, he selected as his book title *Unloving Care: The Nursing Home Tragedy*.[15]

During the 1960s the population of nursing homes rose from about 470,000 to nearly 928,000, largely as a result of Medicaid. A study by the General Accounting Office in 1977 noted that Medicaid was "one of the largest single purchasers of mental health care and the principal Federal program funding the long-term care of the mentally disabled." It also was the most significant "federally sponsored program affecting deinstitutionalization." By 1985 nursing homes had over 600,000 residents diagnosed as mentally ill; the cost of their care was over $10.5 billion, a large proportion of which was paid for by Medicaid. The massive transfer of large numbers of elderly patients who behaved in abnormal ways was not controversial, if only because such individuals posed no obvious threats to community residents. Designed to provide for services for the elderly and indigent, therefore, Medicaid (as well as Medicare) quickly became one of the largest mental health programs in the United States.[16]

Other federal programs had an equally profound effect on the nonelderly mentally ill. In 1956 Congress had amended the Social Security Act to enable eligible persons age fifty and over to receive disability benefits. The Social Security Disability Insurance (SSDI) program continued to become more inclusive in succeeding years, and ultimately covered the mentally disabled. In 1972 the Social Security Act was further amended to provide coverage for individuals who did not qualify for benefits. Under the provisions of Supplemental Security Income for the Aged, the Disabled, and the Blind (more popularly known as SSI), all those whose age or disability made them incapable of holding a job became eligible for income support. This entitlement program was administered and fully funded by the federal government; its affiliation with Social Security had the added virtue of minimizing the stigmatization often associated with welfare. SSI and SSDI encouraged states to discharge severely and persistently mentally ill persons from mental hospitals, since federal payments would presumably enable them to live in the community. Those who were covered under SSI also became eligible for coverage under Medicaid. In addition, public housing programs and food stamps added to the resources of mentally ill persons residing in the community.[17]

The expansion of federal entitlement programs hastened the discharge of large numbers of institutionalized patients during and after the 1970s. This trend was reflected in the changing pattern of mental hospital populations. In the decade following 1955 the decline in inpatient populations was modest, falling from 559,000 to 475,000. The decreases after 1965 were dramatic; between 1970 and 1986 the number of inpatient beds in state and county institutions declined from 413,000 to 119,000. Length-of-stays dropped correspondingly; the median stay for all patients was about twenty-eight days, suggesting that public hospitals still had an important role in providing psychiatric services for a highly disabled population. Moreover, schizophrenics accounted for slightly more than a third of all mental hospital admissions, whereas only 19 percent of psychiatric patients treated in general hospitals fell into this category. Indeed, state hospitals remained the largest provider of total inpatient days of psychiatric care; their clients were disproportionately drawn from the ranks of the most difficult, troubled, and violent-prone.[18]

The growing numbers of severely and persistently mentally ill in communities, in conjunction with the expansion of mental health services and third-party insurance, signaled the emergence of the general hospital as a major supplier of psychiatric services. By 1983 general hospitals accounted for almost two-thirds of the nearly three million inpatient psychiatric episodes. Of these, about 37 percent were for psychoses, 23 percent for alcohol dependence, and 13 percent for neurotic and personality disorders (largely depression). General hospitals, in other words, had become the most frequent site for hospitalization for mental illnesses.[19]

In theory, the combination of entitlement programs and access to psychiatric services outside of mental hospitals should have fostered greater state financial support for community programs. The presumption was that a successful community policy would eventually permit the consolidation of some mental hospitals and closure of others, thus facilitating the transfer of state funds from institutional to community programs. In practice, however, the state mental hospital proved far more resilient than its critics anticipated. Some had powerful support among community residents and employees who feared the dramatic economic consequences that would accompany closure.[20] A shrinking inpatient census, therefore, sometimes led to rising per capita expenditures, since operating costs were distributed among fewer patients. Equally important, there remained a seemingly irreducible group of individuals who were so disabled that institutional care appeared to be a necessity. Using data collected by the NIMH, the authors of one study concluded that there appeared "to be a core of some 100,000 residents for whom there is no alternative to state hospital treatment." On the basis of a careful analysis of the patient population of the Massachusetts Mental Health Center (which had responsibility for the Boston geographic catchment area), two psychiatrists estimated that there were about fifteen persons per 100,000 of population who required "secure, supportive, long-term care in specialized facilities at the regional and state level." If their data were representative, there were perhaps 35,000 persons in the United States requiring mental hospital care or its equivalent.[21]

In retrospect, mental health policy changed dramatically after 1965, but not in the manner envisaged by those active in its formulation. After World War II there was a decided effort to substitute an integrated community system of services for traditional mental hospitals. The system that emerged in the 1970s and 1980s, however, was quite different. First, mental hospitals did not become obsolete even though they lost their central position. They continued to provide both care and treatment for the most severely disabled part of the population. Second, community mental health programs expanded dramatically, and inpatient and outpatient psychiatric services became available in both general hospitals and CMHCs. A significant proportion of their clients, however, represented new populations. Finally, a large part of the burden of supporting severely mentally ill persons in the community fell to a variety of federal entitlement programs that existed quite apart from the mental health care system. Since the 1970s, therefore, severely and persistently mentally ill persons have come under the jurisdiction of two quite distinct systems—entitlements and mental health—that often lacked any formal programmatic or institutional linkages.

Whatever its contradictory and tangled origins, deinstitutionalization had positive consequences for a large part of the nation's severely and persistently mentally ill population. Data from the Vermont Longitudinal Research Project offered some dramatic evidence that individuals with severe mental illness who were provided with a range of comprehensive services could live in the community. Between 1955 and 1960 a multidisciplinary team initiated a program of comprehensive rehabilitation and community placement for 269 patients who were considered to be among the most severely disabled and chronically mentally ill in the Vermont State Hospital. Middle-aged, poorly educated, and lower class, they had histories of illness that averaged sixteen years, had been hospitalized from one to ten times, and as a group averaged six years of continuous institutionalization. More than 80 percent were single, divorced, separated, or widowed, and were rarely visited by friends or relatives. Their disabilities were characteristic of schizophrenics. As a group, they were

> very slow, concentrated poorly, seemed confused and frequently had some impairment or distortion of recent or remote memory. They were touchy, suspicious, temperamental, unpredictable, and over-dependent on others to make minor day-to-day decisions for them. They had many peculiarities of appearance, speech, behavior, and a very constricted sense of time, space, and other people so that their social judgment was inadequate. Very often they seemed to be goalless or, if they had goals, they were quite unrealistic. They seemed to lack initiative or concern about anything beyond their immediate surroundings. . . .
>
> These patients also suffered a high incidence of chronic physical disabilities. Their psychomotor performance in a wide variety of tests was impaired so that their reaction times were prolonged and their ability to perform any type of skilled or precise activity was impaired. They suffered an increased incidence of many degenerative and chronic diseases.

Initially the multidisciplinary team constructed a new inpatient program that consisted of "drug treatment, open-ward care in homelike conditions, group therapy, graded privileges, activity therapy, industrial therapy, vocational counseling, and self-help groups." In the community treatment component, the same clinical team established halfway houses and outpatient clinics, located and placed individuals in jobs, and linked patients to support networks. Periodic follow-up evaluations were conducted over the next twenty-five years. The results indicated that two-thirds "could be maintained in the community if sufficient transitional facilities and adequate aftercare was provided." These results were confirmed by four other longitudinal studies, including Manfred Bleuler's twenty-three year study of 208 patients in Zurich, Ciompi and Muller's thirty-seven year study of 289 patients in Lausanne, Huber and colleagues' twenty-two year study of 502 subjects in Bonn, and Tsuang and colleagues' Iowa study.[22]

In reflecting upon a twenty-year battle with schizophrenia, a former patient offered a sketch of her experiences. In high school she had become withdrawn and sullen, lonely, and alienated. Her first psychotic episode came in college when she began to hear voices. During a two year period she was hospitalized on five occasions, the longest lasting for one year. After being discharged, she experienced a failed marriage. A second marriage to a psychiatrist succeeded, and the persistent and disabling symptoms did not recur for nearly a decade. When they reappeared, she had another unhappy experience in a mental hospital. Leaving the institution, she entered a private psychiatric residential halfway house, where she participated in a program that enabled her to rebuild her confidence and coping skills.

Mental hospitals, she concluded, had their place in the treatment and stabilization of acute psychiatric problems. The best long-term gains in functioning, however, occurred in good community support programs.

> Living in a community allows individuals with a psychiatric illness to gain understanding and acceptance from members of a treatment program. Peers, family, and friends can also provide recognition of and respect for clients' individuality and specific needs.
>
> A community support program can help residents develop a predictable daily schedule to offset their chaotic inner existence and thus make life easier. Any number of structured activities could satisfy this need, but I have found work—a paying job—to be the most helpful.
>
> Peer-run support groups can be extremely valuable to clients by offering support, friendship, hope for the future, and peer-group modeling. . . .
>
> My illness is a sobering reality, yet I am not as vulnerable to it as I once was because of regular use of coping strategies. . . .
>
> Although it takes time, those of us with a mental illness can overcome the disease by compensating for our handicaps. I did not choose to be ill, but I can choose to deal with schizophrenia and learn to live with it. I know I must confront my disorder with courage and struggle with my symptoms persistently, never viewing relapse as a permanent defeat and always acknowledging remission as a hard-earned victory.

A variety of recent studies have confirmed her belief that individuals with severe mental disorders prefer and do better in community settings that provide economic resources, particularly vocational rehabilitation, and status in terms of empowerment that provides a feeling of mastery rather than a sense of dependency.[23]

––––––––––

Under the best of circumstances deinstitutionalization would have been difficult to implement. The multiplication of programs and absence of formal integrated linkages, however, complicated the task of both clients and those responsible for providing care and treatment. Moreover, the decades of the 1970s and 1980s were hardly propitious for the development and elaboration of programs to serve disadvantaged populations such as the severely and persistently mentally ill. The dislocations and tensions engendered by the Vietnam War, the rise of antigovernment ideologies, and an economic system that no longer held out as great a promise of mobility and affluence, all combined to create a context that made experimentation and innovation more difficult. The founding of the National Alliance for the Mentally Ill (NAMI) in 1979 helped in part to redress the balance. It brought together families of the mentally ill in an advocacy organization that began to play an increasingly important role in the politics of mental health during and after the 1980s.

Equally important, the problems that followed the advent of deinstitutionalization were compounded by a partial misunderstanding of the nature of the mentally ill population as well as a service system that diffused rather than concentrated responsibility. As a policy, deinstitutionalization was based on the premise that the population found in mental hospitals was relatively homogeneous.

The first major wave of discharges came after 1965, and occurred among a group of individuals who had been institutionalized for relatively long periods of time or else had been admitted later in their lives. These individuals were relocated in chronic care facilities or else returned to the community where many made somewhat satisfactory adjustments. In its initial stage, therefore, deinstitutionalization dealt with individuals who had constituted the bulk of the traditional inpatient population. This phase was not controversial nor did it create difficulties, since few of these individuals seemed to pose a threat to others.

After 1970 a quite different situation prevailed due to basic demographic trends in the population as a whole and changes in the mental health service system. At the end of World War II there was a sharp rise in the number of births that peaked in the 1960s. Between 1946 and 1960 more than fifty-nine million births were recorded. The disproportionately large size of this age cohort meant that the number of persons at risk for developing severe mental disorders was very high. Morton Kramer warned that large increases were to be expected between 1975 and 1990 "in numbers of persons in high-risk age groups for the use of mental health facilities, and correctional institutions, homes for the aged and dependent and other institutions that constitute the institutional population." Moreover, younger people tended to be highly mobile.

Whereas 40 percent of the general population moved between 1975 and 1979, between 62 and 72 percent of individuals in their twenties changed residences. Like others in their age cohort, the large numbers of young adult severely and persistently mentally ill persons also moved frequently both within and between cities and in and out of rural areas.[24]

At the same time that the cohort born after 1945 was reaching their twenties and thirties, the mental health service system was undergoing fundamental changes. Prior to 1970 persons with severe and persistent mental disorders were generally cared for in state hospitals. If admitted in their youth, they often remained institutionalized for decades, or else were discharged and readmitted. Hence their care and treatment was centralized within a specific institutional context, and in general they were not visible in the community at large. Although chronically mentally ill persons were always found in the community, their relatively small numbers posed few difficulties and in general did not arouse public concern.

After 1970, however, a subgroup of the severely mentally ill—composed largely of young adults—were adversely affected by the changes in the mental health service system. Young chronically mentally ill persons were rarely confined for extended periods within mental hospitals. Restless and mobile, they were the first generation of psychiatric patients to reach adulthood within the community. Although their disorders were not fundamentally different than their predecessors, they behaved in quite different ways. They tended to emulate the behavior of their age peers who were often hostile toward conventions and authority. The young adult mentally ill exhibited aggressiveness, volatility, and were noncompliant. They generally fell into the schizophrenic category, although affective disorders and borderline personalities were also present. Above all, they lacked functional and adaptive skills. As one knowledgeable psychiatrist and his associates noted, these dysfunctional young adults

> seem to be stuck in the transition to adult life, unable to master the tasks of separation and independence. If we examine the nature of their failures, we find them to be based on more or less severe and chronic pathology: thought disorder; affective disorder; personality disorder; and severe deficits in ego functions such as impulse control, reality testing, judgment, modulation of affect, memory, mastery and competence, and integration. In terms of the necessary equipment for community life—the capacity to ensure stress, to work consistently toward realistic goals, to

relate to other people comfortably over time, to tolerate uncertainty and conflict—these young adults are disabled in a very real and pervasive sense.[25]

Complicating the clinical picture were high rates of alcoholism and drug abuse among these young adult chronic patients, which only exacerbated their volatile and noncompliant behavior. Their mobility and lack of coping skills also resulted in high rates of homelessness. Many of them traveled and lived together on the streets, thereby reinforcing each other's pathology. Urban areas in particular began to experience the presence of young adult severely and persistently ill individuals. But even rural states such as Vermont found that their chronic cases were made up of transients who required treatment, welfare, and support services. An APA report on the homeless mentally ill emphasized the tendency of these young persons to drift.

> Apart from their desire to outrun their problems, their symptoms, and their failures, many have great difficulty achieving closeness and intimacy.
>
> They drift also in search of autonomy, as a way of denying their dependency, and out of a desire for an isolated life-style. Lack of money often makes them unwelcome, and they may be evicted by family and friends. And they drift because of a reluctance to become involved in a mental health treatment program or a supportive out-of-home environment . . . [T]hey do not want to see themselves as ill.[26]

The case history of "Sam"—a real individual—is illustrative. His problems emerged in high school when he began to use drugs and underwent a change in personality. At eighteen he had already attempted suicide on several occasions, usually under the influence of alcohol. At this time he still lived at home, and was often caught in the middle between parents constantly bickering with each other. He had a history of drug abuse and experienced paranoid episodes. In the succeeding nine years he was hospitalized no less than seven times for anxiety, depression, confusion, and paranoid delusions. He wandered in and out of treatment programs. Diagnosed as schizophrenic and placed on medication, he repeatedly halted his medication, dropped out of treatment, and continued his dependency on alcohol and marijuana.

Another young man of twenty-three—"Ed"—presented slightly different problems. In speaking with him in Penn Station in New York City in 1980, an interviewer found him "quite disturbed—at times tearful—about his situation." During the conversation Ed alluded to "the Lamb of God, because God wants it that way." He indicated he had been happier when living in his own apartment where he could listen to the radio, smoke a cigarette, and have a cup of coffee. As the investigator recorded in notes:

> We talked in a windswept stairwell, Ed resisting my repeated suggestion to move somewhere warmer. Wolfed down a bagel and a carton of milk, but refused coffee because it made him jittery, speedy. Rapid shifts in conversation and mood: "Do you believe in war?" he asked. To my negative answer, he turns away, then shouts "Armageddon!" and goes on to mumble something about his arm. Slept last night in a warehouse, but can always, when really hard up, return to father's house in Brooklyn for food and clothing. Plagued by the sacrificial image of himself.[27]

The varied career of the young adult chronic patient can be followed in the checkered career of Mr. "J", who first came to the attention of the Rockland County CMHC in 1968. Diagnosed as a schizophrenic, he wandered in and out of treatment programs for more than a decade. He experimented with a number of drugs (including heroin), and was an alcoholic as well. Mr. J. often used and abused the emergency medical services at the Center, remained unemployed, and was socially isolated. Resisting recommendations to enter any systematic treatment programs, he continued to employ drugs to lessen the anxiety and tensions which were an integral part of his daily existence.[28]

These three young adults suffering from chronic mental illness were by no means atypical. Virtually every community experienced their presence on the streets, in emergency medical facilities, and in correctional institutions. Recent estimates have suggested that perhaps a quarter to a third of the single adult homeless population have a severe mental disorder. Many have a dual diagnosis of severe mental illness and substance abuse. Studies of these individuals found that they "were more likely to experience extremely harsh living conditions." More so than other groups, they suffered from "psychological distress and demoralization," granted "sexual favors for food and money," and were often "picked up by the police and . . . incarcerated." They had few contacts with their families, "were highly prone to victimization," were socially isolated, mistrusted people and institutions, and were resistant to accepting assistance.[29]

At the same time that young adult chronic patients were becoming more prominent, the mental hospital was losing its central position and the traditional links between care and treatment were shattered. Treatment was subsumed under a decentralized medical and psychiatric service system that served a varied and diversified client population. Care, by contrast, increasingly came under the jurisdiction of a series of federal entitlement programs which presumed that income maintenance payments would enable disabled persons to live within their community. Indeed, such programs increasingly drove the process of deinstitutionalization, since the release of patients from state institutions to communities meant an implicit transfer of funding responsibilities from states to the federal government.

The combination of a decentralized psychiatric system and the emergence of a young adult chronic population had profound consequences. Before 1965 mental hospitals retained responsibility for the severely mentally ill population. After 1970 a quite different situation prevailed among the new subgroup of young mentally ill adults. Many from this group tended to be pervasive but unsystematic users of psychiatric facilities. They entered and left mental hospitals after brief length-of-stays; they used emergency and psychiatric wards of general hospitals and other inpatient and outpatient facilities; and they could be found as well in correctional and penal institutions. Their high use of services tended to resemble a revolving door. Because of their mobility and restlessness, they moved quickly from one service to another. They proved to be noncompliant; their use of medication was sporadic and inconsistent; their refusal or inability to follow a sustained and rational treatment plan meant that the benefits gained were transient and minimal; and they often had a dual diagnosis of serious mental disorder and substance abuse.

Such patients tended to arouse negative reactions from mental health professionals. Chronicity and substance abuse contradicted the medical dream of cure. The management of such young and intransigent cases was often frustrating, and created powerful emotions of helplessness and inadequacy among professionals whose background and training had not prepared them for such a clientele. Equally significant, those who worked with young adult chronic persons received little or no peer support from their colleagues who dealt with different types of patients, and they found themselves outside the mainstream of psychiatry. "One of the highest 'costs' of the current pattern of interaction with these patients," conceded two psychiatrists,

> is the response of the caretakers themselves. As patients alternately demand and reject care, as they alternate between dependency, manipulation, withdrawal, anger, depression, and other interactive styles and

emotional states, even the most tolerant and resourceful clinician is likely to experience increasing anger, bitterness, frustration, and helplessness. These responses, in turn, can lead to even more inappropriate
treatment decisions, which are not in anyone's long-term interests but
only serve to remove the patient, temporarily, from the responsibility of
a given caretaker.[30]

Deinstitutionalization, as conceived in the postwar decades and
implemented after the 1960s, assumed the release of long-term institutional patients into the community. They were to receive treatment and
care from a series of linked and integrated aftercare institutions and programs. Such a policy, however, was largely irrelevant to many of the
young patients who were highly visible after 1970. They had little or no
experiences with prolonged institutionalization, and hence had not
internalized the behavioral norms of a hospital community. To be sure,
many of the norms of patienthood in institutions were objectionable, but
at the very least they provided individuals with some kind of structure.
Lacking such guidance, many young chronic mentally ill patients—
especially those with a dual diagnosis—developed a common cultural
identity quite at variance with the society in which they lived. The
mobility of such individuals, the absence of a family support system, and
programmatic shortcomings complicated their access to such basic
necessities as adequate housing and social support networks. The dearth
of many basic necessities of life further exacerbated their severe mental
disorders. Ironically, at the very time that unified, coordinated, and integrated medical and social services were needed to deal with a new
patient population, the policy of deinstitutionalization had created a
decentralized system that often lacked any clear focus and diffused
responsibility and authority.The outcome of the presidential election of
1980 further exacerbated to the problems of the mental health system.
However the presidency of Jimmy Carter may be evaluated on other
issues, there is little doubt that his administration was seeking to develop more effective policies to deal with some of the unanticipated and
undesirable consequences of deinstitutionalization. Stimulated by the
President's Commission on Mental Health, the Department of Health
and Human Services and a number of constituent groups developed a
National Plan for the Chronically Mentally Ill. Released a month after
Carter's defeat, the plan focused on the severely and chronically mentally ill. It acknowledged the importance of such programs as SSI, SSDI,
Medicaid, and Medicare, and offered a series of incremental recom-

mendations to modify and integrate them within a more effective national system.[31]

The inauguration of Ronald Reagan in early 1981, however, aborted efforts to integrate federal entitlement and disability programs with the mental health system. The new administration wanted to diminish sharply, if not reverse, the growth of federal domestic spending and thus to reduce taxes. The National Plan was shelved and the Mental Health Systems Act repealed. Equally important, there were sustained efforts to limit programs dealing with the dependent and disabled and to eliminate other programs, including public housing. Aside from efforts to convince Congress to alter the federal role in social policy issues, the White House also began to use its administrative authority to implement its political agenda.

A provision in the Disability Amendments legislation of 1980 gave the administration an opening. This act had mandated that the Social Security Administration should review the eligibility of all SSI and SSDI recipients once every three years. By this time Congress had begun to be concerned with the dramatic increase in entitlement expenditures, and wanted to guard against potential abuse. In 1980 the presumption was that such reviews would result in a modest saving of $218 million by 1985. At the time that Reagan took office, there were about 550,000 disabled persons receiving assistance under these programs, including the mentally ill. The administration seized upon this clause to deny benefits to thousands of new applicants and to purge thousands of others from the rolls. The mentally disabled were especially hard hit. They accounted for 11 percent of SSDI recipients, but represented 30 percent of those cut. The administration projected a savings of nearly $3.5 billion by 1985, and even larger savings in the future, since the mentally disabled who were receiving benefits were young and therefore would be on the roles for decades. The massive reduction in the eligibility rolls was achieved when the Social Security Administration developed a definition of disability and procedures that was quite at variance with earlier practices as well as with existing definitions of the nature of mental disorder.

When the magnitude of the cuts became evident, a public uproar followed. Testimony by individuals from the General Accounting Office brought into question the entire process, which was patently designed to reduce federal expenditures rather than eliminating ineligible recipients. Congressman Claude Pepper, the venerable champion of the aged and dependent, accused the administration of "cruel and callous policies designed to strike terror into the hearts of crippled people all across America." The actions of Social Security officials and the administration received even more negative publicity when news reports revealed that Sergeant Roy Benavidez, a wounded Vietnam veteran and winner of the Congressional Medal of Honor, had been cut off from receiving disability benefits. Besieged by judicial challenges and under attack by state officials, the administration in mid-1983 yielded to growing public criticism and reversed its policy. The incident, however, suggested the lengths that a Republican administration was prepared to go to achieve their social and political objectives.[32]

A superficial analysis of the mental health scene in the recent past can easily lead to depressing conclusions. The combined presence of large numbers of young adult chronic individuals as well as larger numbers of homeless people undoubtedly reinforced feelings of public apprehension and professional impotence. Indeed, the popular image of mental illnesses and the mental health service system was often shaped by spectacular exposes in the media—visual and printed—that seemed to reveal sharp and perhaps irreconcilable tensions. Two cases in particular illustrated the perennial stresses and anxieties caused by the presence of severely mentally ill individuals on the streets. In them could be seen the conflict between absolutist definitions of freedom and other humanitarian and ethical principles, as well as the concerns that the well-being, if not the very safety, of the community seemed endangered.

The first involved Joyce Brown, who in a delusional state began to refer to herself as Billy Boggs. An employee of a New Jersey public agency, she lost her position after becoming mentally disordered and a user of addictive drugs. Upon eviction from a shelter following a two-week stay at a general hospital, she was cared for at considerable psychological cost by her sisters, all of whom had grown up in a religious and cohesive African-American family. Given to chaotic behavioral eruptions, Brown disappeared, and then began to live on the streets of Manhattan in 1987. By any conventional standards, she suffered from either a severe mental illness or personality disorder. She urinated and defecated on the streets, destroyed money gained by panhandling, ran recklessly into heavily trafficked streets, and exposed herself when assistance was offered. A local outreach program attempted to hospitalize her on various occasions, but she was quickly released when the attending psychiatrist diagnosed her as psychotic but not dangerous.

At about this time city authorities had undertaken an effort to remove the severely mentally ill from the streets particularly when their lives might be endangered by severe weather. When Brown was picked up, the New York Civil Liberties Union came to her defense. The case quickly became a cause célèbre, and the complex legal proceedings received wide publicity in the press and media. After initial commitment proceedings a lower court judge issued a fuzzy ruling that Brown was not dangerous and hence authorized her release. His decision, however, evaded the issue of whether or not she was mentally ill. At a subsequent hearing the appellate court overruled the decision, but arranged for an independent evaluation. The psychiatrist conceded that Brown suffered from a serious mental illness, but had an "unusual degree of capacity." She was coherent in the courtroom and understood the benefits and complications of antipsychotic medication. Hence the psychiatrist recommended against involuntary medication. When the court ruled that Brown could not be treated against her will, she was discharged by Bellevue officials, who insisted that without psychiatric and drug treatment there was no justification for further confinement.

After her discharge, Brown briefly became a national celebrity. She possessed remarkable reconstitutive qualities even though she would revert to the bizarre behavior that had led originally to her commitment. Consequently, she appeared on national television and lectured on homelessness before enthusiastic students at the Harvard Law School. But the underlying pathology quickly reappeared, and she returned to the streets, began to use drugs, and resumed her bizarre behavioral pattern.[33]

Several years later readers of the *New York Times* and viewers of the popular television program "Sixty Minutes" learned about Larry Hogue, a substance abuser who was also diagnosed as being mentally ill. Hogue had terrorized a block in upper Manhattan by his behavior. He screamed at residents and threatened them with physical harm. A retired teacher testified that she had witnessed Hogue "assault an elderly woman, stuff burning papers into parked cars, smash a heavy piece of marble through the window of her parked car and, on numerous occasions, jump into traffic from a couched position." He had been institutionalized many times, during which his symptoms were brought under control by psychoactive drugs. Following his release, he reverted to the use of crack cocaine and once again began to behave in ways that alarmed area residents. Demands that he be institutionalized because he might pose a threat met with resistance from both the court and mental health officials. The former ruled that when individuals no longer posed an immediate threat to themselves or others, they could not be indefinitely confined against their will. Similarly, state mental health officials insisted that the mental health system could not act as a surrogate for the criminal justice system. Ultimately a New York State appeals court ruled that Hogue was mentally ill and "invariably" dangerous, and directed that he be involuntarily hospitalized and that his status be reevaluated after six months.[34] The cases of Joyce Brown and Larry Hogue illustrated striking discontinuities within the mental health system, and superficially seemed to dramatize the failures of the policy of deinstitutionalization. Moreover, they demonstrated that many of the statutes pertaining to the mentally disabled addressed only their immediate condition, but did not respond to the reality of individuals on the brink of destabilization because of their refusal to continue taking psychiatric medication or tendency to become substance abusers.

The image of deinstitutionalization so often portrayed in the press and on television, nevertheless, represented a gross simplification that ignored a far more complex reality. The popular image of severely and persistently mentally ill adults, using drugs, wandering the streets of virtually every urban area, threatening residents, and resisting treatment and hospitalization, was true but represented only a subgroup of a much larger seriously mentally ill population. Often overlooked were innovative programs that were specifically designed to deal with the severely and chronically mentally ill in the 1970s and 1980s.

Even as the policy of deinstitutionalization was being implemented, psychiatrists and sociologists were emphasizing some of its shortcomings. Bert Pepper, a psychiatrist who directed the Rockland County CMHC in New York State, reiterated that there were "overwhelming dimensions of unmet human needs," and that psychiatric services, however important, had to "wait until fundamental problems of shelter and survival" were addressed. Similarly, John Talbott, a psychiatrist at Cornell Medical College, insisted in 1979 that "a reconceptualization of the problem" was required that addressed both the psychiatric and human needs of a severely disabled population. David Mechanic, perhaps the preeminent sociologist of mental health, emphasized time and time again the importance of strategies to integrate mental health services in ways that overcame the barriers associated with decentralized and uncoordinated systems of treatment, care, and financing.[35]

Paradoxically, the presence of flaws in the existing systems was recognized by the NIMH, the federal agency that had played a central role in the passage of the Community Mental Health Centers act of 1963. Employing its relatively broad mandate to sponsor research and related activities, the agency launched a new initiative when it created the Community Support Program in 1977. Modestly financed at the outset with an allocation of $3.5 million and rising to $15 million a decade later, the program involved a federal/state partnership designed to assist in the development of community support programs for adults with severe mental disorders. It consisted of ten distinct components, including housing, income, psychiatric and medical treatment, and support services, most of which had been specified (but never realized) in the regulations governing the original legislation of 1963. The initiative was not intended to support services, but rather to encourage states to introduce changes in the mental health system. Although the program was unpopular in the Reagan administration, Congress enacted legislation in 1984 that gave it legal standing. The State Comprehensive Mental Health Services Plan Act two years later built upon this initiative. In 1989 the Community Support Program was redesigned to test the effectiveness of different specific approaches, thus ending its role as a means of encouraging system change.[36]

Some of the initial results in the early 1980s with community support systems programs were encouraging. They served a chronic population; the ten services defined by the NIMH were actually in use; and those with the greatest needs were the beneficiaries. Outward appearances to the contrary, the condition of many severely and persistently ill persons improved during the remainder of the decade as many states attempted to integrate such federal entitlement programs as SSDI, SSI, Medicaid, and Medicare with community mental health services. Nevertheless, the impact of these developments was often overshadowed by massive problems posed by homelessness, the presence of individuals who were both severely mentally ill and substance abusers, and an angry and sometimes alienated public fearful that their security was being endangered.[37]

A quite different perspective on community programs became evident during these years. From World War II to the 1960s, community mental health had been portrayed in terms of an all-embracing panacea;

its supporters employed rhetoric and largely ignored the absence of a body of empirical data that might validate their assertions. Exaggerated claims inevitably prepared the ground for a reaction that threatened to inhibit or undermine efforts to deal with the needs of a severely disabled population. In succeeding decades, by contrast, community care and treatment came to have a quite different meaning. The focus on cure and prevention, although still pervasive, became less significant. The emphasis shifted to the need to limit disability and to preserve function. Moreover, advocates of experimental community programs were more prone to concede that cure, independence, and total integration into normal society was often not achievable, and that many (but not all) severely and persistently mentally ill persons might require comprehensive assistance and services for much of their adult lives. In sum, the challenge was to create a system that provided all of the elements incorporated into traditional mental hospitals, but without the liabilities that accompanied protracted institutionalization.

The integrated and comprehensive community programs created during and after the 1970s provided evidence of the difficulties that lay ahead. To administer a program responsible for a variety of different patients proved a formidable undertaking, especially in view of the need to deal with multiple sources of funding. Nor was it inexpensive or easy to replicate elsewhere the results achieved in any given community. Yet at the very least such programs offered guidelines.

Perhaps the best known of the community mental health care programs was developed in Madison, Wisconsin, by Leonard Stein, Mary Ann Test, and others. Its origins went back to the late 1960s, when efforts were made to combat the negative effects of long-term hospitalization that tended to infantilize patients and reduce them to a state of near total dependency. Initially the emphasis was on psychosocial rehabilitation, which was designed to assist patients to become more independent and thus to leave the hospital and live in the community. Although successful, there was little carryover when patients were returned to the community. Moreover, data from a variety of outpatient treatment experiments indicated that individuals in such programs deteriorated once their involvement ceased. By 1970 Stein and his colleagues had launched the first phase of a program designed to prevent hospitalization. Out of this emerged the Training in Community Living project. An unselected group of patients seeking admission to a mental hospital were randomly assigned to experimental and control groups.

The latter received hospital treatment linked with aftercare services. The experimental group received intensive services designed to provide them with the skills required to cope while residing in the community, thus avoiding rehospitalization. In succeeding years the Madison model underwent significant changes. Patients in the experimental program were taught such simple living skills as how to budget their money and how to use public transportation. They were provided with assistance with housing and jobs, and received a wide range of social support services. Provision was made for ongoing monitoring, including crisis intervention, and—where possible—family members were involved in the program. The model that evolved over time deemphasized traditional office psychiatry and the use of professional facilities. Its central concern was with the provision of care to patients in the community and at their place of residence.

Although subject to debate, the results of the Madison experiment seemed to suggest that it was possible for highly impaired persons to be cared for in the community (thought not necessarily at less cost than in other settings). Clinical interventions appeared to have a more beneficial impact on those in the program, as compared with those in the control group. The former also tended to have better outcomes in terms of personal relationships, derived greater satisfaction, and had lower rates of hospitalization. Nevertheless, they remained marginalized and dependent—an indication that cure and recovery remained distant and remote possibilities.[38]

There were a number of attempts to replicate the Madison model both in the United States and abroad. Most had to make significant changes, if only because of the existence of important differences between Madison and the areas in which the model was duplicated. The most consistent finding was that assertive community care and treatment reduced hospitalization. The meaning of this finding, however, remained unclear. Were reductions in hospitalization, for example, accompanied by compensatory increases in other forms of supervision? Did such programs shift burdens to the families of patients? Until these and other questions would be answered, the relevance of the Madison experiment remained murky.[39]

In an effort to improve services to the chronically mentally ill population, the Robert Wood Johnson Foundation—the nation's largest foundation concerned with health—created the Program on Chronic Mental Illness in 1985. Under this program, nine cities were given resources to

create a central mental health authority to deliver services to chronically mentally ill persons.* Drawing upon the experiences of Madison as
well as those of the Massachusetts Mental Health Center in Boston, the
program grew out of the realization that individuals in urban areas fell
under a variety of jurisdictions. Many urban governments, for example,
had little or no responsibility for mental health services, but dealt with
homelessness, welfare, and housing. The absence of linkages in most
cities precluded continuity of care, thus vitiating efforts to assist the
chronically mentally ill. The Robert Wood Johnson Foundation Program
on Chronic Mental Illness was designed to demonstrate that community care could become a reality rather than a possibility if resources could
be concentrated under a single mental health authority.

Preliminary findings suggested that in the nine cities services were
being directed toward the care of the severely and persistently mentally ill; that a central authority was more likely to be concerned with the
ways in which the system as a whole was serving client needs rather
than being preoccupied with individual programs; that centralization
improved levels of financial support; and perhaps most important, that
change was possible. Whether or not the Robert Wood Johnson Program on Chronic Mental Illness and others will succeed in redressing
existing shortcomings remains an open question. "There is no quick fix
for the problems that plague public mental health systems," David
Mechanic conceded. "The problems are deeply entrenched and difficult
to solve. Many public officials are concerned that investments in mental health will not yield significant visible benefits that justify taking
political risks." Nevertheless, he insisted that the integration of different
strategies—including the integration of assertive community treatment,
approaches that unified diverse sources of funding and directed them
toward meeting needs of disabled persons, strong local mental health
authorities, and rational reimbursement structures—offered at least the
potential for improvement.[40]

The persistence of problems, however, should not be permitted to
conceal the more important fact that a large proportion of severely and
persistently mentally ill persons have made a more or less successful
transition to community life as a result of the expansion of federal dis-

*The nine cities were Austin, Texas; Baltimore, Maryland; Charlotte, North Carolina; Cincinnati,
Columbus, and Toledo, Ohio; Denver, Colorado; Honolulu, Hawaii; and Philadelphia, Pennsylvania.

ability and entitlement programs. To be sure, the media and the public are prone to focus on a subgroup of young adults or others who have a dual diagnosis of mental illness and substance abuse and who tend to be homeless. Their visibility on the streets often overshadows the inadvertent success of "deinstitutionalization." "In fact," two authorities have recently written, "the situation is indeed much better for many people, and overall it is much better than it might have been. . . . While many people still do not have adequate incomes or access to the services theoretically provided through Medicaid and Medicare, the fact that the structure exists within these federal programs to meet the needs of these individuals represents a major step forward."[41]

It would be useful if knowledge of past policies could offer a sound prescription for the present and future. Unfortunately the "lessons" of history are less than clear and often fraught with contradictions and ambiguities. Individuals persist in selecting examples or making analogies that allegedly support their preferred policies. Yet historical knowledge can deepen the way in which we think about contemporary issues and problems; it can also sensitize us to the dangers of simplistic thinking or utopian solutions. The presumption that conscious policy decisions will lead unerringly to stipulated consequences, for example, ignores the reality that individuals and groups often adjust their behavior and reshape laws and regulations and policies in unanticipated and sometimes unwelcome ways.

The history of the care and treatment of the mentally ill in America for almost four centuries offers a sobering example of a cyclical pattern that has alternated between enthusiastic optimism and fatalistic pessimism. In the nineteenth century an affinity for institutional solutions led to the creation of the asylum, an institution designed to promote recovery and to enable individuals to return to their communities. When early hospitals seemed to enjoy a measure of success, institutional care and treatment became the basis of public policy. States invested large sums in creating a public hospital system that integrated care with treatment. The adoption of this new policy reflected a widespread faith that insanity was a treatable and curable malady, and that chronicity would only follow the failure to provide effective hospital treatment.

No institution ever lives up to the claims of its promoters, and the mental hospital was no exception. Plagued by a variety of problems, its reputation and image was slowly tarnished. When it became clear that hospitals were caring for large numbers of chronic patients, the stage was set for an attack on its legitimacy after World War II. Its detractors insisted that a community based policy could succeed where an institutional policy had failed, and that it was possible to identify mental illnesses in the early stages, at which time treatment would prevent the advent of chronicity. Between the 1940s and 1960s there was a sustained attack on institutional care. This assault finally succeeded when Congress enacted legislation that shifted the locus of care and treatment back to the community. The community mental health policy proved no less problematic than its institutional predecessor. Indeed, the emergence of a new group of young chronic mentally ill persons in the 1970s and 1980s created entirely new problems, for the individuals who constituted this group proved difficult to treat and to care for under any circumstances. Yet unforseen developments—notably the expansion of federal disability and entitlement programs—made it possible for many severely and chronically mentally ill people to live in the community.

Each of these stages was marked by unrealistic expectations and rhetorical claims that had little basis in fact. In their quest to build public support and legitimate their cherished policy, psychiatric activists invariably insisted they possessed the means to prevent and cure severe mental disorders. When such expectations proved unrealistic, they placed the blame either upon callous governments, an uninformed public, or an obsolete system that failed to incorporate the findings of medical science.

If American society is to deal effectively, compassionately, and humanely with the seriously mentally ill, we must acknowledge that this group includes individuals with quite different disorders, prognoses, and needs, the outcome of which varies considerably over time. Some schizophrenics, for example, have reasonably good outcomes; others lapse into chronicity and become progressively more disabled. We must also confront the evidence that serious mental disorders are often exacerbated by other social problems of a nonmedical nature—poverty, racism, and substance abuse.[42] Although psychiatric therapies can alleviate symptoms and permit individuals to live in the community, there is no "magic bullet" that will cure all cases of serious mental illnesses. Like cardiovascular, renal, and other chronic degenerative disorders, serious mental disorders require both therapy and management.

Serious mental illnesses can strike at any time and among all elements of the population. The ensuing impact on the individual, family, and society is immense, for it often leads to disability and dependency. Rhetorical claims to the contrary, little is known about the etiology of serious mental disorders. Treatment—whether biological or psychosocial—does not necessarily eliminate the disorder. The absence of curative therapies, however, ought not to be the occasion to disparage efforts to find ways to alleviate some of the adverse consequences of illness. Many therapies assist seriously ill persons in coping with and managing their condition. "In the last analysis," a group of investigators recently concluded, "systems of treatment are not as yet able to cure, but they should be able to remove the obstacles that stand in the way of natural self-healing processes."[43]

For too long mental health policies have embodied an elusive dream of magical cures that would eliminate age-old maladies. Psychiatrists and other professionals have justified their raison d'être in terms of cure and overstated their ability to intervene effectively. The public and their elected representatives often accepted without question the illusory belief that good health is always attainable and purchasable. The result has been periods of prolonged disillusionment that have sometimes led to the abandonment of severely incapacitated persons. Public policy has thus been shaped by exaggerated claims and by unrealistic valuative standards. Largely overlooked or forgotten are ethical and moral considerations. All societies, after all, have an obligation toward individuals whose disability leads to partial or full dependency. Even if the means of complete cure are beyond our grasp, it does not follow that we ought to ignore those whose illness incapacitates them. To posit an absolute standard of cure leads to a paralyzing incapacity to act in spite of evidence that programs that integrate mental health services, entitlements, housing, and social supports often minimize the need for prolonged hospitalization and foster a better quality of life. It has often been noted that a society will be judged by the manner in which it treats its most vulnerable and dependent citizens. In this sense the severely mentally ill have a moral claim upon our sympathy, compassion, and above all, upon our assistance.

NOTES

Prologue

1. Paul S. Appelbaum, "Crazy in the Streets," *Commentary* 83 (May 1987): 34.
2. The quotes in this paragraph are taken from Dorothea L. Dix, *Memorial to the Legislature of Massachusetts 1843* (Boston, 1843), p. 4; *Memorial Soliciting a State Hospital for the Insane Submitted to the Legislature of New Jersey, January 23, 1845* (Trenton, 1845), p. 3; and *Memorial Soliciting Enlarged and Improved Accommodation for the Insane of the State of Tennessee* (Nashville, 1847), pp. 1–2.
3. Unless otherwise noted, all statistical data have been drawn from the annual volumes *Patients in Mental Institutions*, 1940–1966 (through 1946 these volumes were gathered by the U.S. Bureau of the Census; beginning in 1947 the National Institute of Mental Health (NIMH) assumed responsibility). The data on psychiatrists have been compiled from *List of Fellows and Members of the American Psychiatric Association 1940/1941* (n.p., 1942). In this directory, 1,458 members listed an institutional address and 841 a private address (which did not necessarily imply a private or noninstitutional practice).
4. This is the definition used by the group that formulated a national agenda at the close of the Carter presidency. See Department of Health and Human Services, *Toward a National Plan for the Chronically Mentally Ill* (Washington, D.C., 1980).

Chapter 1. Caring for the Insane in Colonial America

1. Mary Ann Jimenez, *Changing Faces of Madness: Early American Attitudes and Treatment of the Insane* (Hanover, 1987), pp. 36, 53–54.
2. Legislation pertaining to the mentally ill in the Bay Colony can be found

in *The Colonial Laws of Massachusetts. Reprinted from the Edition of 1660, with the Supplements to 1672* (Boston, 1889), pp. 35, 45; *The Colonial Laws of Massachusetts. Reprinted from the Edition of 1672, with Supplements through 1686* (Boston, 1887), p. 248; *The Acts and Resolves, Public and Private, of the Province of the Massachusetts Bay* (21 vols. Boston, 1869–1922), I, pp. 151–152, II, pp. 622–624, V, pp. 594–595.

3. See Gerald N. Grob, *Mental Institutions in America: Social Policy to 1875* (New York, 1973), chapter 1.

4. Michael MacDonald, *Mystical Bedlam: Madness, Anxiety, and Healing in Seventeenth-Century England* (New York, 1981), p. 215

5. Roy Porter, *Mind-Forg'd Manacles: A History of Madness in England from the Restoration to the Regency* (Cambridge, 1987), pp. 21, 28–29, 63–66, 169; Richard Hunter and Ida Macalpine, *Three Hundred Years of Psychiatry 1535–1860: A History Presented in Selected English Texts* (London, 1963), pp. 94–99. For an incisive overview see Stanley W. Jackson, *Melancholia and Depression: From Hippocratic Times to Modern Times* (New Haven, 1986).

6. This discussion of Mather is drawn from Jimenez, *Changing Faces of Madness*, pp. 12–23, and her article, "Madness in Early American History: Insanity in Massachusetts from 1700 to 1830," *Journal of Social History*, 20 (1986): 31.

7. Richard H. Shryock, *Medicine and Society on America, 1660–1860* (New York, 1960), p. 57.

8. Cotton Mather, *The Angel of Bethesda*, ed. by Gordon W. Jones (Barre, Mass., 1972), pp. 129–137.

9. Jimenez, *Changing Faces of Madness*, pp. 24–25.

10. See Norman Dain, *Concepts of Insanity in the United States, 1789–1865* (New Brunswick, 1964), chapter 1, and Charles E. Rosenberg, "Body and Mind in Nineteenth-Century Medicine: Some Clinical Origins of the Neurosis Construct," *Bulletin of the History of Medicine*, 63 (1989): 185–197.

11. Charles E. Rosenberg, "Medical Text and Social Context: Explaining William Buchan's *Domestic Medicine*," *Bulletin of the History of Medicine*, 57 (1983): 22–42; Dain, *Concepts of Insanity*, pp. 38–39. Buchan's book appeared originally as *Domestic Medicine: or, The Family Physician: Being an Attempt to Render the Medical Art More Generally Useful, by Shewing People What Is in Their Own Power Both with Respect to the Prevention and Cure of Diseases. Chiefly Calculated to Recommend a Proper Attention to Regimen and Simple Medicines* (Edinburgh, 1769). The first American edition was published in Philadelphia in 1772.

12. Glenn W. LaFantasie, ed., *The Correspondence of Roger Williams*, (2 vols., Hanover, 1988), I, pp. 329–331; Bradford F. Swan, "Roger Williams and the Insane," *Rhode Island History*, 5 (1946): 66.

13. Jimenez, *Changing Faces of Madness*, pp. 31–37.

14. *Ibid.*, p. 42.

15. Albert Deutsch, *The Mentally Ill in America: A History of Their Care and Treatment from Colonial Times* (New York, 1946), p. 42.

16. *The Early Records of the Town of Providence* (20 vols., Providence, 1893–1909), II, p. 89; Swan, "Roger Williams and the Insane," pp. 68–69; Jimenez, *Changing Faces of Madness*, pp. 40–42; Deutsch, *Mentally Ill in America*, p. 50.

17. Wyndham B. Blanton, *Medicine in Virginia in the Seventeenth Century* (Richmond, 1930), p. 131; Deutsch, *Mentally Ill in America*, p. 51.

18. *Report of the Record Commissioners of the City of Boston* (39 vols., Boston, 1876–1909), XX, p. 190; Jimenez, *Changing Faces of Madness*, p. 54. See especially Josiah H. Benton, *Warning Out in New England 1656–1817* (Boston, 1911).

19. *Report of the Record Commissioners of the City of Boston*, XIII, p. 194, XIV, pp. 77, 89, 101, 198, XVI, pp. 126, 139–140, 179–180, 184, 207, 215, XVII, p. 133, XX, p. 98. Brief accounts of colonial almshouses can be found in Carl Bridenbaugh's two books, *Cities in the Wilderness: The First Century of Urban Life in America 1625–1742* (New York, 1938) and *Cities in Revolt: Urban Life in America, 1743–1776* (New York, 1955), as well as David J. Rothman's *The Discovery of the Asylum: Social Order and Disorder in the New Republic* (Boston, 1971).

20. Charles E. Rosenberg, *The Care of Strangers: The Rise of America's Hospital System* (New York, 1987), p. 20 *et passim*.

21. Sydney V. James, *A People Among Peoples: Quaker Benevolence in Eighteenth-Century America* (Cambridge, 1963), pp. 193–215.

22. Benjamin Franklin, *Some Account of the Pennsylvania Hospital; From its First Rise, to . . . May, 1754* (Philadelphia, 1754), pp. 3–4.

23. Thomas G. Morton, *The History of the Pennsylvania Hospital 1751–1895* (Philadelphia, 1895), pp. 7–22; James, *A People among Peoples*, pp. 206–215.

24. Franklin, *Some Account of the Pennsylvania Hospital*, p. 36; *Letters of Benjamin Rush*, ed. by Lyman H. Butterfield (2 vols.: Princeton, 1951), I, p. 443; Morton, *History of the Pennsylvania Hospital*, p. 167.

25. Samuel Bard, *A Discourse Upon the Duties of a Physician, with Some Sentiments, on the Usefulness and Necessity of a Public Hospital* (New York,

1769), pp. 15–18; *Charter of the Society of the New-York Hospital* (New York, 1856), pp. 3–14; William L. Russell, *The New York Hospital: A History of the Psychiatric Service 1771–1936* (New York, 1945), pp. 35–36, 45.

26. William W. Hening, ed., *The Statutes at Large: Being a Collection of All the Laws of Virginia from the First Session of the Legislature in the Year 1619* (13 vols., Richmond, 1809–1823), VIII, pp. 378–381.

27. The history of the origins and early development of the Virginia institution can be followed in Norman Dain's *Disordered Minds: The First Century of Eastern State Hospital in Williamsburg, Virginia 1766–1866* (Williamsburg, 1971), quote from pp. 26–27.

Chapter 2. Inventing the Asylum

1. Statistical data can be found in U.S. Bureau of the Census, *Historical Statistics of the United States, Colonial Times to 1970* (2 vols., Washington, D.C., 1975), I, p. 11, and Adna F. Weber, *The Growth of Cities in the Nineteenth Century* (New York, 1899), p. 22. Peter Knights has dealt with geographical mobility in his book *The Plain People of Boston, 1830–1860: A Study in City Growth* (New York, 1971), pp. 60, 121.

2. For recent contributions by social historians detailing social changes in nineteenth-century America, see the collection of historiographical essays, "The Promise of American History: Progress and Prospects," Stanley I. Kutler and Stanley N. Katz, eds., *Reviews in American History*, 10 (1982): 1–330.

3. There is an extraordinarily large and controversial literature dealing with the origins of the asylum, including Michel Foucault, *Madness and Insanity: A History of Madness in the Age of Reason* (New York, 1965), David J. Rothman, *The Discovery of the Asylum: Social Order and Disorder in the New Republic* (Boston, 1971), Gerald N. Grob, *Mental Institutions in America: Social Policy to 1875* (New York, 1973), and Andrew Scull, *Social Order/Mental Disorder: Anglo-American Psychiatry in Historical Perspective* (Berkeley, 1989).

4. Oscar Handlin, *Boston's Immigrants: A Study in Acculturation* (rev. ed.: Cambridge, 1959), pp. 114–115.

5. William Battie, *A Treatise on Madness* (1758), in Richard Hunter and Ida Macalpine, eds., *Three Hundred Years of Psychiatry 1535–1860: A History Presented in Selected English Texts* (London, 1963), pp. 402–410.

6. Philippe Pinel, *A Treatise on Insanity* (Sheffield, England, 1806), pp. 2, 45. The original French edition was published under the title *Traite médico-*

philosophique sur L'aliénation mentale, ou la Manie (Paris, 1801). See also George Rosen, "The Philosophy of Ideology and the Emergence of Modern Medicine in France," *Bulletin of the History of Medicine*, 20 (1946): 328–331.

7. This description is drawn from Pinel's *Treatise on Insanity*, p. 113, and Dora B. Weiner's "Philippe Pinel's 'Memoir on Madness' of December 11, 1794: A Fundamental Text of Modern Psychiatry," *American Journal of Psychiatry*, 149 (1992): 725–732.

8. Pinel, *Treatise on Insanity*, p. 184; Weiner, "Philippe Pinel's 'Memoir on Madness,'" p. 727; Jean E. D. Esquirol, *Des Passions* (1805), cited in Eric T. Carlson and Norman Dain, "The Psychotherapy that was Moral Treatment," *American Journal of Psychiatry*, 117 (1960): 519.

9. Pinel, *Treatise on Insanity*, pp. 63, 91 (see also pp. 59–60, 83, 99, 190, 215–216); Weiner, "Philippe Pinel's 'Memoir on Madness,'" p. 732.

10. See especially Samuel Tuke, *Description of the Retreat, an Institution Near York for Insane Persons of the Society of Friends* (York, England, 1813), and Anne Digby, *Madness, Morality and Medicine: A Study of the York Retreat, 1796–1914* (Cambridge, England, 1985), quote from p. 25.

11. Tuke, *Description of the Retreat*, pp. 112–112, 141–143, 150, 157–159. The most authoritative history of this institution is Digby's *Madness, Morality and Medicine*.

12. Thomas S. Kirkbride to the Superintendent and Managers of the Utica Asylum, March 28, 1846, Kirkbride Papers, Institute of the Pennsylvania Hospital, Philadelphia.

13. Thomas Eddy, *Hints for Introducing an Improved Mode of Treating the Insane in the Asylum* (New York, 1815), pp. 4–5; Samuel N. Knapp, *The Life of Thomas Eddy* (New York, 1834), pp. 95–98. For the dissemination of psychiatric ideas in the early nineteenth century see Norman Dain's *Concepts of Insanity in the United States, 1789–1865* (New Brunswick, 1964).

14. For a general discussion of the relationship between religion and reform, see William G. McLoughlin, *Revivals, Awakenings, and Reform: An Essay on Religion and Social Change in America, 1607–1977* (Chicago, 1978), quote from pp. 138–139.

15. Orestes A. Brownson, "The Laboring Classes," *Boston Quarterly Review*, 3 (1840), quoted in Oscar and Mary F. Handlin, *Commonwealth: A Study of the Role of Government in the American Economy: Massachusetts, 1774–1861* (rev. ed., Cambridge, 1969), p. 225. First published in 1947, *Commonwealth* remains a classic study that is indispensable for an understanding of the activities of nineteenth-century state government.

16. This account is based on M.A. DeWolfe Howe, *The Humane Society of the Commonwealth of Massachusetts: An Historical Review 1785–1916* (Boston, 1918), pp. 199–201; Nathaniel I. Bowditch, *A History of the Massachusetts General Hospital* (2nd ed., Boston, 1872), pp. 3–9, 64–65, 423–431; Leonard K. Eaton, *New England Hospitals 1790–1833* (Ann Arbor, 1957), pp. 29–34, 45–55; *Address of the Trustees of the Massachusetts General Hospital to the Subscribers and to the Public* (n.p., n.d. [c. 1822]), pp. 4–5.

17. *Account of the Rise and Progress of The Asylum, Proposed to be Established, near Philadelphia, for the Relief of Persons Deprived of the Use of Their Reason* (Philadelphia, 1814), pp. 3–11; *Journal of the Life and Religious Labors of Thomas Scattergood* (Philadelphia, n.d.), p. 202; *Memoirs of Thomas Scattergood* (London, 1845), p. 382.

18. *Reprint of the Proceedings of the Connecticut Medical Society from 1792 to 1829 Inclusive* (Hartford, 1884), pp. 172, 178, 184; *Society for the Relief of the Insane . . . Annual Meeting at Hartford, 2d Wednesday of May* (Hartford, 1823), p. 22; *Report of a Committee of the Connecticut State Medical Society, Respecting an Asylum for the Insane* (Hartford, 1821), also reprinted (but with an erroneous date) in Henry M. Hurd, ed., *The Institutional Care of the Insane in the United States and Canada* (4 vols., Baltimore, 1916–1917), II, pp. 93–102.

19. Eaton, *New England Hospitals*, pp. 66–67; Charles R. Keller, *The Second Great Awakening in Connecticut* (New Haven, 1942); Gerald N. Grob, *Mental Institutions in America: Social Policy to 1875* (New York, 1973), pp. 58–62.

20. The account of Bloomingdale is based upon Pliny Earle, *History, Description and Statistics of the Bloomingdale Asylum for the Insane* (New York, 1848); William L. Russell, *The New York Hospital: A History of the Psychiatric Service 1771–1936* (New York, 1945); Thomas Eddy, *Hints for Introducing an Improved Mode of Treating the Insane*.

21. The description of these cases is drawn from Russell, *New York Hospital*, pp. 104–115.

22. *Ibid.*, pp. 97–115. See also Francis J. Braceland, *The Institute of Living: The Hartford Retreat 1822–1972* (Hartford, 1972), and S. B. Sutton, *Crossroads in Psychiatry: A History of the McLean Hospital* (Washington, D.C., 1986).

23. The primary sources for the data in this paragraph can be found in Grob, *Mental Institutions in America*, p. 68.

24. Luther V. Bell to Robert H. Ives, February 14, 1856, Butler Hospital Papers, John Carter Brown Library, Brown University, Providence; Grob, *Mental Institutions in America*, p. 70.

25. New York State *Assembly Document No. 263* (March 10, 1831): 29; New York Hospital and Bloomingdale Asylum, *Annual Report*, 1851, pp. 15–16, 1856, pp. 19–20, 1862, p. 11, 1866, pp. 17–25; Russell, *New York Hospital*, pp. 150–155; Grob, *Mental Institutions in America*, pp. 71–73.

26. John W. Sawyer to Dorothea L. Dix, September 16, 1870, Dix Papers, Houghton Library, Harvard University, Cambridge.

27. Samuel B. Woodward to Thomas H. Gallandet, February 21, 1840, Woodward Papers, American Antiquarian Society, Worcester, Mass.; McLean Asylum for the Insane, *Annual Report*, 22 (1839), in Massachusetts General Hospital, *Annual Report*, 1839, p. 16; Connecticut Retreat for the Insane, *Annual Report*, 43 (1867): 33.

28. [Josiah Quincy], *Report to Whom was Referred the Consideration of the Pauper Laws of the Commonwealth. Submitted to the Massachusetts Legislature, 1821* (Boston, 1821), pp. 3–4, 9; Report submitted by John V. N. Yates, in New York State *Senate Journal*, 47th Session, 1824, pp. 102, 104, 107–108; *Report of the Committee Appointed by the Board of Guardians of the Poor of the City and Districts of Philadelphia, to Visit the Cities of Baltimore, New-York, Providence, Boston, and Salem* (Philadelphia, 1827). See also Benjamin Klebaner, "Public Poor Relief in America 1790–1860," Ph.D. dissertation, Columbia University, 1952, pp. 73–99, and Michael B. Katz, *In the Shadow of the Poorhouse: A Social History of Welfare in America* (New York, 1986).

29. Virginia Western Lunatic Hospital, *Annual Report*, 9 (1836): 7, 9–10.

30. Kentucky Eastern Lunatic Asylum, *Annual Report*, 1844, pp. 19–21; Samuel Theobold, "Some Account of the Lunatic Asylum of Kentucky, with Remarks, &c," *Transylvania Journal of Medicine and the Associate Sciences*, 2–3 (1829–1830): 91, 509–511; [Edward Jarvis], "Insanity in Kentucky," *Boston Medical and Surgical Journal*, 24 (1841): 166–168.

31. For the early history of the South Carolina Lunatic Asylum, see Peter McCandless, "'A House of Cure': The Antebellum South Carolina Lunatic Asylum," *Bulletin of the History of Medicine*, 64 (1990): 220–242, and Daniel H. Trezevant, *Letters to His Excellency Governor Manning on the Lunatic Asylum* (Columbia, 1854).

32. William Jenks, "Memoir of Rev. Louis Dwight," in *Reports of the Prison Discipline Society* (Boston, 1855), I, p. 22; Boston Prison Discipline Society, *Annual Report*, 2 (1827): 19–20. For a detailed history of the founding and significance of the Bay State's first public institution, see Gerald N. Grob, *The State and the Mentally Ill: A History of Worcester State Hospital in Massachusetts, 1830–1920* (Chapel Hill, 1966).

33. *Independent Chronicle & Boston Patriot*, February 7, 1830.
34 Grob, *The State and the Mentally Ill*, chapters 1 and 2; Pliny Earle, *The Curability of Insanity: A Series of Studies* (Philadelphia, 1887), pp. 25–26.
35. See Grob, *Mental Institutions in America*, chapter 3 and appendix 1.
36. Dorothea L. Dix, "Memorial to the Legislature of Massachusetts 1843," *Old South Leaflets*, 6, No. 148 (Boston, n.d.); Grob, *The State and the Mentally Ill*, pp. 104–112. For Dix's career see Francis Tiffany, *Life of Dorothea Lynde Dix* (Boston, 1890), and Helen E. Marshall, *Dorothea Dix: Forgotten Samaritan* (Chapel Hill, 1937).
37. Amariah Brigham to Thomas S. Kirkbride, March 3, 1845, Kirkbride Papers; Isaac Ray to John W. Sawyer, December 11, 1873, Butler Hospital, Providence.
38. Lunatic, Idiot and Epileptic Asylum of the State of Georgia, *Annual Report*, 1 (1842/1844): 8–9; D. Tilden Brown to Pliny Earle, January 22, 1846, Earle Papers, American Antiquarian Society; *Reports of Jas. F. Bozeman, M.D., and Wm. Henry Cumming, M.D., on the State Lunatic Asylum, Under Resolution of the General Assembly . . . 1872* (Atlanta, 1872), p. 29.
39. Worcester State Lunatic Hospital, *Annual Report*, 23 (1855): 45; Illinois Board of State Commissioners of Public Charities, *Biennial Report*, 1 (1869/1870): Table 2 between pp. 288–289.
40. See L. Ray Gunn, *The Decline of Authority: Public Economic Policy and Political Development in New York 1800–1860* (Ithaca, 1988).
41. Edward Jarvis, "The Influence of Distance from and Proximity to an Insane Hospital, on its Use by any People," *Boston Medical and Surgical Journal*, 42 (1850): 209–222, and "On the Supposed Increase of Insanity," *American Journal of Insanity*, 8 (1852): 344. For an extended treatment see Gerald N. Grob, *Edward Jarvis and the Medical World of Nineteenth-Century America* (Knoxville, 1978).
42. *Report of the Commissioners of the Alms House, Bridewell and Penitentiary* [1837], New York City Board of Aldermen *Document No. 32* (1837): 208; "Account of a visit to 9 institutions in 1845 by Dr. Thomas S. Kirkbride and Mr. Jacob Morris," Kirkbride Papers; Charles Dickens, *American Notes and Pictures from Italy* (first edition 1842: London, 1957), pp. 92–94. For a more extensive analysis of urban asylums see Grob, *Mental Institutions in America*, pp. 118–130.
43. *Report of the Investigation of the Board of Supervisors of Kings County, in the Matter of Alleged Abuses at the Lunatic Asylum . . . 1877* (New York, 1877), p. 6.
44. John C. Bucknill, *Notes on Asylums for the Insane in America* (London,

1876), pp. 40–53; Isaac Ray in *American Journal of Insanity*, 33 (1876): 262–266, 294–295, 300–307; Ray, "What Shall Philadelphia Do for Its Paupers?" *Penn Monthly*, 4 (1873): 226–238.

45. Grob, *Mental Institutions in America*, pp. 125–128.
46. Stanford Chaillé, *A Memoir of the Insane Asylum of the State of Louisiana, at Jackson* (New Orleans, 1858), pp. 11–12.
47. Grob, *Mental Institutions in America*, p. 130.

Chapter 3. The Emergence of American Psychiatry

1. The creation of the specialty of psychiatry in early and mid-nineteenth-century America can be followed in Gerald N. Grob, *Mental Institutions in America: Social Policy to 1875* (New York, 1973), and Constance M. McGovern, *Masters of Madness: Social Origins of the American Psychiatric Profession* (Hanover, 1985).
2. Samuel B. Woodward, "Religious Beliefs" (1845) and "History of the Medical Sciences" (c. 1833), Woodward Papers, American Antiquarian Society, Worcester, Mass. See also Gerald N. Grob, "Samuel B. Woodward and the Practice of Psychiatry in Early Nineteenth-Century America," *Bulletin of the History of Medicine*, 36 (1962): 420–443, and McGovern, *Masters of Madness*, pp. 53–54 *et passim*.
3. My description of Kirkbride is drawn from Nancy Tomes, *A Generous Confidence: Thomas Story Kirkbride and the Art of Asylum-keeping, 1840–1883* (New York, 1984).
4. For an analysis of nineteenth-century concepts of health and disease see Charles E. Rosenberg, *Explaining Epidemics and Other Studies in the History of Medicine* (New York, 1992), and John H. Warner, *The Therapeutic Perspective: Medical Practice, Knowledge, and Identity in America, 1820–1885* (Cambridge, 1986).
5. Utica State Lunatic Hospital, *Annual Report*, 1 (1843): 36; Worcester State Lunatic Hospital, *Annual Report*, 7 (1839): 72; 9 (1841): 40–41; 10 (1842): 39; 13 (1845): 50–51; Pliny Earle to Clark Bell (copy), April 16, 1886, Earle Papers, American Antiquarian Society, Worcester, Mass. For an overview of the history of psychiatric classification, see Gerald N. Grob, "Origins of DSM-I: A Study in Appearance and Reality," *American Journal of Psychiatry*, 148 (1991): 421–431.
6. Edward Jarvis, "Causes of Insanity," *Boston Medical and Surgical Journal*, 45 (1851): 294.

7. Worcester State Lunatic Hospital, Case Book No. 1, pp. 1, 298–99, Case Book, No. 8, pp. 346–47, Case Book No. 19, p. 526, Countway Library of Medicine, Harvard Medical School, Boston; Worcester State Lunatic Hospital, *Annual Report*, 1 (1833): 16; 2 (1834): table opposite p. 20; 7 (1839): 31; 13 (1845): 60.

8. Worcester State Lunatic Hospital, *Annual Report*, 13 (1845): 7.

9. Edward Jarvis, "On the Supposed Increase of Insanity," *American Journal of Insanity*, 8 (1852): 333–364. See also Grob, *Mental Institutions in America*, pp. 155–159.

10. Grob, *Mental Institutions in America*, p. 157; Ohio Lunatic Asylum, *Annual Report*, 4 (1842): 18; [Edward Jarvis] *Report on Insanity and Idiocy in Massachusetts, by the Commission on Lunacy, Under Resolve of the Legislature of 1854*, Massachusetts *House Document No. 144* (1855): 61–62.

11. Connecticut Retreat for the Insane, *Annual Report*, 41 (1865): 14–15.

12. Edward Jarvis, "The Production of Vital Force," *Medical Communications of the Massachusetts Medical Society*, 2nd ser., IV (Boston, 1854), pp. 1–40; *idem*, "Law of Physical Life," *Christian Examiner*, 35 (September 1843): 1–31. For Jarvis's career see Gerald N. Grob, *Edward Jarvis and the Medical World of Nineteenth-Century America* (Knoxville, 1978).

13. Worcester State Lunatic Hospital, *Annual Report*, 4 (1836): 56–57.

14. *Ibid.*, 3 (1835): 34–35; 4 (1836): 49–50; 9 (1841): 79; 10 (1842): 64; 12 (1844): 70–82; Woodward, "Observations on the Medical Treatment of Insanity," *American Journal of Insanity*, 7 (1850): 1–34.

15. Amariah Brigham, *An Inquiry Concerning the Diseases and Functions of the Brain, the Spinal Cord, and the Nerves* (New York, 1840), p. 294; Tomes, *A Generous Confidence*, pp. 194–197; Samuel B. Thielman, "Madness and Medicine: Trends in American Medical Therapeutics for Insanity, 1820–1860," *Bulletin of the History of Medicine*, 61 (1987): 25–46.

16. McLean Asylum for the Insane, *Annual Report*, 24 (1841): 22–32.

17. Worcester State Lunatic Hospital, *Annual Report*, 7 (1839): 97; Woodward to Charles Sedgwick, January 16, 1844, in Woodward, "Collected Writings," vol. III, Worcester State Hospital Library, Worcester, Mass.

18. Tomes, *A Generous Confidence*, pp. 198–202; Gerald N. Grob, *The State and the Mentally Ill: A History of Worcester State Hospital in Massachusetts 1830–1920* (Chapel Hill, 1966), pp. 65–66.

19. Ellen Dwyer, *Homes for the Mad: Life Inside Two Nineteenth-Century Asylums* (New Brunswick, 1987), pp. 27, 126; Grob, *Mental Institutions in America*. p. 179; Judson B. Andrews, "Asylum Periodicals," *American Journal of Insanity*, 33 (1876): 42–49.

20. Tomes, *A Generous Confidence*, p. 206; Worcester State Lunatic Hospital, *Annual Report*, 7 (1839): 80.

21. Worcester State Lunatic Hospital, *Annual Report*, 12 (1844): 89; Kentucky Eastern Lunatic Asylum, *Annual Report*, 1845, p. 24; Isaac Ray, "Observations on the Principal Hospitals for the Insane in Great Britain, France and Germany," *American Journal of Insanity*, 2 (1846): 387–388.

22. Tomes, *A Generous Confidence*, pp. 210ff.

23. Thomas S. Kirkbride, *On the Construction, Organization, and General Arrangements of Hospitals for the Insane* (Philadelphia, 1854), p. 59 (2nd ed., Philadelphia, 1880), p. 248.

24. Joseph G. Rogers, "A Century of Hospital Building for the Insane," *American Journal of Insanity*, 57 (1900): 1.

25. The propositions adopted by the AMSAII appeared in *ibid.*, 8 (1851): 79–81 and 10 (1853): 67–69. See also Kirkbride's article "Remarks on the Construction and Arrangements of Hospitals for the Insane," *American Journal of the Medical Sciences*, n.s. 13 (1847): 40–56, and his book *On the Construction, Organization, and General Arrangements of Hospitals for the Insane*.

26. See especially Arthur E. Bestor, Jr., "Patent-Office Models of the Good Society: Some Relationships Between Social Reform and Westward Expansion," *American Historical Review*, 58 (1953): 505–526.

27. See the discussion in Tomes, *A Generous Confidence*, chapter 4.

28. *American Journal of Insanity*, 10 (1853): 67–69.

29. Kirkbride, *On the Construction, Organization, and General Arrangements of Hospitals for the Insane* (1854 edition), p. 2.

30. See McGovern, *Masters of Madness*.

31. The history of the AMSAII can be followed in McGovern, *Masters of Madness*, and Grob, *Mental Institutions in America*.

32. Woodward to Horace Mann, June 5, 1845, Woodward Papers, American Antiquarian Society, Worcester, Mass.; Brigham to Pliny Earle, February 27, 1845, Earle Papers; *American Journal of Insanity*, 1 (1845): 381–182; 2 (1845): 175–183; *Journal of Prison Discipline and Philanthropy*, 2 (1846): 49–57; N. D. Benedict to Kirkbride, January 31, 1855, Kirkbride Papers, Institute of the Pennsylvania Hospital, Philadelphia; Earle, "Reports of American Hospitals for the Insane," *American Journal of the Medical Sciences*, n.s. 46 (1863): 173–175.

33. *American Journal of Insanity*, 10 (1853): 85; 28 (1871): 205–208, 212; American Medical Association, *Transactions*, 17 (1866): 121ff.; 18 (1867): 399ff.; 19 (1868): 161ff.; 22 (1871): 101–109.

Chapter 4. Realities of Asylum Life

1. Nancy Tomes, *A Generous Confidence: Thomas Story Kirkbride and the Art of Asylum-Keeping, 1840–1883* (New York, 1984), pp. 108–113; Ellen Dwyer, *Homes for the Mad: Life Inside Two Nineteenth-Century Asylums* (New Brunswick, 1987), pp. 86–89; Gerald N. Grob, *Mental Illness and American Society, 1875–1940* (Princeton, 1983), pp. 9–11; Richard W. Fox, *So Far Disordered in Mind: Insanity in California 1870–1930* (Berkeley, 1978), pp. 84ff.

2. Dwyer, *Homes for the Mad*, pp. 90–91, 103; Tomes, *A Generous Confidence*, p. 104.

3. Tomes, *A Generous Confidence*, p. 110; Grob, *Mental Illness and American Society*, p. 9.

4. For data on the institutionalized population in 1880 see U.S. Census Office, *Report on the Defective, Dependent, and Delinquent Classes of the Population of the United States, as Returned at the Tenth Census (June 1, 1880)* (Washington, D.C., 1888), pp. vii–xli.

5. In their classic study of rates of institutionalization from 1840 to 1941, Herbert Goldhamer and Andrew W. Marshall concluded that nineteenth-century hospital admissions contained "a larger proportion of psychotic cases and of severe derangement than do contemporary admissions." See their *Psychosis and Civilization: Two Studies in the Frequency of Mental Disease* (Glencoe, Ill., 1953), pp. 35–43, 91. Nineteenth-century hospital records tend to support this generalization.

   Many charges of wrongful commitment by families are often murky. See especially Carole Haber, "Who's Looney Now?: The Insanity Case of John Armstrong Chaloner," *Bulletin of the History of Medicine*, 60 (1986): 177–193.

6. Tomes, *A Generous Confidence*, pp. 224–225. The Kirkbride Papers at the Institute of the Pennsylvania Hospital in Philadelphia and the Woodward Papers at the American Antiquarian Society in Worcester contain letters from former patients.

7. Luther V. Bell to Dorothea L. Dix, February 14, 1843, Dix Papers, Houghton Library, Harvard University, Cambridge.

8. Robert Fuller, *An Account of the Imprisonments and Sufferings of Robert Fuller, of Cambridge* (Boston, 1833), pp. 24–29.

9. Barbara Sapinsley, *The Private War of Mrs. Packard* (New York, 1991), *passim*; Elizabeth W. Packard, *Modern Persecution, or Insane Asylums Unveiled* (2 vols., Hartford, 1873). See also Grob, *Mental Institutions in America: Social Policy to 1875* (New York, 1973), pp. 263–266, and "Abuse

in American Mental Hospitals in Historical Perspective: Myth and Reality,"
International Journal of Law and Psychiatry, 3 (1980): 295–310.

10. Stephen Smith, "Care of the Filthy Classes of Insane," National Conference of Charities and Correction, *Proceedings*, 12 (1885): 148–153.

11. Isaac Ray to Dorothea L. Dix, December 8, 1851, November 3, 1852, March 7, April 15, 1854, Dix Papers; Ray, "American Hospitals for the Insane," *North American Review*, 79 (1854): 66–90.

12. Worcester State Lunatic Hospital, *Annual Report*, 7 (1839): 89.

13. Ohio Lunatic Asylum, *Annual Report*, 13 (1851): 22–23.

14. New York City Lunatic Asylum, Blackwell's Island, *Annual Report*, 1858, p. 12.

    Many antebellum Americans inferred that immigrants were more susceptible to insanity, a conclusion that fortified nativist sentiment. The development of more sophisticated techniques of statistical analysis after 1900, however, called into question the allegation that immigrants provided a disproportionate share of admissions to mental hospitals. For a more detailed analysis of this point see chapter 6, n. 49.

15. *American Journal of Insanity*, 14 (1857): 79, 103; 27 (1870): 158–159; Ray, "Doubtful Recoveries," *ibid.*, 20 (1863): 33.

16. Worcester State Lunatic Hospital, *Annual Report*, 22 (1854): 10–11.

17. *Ibid.*, 15 (1847): 33; 26 (1858): 56–57; *American Journal of Insanity*, 16 (1859): 106–107. The impact of ethnic tensions in Massachusetts can be followed in Gerald N. Grob, *The State and the Mentally Ill: A History of Worcester State Hospital in Massachusetts 1830–1920* (Chapel Hill, 1966). The nature of urban asylums is analyzed in Grob, *Mental Institutions in America*.

18. Charles H. Nichols to Kirkbride, April 24, 1855, Kirkbride Papers, Institute of the Pennsylvania Hospital, Philadelphia.

19. Grob, *Mental Institutions in America*, pp. 244–245; *Report of the Commissioners of the Alms House, Bridewell and Penitentiary*, New York City Board of Alderman *Document No. 32* (1837): 204.

20. Virginia Eastern Asylum, *Annual Report*, 1846, p. 4; 1848, pp. 23–29; 1849, pp. 5–6, 17; Virginia Western Lunatic Asylum, *Annual Report*, 18 (1845): 7–8, 29–31; 21 (1848): 4–5, 32–34, *Biennial Report*, 1867/1868–1868/1869, pp. 6–7; Norman Dain, *Disordered Minds: The First Century of Eastern State Hospital in Williamsburg, Virginia 1766–1866* (Williamsburg, 1971), pp. 19, 105, 109–113; Grob, *Mental Institutions in America*, pp. 248–254.

21. E. B. and Augustin Fleming, *Three Years in a Mad-House* (Chicago, 1893), pp. 25–27.

22. Nancy Tomes, "Historical Perspectives on Women and Mental Illness," in *Women, Health, and Medicine in America: A Historical Handbook*, Rima D. Apple, ed. (New York, 1990), pp. 165–166; Constance M. McGovern, "Doctors or Ladies? Women Physicians in Psychiatric Institutions," *Bulletin of the History of Medicine*, 55 (1981): 88–107; U.S. Bureau of the Census, *Insane and Feeble-Minded in Hospitals and Institutions 1904* (Washington, D.C., 1906), p. 18, and *Insane and Feeble-Minded in Institutions 1910* (Washington, D. C., 1914), pp. 41–44.

23. Statistics on hospital populations can be found in Grob, *Mental Institutions in America*, pp. 373–395.

24. George Chandler, "On the proper number of patients for an institution . . . ," undated manuscript, c. 1848, Chandler Papers, American Antiquarian Society, Worcester, Mass.

25. Robert Gardiner Hill, *A Lecture on the Management of Lunatic Asylums, and the Treatment of the Insane* (London, 1839), reprinted in *Three Hundred Years of Psychiatry 1535–1860: A History Presented in Selected English Texts*, Richard Hunter and Ida Macalpine, eds. (London, 1963), p. 890. See also "John Conolly: A Victorian Psychiatric Career," in Andrew Scull, *Social Order/Mental Disorder: Anglo-American Psychiatry in Historical Perspective* (Berkeley, 1989), pp. 164–212.

26. Worcester State Lunatic Hospital, *Annual Report*, 22 (1854): 30–31. See also Grob, *Mental Institutions in America*, pp. 206ff.

27. *Report of the Resident Physician of the Alms-House Establishment*, New York City Board of Alderman *Document No. 119* (May 8, 1843): 1405–1406; New York City Asylum for the Insane, Ward's Island, *Annual Report*, 4 (1875): 21–25; Grob, *State and the Mentally Ill*, p. 326. For a cogent analysis of attendants see Dwyer, *Homes for the Mad*, pp. 163–185.

28. See [Edward Jarvis] *Report on Insanity and Idiocy in Massachusetts by the Commission on Lunacy Under Resolve of the Legislature of 1854* (Mass. House Document No. 144 [1855]: Boston, 1855), p. 18.

29. For a fuller discussion see Grob, *Mental Institutions in America*, Chapter 5.

30. *Memorial of D. L. Dix, Praying a Grant of Land for the Relief and Support of the Indigent, Curable and Incurable Insane*, 30th Cong., 1st Sess., *Senate Miscellaneous Document No. 150*; 33rd Cong., 1st Sess., *House Report No. 125* (March 29, 1854). The newspaper clippings in the Dix Papers detail reactions to Pierce's veto.

31. *American Journal of Insanity*, 21 (1864): 152–155, 266–267; 32 (1876): 345–355; Illinois Board of Commissioners of Public Charities, *Biennial Report*, 4 (1875–1876): 73–76. For an extended discussion of the growth of state regulation see Grob, *Mental Institutions in America*, Chapter 7.

32. Ohio Lunatic Asylum, *Annual Report*, 4 (1842): 57; Worcester State Lunatic Hospital, *Annual Report*, 3 (1835): 35; 4 (1836): 56–57; 9 (1841): 57, 67–68.

33. Pliny Earle, *The Curability of Insanity: A Series of Studies* (Philadelphia, 1887), pp. 9–22. This book was an outgrowth of studies undertaken while Earle was superintendent of the Northampton (Massachusetts) State Lunatic Hospital in the 1870s. In his published work in the 1840s, however-er, Earle did not indict the concept of curability.

34. Woodward to Earle, March 18, 1842, Woodward Papers; Worcester State Lunatic Hospital, *Annual Report*, 8 (1840): 47; 9 (1841): 68; 10 (1842): 62.

35. Worcester State Lunatic Hospital, *Annual Report*, 49 (1881): 12–14; 61 (1893): 70; Norman Dain, *Disordered Minds: The First Century of the Eastern State Hospital in Williamsburg, Virginia 1776–1866* (Williamsburg, 1971), pp. 45–46; Dwyer, *Homes for the Mad*, pp.150–157; Tomes, *A Generous Confidence*, pp. 324–326.

   More contemporary data suggest that the attitudes of the therapist and the institutional environment play key roles in successful outcomes. Hence it is possible to speculate that the internal environment of nineteenth-century hospitals and the charismatic personalities of early superintendents may have combined to create asylum environments that had beneficial effects upon patients. For an elaboration of this theme, see Grob, *Mental Institutions in America*, pp. 182–185.

36. Worcester State Lunatic Hospital, *Annual Report*, 10 (1842): 17–27; 38 (1870): 38–60; Virginia Western Lunatic Asylum, *Annual Report*, 23 (1850): 14–23; California Insane Asylum, *Annual Report*, 8 (1860): 16–32; Dwyer, *Homes for the Mad*, p. 150.

Chapter 5. The Problem of Chronic Mental Illnesses, 1860–1940

1. Ellen Dwyer, *Homes for the Mad: Life Inside Two Nineteenth-Century Asylums* (New Brunswick, 1987), pp. 142–143.

2. [Edward Jarvis] *Report on Insanity and Idiocy in Massachusetts by the Commission on Lunacy Under Resolve of the Legislature of 1854* (Mass. House Document No. 144 [1855]: Boston, 1855), pp. 17–18. A reprint edition edited by Gerald N. Grob was issued in 1971 by Harvard University Press. All of the manuscript returns are available in the "Report of the Physicians of Massachusetts. Superintendents of Hospitals . . . and Others Describing the Insane and Idiotic Persons in the State of Massachusetts in 1855. Made to the Commissioners on Lunacy," manuscript volume in the Countway Library of Medicine, Harvard Medical School, Boston. See also Samuel B. Thielman. "Community Management of Mental Disorders in

Antebellum America," *Journal of the History of Medicine and Allied Sciences*, 44 (1989): 351–374.

3. "Report of the select committee on report and memorial of county superintendents of the poor, on lunacy and its relation to pauperism," New York *Senate Document No. 71* (March 5, 1856): 13.

4. Jarvis, *Report on Insanity and Idiocy*, pp. 183–184.

5. Gerald N. Grob, *Mental Institutions in America: Social Policy to 1875* (New York, 1973), pp. 308–309.

6. New York State *Senate Document No. 17* (January 23, 1856), *No. 71* (March 5, 1856), *No. 8* (January 9, 1857). For an extended discussion see Dwyer, *Homes for the Mad*, pp. 40ff.

7. John P. Chapin, "Insanity in the State of New York," *American Journal of Insanity*, 13 (1856): 39–52.

8. Sylvester D. Willard, *Report on the Condition of the Insane Poor in the County Poor Houses of New York*, New York *Assembly Document No. 19* (January 13, 1865), *passim*.

9. Dwyer, *Homes for the Mad*, p. 136.

10. "The Willard Asylum, and Provision for the Insane," *American Journal of Insanity*, 22 (1865): 192–212; George Cook to Dorothea L. Dix, March 15, 1866, D. T. Brown to Dix, March 31, April 7 (2 letters), 1866, Chapin to Dix, February 11, 20, 1867, John P. Gray to Dix, January 10, 1869, Dix Papers, Houghton Library, Harvard University, Cambridge; Chapin to Edward Jarvis, April 24, 1868, Jarvis Papers, Countway Library of Medicine.

11. *American Journal of Insanity*, 23 (1866): 147–250.

12. Frederick H. Wines to Pliny Earle, April 26, 1879, Earle Papers, American Antiquarian Society, Worcester, Mass.; Wines, "Hospital Building for the Insane," Conference of Charities, *Proceedings*, 5 (1878): 143–150. For an extended treatment of the debate over incurable institutions see Grob, *Mental Institutions in America*, chapter 8. The history of Willard is dealt with in Dwyer, *Homes for the Mad*.

13. John M. Galt, "The Farm of St. Anne," *American Journal of Insanity*, 11 (1855): 352–357; Virginia Eastern Asylum, *Report*, 1853/1854 and 1854/1855, p. 24; 1855/1856 and 1856/1857, pp. 20–30. For examples of the hostile reaction to Galt see *American Journal of Insanity*, 12 (1855): 42ff.; D. Tilden Brown to Thomas S. Kirkbride, May 3, 11, 1855, Charles H. Nichols to Kirkbride, April 14, 24, July 3, October 10, 1855, Kirkbride Papers, Institute of the Pennsylvania Hospital, Philadelphia.

14. See J. Parigot, "The Gheel Question: From an American Point of View," *American Journal of Insanity*, 19 (1863): 332–354.

15. Worcester State Lunatic Hospital, *Annual Report*, 33 (1865): 4, 58–63; 34 (1866): 78–80; 35 (1867), 5–6, 76–78; 36 (1868): 54–83; 37 (1869): 75; Massachusetts Board of State Charities, *Annual Report*, 4 (1867): xli–xlii.

16. Northampton State Lunatic Hospital, *Annual Report*, 16 (1871): 28–39; 17 (1872): 36–42; Isaac Ray to Pliny Earle, February 18, 1872, Kirkbride to Earle, March 3, 1873, Earle Papers; Ray to John Sawyer, February 15, 1873, Butler Hospital Library, Providence. For a detailed analysis of the conflict see Gerald N. Grob, *The State and the Mentally Ill: A History of Worcester State Hospital in Massachusetts, 1830–1920* (Chapel Hill, 1966), pp. 208–228.

17. Massachusetts Board of State Charities, *Annual Report*, 14 (1877): xxxvii; Chap. CCXXVII, Act of May 15, 1877 and Chap. CCXXXIX, Act of May 2, 1887 (in Massachusetts *Acts and Resolves*, 1877, 1887).

18. Illinois Board of State Commissioners of Public Charities, *Biennial Report*, 1 (1869–1870): 82–101.

19. *Ibid.*, 5 (1877–1878): 64–67; 7 (1881–1882): 120; 8 (1883–1884): 88–92; Richard S. Dewey, *Recollections of Richard Dewey: Pioneer in American Psychiatry* (Chicago, 1936), *passim*; *idem*, "Differentiation in Institutions for the Insane," *American Journal of Insanity*, 39 (1882): 1–21, and "Congregate and Segregate Buildings for the Insane," National Conference of Charities and Correction, *Proceedings*, 10 (1883): 441–456.

20. Wisconsin State Board of Charities and Reform, *Annual Report*, 6 (1876): 8–12; 7 (1877): 13–20; 10 (1880): 21, 40, 48–50, 124, 173–185; 11 (1881): xii, 270; Dale W. Robison, *Wisconsin and the Mentally Ill* (New York, 1979), *passim*.

21. Pennsylvania Board of Commissioners of Public Charities, *Annual Report*, 9 (1878): 6–9; 27 (1896): 3–7; 28 (1897): 3–4; Pennsylvania Committee on Lunacy, *Annual Report*, 14 (1896): 14–18, 67–76; 15 (1897): 7–15, 43–51; 16 (1898): 7–10; Pennsylvania Department of Welfare, Secretary of Welfare, *Biennial Report*, 5 (1929–1930): 75; Wisconsin State Board of Control, *Biennial Report*, 20 (1928–1930): xxii; 21 (1930–1932): 90.

22. Dwyer, *Homes for the Mad*, pp. 50–54, 117–162.

23. D. H. Tuke, *The Insane in the United States and Canada* (London, 1885), pp. 79, 174, 260; Illinois Board of State Commissioners of Public Charities, *Biennial Report*, 15 (1897–1898): 45–46; Illinois Board of Administration, *Annual Report*, 2–3 (1911–1912): 491; Adolf Meyer to G. Alder Blumer, October 23, 1894, Meyer Papers, Series I, Johns Hopkins Medical School, Baltimore, Md.; *The Collected Papers of Adolf Meyer*, ed. Eunice Winters (4 vols.: Baltimore, 1950–1952), II, p. 39, IV, pp. 24–29.

24. National Conference of Charities and Correction, *Proceedings*, 9 (1882): 97–119, 231–240, 259–261; *American Journal of Insanity*, 22 (1865): 68–74; 23 (1866): 147–250; Grob, *Mental Institutions in America*, pp. 313ff.

25. C. Floyd Haviland, *The Treatment and Care of the Insane in Pennsylvania Being the Report of a Survey of All the Institutions in Pennsylvania Caring for the Insane* (Philadelphia, 1915), pp. 12–13, 20–21, 68–69, 80–94; Pennsylvania Committee on Lunacy, *Annual Report*, 27 (1909): 10–21; 33 (1914–1915): 279–284; 34 (1915–1916): 275–322; 35 (1916–1917): 253–259. The generalizations about the Wisconsin plan are based on a reading of the Wisconsin State Board of Control's *Annual Reports*, 1–23 (1890/1892–1934/1936) and Robison, *Wisconsin and the Mentally Ill*, pp. 98–102, 231–232, 240–242, 259–260, 293–296.

26. For an elaboration of this theme see Carole Haber, *Beyond Sixty-Five: The Dilemma of Old Age in America's Past* (New York, 1983), chapter 5 (quotes from p. 89).

27. *Report of Select Committee appointed to visit Charitable Institutions supported by the State, and all city and county poor and work houses and jails*, New York *Senate Document No. 8* (January 9, 1857): 3–5. See especially Michael B. Katz, *In the Shadow of the Poorhouse: A Social History of Welfare in America* (New York, 1986), chapter 1.

28. Michael B. Katz, *Poverty and Policy in American History* (New York, 1983), pp. 57–89; U.S. Bureau of the Census, *Paupers in Almshouses 1910* (Washington, D.C., 1915), pp. 42–43.

29. Katz, *In the Shadow of the Poorhouse*, p. 35. The statistics in this and the preceding paragraph are compiled from U.S. Bureau of the Census, *Historical Statistics of the United States: Colonial Times to 1970* (2 vols.: Washington, D.C., 1975), I, p. 15; *idem, Paupers in Almshouses 1910*, p. 43, and *Paupers in Almshouses 1923* (Washington, D.C., 1925), pp. 5, 33.

30. Gerald N. Grob, *Mental Illness and American Society, 1875–1940* (Princeton, 1983), pp. 181–182; Herbert Goldhamer and Andrew W. Marshall, *Psychosis and Civilization: Two Studies in the Frequency of Mental Disease* (Glencoe, Ill., 1953), pp. 54, 91.

31. New York State Department of Mental Hygiene, *Annual Report*, 52 (1939–1940): 174–175; Benjamin Malzberg, "A Statistical Analysis of the Ages of First Admissions to Hospitals for Mental Disease in New York State," *Psychiatric Quarterly*, 23 (1949): 346; *idem*, "A Comparison of First Admissions to the New York Civil State Hospitals During 1919–1921 and 1949–1951," *ibid.*, 28 (1954): 314; American Psychiatric Association, *Report on Patients over 65 in Public Mental Hospitals* (Washington, D.C., 1960), p. 5.

32. The passage of state care acts can be followed in Grob, *Mental Illness and American Society*, chapters 4 and 7, and Ellen Dwyer, *Homes for the Mad*, *passim*.

33. New York State Commission in Lunacy, *Annual Report*, 12 (1900): 26–29.

34. U.S. Public Health Service, *Mental Health in Later Maturity: Papers Presented at a Conference Held in Washington, D.C. May 23–24, 1941* (Washington, D.C., 1942); Aubrey Lewis, "Ageing and Senility: A Major Problem of Psychiatry," *Journal of Mental Science*, 92 (1946): 150–170. The proliferation of articles and books dealing with senility and psychiatry after 1900 is striking, and a listing would be far too lengthy.

35. New York State Commission in Lunacy, *Annual Report*, 12 (1900): 22–36.

36. "The Care of the Mentally Disordered in Illinois: The State Hospitals" c. 1931, pp. 7–8, typescript copy in American Foundation for Mental Hygiene Papers, Archives of Psychiatry, New York Hospital-Cornell Medical Center, New York.

37. Lawrence Kolb, "The Psychiatric Significance of Aging as a Public Health Problem," in *Mental Health in Later Maturity*, p. 17; Robert M. Elliott, "Dotards in State Hospitals," New York State Commission in Lunacy, *Annual Report*, 19 (1907): 161–168.

38. Earl S. Pollock, B. Z. Locke, and M. Kramer, "Trends in Hospitalization and Patterns of Care of the Aged Mentally Ill," in *Psychopathology of Aging*, Paul H. Hoch and Joseph Zubin, eds. (New York, 1961), p. 36; Morton Kramer, H. Goldstein, R. H. Israel, and N.A. Johnson, *A Historical Study of the Disposition of First Admissions to a State Mental Hospital: Experience of the Warren State Hospital during the Period 1916–50* (Public Health Service Publication 445 Washington, D.C., 1955), p. 12; *idem, Mental Disorders/Suicide* (Cambridge, 1972), pp. 27–28; Oswaldo Camargo and G. H. Preston, "What Happens to Patients who are Hospitalized for the First Time When over Sixty-five Years of Age," *American Journal of Psychiatry*, 102 (1945): 168–173.

39. E. E. Southard and H. C. Solomon, *Neurosyphilis: Modern Systematic Diagnosis and Treatment* (Boston, 1917), pp. 86–87, 90, 115–116.

40. New York State Department of Mental Hygiene, *Annual Report*, 52 (1939–1940): 176; Horatio M. Pollock, *Mental Disease and Social Welfare* (Utica, 1941), chapter 6; Benjamin Malzberg, *Social and Biological Aspects of Mental Disease* (Utica, 1940), pp. 30–32; American Psychopathological Association, *Trends of Mental Disease* (New York, 1945), p. 31; Edith M. Furbish, "General Paralysis in State Hospitals for Mental Disease," *Mental*

Hygiene, 7 (1923): 565–578; Neil M. Dayton, *New Facts on Mental Disorders: Study of 89,190 Cases* (Springfield, Ill., 1940), *passim*.

41. Pollock, *Mental Disease and Social Welfare*, pp. 98–109.
42. Data collected from U.S. Bureau of the Census annual compilations of hospital statistics. The first volume, *Patients in Hospitals for Mental Disease 1923* was published in 1926; from 1926 to 1946 comparable volumes, sometimes with slightly varying titles, were published (some covering more than one year). See also Morton Kramer, *Psychiatric Services and the Changing Institutional Scene, 1950–1985* (Washington, D.C., 1976), p. 82.
43. Benjamin Malzberg, *Mortality Among Patients with Mental Disease* (Utica, 1934), pp. 15–16, 29, 84, 119, 143, 166, 179.
44. U.S. Bureau of the Census, *Insane and Feeble-Minded in Hospitals and Institutions 1904* (Washington, D.C., 1906), p. 37; *idem, Insane and Feeble-Minded in Institutions 1910* (Washington, D.C., 1914), p. 59; *idem, Patients in Hospitals for Mental Disease 1923* (Washington, D.C., 1926), p. 36.

Chapter 6. A New Psychiatry

1. Thomas S. Kirkbride, *On the Construction, Organization, and General Arrangements of Hospitals for the Insane* (2nd ed., Philadelphia, 1880), pp. 26, 300.
2. Elizabeth T. Stone, *A Sketch of the Life of Elizabeth T. Stone, and of Her Persecutions, with an Appendix of Her Treatment and Sufferings While in the Charlestown McLean Asylum, Where She Was Confined Under the Pretence of Insanity* (n.p., 1842), pp. 35–36. See also Robert Fuller, *An Account of the Imprisonments and Sufferings of Robert Fuller, of Cambridge* (Boston, 1833), and Isaac H. Hunt, *Astounding Disclosures! Three Years in a Madhouse by a Victim* (n.p., 1852).
3. Massachusetts *House Report No. 277* (April 20, 1863): 3–11.
4. Gerald N. Grob, *Mental Institutions in America: Social Policy to 1875* (New York, 1973), chapter 7, and *Mental Illness and American Society, 1875–1940* (Princeton, 1983), chapter 3.
5. See especially Bonnie E. Blustein, *Preserve Your Love of Science: Life of William A. Hammond, American Neurologist* (New York, 1991), and F. G. Gosling, *Before Freud: Neurasthenia and the American Medical Community, 1870–1910* (Urbana, 1987).
6. *Journal of Nervous and Mental Disease*, 1 (1874): 225.
7. William A. Hammond, "The Non-Asylum Treatment of the Insane," Medical Society of the State of New York, *Transactions*, (1879): 280–297. The

conflict can be followed in Grob, *Mental Illness and American Society*, pp. 51–55, and Blustein, *Preserve Your Love for Science*.

8. *National Association for the Protection of the Insane and the Prevention of Insanity* (Boston, 1880); *Papers and Proceedings of the National Association for the Protection of the Insane and the Prevention of Insanity . . . 1882* (New York, 1882).

9. Dorman B. Eaton, "Despotism in Lunatic Asylums," *North American Review*, 132 (1881): 263–275.

10. This discussion is based upon Charles E. Rosenberg's *The Trial of the Assassin Guiteau: Psychiatry and Law in the Gilded Age* (Chicago, 1968). See also Robert J. Waldinger, "Sleep of Reason: John P. Gray and the Challenge of Moral Insanity," *Journal of the History of Medicine and Allied Sciences*, 34 (1979): 163–179. Guiteau's trial transcript has been reprinted as *Supreme Court Holding a Criminal Term, No. 14056: The United States vs. Charles J. Guiteau* (2 vols., New York, 1973).

11. Orpheus Everts, "The American System of Public Provision for the Insane, and Despotism in Lunatic Asylums," *American Journal of Insanity*, 38 (1881): 186–231.

12. John B. Chapin, "Public Complaints Against Asylums for the Insane, and the Commitment of the Insane," *ibid.*, 40 (1883): 33–49.

13. *Journal of Nervous and Mental Disease*, 21 (1894): 413–437, 443–473, 512–515, 597–604; 22 (1895); 181–183, 718–728; *American Journal of Insanity*, 51 (1894): 171–181.

14. Henry Smith Williams, "Politics and the Insane," *North American Review*, 161 (1895): 394–404.

15. *American Journal of Insanity*, 52 (1896): 446–452.

16. For a discussion of the role of women see Constance M. McGovern, "Doctors or Ladies? Women Physicians in Psychiatric Institutions, 1872–1900," *Bulletin of the History of Medicine*, 55 (1981): 88–107, and Grob, *Mental Illness and American Society*, pp. 65–66.

17. Mary M. Wolfe, "The Present Status of Women Physicians in Hospitals for the Insane," American Medico-Psychological Association, *Proceedings*, 16 (1909): 349–356. For Rabinovitch's criticisms of her psychiatric colleagues, see the various issues of the *Journal of Mental Pathology*, which published sporadically between 1901 and 1909.

18. *American Journal of Insanity*, 42 (1885): 60–77.

19. *Ibid.*, 44 (1887): 128; 45 (1888): 50–57, 127–143.

20. *Ibid.*, 49 (1892): 276–287; William Malamud, "The History of Psychiatric Therapies," in *One Hundred Years of American Psychiatry*, J. K. Hall, ed.

(New York, 1944), pp. 291ff., 320–321; Edward Cowles, "The Advancement of Psychiatry in America," *American Journal of Insanity*, 52 (1896): 364–386.

21. Bernard Sachs, "Advances in Neurology and Their Relation to Psychiatry," *American Journal of Insanity*, 54 (1897): 17. The annual speeches of AMPA presidents (published annually in the *American Journal of Insanity*) all echoed Sachs's theme.

22. Meyer, "A Short Sketch of the Problems of Psychiatry," *American Journal of Insanity*, 53 (1896–1897), in *The Collected Papers of Adolf Meyer*, ed. Eunice Winters (4 vols., Baltimore, 1950–1952), II, pp. 273–282. Biographical data on Meyer can be found in the following: *Collected Papers, passim*; Alfred Lief, ed., *The Commonsense Psychiatry of Adolf Meyer: Fifty-Two Selected Papers, Edited, with Biographical Narrative* (New York, 1948); Grob, *Mental Illness and American Society*; Theodore Lidz, "Adolf Meyer and the Development of American Psychiatry," *American Journal of Psychiatry*, 123 (1966): 320–332; and Ruth Leys and Rand B. Evans, ed., *Defining American Psychology: The Correspondence Between Adolf Meyer and Edward Bradford Titchner* (Baltimore, 1990).

23. Meyer to William Healy, October 29, 1917, Meyer Papers, Series I, Johns Hopkins Medical Institutions, Baltimore; Smith Ely Jelliffe to Harry Stack Sullivan, June 1, 1937, Jelliffe Papers, Library of Congress, Washington, D.C.

24. Jelliffe and White, *Diseases of the Nervous System* (4th edition), quoted in John C. Burnham, *Jelliffe: American Psychoanalyst and Physician* (Chicago, 1983), pp. 64–66. See also White's two autobiographical accounts: *Forty Years of Psychiatry* (New York, 1933) and *William Alanson White: The Autobiography of a Purpose* (Garden City, N.Y., 1938).

25. Jelliffe to L. Kerschbaumer, April 18, 1940, Jelliffe Papers.

26. The rise of the modern hospital and the creation of health policies are superbly dealt with in three recent works: Charles E. Rosenberg, *The Care of Strangers: The Rise of America's Hospital System* (New York, 1987); Rosemary Stevens, *In Sickness and in Wealth: American Hospitals in the Twentieth Century* (New York, 1989); and Daniel M. Fox, *Health Policies, Health Politics: The British and American Experience, 1911–1965* (Princeton, 1986).

27. Ira Van Giesen to Meyer, April 26, 1900, Meyer Papers, Series I.

28. H. L. Palmer to Meyer, November 13, 1903, Series II, Meyer Papers; Robert M. Schley to Meyer, December 23, 1908, Series I, Meyer Papers; C. P. Oberndorf, *A History of Psychoanalysis in America* (New York, 1953), p. 84.

29. E. E. Southard to Thomas W. Salmon, July 24, 1919, Salmon Boxes in

American Foundation for Mental Hygiene Papers, Archives of Psychiatry, New York Hospital-Cornell Medical Center, New York. See also Grob, *Mental Illness and American Society*, pp. 126–135.

30. Salmon to Southard, July 21, 1919, Salmon Boxes in American Foundation for Mental Hygiene Papers.

31. J. Montgomery Mosher, "Pavilion F, a Department for Mental Diseases of the Albany Hospital," National Conference of Charities and Correction, *Proceedings*, 34 (1907): 423.

32. Meyer and C. M. Campbell, "The Henry Phipps Psychiatric Clinic," c. 1920, typescript, Meyer to Harvey Cushing, April 26, 1919, Meyer to David T. Layman, Jr., June 21, 1922, Richard S. Lyman, "Dr. Lyman's Impressions of the HPPC at the Start, about 1925 & today," March 23, 1939, Series I, Meyer Papers; Alan M. Chesney, *The Johns Hopkins Hospital and the Johns Hopkins University School of Medicine* (3 vols.; Baltimore, 1943–1963), III, pp. 90–94, 188–192, 233–242.

33. See E. E. Southard, "The Psychopathic Hospital Idea," *Journal of the American Medical Association*, 61 (1913): 1973; Massachusetts State Board of Insanity, *Annual Report*, 11 (1909): 46; 12 (1910): 77–78, 85; 13 (1911): 35–36; 15 (1913): 43–47; 17 (1915): 50; Massachusetts Commission on Mental Diseases, *Annual Report*, 2 (1917): 41–42; Southard, "A Study of the Dementia Praecox Group," *American Journal of Insanity*, 67 (1910): 119–176; Frederick P. Gay, *The Open Mind: Elmer Ernest Southard 1876–1920* (n.p., 1938).

34. Milton Greenblatt et al., *From Custodial to Therapeutic Care in Mental Hospitals* (New York, 1955), pp. 40–41.

35. Elizabeth Lunbeck, "'A New Generation of Women': Progressive Psychiatrists and the Hypersexual Female," *Feminist Studies*, 13 (1987): 513–543; "Report of the Director of Psychopathic Hospital to the Trustees of the Boston State Hospital, February, 1915," in "Report of the Director of the Psychopathic Department of the Boston State Hospital 1915," and "Report of the Director of the Psychopathic Department of Boston State Hospital . . . May, 1916," in "Notes of Trustees 1916," mss. vols. in Countway Library of Medicine, Harvard Medical School, Boston; L. Vernon Briggs and collaborators, *History of the Psychopathic Hospital, Boston, Massachusetts* (Boston, 1922), p. 158. See also Estelle B. Freedman, "'Uncontrolled Desires': The Response to the Sexual Psychopath, 1920–1960," *Journal of American History*, 74 (1987): 83–106.

36. Thomas W. Salmon, "Some New Fields in Neurology and Psychiatry," *Journal of Nervous and Mental Disease*, 46 (1917): 90–99.

37. Clifford W. Beers, *A Mind That Found Itself* (first ed., 1908; Pittsburgh, 1981), pp. 35–36.

38. For discussions of his career and work see Norman Dain's authoritative *Clifford W. Beers: Advocate for the Insane* (Pittsburgh, 1980), and Grob, *Mental Illness and American Society*, chapter 6.

39. Beers, "To Whom It May Concern," January 1, 1905, American Foundation for Mental Hygiene Papers; William James to Beers, April 21, 1907, James Papers, Houghton Library, Harvard University, Cambridge. My discussion of Beers's early career is based on a careful reading of the voluminous manuscript materials in the American Foundation for Mental Hygiene Papers, the William James Papers, and the Adolf Meyer Papers. The limitations of space preclude complete citations; see Dain, *Beers* and Grob, *Mental Illness and American Society* for more detailed data.

40. Meyer to Henry S. Noble, February 28, 1908. Meyer Papers, Series II; *North American Review*, 187 (1908): 611–614. Eunice Winters's "Adolf Meyer and Clifford Beers, 1907–1910," *Bulletin of the History of Medicine* 43 (1969): 414–443 is a useful analysis, but has major shortcomings relating to the author's close association with Meyer, which led her to accept Meyer's claims at face value and dismiss Beers's views.

41. Beers to Meyer, October 27, December 22, 23, 31, Meyer to Beers, December 19, 22, 1908, American Foundation for Mental Hygiene Papers.

42. "Minutes for the Founding of a National Committee of Mental Hygiene. February 19, 1909," William James to Beers, February 21, 26, 1909, *ibid.*; Dain, *Clifford W. Beers*, pp. 132–133.

43. Meyer to Beers, November 30, 1909, Meyer to Anson Stokes Phelps, February 25, 1910, Meyer to James, February 28, 1910, Beers to James, March 10, 16, 1910, American Foundation for Mental Hygiene Papers; James to Beers, March 3, 5, 1910, James Papers.

44. Arthur P. Herring, *Report to Hon. Richard I. Manning . . . on the State Hospital for the Insane at Columbia* (Columbia, S.C., 1915); C. Floyd Haviland, *The Treatment and Care of the Insane in Pennsylvania* (Philadelphia, 1915); Grob, *Mental Illness and American Society*, pp. 157–160.

45. "Proceedings of the 9th Annual Meeting of the National Committee for Mental Hygiene . . . 1917," pp. 14–15, typed copy in American Foundation for Mental Hygiene Papers; Frankwood E. Williams to Edwin R. Embree, May 1, 1925, together with "Statement in Reference to a Proposal for a Study of the Psychopathology of Dependency," Record Group 1.1, Series 200 (NCMH), Rockefeller Archive Center, Pocantico Hills, North Tarrytown, N.Y. The involvement of the NCMH with children can be followed in

Margo Horn, *Before It's Too Late: The Child Guidance Movement in the United States, 1922–1945* (Philadelphia, 1989) and Theresa R. Richardson, *The Century of the Child: The Mental Hygiene Movement and Social Policy in the United States and Canada* (Albany, 1989).

46. See especially Dain, *Clifford W. Beers*, chapters 14–20.

47. Meyer to Dr. William Gerry Morgan, July 2, 1930, Meyer Papers, Series I; Maxwell Gitelson to Dr. Earl Saxe, December 19, 1939, Gitelson Papers, Library of Congress, Washington, D.C.

48. Frankwood E. Williams, "Is There a Mental Hygiene," *Psychoanalytic Quarterly*, 1 (1932), 113–120; V. V. Anderson, *Psychiatry in Industry* (New York, 1929) and *Psychiatry in Education* (New York, 1932); "News Letter of the Association for the Psychiatric Study of Social Issues" (1939) with form letter to John C. Whitehorn, September 7, 1939, Whitehorn Papers, Archives of the American Psychiatric Association, Washington, D.C.

49. Irving Fisher to Meyer, November 19, 24, 1923, with "Report of the Committee on Selective Immigration of the Eugenics Committee of the United States of America," Meyer to Fisher, November 23, 1923, Meyer Papers, Series II.

    When the institutionalized population was analyzed in terms of the age distribution of the entire native and foreign-born population, the relative proportion of immigrants in asylums declined precipitously. The mental hospital population was composed entirely of individuals over the age of twenty. Yet a large proportion of the native-born white population was under the age of twenty, whereas a much smaller proportion of immigrants was less than twenty. "The age difference," noted the authors of the census of 1910, "probably goes further than any other factor toward explaining the contrast between the native white and the foreign-born white in respect to the proportionate numbers admitted to hospitals for the insane," and they suggested that other differences might be accounted for by sex distribution or urban-rural residence. Such data called into question claims about the allegation that immigrants, particularly Catholics and Jews from Eastern and Southern Europe, were more susceptible to insanity because of innate traits. U.S. Bureau of the Census, *Insane and Feeble-Minded in Institutions 1910* (Washington, D.C., 1914), pp. 26–27.

50. See Philip R. Reilly, *The Surgical Solution: A History of Involuntary Sterilization in the United States* (Baltimore, 1991); Mark Haller, *Eugenics: Hereditarian Attitudes in American Thought* (New Brunswick, 1963); and Daniel Kevles, *In the Name of Eugenics: Genetics and the Uses of Human Heredity* (New York, 1985).

51. Statistical data from mimeographed "Table of Sterilization . . . 1940," Association for Voluntary Sterilization Papers (Box 6, Folder 56), Social History Welfare Archives, University of Minnesota, Minneapolis. See also Reilly, *Surgical Solution, passim.*

52. William A. White to Dr. Fisher, c. 1919, White Papers, RG 418, National Archives, Washington, D.C.; J. K. Hall, "Sterilization," *Southern Medicine and Surgery*, 99 (1937): 514; American Neurological Association, *Eugenical Sterilization: A Reorientation of the Problem* (New York, 1936), *passim.*

53. Richard Dewey to William A. White, January 4, 1906, White to Dewey, n.d. (c. January 1906), White Papers; White, "Presidential Address," *American Journal of Psychiatry*, 82 (1925): 1–20.

54. Charles W. Burr, "The Teaching of Psychiatry," *Journal of the American Medical Association*, 60 (1913): 1054–1057.

55. "Report of the Division of Psychiatric Education of the National Committee for Mental Hygiene for the Year 1931–1932," copy in Adolf Meyer Papers, Series II; Ralph A. Noble, *Psychiatry in Medical Education: An Abridgement of a Report Submitted to the Advisory Committee of Psychiatric Education of the National Committee for Mental Hygiene* (New York, 1933), *passim.*

56. James V. May, "The Establishment of Psychiatric Standards by the Association," *American Journal of Psychiatry*, 90 (1933): 8, 14.

57. *Ibid*, 91 (1934): 713; 92 (1935): 226–229, 426–430, 475–477; 95 (1938): 477–479; Walter Freeman, Franklin Ebaugh, and David A. Boyd, "The Founding of the American Board of Psychiatry and Neurology, Inc.," *ibid*, 115 (1959): 769–778.

Chapter 7. Depression, War, and the Crisis of Care

1. U.S. Bureau of the Census, *Insane and Feeble-Minded in Institutions 1910* (Washington, D.C., 1914), p. 22; Samuel W. Hamilton et al, *A Study of the Public Mental Hospitals of the United States 1937–39* (Washington, D.C., 1941), p. 39; N.Y.S. Department of Mental Hygiene, *Annual Report-Statistical Section*, 1962–1963, pp. 18, 47.

2. Morton Kramer, H. Goldstein, R. H. Israel, and N. A. Johnson, *A Historical Study of the Disposition of First Admissions to a State Mental Hospital: Experiences of the Warren State Hospital During the Period 1916–50* (Public Health Service *Publication 445*: Washington, D.C., 1955), p. 9.

3. U.S. Bureau of the Census, *Insane and Feeble-Minded in Institutions 1910*, pp. 22, 47–48.

4. Hamilton, *Study of Public Mental Hospitals*, p. 81; Gerald N. Grob, *Mental Illness and American Society, 1875–1940* (Princeton, 1983), p. 219, and *From Asylum to Community: Mental Health Policy in Modern America* (Princeton, 1991), p. 161.

5. Hester B. Crutcher, *Foster Home Care for Mental Patients* (New York, 1944), *passim*; Hans B. Molholm and Walter E. Barton, "Family Care, a Community Resource in the Rehabilitation of Mental Patients," *American Journal of Psychiatry*, 98 (1941): 33–41; Edith M. Stern, "Family Care for the Mentally Ill," *Survey Graphic*, 31 (January 1942): 31; Grob, *Mental Illness and American Society*, pp. 83–86.

6. Molholm and Barton, "Family Care," p. 34.

7. U.S. Bureau of the Census, *Patients in Mental Institutions 1940* (Washington, D.C., 1943), p. 63; NCMH, *State Hospitals in the Depression: A Survey of the Effects of the Economic Crisis on the Operations of the Institutions for the Mentally Ill in the United States* (New York, 1934), *passim*.

8. NCMH, *State Hospitals in the Depression*, pp. 90–94, 117–119.

9. Clarence M. Hincks to Edward Sydenstricker, November 26, 1934, American Foundation for Mental Health Papers, Archives of Psychiatry, New York Hospital-Cornell Medical Center, New York; Hamilton, *Study of the Public Mental Hospitals*, p. 22; *PM*, August 4–8, 1941.

10. GAP Circular Letter No. 12 (November 20, 1946), GAP Papers, Archives of Psychiatry; Harry J. Worthing to J. K. Hall, November 26, 1942, Hall Papers, Southern Historical Collection, University of North Carolina, Chapel Hill; Dorothy Deming, "Mental Hospitals in Wartime," *American Journal of Nursing*, 43 (1943): 1013–1017.

11. GAP Circular Letter No. 12 (November 20, 1946), Archives of Psychiatry. See also "Public Psychiatric Hospitals," GAP *Report No. 5* (April 1948), and *New York Times*, January 22, 1945.

12. John M. Gessell, "State Hospital Scandal," *Christian Century*, 63 (1946): 1245.

13. U.S. Bureau of the Census, *Summary of State Laws Relating to the Dependent Classes 1913* (Washington, D.C., 1914), pp. 312–321 *et passim*.

14. Winfred Overholser, "The Desiderata of Central Administrative Control of State Mental Hospitals," *American Journal of Psychiatry*, 96 (1939): 519–521.

15. U.S. Bureau of the Census, *Mental Patients in State Hospitals 1931 and 1932* (Washington, D.C., 1934), p. 62; J. K. Hall to Douglas Southall Freeman, May 18, 1936, Hall to Hugh C. Henry, February 24, 1939, Hall Papers.

16. This theme was admirably developed by Oscar and Mary F. Handlin in

their classic *Commonwealth: A Study of the Role of Government in the American Economy: Massachusetts, 1774–1861* (Cambridge, 1947).

17. *American Journal of Psychiatry*, 79 (1922): 330; 81 (1924): 385ff.; 82 (1925): 300–306; 83 (1926): 362; 84 (1927): 328–329; 86 (1929): 409–410.

18. *Ibid.*, 91 (1934): 414–420; 92 (1935): 480–482; Arthur P. Noyes to Clarence B. Farrar, January 9, 1934, March 11, 1935, April 20 and July 10, 1936, Farrar to Noyes, January 15, 1934, July 13, 1936, "Summary of Reports From Various States" (manuscript), *passim*, Farrar Papers, Archives of the American Psychiatric Association, Washington, D.C.

19. The Winfred Overholser Scrapbooks at the Library of Congress, Washington, D.C., contain an extensive number of newspaper clippings. The American Foundation for Mental Hygiene Papers and the Clarence Farrar Papers include correspondence by many of the participants. The report of the Massachusetts Special Commission can be found in Massachusetts *House Document No. 320* (January 1938). See also Grob, *Mental Illness and American Society*, pp. 224–228.

20. Overholser, "The Desiderata of Central Administrative Control," 517–534, 563–574.

21. See especially Allan M. Brandt, *No Magic Bullet: A Social History of Venereal Disease in the United States Since 1880* (New York, 1985), and Claude Quétel, *History of Syphilis* (Cambridge, England, 1990).

22. William A. White to H. W. Mitchell, April 25, 1923, White Papers, R.G. 418, National Archives, Washington, D.C.

23. Watson W. Eldridge to White, June 21 and 27, 1930, White to Eldridge, June 24 and 28, 1930, *ibid.*

24. John H. Stokes, "Critical Treatment Problems in Today's Syphilology," *Journal of the American Medical Association*, 94 (1930): 1033; A. E. Bennett, "Evaluation of Artificial Fever Therapy for Neuropsychiatric Disorders," *Archives of Neurology and Psychiatry*, 40 (1938): 1141–1155; Oskar Diethelm, "An Historical View of Somatic Treatment in Psychiatry," *American Journal of Psychiatry*, 95 (1939): 1165–1179.

25. See Manfred Sakel's *The Pharmacological Shock Treatment of Schizophrenia* (New York, 1938), and "The Origin and Nature of the Hypoglycemic Therapy of the Psychoses," *Bulletin of the New York Academy of Medicine*, 13 (1937): 97–109.

26. White to C. M. Hincks, October 27, 1936, Overholser to Hincks, October 27, 1936, American Foundation for Mental Health Papers; A. A. Brill to White, October 31, 1936, White Papers; Meyer to White, December 17, 1936, Meyer Papers, Series I, Johns Hopkins Medical Institutions, Baltimore; J. K. Hall to D. H. Duncan, March 2, 1940, Hall Papers.

27. Ladislas von Meduna, *Die Konvulsiontherapie der Schizophrenia* (Halle, 1937).

28. Lawrence C. Kolb and Victor H. Vogel, "The Use of Shock Therapy in 305 Mental Hospitals," *American Journal of Psychiatry*, 99 (1942): 90–100; (New York State) Temporary Commission on State Hospital Problems, *Insulin Shock Therapy* (New York, 1944), p. 81; Lothar B. Kalinowsky and Paul H. Hoch, *Shock Treatments and Other Somatic Procedures in Psychiatry* (New York, 1946), p. ix.

29. The most authoritative analysis of psychosurgery is Jack Pressman's "Uncertain Promise: Psychosurgery and the Development of Scientific Psychiatry in America, 1933 to 1955" (Ph.D. dissertation, University of Pennsylvania, 1986), which will be published in revised form by Cambridge University Press. See also Pressman's "Sufficient Promise: John F. Fulton and the Origins of Psychosurgery," *Bulletin of the History of Medicine*, 62 (1988): 1–22. Elliot S. Valenstein's *Great and Desperate Cures: The Rise and Decline of Psychosurgery and Other Radical Treatments for Mental Illness* (New York, 1986) is useful for Freeman's career, but is marred by an ahistorical and moralistic approach that results in a misunderstanding of therapies—psychiatric and others—in general. One of the most illuminating primary sources is the *Proceedings* (1–3 [1949–1951]) of the U.S. Public Health Service's Research Conference on Psychosurgery.

30. Kalinowsky and Hoch, *Shock Treatments*, p. 243.

31. "Electroshock: A Round Table Discussion," *American Journal of Psychiatry*, 100 (1943): 362.

32. Thelma G. Alper, "An Electric Shock Patient Tells His Story," *Journal of Abnormal and Social Psychology*, 43 (1948): 201–210.

33. Benjamin Malzberg, "Outcome of Insulin Treatment of One Thousand Patients with Dementia Praecox," *Psychiatric Quarterly*, 12 (1938): 528–553, and "A Follow-Up Study of Patients with Dementia Praecox Treated with Insulin in the New York Civil State Hospitals," *Mental Hygiene*, 23 (1939): 641–651; Horatio M. Pollock, "A Statistical Study of 1,140 Dementia Praecox Patients Treated with Metrazol," *Psychiatric Quarterly*, 13 (1939): 558–568.

34. A. E. Bennett, "Evaluation of Progress in Established Physiochemical Treatments in Neuropsychiatry. III. The Use of Electroshock in the Total Psychiatric Treatment Program," *Diseases of the Nervous System*, 10 (1949): 195–206.

35. Solomon Katzenelbogen, "A Critical Appraisal of the 'Shock Therapies' in the Major Psychoses," *Psychiatry*, 2 (1939): 493–505, and 3 (1940): 211–228, 409–420.

36. Rylander's work is summarized in Lawrence C. Kolb, "An Evaluation of Lobotomy and its Potentialities for Future Research in Psychiatry and the Basic Sciences," *Journal of Nervous and Mental Disease*, 110 (1949): 113–114, 127.

37. Research Conference on Psychosurgery, *Proceedings*, 1 (1949): 5; 3 (1951): 4; Carney Landis, "A Statistical Evaluation of Psychotherapeutic Methods," in Leland E. Hinsie, *Concepts and Problems of Psychotherapy* (New York, 1937), pp. 155–169. My discussion of psychosurgery is based upon Pressman's outstanding work, "Uncertain Promise," *passim*.

38. Horatio M. Pollock, "Trends in the Outcome of General Paresis," *Psychiatric Quarterly*, 9 (1935): 194–211; Henry D. Sheldon, "Certain Trends Reflected in Census Statistics on Patients in Hospitals for Mental Disease 1933 to 1942," in American Psychopathological Association, *Trends of Mental Disease* (New York, 1945), pp. 34ff.; Benjamin Malzberg, *Social and Biological Aspects of Mental Disease* (Utica, 1940), p. 353.

39. Kramer et al., *A Historical Study of the Disposition of First Admissions to a State Mental Hospital, passim*.

40. See James Jones, *Bad Blood: The Tuskegee Syphilis Experiment* (New York, 1981).

41. Hamilton, *Study of the Public Mental Hospitals*, pp. 15–16; Winfred Overholser, "Facts and Fiction About Our State Hospitals," *Ohio State Medical Journal*, 36 (1940): 1167; Charles C. Burlingame, "Can the Point of View and Technique of Private Practice be Carried Into the Mental Hospital," paper delivered at the Southern Psychiatric Association, October 9, 1937, quoted in Pressman, "Uncertain Promise," p. 164.

Chapter 8. World War II and New Models of Mental Disorders

1. Karl A. Menninger, "The Future of Psychiatric Care in Hospitals," *Modern Hospital*, 64 (May 1945): 43. See also Victor H. Vogel, "Our Inadequate Treatment of the Mentally Ill as Compared with Treatment of Other Sick People," *Public Health Reports*, 56 (1941): 1941–1947.

2. Albert Deutsch, "Military Psychiatry: World War II 1941–1943," in *One Hundred Years of American Psychiatry*, ed. J. K. Hall (New York, 1944), pp. 421–427; David J. Flicker, "Psychiatric Induction Examination," *War Medicine* 2 (1942): 935–936, cited in *ibid*.

3. Rebecca S. Greene, "The Role of the Psychiatrist in World War II" (Ph.D. dissertation, Columbia University, 1977), pp. 59–208, 323–350; U.S. Army Medical Department, *Neuropsychiatry in World War II* (2 vols., Washing-

ton, D.C., 1966–1973), I, pp. 153–191, 740–744, 768; Gerald N. Grob, "World War II and American Psychiatry," *Psychohistory Review*, 19 (1990): 41–69.

4. Herbert X. Spiegel, "Psychiatry with an Infantry Battalion in North Africa," in U.S. Army Medical Department, *Neuropsychiatry in World War II*, II, pp. 120–121.

5. U.S. Army Medical Department, *Neuropsychiatry in World War II*, I, pp. 390–391, 406–407, II, pp. 995, 1017–1021; William C. Menninger, "Psychiatric Experience in the War, 1941–1946," *American Journal of Psychiatry*, 103 (1947): 580.

6. See Roy R. Grinker and John P. Spiegel, *War Neuroses* (Philadelphia, 1945), p. 70, and *Men Under Stress* (Philadelphia, 1945); John W. Appel and Gilbert W. Beebe, "Preventive Psychiatry: An Epidemiologic Approach," *Journal of the American Medical Association*, 131 (1946): 1469–1475; Herbert X. Spiegel, "Psychiatric Observations in the Tunisian Campaign," *American Journal of Orthopsychiatry*, 14 (1944): 381–385, and "Preventive Psychiatry with Combat Troops," *American Journal of Psychiatry*, 101 (1944): 310–315; Leo H. Bartemeier et al., "Combat Exhaustion," *Journal of Nervous and Mental Disease*, 104 (1946): 358–389, 489–525; Harry C. Solomon and Paul I. Yakovlev, eds., *Manual of Military Neuropsychiatry* (Philadelphia, 1944), p. 528 *et passim*.

7. U.S. Army Medical Department, *Neuropsychiatry in World War II*, II, pp. 275–333; William C. Menninger, "Psychiatric Experiences in the War," p. 579.

8. Albert J. Glass, "Lessons Learned," U.S. Army Medical Department, *Neuropsychiatry in World War II*, II, pp. 999–1000.

9. Appel and Beebe, "Preventive Psychiatry," p. 147. See also William C. Menninger, *Psychiatry in a Troubled World: Yesterday's War and Today's Challenge* (New York, 1948), pp. 410–437.

10. Robert H. Felix and R. V. Bowers, "Mental Hygiene and Socio-Environmental Factors," *Milbank Memorial Fund Quarterly*, 26 (1948): 125–147 and Felix, "Mental Public Health: A Blueprint," presentation at St. Elizabeths Hospital, April 21, 1945, Felix Papers, National Library of Medicine, Bethesda, Md.

11. Thomas A. C. Rennie and Luther E. Woodward, *Mental Health in Modern Society* (New York, 1948), pp. vii–xi *et passim*; Nolan D. C. Lewis, "What the Wars' Experiences Have Taught Us in Psychiatry," in N.Y. Academy of Medicine, *Medicine in the Postwar World* (New York, 1948), p. 65.

12. U.S. Army Medical Department, *Neuropsychiatry in World War II*, I, pp.

33–66; William C. Menninger, "Development of Psychiatry in the Army in World War II," *War Medicine* 8 (1945): 230–231.

13. Karl Menninger's career can be followed in Lawrence Friedman's *Menninger: The Family and the Clinic* (New York, 1990). See also Howard J. Faulkner and Virginia D. Pruitt, eds., *The Selected Correspondence of Karl A. Menninger, 1919–1945* (New Haven, 1988).

14. Clarence B. Farrar to Clarence O. Cheyney, February 11, Farrar to William L. Russell, March 8, Russell to Winfred Overholser, February 26, 1945, Farrar Papers, APA Archives, Washington, D.C. The conflict within the APA is described at length in Gerald N. Grob, "Psychiatry and Social Activism: The Politics of a Specialty in Postwar America," *Bulletin of the History of Medicine*, 60 (1986): 477–501, and *From Asylum to Community: Mental Health Policy in Modern America* (Princeton, 1991), chapter 2.

15. *American Journal of Psychiatry*, 102 (1946): 388–389, 694–700; GAP, Minutes of the First, Second, and Third Informal Gathering, May 26–28, 1946, GAP Papers, Archives of Psychiatry, New York Hospital-Cornell Medical Center, New York, N.Y.

16. See GAP *Reports Nos. 1–13* (1947–1950). The quote is from "The Social Responsibility of Psychiatry, A Statement of Orientation," *ibid.*, 13 (July 1950): 1–5.

17. Farrar to Overholser, December 20, 1946 (with enclosed constitution), Farrar Papers.

18. Overholser to Farrar, February 15, June 26, 1947, May 11, 1949, June 6, 1951, Overholser to Walter Treadway, July 3, 1951, C. C. Burlingame to Farrar, November 26, December 19, 1947, Farrar to Burlingame, December 2, 1947, William C. Menninger to Farrar, December 2, 1946, January 18, 1947, Farrar to Menninger, December 6, 1946, March 6, 1947, Farrar to Samuel Hamilton, December 6, 1946, January 31, 1947, Hamilton to Farrar, February 17 (two letters), February 28, March 6, 1947, Farrar Papers.

19. *American Journal of Psychiatry*, 105 (1949): 858–860; Dexter Bullard interview, August 5, 1964, Oral History 148, pp. 31–34, APA Archives.

20. *New York Daily Compass*, May 24, 1949.

21. Form letter from Theodore Robie and letter from the Committee for the Preservation of Medical Standards in Psychiatry to all APA members, ca. late December 1948 or early January 1949, Records of the Medical Director's Office, 200–25, APA Archives; Committee for the Preservation of Medical Standards in Psychiatry, *Newsletter*, 1–3 (January-March 1949), copies in GAP Papers.

22. D. Ewen Cameron to Daniel Blain, April 26, May 12, 1949, Records of the

Medical Director's Office, 100–3, APA Archives; "Report to the Council from the Committee on Reorganization," May, 1949, *ibid.*, 200–20; *American Journal of Psychiatry*, 105 (1949): 548–549, 704–705, 794; Grob, *From Asylum to Community*, pp. 39–41.

23. This generalization is based on a 10 percent (n=943) sample of the total membership of the APA for 1957, using the *Biographical Directory of Fellows & Members of the American Psychiatric Association as of October 1, 1957* (New York, 1958).

24. *New York Times*, October 3, 1946; Commission to Investigate the Management and Affairs of the Department of Mental Hygiene of the State of New York and the Institutions Operated by It, *The Care of the Mentally Ill in the State of New York* (Albany, 1944); Grob, *From Asylum to Community*, pp. 71–72.

25. Albert Deutsch, *The Mentally Ill in America: A History of Their Care and Treatment from Colonial Times* (Garden City, N.Y., 1937); Jeanne Brand, "Albert Deutsch: The Historian as Social Reformer," *Journal of the History of Medicine and Allied Sciences*, 18 (1963): 149–157.

26. Most of Deutsch's articles appeared in *PM* between March 1946 and September 1947. A complete list of the reviews of *The Shame of the States* (New York, 1948) can be found in the Deutsch Papers, APA Archives.

27. Deutsch, *Shame of the States*, pp. 182–188; Deutsch to Dora S. Heffner, December 21, 1948, Deutsch Papers, APA Archives.

28. Albert Q. Maisel, "Bedlam 1946," *Life*, 20 (May 6, 1946): 103–118; *Christian Century*, 63 (1946): 611–612; *Commonweal*, 44 (1946): 107.

29. Alan Gregg to John D. Rockefeller, Jr., March 18, 1946, RG 1.2, Series 200A, Rockefeller Foundation Papers, Rockefeller Archive Center, North Tarrytown, N.Y.; Frank L. Wright, Jr., *Out of Sight Out of Mind* (Philadelphia, 1947).

30. Gorman's articles in the *Daily Oklahoman* were reprinted in pamphlet form under the following titles: *Misery Rules in State Shadowland* (Norman, 1946), *Let There Be Light* (Norman, 1947), and *If We Can Love* (Norman, 1947); Gorman, "Oklahoma Attacks Its Snakepits," *Reader's Digest*, 53 (September 1948): 139–160; Karl A. Menninger to George Stevenson (with enclosure), April 16, 1948, Karl A. Menninger Papers, Menninger Foundation Archives, Topeka, Kansas.

31. Mary Jane Ward, *The Snake Pit* (New York, 1946), condensed in *Reader's Digest*, 48 (May 1946): 129–168; Krin and Glen O. Gabbard, *Psychiatry and the Cinema* (Chicago, 1987), pp. 68–71; Grob, *From Asylum to Community*, pp. 76–77.

32. Grob, *From Asylum to Community*, pp. 78–82. The APA Archives contain both the Records of the Medical Director's Office and the Central Inspection Board Papers, which provide extensive data on the organization's activities in the postwar years. The views of the NCMH can be found in George S. Stevenson's "Needed: A Plan for the Mentally Ill," *New York Times Magazine*, July 27, 1947, pp. 11, 18–19.

33. See especially Friedman, *Menninger*.

34. World War II in particular had a dramatic effect on the social sciences, for it strengthened faith in the efficacy of social engineering. See Peter Buck, "Adjusting to Military Life: The Social Sciences Go to War, 1941–1950," in *Military Enterprise and Technological Change: Perspectives on the American Experience*, ed. Merritt Roe Smith (Cambridge, 1985), pp. 203–252.

35. See President's Scientific Research Board, *Science and Public Policy* (5 vols., Washington, D.C.); Daniel M. Fox, *Health Policies, Health Politics: The British and American Experience, 1911–1965* (Princeton, 1986); and Stephen P. Strickland, *Politics, Science, and Dread Disease: A Short History of United States Medical Research Policy* (Cambridge, 1972).

36. See Franklin G. Ebaugh, *The Care of the Psychiatric Patient in General Hospitals* (Chicago, 1940).

37. The hearings are found in 79-1 Congress, *National Neuropsychiatric Institute Act. Hearing before a Subcommittee of the Committee on Interstate and Foreign Commerce, House of Representatives . . . 1945* (Washington, D.C., 1945), and 79–2 Congress, *National Neuropsychiatric Institute Act. Hearings before a Subcommittee of the Committee on Education and Labor, United States Senate . . . 1946* (Washington, D.C., 1946).

38. The passage of the law can be followed in Grob, *From Asylum to Community*, chapter 3.

39. Chap. 538, *U.S. Statutes at Large*, 60:421–426 (1946).

40. See Robert H. Felix interview by Harlan Phillips, February 8, 1963, Felix interview by Jeanne Brand, April 2, 1964, National Library of Medicine, Bethesda, Md.; Felix interview by Milton J. Senn, March 8, 1979, Senn Collection (OH76), National Library of Medicine; Felix interview by Daniel Blain, May 15, 1972, Blain Papers, APA Archives; Felix interview by Eli Rubenstein, 1977, NIMH, Rockville, Md.

41. Felix, "Mental Disorders as a Public Health Problem," *American Journal of Psychiatry*, 106 (1949): 401–406. See also Paul V. Lemkau, *Mental Hygiene in Public Health* (New York, 1st ed., 1949; 2nd ed., 1955).

42. See Felix interview by Brand, National Library of Medicine.

43. Jeanne L. Brand and Philip Sapir, eds., "An Historical Perspective on the

National Institute of Mental Health," February, 1964, mimeograph document prepared as Section I of the NIMH Report to Dean E. Woolridge, chairperson, National Institutes of Health Study Committee, copy provided by Jeanne L. Brand; NIMH, *Mental Health Series*, No. 4 (Public Health Service *Publication 20*: rev. ed., 1950), pp. 1–20. See also John Clausen, *Sociology and the Field of Mental Health* (New York, 1956).

44. Public Health Service Mental Hygiene Division, "Annual Report for Fiscal Year 1947," pp. 5–6, typed copy in NIMH Records, Subject Files, 1940–51, Box 82, Washington National Records Center, Suitland, Md.; 80–2 Congress, House of Representatives Subcommittee of the Committee on Appropriations, *Department of Labor–Federal Security Agency Appropriation for 1949: Hearings* (Washington, D.C., 1948), Part 2, p. 271; Felix, "The Relation of the National Mental Health Act to State Health Authorities," *Public Health Reports*, 62 (1947): 46–47; *idem.*, "The National Mental Health Program—A Progress Report," *ibid.*, 63 (1948): 837–839; *New York Times*, April 4, 1947.

45. Public Health Service Mental Hygiene Division, "Annual Report, Fiscal 1948," p. 4, NIMH, "Annual Report, Fiscal 1949," p. 9 and Table V, typed copies in NIMH Records, Subject Files, 1940–51, Box 82, NIMH records; NIMH, "Objectives and a Balanced Program for the NIMH," draft, October 15, 1951, p. 15, Central Files 1951–54, Box 10, *ibid.*; 81–2 Congress, House of Representatives Subcommittee of the Committee on Appropriations, *Department of Labor-Federal Security Agency Appropriations for 1951: Hearings* (Washington, D.C., 1950), p. 539; 83–1, House of Representatives Subcommittee of the Committee on Appropriations, *Department of Labor-Federal Security Agency Appropriations for 1954: Hearings* (Washington, D.C., 1953), Part 1, p. 1034; Jerry W. Carter, "The Community Services Program of the National Institute of Mental Health, U.S. Public Health Service," *Journal of Clinical Psychology*, 6 (1950): 113–114; Anita K. Bahn and V. B. Norman, *Outpatient Psychiatric Clinics in the United States 1954–55* (Public Health Service, *Public Health Monograph No. 49*: Washington, D.C., 1957), p. 40.

46. Carter, "Community Services Programs," p. 14; National Advisory Mental Health Council, Minutes of Meeting, November 8–9, 1954, p. 8, RG 90, National Archives, Washington, D.C. See especially the Community Services State Files 1949–1954, and the Annual Summaries of State Mental Health Programs 1947–60, in NIMH Records.

47. National Advisory Mental Health Council, Minutes of Meeting, December 11–12, 1950, pp. 11–14, March 9–11, 1955, pp. 5–7, RG 90, National

Archives; NIMH, *Evaluation in Mental Health . . . Report of the Subcommittee on Evaluation of Mental Health Activities, Community Services Committee, National Advisory Mental Health Council* (Public Health Service *Publication 413*: Washington, D.C., 1955), pp. 1, 3, 57.

48. For the state of psychiatric classification in the postwar period see *Diagnostic and Statistical Manual: Mental Disorders* (often referred to as DSM-I), prepared by the Committee on Nomenclature and Statistics of the APA (Washington, D.C., 1952). The background of DSM-I can be followed in Gerald N. Grob, "Origins of DSM-I: A Study in Appearance and Reality," *American Journal of Psychiatry*, 148 (1991): 421–431.

49. Felix to William C. Menninger, February 11, enclosed with "Report of the Sub-Committee on Integrative Policy to the Committee on Training, Division of Mental Hygiene, U.S. Public Service," Felix to Menninger, July 23, 1948, William C. Menninger Papers, Menninger Foundation Archives.

50. The data for 1948–1951 are included in William C. Jenkins to R. R. Willey, September 8, 1952, NIMH Records, Central Files 1951–54, Box 7. The data are suggestive rather than definitive. NIMH had data on only about 60 percent of trainees, and the information was limited to the first position accepted by individuals. Nor did the data delineate situations that included multiple employment. Information for the 1960s can be found in the following: *Current Professional Status of Mental Health Personnel Supported under National Institute of Mental Health Training Grants* (Public Health Service *Publication 1088*: 1963); *A Study of the Current Status of Mental Health Personnel Supported under National Institute of Mental Health Training Grants* (Public Health Service *Publication 1541*: 1966); and Franklyn N. Arnhoff, B. M. Shiver, and R. M. VanMatre, "Subsequent Career Activities of National Institute of Mental Health Trainees in Psychiatry," *Journal of Medical Education*, 42 (1967): 855–862.

51. See Memo of Harold P. Halpert to Robert Felix and Staff, October 3, 1952 ("Draft of Long-Range Plan for P & R Section"), Central Files 1951–54, Box 11, NIMH Records; and Richard H. Williams, "Some Issues of Planning and Policy in the National Institute of Mental Health," Mental Health Subject Files 1957–60, Box 14, *ibid.*

Chapter 9. The Foundations of Change in Postwar America

1. See Harold Maine, "We Can Save the Mentally Sick," *Saturday Evening Post*, 220 (1947): 20–21, 160, 162, 165–166, and *If a Man be Mad* (Garden

City, N.Y., 1947). Lawrence J. Friedman's *Menninger: The Family and the Clinic* (New York, 1990) provides detailed descriptions and analyses of one of the nation's most important postwar psychiatric institutions.

2. Jerome D. Frank, *Persuasion and Healing: A Comparative Study of Psychotherapy* (Baltimore, 1961), pp. 11–13, 231–232.

3. Leo H. Bartemeier, "Presidential Address," *American Journal of Psychiatry*, 109 (1952): 1–7; Jules H. Masserman, "Faith and Delusion in Psychotherapy," *ibid.*, 110 (1953): 324–333; Samuel H. Hadden, "Historic Background of Group Psychotherapy," *International Journal of Group Psychotherapy*, 5 (1955): 162–168; American Psychological Association, Conference on Research in Psychotherapy, *Proceedings*, I (1958): 292.

4. Maxwell Jones, *The Therapeutic Community: A New Treatment Method in Psychiatry* (New York, 1953), pp. 156–157 (first published in England in 1952 under the title *Social Psychiatry*). See also his "The Treatment of Personality Disorders in a Therapeutic Community," *Psychiatry*, 20 (1957): 212–217, and Albert Deutsch's interview with Jones and Harry Wilmer, August 29, 1959, Deutsch Papers, APA Archives, Washington, D.C.

5. J. Fremont Bateman and H. Warren Dunham, "The State Mental Hospital as a Specialized Community Experience," *American Journal of Psychiatry*, 105 (1948): 445–448.

6. Alfred H. Stanton and Morris S. Schwartz, *The Mental Hospital: A Study of Institutional Participation in Psychiatric Illness and Treatment* (New York, 1954); Milton Greenblatt, R. H. York, E. L. Brown, and R. W. Hyde, *From Custodial to Therapeutic Patient Care in Mental Hospitals* (New York, 1955), pp. 237, 424; Robert N. Rapoport, *Community as Doctor* (London, 1960), p. 10. Some other works in this tradition included Otto von Mering and Stanley H. King, *Remotivating the Mental Patient* (New York, 1957); Ivan Belknap, *Human Problems of a State Mental Hospital* (New York, 1956); William Caudill, *The Psychiatric Hospital as a Small Society* (Cambridge, 1958); H. Warren Dunham and S. K. Weinberg, *The Culture of the State Mental Hospital* (Detroit, 1960). The literature on the therapeutic community is immense; additional references can be found in Charlotte G. Schwartz, *Rehabilitation of Mental Hospital Patients: Review of the Literature* (Public Health Service, *Publication 297*: Washington, D.C., 1953); Greenblatt et al., *From Custodial to Therapeutic Patient Care*, pp. 431–484, and Mering and King, *Remotivating the Mental Patient*, pp. 201–207.

7. Gerald N. Grob, *From Asylum to Community: Mental Health Policy in Modern America* (Princeton, 1991), pp. 145–146.

8. My discussion of the development and introduction of psychoactive drugs

is based on Judith P. Swazey's excellent monograph, *Chlorpromazine in Psychiatry: A Study of Therapeutic Innovation* (Cambridge, 1974).

9. *Ibid.*, chapters 1–4.

10. *Ibid.*, pp. 111–141. The quotation is from Jean Delay and Pierre Deniker, "Les neuroplégiques en thérapeutique psychiatrique," *Thérapie*, 8 (1953): 361.

11. Swazey, *Chlorpromazine in Psychiatry*, chapters 6–8. See also Norman Rosenzweig, "Developments in Psychiatry over the Past Decade," *Bulletin of the Sinai Hospital of Detroit*, 10 (1963): 304–368.

12. APA, "A Statement on the Contribution of the Tranquilizing Drugs," press release, June 7, 1956, Records of the Medical Directors Office, 200–21, APA Archives; Winfred Overholser, "Has Chlorpromazine Inaugurated a New Era in Mental Hospitals?" *Journal of Clinical and Experimental Psychopathology*, 17 (1956): 197–201.

13. Morton Kramer, *Facts Needed to Assess Public Health and Social Problems in the Widespread Use of the Tranquilizing Drugs* (Public Health Service, *Publication No. 486*: Washington, D.C., 1956); Mike Gorman speech, Trenton, N.J., February 4, 1957, copy in Gorman Papers, National Library of Medicine, Bethesda, Md.; Gorman, *Every Other Bed* (Cleveland, 1956), pp. 89–132; William C. Menninger to Albert Deutsch, February 28, Deutsch to Mary Lasker, March 5, 1956, Deutsch to Norman Reider, February 16, Deutsch to David Rapaport, February 17, 1957, Deutsch Papers; NIMH Psychopharmacology Service Center Collaborative Study Group, "Phenothiazine Treatment in Acute Schizophrenia," *Archives of General Psychiatry*, 10 (1964): 246–261. For an overview of the debate see Grob, *From Asylum to Community*, pp. 146–156.

14. Council of State Governments, *The Mental Health Programs of the Forty-Eight States: A Report to the Governors' Conference* (Chicago, 1950). See also the Council's subsequent study, *Training and Research in State Mental Health Programs: A Report to the Governors' Conference* (Chicago, 1953),

15. *State Government*, 23 (1950): 4–5, 183–184.

16. Grob, *From Asylum to Community*, pp. 163–164. APA State Surveys can be found in the APA Archives; between 1955 and 1959 there were at least eight.

17. Data on patient-staff ratios drawn from APA Joint Information Service, *JIS Fact Sheet*, 1 (1957): 2; data on expenditures compiled from NIMH's annual *Patients in Mental Institutions*.

18. Harry C. Solomon, "The American Psychiatric Association in Relation to American Psychiatry," *American Journal of Psychiatry*, 115 (1958): 1–9;

Robert C. Hunt to Solomon, June 17, Solomon to Hunt, June 19, 1958, Solomon Papers, APA Archives; Hunt "The State Hospital Stereotype", in "Minutes . . . [APA] Commission on Long Term Policies," October 30, 1959, Jack R. Ewalt Papers, Countway Library of Medicine, Harvard Medical School, Boston.

19. There is a large and growing literature on the influence of gender on medicine. See especially Regina Morantz-Sanchez, *Sympathy and Science: Women Physicians in American Medicine* (New York, 1985), and a forthcoming work edited by Ellen More, *The Empathic Practitioner: Empathy, Gender, and the Therapeutic Relationship*, to be published in 1994 by Rutgers University Press.

20. Data on general hospital psychiatric units can be found in the *Journal of the American Medical Association*, 147 (1951): 1020; *American Journal of Psychiatry*, 107 (1951): 321–327; Raymond Giesler, P. L. Hurley, and P. H. Person, Jr., *Survey of General Hospitals Admitting Psychiatric Patients* (Public Health Service, *Publication 1462*: Washington, D.C., 1966), p. 2; Morton Kramer, *Psychiatric Services and the Changing Institutional Scene, 1950–1985* (DHEW Publication No. [ADM] 77–433: Washington, D.C., 1977), p. 75.

21. The following publications of the Milbank Memorial Fund conferences suggest the wide range of its interests: *Epidemiology of Mental Disorder* (New York, 1950); *The Biology of Mental Health and Disease* (New York, 1952); *Interrelations between the Social Environment and Psychiatric Disorders* (New York, 1953); *The Elements of a Community Mental Health Program* (New York, 1956); *Programs for Community Mental Health* (New York, 1957); *An Approach to the Prevention of Disability from Chronic Psychoses* (New York, 1958); *Planning Evaluations of Mental Health Programs* (New York, 1958); *Progress and Problems of Community Mental Health Services* (New York, 1959); *Steps in the Development of Integrated Psychiatric Services* (New York, 1960); and *Decentralization of Psychiatric Services and Continuity of Care* (New York, 1962). See also Grob, "The Origins of American Psychiatric Epidemiology," *American Journal of Public Health*, 75 (1985): 229–236.

22. This and the preceding paragraph are based on the following: *New York Times*, January 5, 7, 26, February 2, 14, 1954; Robert C. Hunt and H. M. Forstenzer, "The New York State Community Mental Health Services Act: Its Birth and Early Development," *American Journal of Psychiatry*, 113 (1957): 680–684; Forstenzer and Hunt, "The New York State Community Mental Health Services Act: Its Origins and First Four Years of Develop-

ment," *Psychiatric Quarterly, Supplement*, pt. 1, 32 (1958): 41–54; New York State Department of Mental Hygiene, *Annual Report*, 73 (1960–1961): 5.

23. Data on California taken from California Senate Interim Committee on the Treatment of Mental Illness, *Partial Report*, 1–5 (1955–1958); Uri Aviram and S. Segal, "From Hospital to Community Care: The Change in the Mental Health Treatment System in California," *Community Mental Health Journal*, 13 (1977): 159–160; and Eugene Bardach, *The Skill Factor in Politics: Repealing the Mental Commitment Laws in California* (Berkeley, 1972).

24. APA Joint Information Service, "Highlights of Recent Community Mental Health Legislation," *JIS Fact Sheet*, 8 (January 1959): *passim*; Public Health Service, *State Mental Health Programs . . . 1954 and 1955* (Public Health Service, *Publication 374*: Washington, D.C., 1954); Anita K. Bahn and V. B. Norman, *Outpatient Psychiatric Clinics in the United States 1954–55* (Public Health Service, *Publication 538*: Washington, D.C., 1957), p. 5; "Gains in Outpatient Psychiatric Services, 1959," *Public Health Reports*, 75 (1960): 1092–1093.

25. Albert Deutsch, "States Astir against Mental Disease," *Mental Hygiene*, 40 (1956): 16–17.

26. Harold Sampson, D. Ross, B. Engle, and F. Livson, *A Study of the Suitability for Outpatient Clinic Treatment of State Mental Hospital Admissions* (California Department of Mental Hygiene, *Research Report No. 1*: 1957 [a briefer version appeared under the title "Feasibility of Community Clinic Treatment for State Mental Hospital Patients," *Archives of Neurology and Psychiatry*, 80 (1958): 71–77]); Benjamin Pasamanick, F. R. Scarpitti, and S. Dinitz, *Schizophrenics in the Community: An Experimental Study in the Prevention of Hospitalization* (New York, 1967), pp. vii–x, 267–270.

27. GAP *Report No. 10* (July 1949); *American Psychologist*, 4 (1949): 445; George E. Gardner to William C. Menninger, October 6, 1949, W. C. Menninger Papers, Menninger Foundation, Topeka, Kansas; William C. Menninger, "The Relationship of Clinical Psychology and Psychiatry," *Bulletin of the Menninger Clinic*, 14 (1950): 1–21 (also printed in *American Psychologist*, 5 [1950]: 3–15).

28. *American Journal of Psychiatry*, 111 (1954): 385–386; Fillmore H. Sanford, "Relations with Psychiatry," *American Psychologist*, 8 (1953): 169–173. For a description and analysis of the relations between clinical psychology and psychiatry see Grob, *From Asylum to Community*, pp. 102–112.

29. William J. Goode, "Encroachment, Charlatanism, and the Emerging Profession: Psychology, Sociology, and Medicine," *American Sociological Review*, 25 (1960): 902–914.

30. The development of nonmedical mental health specialties can be followed in Grob, *From Asylum to Community*, pp. 114–122.

31. Kenneth E. Appel, "A Program for Public Support," APA Mental Hospital Institute, *Proceedings*, 5 (1953): 1–8; "Summary of Joint Meeting" (AMA Council on Mental Health and APA Executive Committee), January 7–8, 1955, Box 6, and "Proceedings of Meeting of Joint Commission . . . April 7–8, 1955," pp. 213–215, Box 5, Joint Commission of Mental Illness and Health (JCMIH) Papers, APA Archives.

    Appel's proposal was modeled after the famous report by Abraham Flexner for the Carnegie Foundation for the Advancement of Teaching. Published in 1910, *Medical Education in the United States and Canada* presumably had led to the modernization of medical education. Why could not a comparable report on mental health policy ultimately lead to fundamental changes in the ways in which American society acted toward its mentally ill citizens? (In reality Flexner had built on a conceptual revolution that had transformed the ways in which physicians were educated; his report confirmed but did not originate the changes that followed.)

32. 84–1 Congress, *Mental Health. Hearings before the Subcommittee on Health of the Committee on Labor and Public Welfare . . . Senate . . . 1955* (Washington, D.C., 1955); 84–1 Congress, *Mental Health Study Act of 1955. Hearings before a Subcommittee of the Committee on Interstate and Foreign Commerce House of Representatives . . . 1955* (Washington, D.C., 1955): *U.S. Statutes at Large*, 69:381–383 (1955).

33. Originally the Joint Commission was to deal with mental illness and mental retardation. The latter, however, was quickly dropped. The care and treatment of the mentally retarded had always been of marginal concern to psychiatrists, and by the 1950s evidence of conflict between mainstream psychiatrists and those involved with retardation was evident. Indeed, the American Association on Mental Deficiency (which held membership in the Commission) opposed the inclusion of retardation, favoring instead a separate study.

34. "Minutes of the Organizational Meeting of the Board of Trustees," September 11, 1955, Box 5, JCMIH Papers.

35. JCMIH, *Annual Report*, 1 (1956): appendix D (mimeographed), pp. 4–5, appendix F, pp. 2–8, copy in Countway Library of Medicine. See also Ewalt, "Goals of the Joint Commission on Mental Illness and Health," *American Journal of Public Health*, 47 (1957): 19–24.

36. Jack Ewalt, Staff Memo, June 5, 1957, Box 6, JCMIH Papers.

37. Ewalt, "Evaluating Mental Health Programs," p. 15, presentation at the

National Opinion Research Center, August 9, 1956, copy in Box 2, *ibid.*; Ewalt, "Goals of the Joint Commission," p. 22.

38. The published reports include the following: Rashi Fein, *Economics of Mental Illness* (New York, 1958); Marie Jahoda, *Current Concepts of Positive Mental Health* (New York, 1958); George W. Albee, *Mental Health Manpower Trends* (New York, 1959); Gerald Gurin, J. Veroff, and S. Field, *Americans View Their Mental Health* (New York, 1960); Reginald Robinson, D. F. DeMarche, and M. K. Wagle, *Community Resources in Mental Health* (New York, 1960); Wesley Allinsmith and G. W. Goethals, *The Role of the Schools in Mental Health* (New York, 1962); Richard V. McCann, *The Churches and Mental Health* (New York, 1962); Richard J. Plunkett and H. E. Gordon, *Epidemiology and Mental Illness* (New York, 1960); Morris S. and C. G. Schwartz et al., *Social Approaches to Mental Patient Care* (New York, 1964). William F. Soskin's report on research resources in mental health was never published.

39. "Summary of Discussion of the Meeting of the Committee on the Studies," November 15, 1957, pp. 2, 23, "Summary of the Minutes of the Meeting of the Committee on the Studies," March 9, 1958, p. 10, Box 1, JCMIH Papers; Walter Barton, "Viewpoint of a Clinician," in Jahoda, *Current Concepts*, pp. 111–119; Ewalt to Members of the Committee on the Studies, June 12, Barton to Ewalt, July 5, Ewalt to Barton and M. Ralph Kaufman, August 8, Barton to Warren T. Vaughan, August 14, Barton to Kaufman, August 14, 1961, Kaufman and Barton, "Dissent," Barton Papers, APA Archives.

40. Mike Gorman interview by Michael Barton, April 7, 1972, pp. 28–29, copy in Daniel Blain Papers, APA Archives.

41. *Action for Mental Health: Final Report of the Joint Commission on Mental Illness and Health 1961* (New York, 1961), pp. 8, 22–23, 26–85.

42. *Ibid.*, pp. xxv, 93, 228, 241–243.

43. *Ibid.*, pp. 213–241.

44. *Ibid.*, pp. 241–260.

45. *Ibid.*, pp. 260–268.

46. *Ibid.*, pp. 267–275.

47. *Ibid.*, pp. 275–281.

48. *Ibid.*, pp. 282–295; Fein, *Economics of Mental Illness*, p. 137.

49. JCMIH Press Release, March 24, 1961, in R. L. Robinson File *Action for Mental Health*, Box 6, JCMIH Papers.

Chapter 10. The New Frontier and the Promise of Community Mental Health

1. Louis Linn, "The Fourth Psychiatric Revolution," *American Journal of Psychiatry*, 124 (1968): 1043–1048; Stephen E. Goldston, ed., *Concepts of Community Psychiatry: A Framework for Training* (Public Health Service, *Publication 1319*: Washington, D.C., l964), pp. 195–197.

2. Gerald Caplan, "Community Psychiatry," in *Concepts of Community Psychiatry*, Goldston, ed., pp. 4, 10; *idem*, "Current Issues Relating to the Education of Psychiatric Residents in Community Psychiatry," in *Mental Health Career Development Program . . . 1964* (Public Health Service, *Publication 1245*: Washington, D.C., 1964), pp. 12–30; *idem*, *Principles of Preventive Psychiatry* (New York, 1964), pp. 16ff.

3. John C. Whitehorn, "Thoughts on 'issues' in regard to our expanding 'community psychiatry,'" December 1965, Whitehorn Papers, APA Archives, Washington, D.C.; Lawrence S. Kubie, "Pitfalls of Community Psychiatry," *Archives of General Psychiatry*, 18 (1968): 257–266, and "The Retreat From Patients," *International Journal of Psychiatry*, 9 (1970/1971): 693–722; Leon Eisenberg, "The Need for Evaluation," *American Journal of Psychiatry*, 124 (1968): 1700–1701; H. Warren Dunham, "Community Psychiatry: The Newest Therapeutic Bandwagon," *Archives of General Psychiatry*, 12 (1965): 303–313.

    For a perceptive analysis of social and community psychiatry see Alfred J. Kahn, *Studies in Social Policy and Planning* (New York, 1969), chapter 6.

4. *Psychiatric News*, 1 (January 1966): 1, 18–19; 3 (January 1968): 5; 4 (May 1969): 3, 8; "The Arlie House Propositions," January 1966, issued by the APA Publications Department, copy in the APA Archives, Washington, D.C.; Henry W. Brosin to Whitehorn, June 13, 1967, Whitehorn Papers, APA Archives; Daniel Blain interview, pp. 3–14, APA Oral History 135, APA Archives; *American Journal of Psychiatry*, 124 (1968): 1015–1016; 126 (1970): 1490–1492, 1543–1554.

5. The minutes of the APA Council and JCMIH Papers in the APA Archives in Washington, D.C., reveal the diversity of views on the recommendations of *Action for Mental Health*. For a summary of the reaction to the report see Gerald N. Grob, *From Asylum to Community: Mental Health Policy in Modern America* (Princeton, 1991), pp. 210–216.

6. The White House Central Files and the President Office Files, as well as the Myer Feldman interview at the John F. Kennedy Library in Boston, Mass., contain vital documents dealing with mental health policy. See also Edward D. Berkowitz, "The Politics of Mental Retardation during the Kennedy Administration," *Social Science Quarterly*, 61 (1980): 128–143.

7. Kennedy to Abraham Ribicoff, December 1, 1961, White House Central

Files, Box 338, Folder HE 1–1, Kennedy Library; Henry A. Foley, *Community Mental Health Legislation: The Formative Process* (Lexington, Mass., 1975), pp. 33–37.

8. "Report of [NIMH] Task Force on the Status of State Mental Hospitals in the United States," March 30, 1962, Bertram Brown Papers, National Library of Medicine, Bethesda, Md.; "Preliminary Draft Report of NIMH Task Force on Implementation of Recommendations of the Report of the Joint Commission on Mental Illness and Health," January 5, 1962, and "A Proposal for a Comprehensive Mental Health Program to Implement the Findings of the Joint Commission on Mental Illness and Health," April 1962, pp. 10, 12, 34–35, *et passim*, NIMH Records, Miscellaneous Records, 1956–67, Box 1, Washington National Records Center, Suitland, Md.

9. Foley, *Community Mental Health Legislation*, pp. 39–41; Lisa Reichenbach, "The Federal Community Mental Health Centers Program and the Policy of Deinstitutionalization," manuscript prepared for the NIMH under Grant No. MH27738-02 (1980), p. 63; Robert H. Atwell to Director, "Proposals for the President's Mental Health Program—A report of the interagency group appointed by the President," draft dated November 1, 1962, Daniel Patrick Moynihan to Boisfeuillet Jones, August 21, 1962, Brown Papers.

10. 88-1 Congress, *Mental Health: Hearings before a Subcommittee of the Committee on Interstate and Foreign Commerce House of Representatives . . . 1963* (Washington, D.C., 1963), pp. 100–106; Foley, *Community Mental Health Legislation*, pp. 41–44.

11. Anthony Celebrezze, W. Willard Wirtz, and J. Gleason to John F. Kennedy, November 30, 1962, White House Central Files, Box 338, Folder HE 1-1, Kennedy Library.

12. *Ibid.*

13. *Wall Street Journal*, January 15, 1963; Myer Feldman interview, vol. 14, pp. 13–15, 24–25, Kennedy Library. See also Bertram Brown interview by John F. Stewart, August 6, 1968, pp. 23–24, *ibid.*, and Felix interview, August 5, 1964, p. 11 (OH120), APA Archives.

14. "Message from the President of the United States Relative to Mental Illness and Mental Retardation," 88-1 Congress, *House Document No. 58* (February 5, 1963). The document was also reprinted in the *American Journal of Psychiatry*, 120 (1964): 729–737.

15. 88-1 Congress, *Mental Health. Hearings . . . House*, pp. 97, 99–106, 147–155, 237–243, 341–342; 88-1 Congress, *Mental Illness and Retardation. Hearings before the Subcommittee on Health of the Committee on Labor and Public Welfare United States Senate . . . March 5, 6, and 7, 1963* (Washington, D.C., 1963), pp. 17–19, 41–44, 87–88, 191, *et passim*.

16. For an analysis of the legislative history of the bill see Grob, *From Asylum to Community*, pp. 231–233, and Foley, *Community Mental Health Legislation*, pp. 68–76.

17. Public Law 88–164, *U.S. Statutes at Large*, 77: 282–299 (1963); Robert Felix, "A Model for Comprehensive Mental Health Centers," *American Journal of Public Health*, 54 (1964): 1965. See also Felix's "The National Mental Health Program," *ibid.*, 1804–1809, and "Community Mental Health: A Federal Perspective," *American Journal of Psychiatry*, 121 (1964): 428–432.

18. Data in this and the preceding paragraph are drawn from a sample of studies produced by the staff of the Biometrics Branch during these years that were relevant to policy. See Kramer, "Long Range Studies of Mental Hospital Patients, an Important Area for Research in Chronic Disease," *Milbank Memorial Fund Quarterly*, 31 (1953): 253–264; Kramer, H. Goldstein, R. H. Israel, and N. A. Johnson, *A Historical Study of the Disposition of First Admissions to a State Mental Hospital: Experiences of the Warren State Hospital during the Period 1916–50* (Public Health Service, *Publication 445*: Washington, D.C., 1955); Kramer, *Facts Needed to Assess Public Health and Social Problems in the Widespread Use of the Tranquilizing Drugs* (Public Health Service, *Publication 486*: Washington, D.C., 1956); Ben Z. Locke, Kramer, C. E. Timberlake, B. Pasamanick, and D. Smeltzer, "Problems in Interpretation of Patterns of First Admissions to Ohio State Public Mental Hospitals for Patients with Schizophrenic Reactions," APA, *Psychiatric Research Reports*, 10 (1958): 172–208; Earl S. Pollack, P. H. Person, Kramer, and Goldstein, *Patterns of Retention, Release, and Death of First Admissions to State Mental Hospitals* (Public Health Service, *Publication 672*: Washington, D.C., 1959); Kramer, Pollack, and R. W. Redick, "Studies of the Incidence and Prevalence of Hospitalized Mental Disorders in the United States: Current Status and Future Goals," in *Comparative Epidemiology of the Mental Disorders*, Paul H. Hoch and J. Zubin, eds. (New York, 1961), pp. 56–100; Kramer, *Some Implications of Trends in the Usage of Psychiatric Facilities for Community Mental Health Programs and Related Research* (Public Health Service, *Publication 1434*: Washington, D.C., 1967); Kramer, "Epidemiology, Biostatistics, and Mental Health Planning," in APA, *Psychiatric Research Reports*, 22 (1967): 1–68; Kramer, C. Taube, and S. Starr, "Patterns of Use of Psychiatric Facilities by the Aged: Current Status, Trends, and Implications," *ibid.*, 23 (1968): 89–150.

19. The regulations can be found in the *Federal Register*, 29 (1964): 5951–5956, and the writing of the regulations is ably traced in Foley, *Community Mental Health Legislation*, pp. 89–98.

20. Annual Conference of the Surgeon General Public Health Service with State and Territorial Mental Health Authorities, *Proceedings*, 1965, pp. 10–11, 39 (Public Health Service, *Publication 1355*: Washington, D.C., 1965); 89-1 Congress, *Research Facilities, Mental Health Staffing . . . Hearings before the Committee on Interstate and Foreign Commerce House of Representatives . . . 1965* (Washington, D.C., 1965); Public Law 89–105, *U.S. Statutes at Large*, 79:427–430 (1965); *Federal Register*, 31 (March 1, 1966): 3246–3248; Foley, *Community Mental Health Legislation*, pp. 103–116.

21. 90-1 Congress, *Mental Health Centers Construction Act Extension: Hearings before the Subcommittee on Public Health and Welfare . . . House . . . 1967* (Washington, D.C., 1967), pp. 13, 18, 82–89; 91-1 Congress, *Community Mental Health Centers Amendments of 1969: Hearings before the Subcommittee on Health . . . Senate . . . 1969* (Washington, D.C., 1969), pp. 17–18, 58, 98–102, 121–134, 140–150; Raymond M. Glasscote, J. Susex, E. Cumming, and L. Smith, *The Community Mental Health Center: An Interim Appraisal* (Washington, D.C., 1969), pp. 5–7; 91-1 Congress, *Community Mental Health Centers Act Extension: Hearings before the Subcommittee on Public Health and Welfare . . . House . . . 1969* (Washington, D.C., 1969), pp. 18–21, 96, 107–140, 148–162, 171–172; Christopher J. Smith, "Geographic Patterns of Funding for Community Mental Health Centers," *Hospital & Community Psychiatry*, 35 (1984): 1133–1140.

22. *New York Times*, May 22, 1989.

23. Herbert C. Modlin to Walter E. Barton, June 29, 1966, GAP Papers, Archives of Psychiatry, New York Hospital-Cornell Medical Center, New York, N.Y.; Glasscote, Susex, Cumming, and Smith, *The Community Mental Health Center: An Analysis of Existing Models* (Washington, D.C., 1964), pp. 28–30; Harvey J. Newton, "The Comprehensive Mental Health Center: Uncharted Horizons for Inpatient Services," *American Journal of Psychiatry*, 123 (1967): 1210–1219.

24. Robert H. Connery *et al.*, *The Politics of Mental Health: Organizing Community Mental Health in Metropolitan Areas* (New York, 1968), p. 479; David Mechanic, *Mental Health and Social Policy* (Englewood Cliffs, N.J., 1969), pp. 148–149; Glasscote, Susex, Cumming, and Smith, *The Community Mental Health Center: An Analysis of Existing Models*, p. 22; August B. Hollingshead and F. C. Redlich, *Social Class and Mental Illness: A Community Study* (New York, 1958), pp. 258 *et passim*; Steven S. Sharfstein, "Will Community Mental Health Survive in the 1980s?" *American Journal of Psychiatry*, 135 (1978): 1364–1365.

25. Grob, *From Asylum to Community*, pp. 253–254.

26. "Report of the Meeting of the Ad Hoc Committee on State Mental Health Program Development October 10–11, 1966," NIMH Records, Subject Files, 1963–66, Box 12; NIMH *Statistical Note 67* (1972), and *Mental Health Statistical Note No. 160* (1981); Glasscote, *The Community Mental Health Center: An Interim Appraisal*, p. 12; *American Journal of Psychiatry*, 136 (1979): 24–27, 406–409; Donald G. Langsley, "The Community Mental Health Center: Does It Treat Patients?" *Hospital & Community Psychiatry*, 31 (1980): 815–819; Sharfstein, "Will Community Mental Health Survive in the 1980s?," p. 1365; James W. Thompson and Roslyn D. Bass, "Changing Staffing Patterns in Community Mental Health Centers," *Hospital & Community Psychiatry*, 35 (1984): 1109; David F. Musto, "Whatever Happened to 'Community Mental Health'?" *Public Interest*, 39 (Spring, 1975): 53–79; Grob, *From Asylum to Community*, pp. 256–257.

27. Alan I. Levenson and Bertram S. Brown, "Social Implications of the Community Mental Health Center Concept," paper delivered at the meeting of the American Psychopathological Association, February 17, 1967, Brown Papers.

28. The conflict can be followed in the various issues of the *New York Times* beginning March 5, 1969.

29. NIMH *Statistical Note 107* (1974), *Statistical Note 146* (1978), 4; Morton Kramer, *Psychiatric Services and the Changing Institutional Scene, 1950–1985* (DHEW Publication No. [ADM] 77–433: Washington, D.C., 1977), p. 80; William Gronfein, "Incentives and Intentions in Mental Health Policy: A Comparison of the Medicaid and Community Mental Health Programs," *Journal of Health and Social Behavior*, 26 (1985): 192–206; Howard H. Goldman, M. H. Adams, and C. Taube, "Deinstitutionalization: The Data Demythologized," *Hospital & Community Psychiatry*, 34 (1983): 133.

30. For detailed statistical data see Grob, *From Asylum to Community*, pp. 257–261.

31. NIMH, *Psychiatric Services in General Hospitals 1969–1970* (NIMH, *Mental Health Statistics*, Series A No. 11 [1972]): 21; Charles Kanno and P. L. Scheidemandel, *Psychiatric Treatment in the Community: A National Survey of General Hospital Psychiatry and Private Psychiatric Hospitals* (Washington, D.C., 1974), pp. 34–35; Kramer, *Psychiatric Services and the Changing Institutional Scene*, p. 17; Raymond Glasscote and C. K. Kanno, *General Hospital Psychiatric Units: A National Survey* (Washington, D.C., 1965), p. 16; NIMH, *Statistical Note No. 70* (February 1973).

32. Horatio M. Pollock, "A Brief History of Family Care of Mental Patients in America," *American Journal of Psychiatry*, 102 (1945): 351–361; Walter E. Barton and W. T. St. John, "Family Care and Outpatient Psychiatry," *American Journal of Psychiatry*, 117 (1961): 644–647; Milton Greenblatt and B. Simon, eds., *Rehabilitation of the Mentally Ill: Social and Economic Aspects* (Washington, D.C., 1959), pp. 157–178; Raymond Glasscote,E. Cumming, I. Rutman, J. Sussex, and S. Glassman, *Rehabilitating the Mentally Ill in the Community: A Study of Psychosocial Rehabilitation Centers* (Washington, D.C., 1971), pp. 8, 41–63; Glasscote, E. Gudeman, *Halfway Houses for the Mentally Ill: A Study of Programs and Problems* (Washington, D.C., 1971), pp. 10–24, 175–177; David Landy and Greenblatt, *Halfway House: A Sociocultural and Clinical Study of Rutland Corner House* (Washington, D.C., 1965); Harold L. and C. L. Raush, *The Halfway House Movement: A Search for Sanity* (New York, 1968); Naomi D. Rothwell and J. M. Doniger, *The Psychiatric Halfway House: A Case Study* (Springfield, Ill., 1966); *Halfway Houses Serving the Mentally Ill and Alcoholics United States 1969–1970* (NIMH, *Mental Health Statistics*, Series A No. 9 [1971]); Walter Barton, *Administration in Psychiatry* (Springfield, Illinois, 1962), pp. 160–161.

33. Howard H. Goldman, D. A. Regier, C. Taube, R. W. Redick, and R. D. Bass, "Community Mental Health Centers and the Treatment of Severe Mental Disorder," *American Journal of Psychiatry*, 137 (1980): 83–86; Goldman, Adams, and Taube, "Deinstitutionalization: The Data Demythologized," pp. 129–134.

34. Krin and G. O. Gabbard, *Psychiatry and the Cinema* (Chicago, 1987), pp. 37–38, 84–114.

35. Stanley F. Yolles, "Past, Present and 1980: Trend Projections," *Progress in Community Mental Health*, 1 (1969): 3–4; Seymour L. Halleck, "Psychiatry and the Status Quo: A Political Analysis of Psychiatric Practice," *Archives of General Psychiatry*, 19 (1968): 257–265; Robert L. Coles, *Wages of Neglect* (with Maria Piers) (Chicago, 1969), p. 6, and *Children of Crisis: A Study of Courage and Fear* (New York, 1968).

36. Joseph Wortis in *Biological Psychiatry*, 2 (1970): 1–2.

37. *New York Times*, July 2, 1947, May 10, 1963; A. Robert Smith, "Siberia, U.S.A.," *The Reporter*, 14 (June 28, 1956): 27–29, Ed Cray, "Enemies of Mental Health," *Nation*, 192 (April 8, 1961): 304–305; Donald Robinson, "Conspiracy USA," *Look*, 29 (January 26, 1965): 30–32.

38. Thomas S. Szasz, *The Manufacture of Madness: A Comparative Study of the Inquisition and the Mental Health Movement* (New York, 1970), pp. xix–xxv. Some of his other major works include *The Myth of Mental Illness: Founda-*

tions of a Theory of Personal Conduct (New York, 1961); and *Law, Liberty, and Psychiatry: An Inquiry Into the Social Uses of Mental Health Practices* (New York, 1963); *Psychiatric Justice* (New York, 1965).

39. R. D. Laing, *The Politics of Experience and the Bird of Paradise* (London, 1967), pp. 98, 100, 107. Laing's other works include *The Divided Self: An Existential Study in Sanity and Madness* (London, 1960), *Self and Others* (London, 1961), and *Sanity, Madness, and the Family* (London, 1964).

40. Erving Goffman, *Asylums: Essays on the Social Situation of Mental Patients and Other Inmates* (Garden City, N.Y., 1961), p. 386.

41. *Ibid,.* p. 384. See also Roger Peele, P. V. Luisada, M. Lucas, D. Russell, and D. Taylor, "*Asylums* Revisited," *American Journal of Psychiatry*, 134 (1977): 1077–1081; Peter Sedgwick, *Psycho-Politics* (New York, 1982); and David Mechanic, "Medical Sociology: Some Tensions Among Theory, Method, and Substance," *Journal of Health and Social Behavior*, 30 (1989): 147–150.

42. Thomas J. Scheff, *Being Mentally Ill: A Sociological Theory* (Chicago, 1966) and "Schizophrenia as Ideology," *Schizophrenia Bulletin*, No. 2 (Fall 1970): 15–19.

43. Roy R. Grinker, Sr., "Emerging Concepts of Mental Illness and Models of Treatment: The Medical Point of View," George Albee, "Emerging Concepts of Mental Illness and Models of Treatment: The Psychological Point of View," and "Letters to the Editor," *American Journal of Psychiatry*, 125 (1969): 870–876, 1744–1746.

44. Foucault's numerous books include *Madness and Civilization: A History of Insanity in the Age of Reason* (New York, 1965), originally issued as *Folie et deraison, Histoire de la folie à l'âge classique* (Paris, 1961); *The Order of Things: An Archaeology of the Human Sciences* (New York, 1970); *The Archaeology of Knowledge and the Discourse on Language* (New York, 1972); *The Birth of the Clinic: An Archaeology of Medical Perception* (New York, 1973); and *Discipline and Punish: The Birth of the Prison* (New York, 1977).

45. Morton Birnbaum, "The Right to Treatment," *American Bar Association Journal*, 46 (1960); 499–505; 87-1 Congress, *Constitutional Rights of the Mentally Ill: Hearings before the Subcommittee on Constitutional Rights of the Committee on the Judiciary . . . Senate . . . 1961* (Washington, D.C., 1961), pp. 2, 273–305; *Rouse v. Cameron*, 373 F.2d 451 (D.C. Cir. 1966); David L. Bazelon, "The Right to Treatment: The Court's Role," *Hospital & Community Psychiatry*, 20 (1969): 129–135; Alan A. Stone, "Overview: The Right to Treatment—Comments on the Law and Its Impact," *American Journal of Psychiatry*, 132 (1975): 1125–1134.

46. Alexander D. Brooks, "Hospitalization of the Mentally Ill: The Legislative Role," *State Government*, 50 (1977): 198–202. Developments in the 1970s can be followed in Brooks's *Law, Psychiatry and the Mental Health System* (Boston, 1974), and the *1980 Supplement* (Boston, 1980) to this volume.

47. K. and G. O. Gabbard, *Psychiatry and the Cinema*, 115–144; Frederick Wiseman, *The Titicut Follies* (distributed by Grove Press, 1967); Ken Kesey, *One Flew Over the Cuckoo's Nest* (New York, 1962); Elliot Baker, *A Fine Madness* (New York, 1964).

48. Fredrick C. Redlich and D. X. Freedman, *The Theory and Practice of Psychiatry* (New York, 1966), p. 459; Morris A. Lipton, "A Consideration of Biological Factors in Schizophrenia," in *Neurobiological Aspects of Psychopathology*, Joseph Zubin and C. Shagass, eds., (New York, 1969), pp. 310–330.

49. David R. Hawkins, A. W. Bortin, and R. P. Runyon, "Orthomolecular Psychiatry: Niacin and Megavitamin Therapy," *Psychosomatics*, 11 (1970): 517–521; Linus Pauling, "Orthomolecular Psychiatry," *Science*, 160 (1968): 265–271, and *Schizophrenia*, 3 (1971): 129–133; *New York Times*, April 20, June 16, 1968, November 23, 1969; *Science*, 160 (1968): 1181; *Science News*, 104 (July 28, 1973): 59–60.

50. Sydney E. Pulver, "Survey of Psychoanalytic Practice 1976: Some Trends and Implications," *Journal of the American Psychoanalytic Association*, 26 (1978): 621.

Chapter 11. Confronting the Mad Among Us in Contemporary America

1. The growth of welfare is well covered in James T. Patterson's *America's Struggle Against Poverty, 1900–1980* (Cambridge, 1981).

2. 91-1 Congress, *Community Mental Health Centers Amendments of 1969: Hearings Before the Subcommittee on Health of the Committee on Labor and Public Welfare United States Senate . . . 1969* (Washington, D.C., 1969), p. 58; Gerald N. Grob, *From Asylum to Community: Mental Health Policy in Modern America* (Princeton, 1991), pp. 249ff.

3. 90-2 Congress, *Departments of Labor, and Health, Education and Welfare Appropriations for Fiscal Year 1969: Hearings before the Subcommittee of the Committee on Appropriations United States Senate* (Washington, D.C., 1968), pp. 612–613; 91-1 Congress, *Departments of Labor, and Health, Education, and Welfare Appropriations for 1970: Hearings before the Subcommittee of the Committee on Appropriations House of Representatives* (Washington, D.C., 1969), part 2, p. 10.

4. Donald G. Langsley, "The Community Mental Health Center: Does It Treat Patients?" *Hospital & Community Psychiatry*, 31 (1980): 815–819; Rosalyn D. Bass, *CMHC Staffing: Who Minds the Store?* (DHEW Publication [ADM] 78–686: Washington, D.C., 1978); David A. Dowell and James A. Ciarlo, "An Evaluative Overview of the Community Mental Health Centers Program," in *Handbook on Mental Health Policy in the United States*, David A. Rochefort, ed. (Westport, Conn., 1989), p. 206.

5. The fight between the administration and Congress can be followed in a number of committee hearings. See especially 92-2 Congress, *Extend Community Mental Health Centers Act: Hearing before the Subcommittee on Public Health and Environment of the Committee on Interstate and Foreign Commerce House of Representatives. . . 1972* (Washington, D.C., 1972); 93-1 Congress, *Public Health Service Act Extension, 1973: Hearing before the Committee on Labor and Welfare United States Senate . . . 1973* (Washington, D.C., 1973); and 93-1 Congress, *Departments of Labor, and Health, Education and Welfare and Related Agencies Appropriations for Fiscal Year 1974: Hearings before a Subcommittee of the Committee on Appropriations United States Senate* (Washington, D.C., 1973) (the Weinberger statement appeared in part 1, pp. 91–92). For analyses of the policy debates of the early 1970s see Henry A. Foley, *Community Mental Health Legislation: The Formative Process* (Lexington, Mass., 1975); Walter E. Barton and Charlotte J. Sanborn, eds., *An Assessment of the Community Mental Health Movement* (Lexington, Mass., 1977); Henry A. Foley and Steven S. Sharfstein, *Madness and Government: Who Cares for the Mentally Ill?* (Washington, D.C., 1983); E. Fuller Torrey, *Nowhere to Go: The Tragic Odyssey of the Homeless Mentally Ill* (New York, 1988); and Lisa Reichenbach, "The Federal Community Mental Health Centers Program and the Policy of Deinstitutionalization," manuscript prepared for the NIMH under Grant No. MH27738-02 (1980).

6. General Accounting Office, "Need for More Effective Management of Community Mental Health Centers Program," August 27, 1974 (B-164031[5]), p. iii. See also this agency's earlier report, "Community Mental Health Centers Program—Improvements Needed in Management," July 8, 1971 (B-164031[2]).

7. Public Law 94-63, *U.S. Statutes at Large*, 89:304–369 (July 29, 1975), Public Law 95-83, *ibid.*, 91:383–399 (August 1, 1977), and Public Law 95-622, *ibid.*, 92:3412–3442 (November 9, 1978).

8. *Report to the President from The President's Commission on Mental Health 1978* (4 vols., Washington, D.C., 1978), I, p. 5, II, p. 324; General Account-

ing Office, *Returning the Mentally Disabled to the Community: Government Needs to Do More* (Washington, D.C., 1977).

9. The recommendations are found in vol. I of the *Report to the President from The President's Commission on Mental Health*. The work of the Commission is discussed in Foley and Sharfstein, *Madness and Government*, pp. 112–116; Torrey, *Nowhere to Go*, pp. 190–195; and David Mechanic, *Mental Health and Social Policy* (3rd ed.: Englewood Cliffs, N.J., 1989), pp. 93–94.

10. *Mental Health Systems: Message from the President of the United States* (May 15, 1979) (Washington, D.C., 1979).

11. 96-1 Congress, *Mental Health Systems Act, 1979: Hearings before the Subcommittee on Health and Scientific Research of the Committee on Labor and Human Resources United States Senate . . . 1979* (Washington, D.C., 1980); 96-1 Congress, *Mental Health Systems Act: Hearings before the Subcommittee on Health and the Environment of the Committee on Interstate and Foreign Commerce House of Representatives . . . 1979* (Washington, D.C., 1979); 96-2 Congress, *Community Mental Health Centers, Oversight: Hearing before the Subcommittee on Health and the Environment of the Committee on Interstate and Foreign Commerce, House of Representatives . . . 1980* (Washington, D.C., 1980); Public Law 96-398, *U.S. Statutes at Large*, 94:1564–1613 (October 7, 1980). The best description of the history of the act is Foley and Sharfstein, *Madness and Government*, pp. 118–134.

12. Sheehan, *Is There No Place on Earth for Me?* (Boston, 1982); Ann E. Moran and R. I. Freedman, "The Journey of Sylvia Frumkin: A Case Study for Policymakers," *Hospital & Community Psychiatry*, 35 (1984): 887–893.

13. The literature dealing with mental health law since the 1960s is immense. For overviews see the following: Alexander D. Brooks, *Law, Psychiatry and the Mental Health System* (Boston, 1974), and the *1980 Supplement* (Boston, 1980) to this volume; Mechanic, *Mental Health and Social Policy*, pp. 213–234; Paul S. Appelbaum, "The Right to Refuse Treatment with Antipsychotic Medications: Retrospect and Prospect," *American Journal of Psychiatry*, 145 (1988): 413–419; Gerald L. Klerman, "The Psychiatric Patient's Right to Effective Treatment: Implications of *Osheroff v. Chestnut Lodge*," *ibid.*, 147 (1990): 409–418; Alan A. Stone, "Law, Science, and Psychiatric Malpractice: A Response to Klerman's Indictment of Psychoanalytic Psychiatry," *ibid.*, 419–427.

14. See Alan Stone, "Overview: The Right to Treatment—Comments on the Law and Its Impact," *American Journal of Psychiatry*, 132 (1975): 1125–1134.

15. GAP, *Report No. 79* (November 1970): 662; Bruce C. Vladeck, *Unloving Care: The Nursing Home Tragedy* (New York, 1980).

16. General Accounting Office, *Returning the Mentally Disabled to the Community*, p. 81; Ann B. Johnson, *Out of Bedlam: The Truth About Deinstitutionalization* (New York, 1990), pp. 94–95; Dorothy P. Rice, S. Kelman, L. S. Miller, and S. Dunmeyer, *The Economic Costs of Alcohol and Drug Abuse and Mental Illness: 1985* (San Francisco, 1990), pp. 76, 108, 110.

17. Public Law 92-603, *U.S. Statutes at Large*, 86:1329–1492 (October 30, 1972); Johnson, *Out of Bedlam*, pp. 96–99. See also Edward D. Berkowitz, *Disabled Policy: America's Programs for the Handicapped* (New York, 1987).

18. NIMH, *Mental Health, United States, 1990*, Ronald W. Manderscheid and Mary A. Sonnenschein, eds. (Washington, D.C., 1990), pp. 31, 158, 160; David Mechanic and D. A. Rochefort, "Deinstitutionalization: An Appraisal of Reform," *Annual Review of Sociology*, 16 (1990); 308–313; Joseph P. Morrissey, "The Changing Role of the Public Mental Hospital," in *Handbook on Mental Health Policy*, Rochefort, ed., pp. 311–338; Howard Goldman, C. A. Taube, D. A. Regier, and M. Witkin, "The Multiple Functions of the State Mental Hospital," *American Journal of Psychiatry*, 140 (1983): 296–300.

19. Charles A. Kiesler and A. E. Sibulkin, *Mental Hospitalization: Myths and Facts About a National Crisis* (Newbury Park, Ca., 1987), chapter 3; Mechanic, *Mental Health and Social Policy*, p. 132.

20. See especially Henry Santiestevan, *Deinstitutionalization: Out of Their Beds and into the Streets*, a pamphlet published by the American Federation of State, County and Municipal Employees in 1975 and reprinted in the *American Journal of Psychiatry*, 132 (1975): 95–137.

21. Howard H. Goldman, N. H. Adams, and C. A. Taube, "Deinstitutionalization: The Data Demythologized," *Hospital & Community Psychiatry*, 34 (1983): 129–134; Jon E. Guderman and Miles F. Shore, "Beyond Deinstitutionalization: A New Class of Facilities for the Mentally Ill," *New England Journal of Medicine*, 311 (1984): 832–835.

The persistence of the state hospital, as a matter of fact, is mirrored in a variety of data. Between 1969 and 1983 expenditures for state hospital systems increased in current dollars from $1.8 to $5.5 billion (in constant dollars there was a slight decline from $1.8 to $1.7 billion). In 1986 there were 286 state and county hospitals, eleven more than in 1955 but down from the high of 334 in 1973. See NIMH, *Mental Health, United States, 1987*, Ronald W. Manderscheid and S. A. Barrett, eds. (Washington, D.C., 1987), pp. 56–57, and Mechanic and Rochefort, "Deinstitutionalization," pp. 308ff.

22. Courtenay M. Harding, George W, Brooks, Takamaru Ashikaga, John S. Strauss, and Alan Breier, "The Vermont Longitudinal Study of Persons with Severe Mental Illness, I: Methodology, Study Sample, and Overall Status 32 Years Later," and "The Vermont Longitudinal Study of Persons with Severe Mental Illness, II: Long-Term Outcome of Subjects Who Retrospectively Met *DSM-III* Criteria for Schizophrenia," *American Journal of Psychiatry*, 144 (1986): 718–735.

23. Esso Leete, "The Treatment of Schizophrenia: A Patient's Perspective," *Hospital & Community Psychiatry*, 38 (1987): 486–491; Sarah Rosenfield, "Factors Contributing to the Subjective Quality of Life of the Chronic Mentally Ill," *Journal of Health and Social Behavior*, 33 (1992): 299–315.

    In an as yet unpublished study, Allan Horwitz interviewed 142 individuals on the threshold of release from a mental hospital. Not a single individual expressed a preference for institutionalization; all looked forward to resuming their lives in the community. Allan Horwitz, personal communication, June, 1993.

24. U. S. Bureau of the Census, *Historical Statistics of the United States, Colonial Times to 1970* (2 vols., Washington, D.C., 1975), I, p. 49; Morton Kramer, *Psychiatric Services and the Changing Institutional Scene, 1950–1985* (DHEW Publication [ADM] 77-433: Washington, D.C., 1977), p. 46; Leona L. Bachrach, "Young Adult Chronic Patients: An Analytical Review of the Literature," *Hospital & Community Psychiatry*, 33 (1982): 189–197.

25. Bert Pepper, H. Ryglewicz, and M. C. Kirschner, "The Uninstitutionalized Generation: A New Breed of Psychiatric Patient," in *The Young Adult Chronic Patient*, Pepper and Ryglewicz, eds. (San Francisco, 1982), p. 5. See also Bachrach, "The Homeless Mentally Ill and Mental Health Services: An Analytical Review of the Literature," in *The Homeless Mentally Ill: A Task Force Report of the American Psychiatric Association*, H. Richard Lamb, ed. (Washington, D.C., 1984), pp. 11–53.

26. Bachrach, "The Concept of Young Adult Chronic Psychiatric Patients: Questions from a Research Perspective," *Hospital & Community Psychiatry*, 35 (1984): 574; Lamb, "Deinstitutionalization and the Homeless Mentally Ill," in *The Homeless Mentally Ill*, p. 65.

27. Pepper and Ryglewicz, *Young Adult Chronic Patient*, pp. 5–6, 38.

28. Pepper, Kirshner, and Ryglewicz, "The Young Adult Chronic Patient: Overview of a Population," *Hospital & Community Psychiatry*, 32 (1981): 465–466. This issue devoted an entire section to the young adult chronic population (*ibid.*, pp. 463–481).

29. Pamela J. Fischer and W. R. Breakey, "The Epidemiology of Alcohol, Drug, and Mental Disorders Among Homeless Persons," *American Psychologist*, 46 (1991): 1115–1128; Deborah L. Dennis, J. C. Buckner, F. R. Lipton, and I. S. Levine, "A Decade of Research and Services for Homeless Mentally Ill Persons," *ibid.*, 1129–1138; Dennis McCarty, M. Algeriou, R. B. Huebner, and B. Lubran, "Alcoholism, Drug Abuse, and the Homeless," *ibid.*, 1139–1148; Robert E. Drake, F. C. Osher, and M. A. Wallach, "Homelessness and Dual Diagnosis," *ibid.*, 1149–1158; Ron Jemelka, E. Trupin, and J. A. Chiles, "The Mentally Ill in Prisons: A Review," *Hospital & Community Psychiatry*, 40 (1989): 481–491. See also *ibid.*, 43 (1992): 1253–1254.

30. Stuart R. Schwartz and S. M. Goldfinger, "The New Chronic Patient: Clinical Characteristics of an Emerging Subgroup," *Hospital & Community Psychiatry*, 32 (1981): 473. See especially the essays in *Barriers to Treating the Chronic Mentally Ill*, Arthur T. Meyerson, ed. (San Francisco, 1987).

31. Department of Health and Human Services, *Toward a National Plan for the Chronically Mentally Ill* (Washington, D.C., 1980).

32. Howard H. Goldman and A. A. Gattozzi, "Murder in the Cathedral Revisited: President Reagan and the Mentally Disabled," *Hospital & Community Psychiatry*, 39 (1988): 505–509, and "Balance of Powers: Social Security and the Mentally Disabled, 1980–1985," *Milbank Quarterly*, 66 (1988): 531–551.

33. My description of this case is drawn from the account by Rael J. Isaac and V. A. Armat, *Madness in the Streets: How Psychiatry and the Law Abandoned the Mentally Ill* (New York, 1990), pp. 256–260, 346–347. The case received extensive coverage in the *New York Times* and on television.

34. For a brief summary see *New York Times*, February 5, 1993, p. B2, March 2, 1993, pp. B1, 6.

35. Pepper and Ryglewicz, *Young Adult Chronic Patient*, p. 121; John A. Talbott, "Deinstitutionalization: Avoiding the Disasters of the Past," *Hospital & Community Psychiatry*, 30 (1979): 623; David Mechanic, "Correcting Misconceptions in Mental Health Policy: Strategies for Improved Care of the Seriously Mentally Ill," *Milbank Quarterly*, 65 (1987): 203–230, and "Strategies for Integrating Public Mental Health Services," *Hospital & Community Psychiatry*, 42 (1991): 797–801.

36. Richard C. Tessler and H. H. Goldman, *The Chronically Mentally Ill: Assessing Community Support Programs* (Cambridge, 1982); Chris Koyanagi and Goldman, "The Quiet Success of the National Plan for the Chronically Mentally Ill," *Hospital & Community Psychiatry*, 42 (1991): 901; Koyanagi and Goldman, *Inching Forward: A Report on Progress Made in Federal Mental Health Policy in the 1980's* (Alexandria, Va., 1991), pp. 55–56.

37. Tessler, A. G. Bernstein, B. M. Rosen, and H. H. Goldman, "The Chronically Mentally Ill in Community Support Systems," *Hospital & Community Psychiatry*, 33 (1982): 208–211; Koyanagi and Goldman, "The Quiet Success of the National Plan," 904.

38. For a review of the Madison model see Kenneth S. Thompson, E. E. H. Griffith, and P. J. Leaf, "A Historical Review of the Madison Model of Community Care," and Mark Olfson, "Assertive Community Treatment: An Evaluation of the Experimental Evidence," *Hospital & Community Psychiatry*, 41 (1990): 625–641. See also Leonard I. Stein, ed., *Innovative Community Mental Health Programs* (San Francisco, 1992).

39. See Olfson, "Assertive Community Treatment," p. 640.

40. Miles F. Shore and M. D. Cohen, "The Robert Wood Johnson Foundation Program on Chronic Mental Illness: An Overview," Goldman, A. F. Lehman, J. P. Morrissey, S. J. Newman, R. G. Frank, and D. M. Steinwachs, "Design for the National Evaluation of the Robert Wood Johnson Program on Chronic Mental Illness," and Goldman, Morrissey, and M. S. Ridgely, "Form and Function of Mental Health Authorities at RWJ Foundation Program Sites: Preliminary Observations," all in *Hospital & Community Psychiatry*, 41 (1990): 1212–1230; David Mechanic, "Strategies for Integrating Public Mental Health Services," pp. 797–801.

41. Koyanagi and Goldman, "The Quiet Success of the National Plan," p. 904.

42. These points have been effectively made by Mechanic, "Correcting Misconceptions in Mental Health Policy," p. 212.

43. Courtenay M. Harding, J. Zubin, and J. S. Strauss, "Chronicity in Schizophrenia: Fact, Partial Fact, or Artifact?" *Hospital & Community Psychiatry*, 38 (1987): 483.

Index

Felix, Robert H. (*cont.*)
  Community Mental Health
    Centers Act of 1963,
    253–254, 258
  director of the National Institute of
    Mental Health, 211–212,
    219–220
  National Mental Health Act of
    1946, 209–210
  role in postwar mental health poli-
    cy, 211ff.
Female professions, 240
Fever, 216
Fever therapy: *see* Therapy, fever
Finch, Robert, 280
Fine Madness, A (E. Baker), 275
Fishbein, Morris, 203
Fisher, Irving, 160
Flexner, Abraham, 353 n. 31
Flexner, Simon, 147
Fogarty, John, 281
Ford, Gerald, 283
Foucault, Michel, 273–274
Fountain House, 267
Francklin, Edmund, 8
Frank, Jerome D., 224
Franklin, Benjamin, 19
Freeman, Walter, 182
Freud, 269
Freud, Sigmund, 143, 270, 273
Friends' Asylum, 29, 31, 33, 36–37,
    57
Frumkin, Sylvia, 287–288
Fuller, Robert, 84
Fulton, John F., 183

Galenic humoral tradition, 7
Galt, John M., 89, 110
Garfield, James A., 134
Gender, and psychiatry, 233
General Accounting Office, 283, 285,
    290, 301

General hospital psychiatric wards,
    209
General hospitals, 291
General paralysis of the insane: *see*
    Paresis
Georgia, 45, 48, 284
Gesell, Gerhard, 282
Gessell, John M., 171
Gheel Colony for the Insane (Bel-
    gium), 110
Giesen, Ira Van, 145–146
Gitelson, Maxwell, 158
Goffman, Erving, 272–273
Goldwater, Barry, 261
Goode, William J., 239
Gorman, Mike, 205–206, 230,
    280
Grant, Madison, 160
Gray, John P., 98, 108–109, 135
Great Society program, 249, 261
Greenblatt, Milton, 227
Gregg, Alan, 205
Grinker, Roy R., 194, 273
Group for the Advancement of Psy-
    chiatry (GAP), 170, 198–201,
    206–207, 238, 269
"Group of Unknowns in Psychiatry"
    (GUP), 199–200
Guadalcanal, 193
Guiteau, Charles J., 134–135

Halfway houses, 267–268
Hall, J. K., 161, 174, 181
Halleck, Seymour, 270
Hamilton, Samuel, 199
Hammond, William A., 133
Hancock, John, 17
Hancock, Thomas, 17
Handy, William, 35–36
Hanson, Frederick, 194
Harris, Oren, 257
Hartford Retreat, 31, 36–37, 39,